100 GREAT PUB WALKS

100 GREAT PUB WALKS

Patrick Kinsella

National Trust

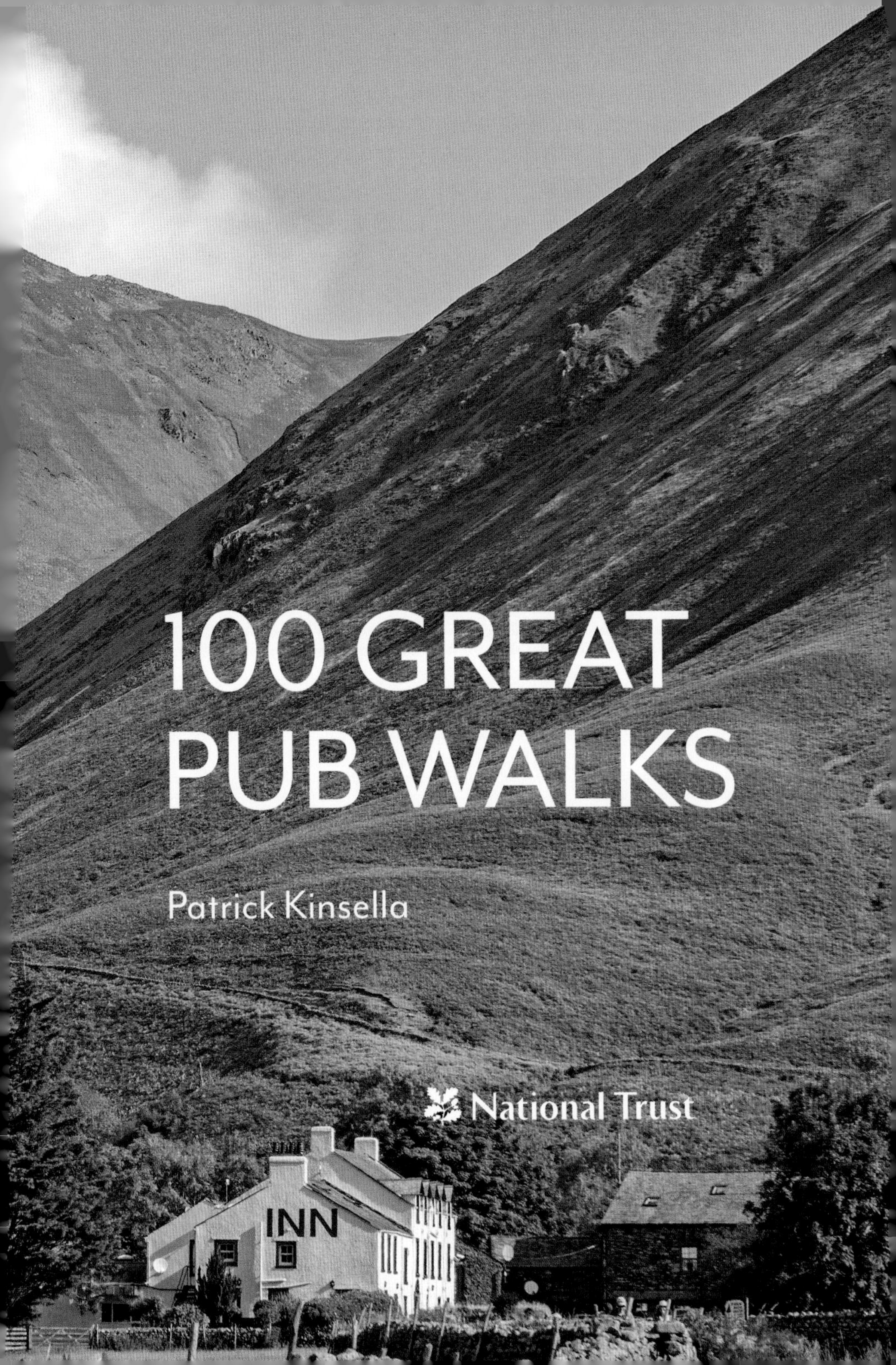

INN

Published by National Trust Books
An imprint of HarperCollins Publishers 1 London Bridge Street
London SE1 9GF www.harpercollins.co.uk

HarperCollins Publishers
Macken House, 39/40 Mayor Street Upper, Dublin 1, D01 C9W8, Ireland

First published 2022

ISBN 978-1-91-165721-7
10 9 8 7 6 5

A catalogue record for this book is available from the British Library.

Printed and bound in India

If you would like to comment on any aspect of this book, please contact us at the above address or national.trust@harpercollins.co.uk

National Trust publications are available at National Trust shops or online at nationaltrustbooks.co.uk

This book is produced from independently certified FSC™ paper to ensure responsible forest management.

For more information visit: www.harpercollins.co.uk/green

Previous page: The Wasdale Head Inn, a brilliant base for exploring fabulous fells in the Lake District, including Scafell Pike (see page 225).

Contents

Midlands

Wales

North West

North East

Northern Ireland

Scotland

The trail from Edale leading on to Kinder Scout in the Dark Peak, Derbyshire (see page 162).

Introduction

The importance of getting outside and sharing positive experiences, green spaces and special places with others has been brought home to us more than ever in recent years and, for my money, there is no better way to do that than by enjoying a good pub walk with friends or family. Britain is famous for its public footpaths and public houses, many of which have been in existence for centuries. Across the country, the two can so often be perfectly paired together to make for a sensational day or afternoon adventure, exploring trails, tasting ales and telling tales.

The paths that crisscross these isles are so much more than mere conduits linking villages, towns and cities to one another. They can be escape routes (invaluable for maintaining our mental health), portals to new places, and also experiences and destinations in their own right – leading to or passing through terrain populated by wonderful wildlife, or with jaw-dropping viewing points and fascinating historical sites.

And the pubs that punctuate these paths are not simply somewhere to go for a drink – although, happily, they are that too. Gathering around a table in a sun-soaked beer garden or near the fire in a low-beamed bar to chat about the adventure you've just enjoyed (or endured) is how funny anecdotes, shared encounters and epic achievements distill into life-long memories. This is where yarns that will be retold many times over, in other pubs along different trails (usually growing with each telling), are born.

Very often, these watering holes are also the heartbeat of rural communities – repositories of local history, full of character and characters. Here, over a beer, you can meet the people and hear the stories that make each little corner of the country completely unique. The buildings might be ancient,

with nooks and crannies that echo with memories of dawdlers and drinkers that have passed this way long ago, and quite a number are as much museums as they are pubs.

Increasingly, pubs are prioritising ales, ciders, wines and spirits produced nearby, and serving great food using locally sourced, seasonal ingredients, so you can literally get a real taste of the area you are exploring. Some have been run by members of one family for decades, others have been taken on by newcomers and completely reinvigorated, with fresh flavours and themes being added to local heritage.

In pursuit of great pub walks, I've hiked from fells to fens, through dales and vales, over peaks and tors, across moors and along the shore of England, Wales, Scotland and Northern Ireland. I know – tough gig, but someone had to do it. Along the way the ales have been every bit as varied as the accents, and I've learned more about my home country while researching this book than I have in all the years previous.

The elements and features that make a pub or a path 'great' are subjective: some people prioritise an excellent menu, while others prefer a diverse range of local ales and ciders; great views and abundant wildlife delight many walkers, but others love to wander through historical remains, passing ruins, standing stones, graves, battlesites and castles. All of these things feature, but I can't promise all of them on every walk. And, of course, your personal favourite pub walk might not appear. There are many additional places I would have liked to include, and plenty more, I'm sure, that I've yet to discover (which is exciting). It's impossible to cover them all in one book, but I'd love to hear your suggestions.

You will note that the walks often start on, and almost always cross, land cared for by the National Trust. To some extent, this is almost inevitable – the National Trust has responsibility for well over 685,000 acres (277,000ha) of countryside and nearly 800 miles of the British coastline, so the odds of passing through a landscape looked after by the charity are large when you're out exploring. Something many people aren't so aware of is that, among the 300 historic buildings maintained by the National Trust, there are around 50 pubs and inns. These are typically licensed properties with a particularly interesting past, set amid extraordinarily stunning surrounds.

There are some caveats, of course. At the time of writing, all the routes described in this book are wonderful to explore, and each features a fantastic pub (sometimes two). But the outdoors is a dynamic place, and things can change quickly. Not all of the land crossed by these walks is cared for by the National Trust. Public paths do get overgrown

Opposite: Signage for the Hunter's Inn, on the Exmoor coast, with Great Hangman lit by the morning sun (see page 38).

Below: A handpump for one of many ales brewed at the Twice Brewed Inn, near Hadrian's Wall in Northumberland (see page 253).

at times, or temporarily dissolve into muddy quagmires after heavy weather, and it's possible they may even suffer from erosion and get diverted. In addition, signage might occasionally become obscured and stiles sometimes break (ideally to be replaced by gates).

Likewise, pubs can change hands and alter their opening hours, or food and drink offering. The ambience might vary and, sadly, some may close down altogether. Many of the featured establishments are several centuries old, with long histories of offering refreshment and hospitality to wayfarers, but even they are not entirely immune from such a fate. It's always worth viewing the website of the pub you intend to visit, or giving them a call to check they're open, before heading out for a day's walk – especially if you're wandering around a quiet area on an out-of-season weekday.

Lastly, while walking and pubs go together beautifully, mixing driving and alcohol is obviously not something we recommend or endorse. Public transport directions have been included for each walk, but some routes are hard to reach without a car. Please be responsible. All pubs serve a wide range of delicious soft drinks and most have low- or no-alcohol beer and cider options.

I hope you enjoy exploring the paths and pubs described in this book, and please do share your tales from the trails with us and other walkers.

Cheers,
Patrick Kinsella

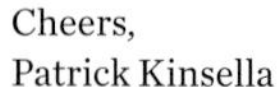

Waymarkers on the Bath Skyline walk, en route to The George Inn (see page 65).

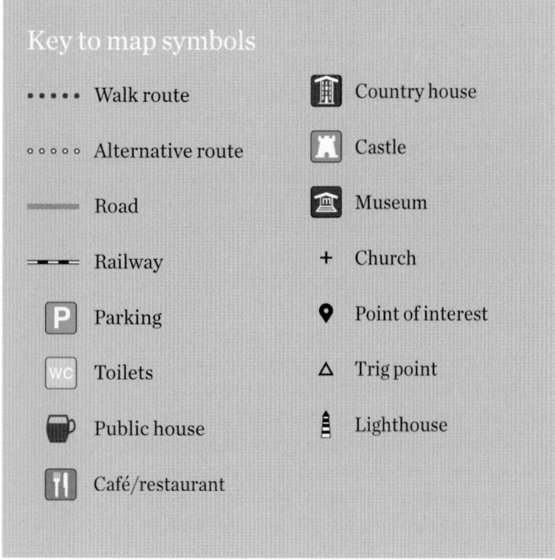

The South West Coast Path leading around Godrevy Point towards The Bucket of Blood pub (see page 24).

Walking Hints and Tips

- Consider taking a mobile phone with you, bearing in mind coverage can be patchy in rural areas.
- If you are walking alone, let someone know where you are and when you expect to return.
- It's advisable to take an Ordnance Survey map with you on country walks to supplement the maps provided.
- As far as possible, our routes follow footpaths across coast and countryside terrain, but almost all of the walks involve one or two road crossings and/or sections that take you along lanes where encounters with motorised vehicles are possible. Be familiar with the Highway Code and how it relates to walkers. The salient points are thus: use paths and pavements whenever possible; cross roads only where and when it's safe; help drivers see you by wearing something bright, fluorescent or reflective (especially if you think you might be out after dusk); and take special care with young children and others who need assistance.
- Take special care of children when walking beside water or along cliff-tops.
- Public transport may change over time, so, if you're thinking of taking a bus or train, always check timetables and routes online or with a local tourist information centre before setting out.

Follow the Countryside Code

Following this code helps everyone better enjoy parks and waterways, coast and countryside:

Respect everyone

- Be considerate to those living in, working in and enjoying the countryside
- Leave gates and property as you find them
- Do not block access to gateways or driveways when parking
- Be nice, say hello, share the space
- Follow local signs and keep to marked paths unless wider access is available

Protect the environment

- Take your litter home – leave no trace of your visit
- Do not light fires and only have barbecues where signs say you can
- Always keep dogs under control and in sight
- Dog poo – bag it and bin it – any public waste bin will do
- Care for nature – do not cause damage or disturbance

Enjoy the outdoors

- Check your route and local conditions
- Plan your adventure – know what to expect and what you can do
- Enjoy your visit, have fun, make a memory

The Canine Code

We want you and your dog to have a fun and stress-free day. We also want to protect farm animals and precious wildlife habitats, as well as ensure everyone can enjoy the countryside, whether or not they have a dog. This is why we've teamed up with Forthglade to put together the Canine Code.

Take the lead: You can help reduce the chance of your dog disturbing ground-nesting birds and livestock by keeping them on a short lead. Remember, if you're approached by cattle, the safest thing to do is let your dog go, and call them back when safe to do so.

Scoop that poop: Picking up your dog's waste keeps the area clean for everyone to enjoy. When you're done, pop it in the bin, or if there isn't one, take it home with you.

Paws for thought: Are you in the right area? Sometimes we might ask you to walk somewhere else to help us protect you, the places we look after and the wildlife that lives there. Keep an eye out for signs and be extra careful on coastal and cliff top paths.

Be on the ball: While lots of us love dogs, some of us don't. That's why it's important to make sure your four-legged friend doesn't run up to other people – especially children.

Following the 'Canine Code' at Lindisfarne Castle on Holy Island (see page 259).

A natural partnership

We share a love of nature and a passion for the great outdoors with Cotswold Outdoor. Through our partnership, we aim to inspire the nation to explore Britain's incredible coast and countryside on foot – whatever the weather.

In partnership with

The outdoor experts at Cotswold Outdoor show us what's inside their kit bag.

Comfy footwear Well-fitting footwear makes a big difference. After all, they are with you every step of the way. Fabric boots are lighter weight, flexible and don't need as much breaking in. Leather is tougher and naturally water resistant, so lasts longer. Also consider what type of terrain you'll be covering; rocky mountain paths will require good ankle support and a deep tread, whereas rambles thought grassy fields are better with softer, suppler footwear.

Quality socks However far you roam, good quality socks will keep your feet dry, happy and blister-free. Pick a pair made with natural materials, such as wool – Merino wool is a firm favourite, known for its softness, durability and temperature controlling properties.

A waterproof jacket Prepare to deal with the famous British weather. We always pack for November in July, just in case. Look for a jacket with taped seams and breathability. High-quality jackets will have a waterproof rating – 10,000mm and above is best for those really stormy days.

A dry bag Keep all your spare layers and electronic devices inside one of these waterproof wonders. Stuff it into your rucksack, and shrug off the rain.

Repair tape From patching torn waterproofs to sealing broken zips, this miracle tape has proven itself countless times.

Don't forget, National Trust supporters receive 15% discount at Cotswold Outdoor in store and online.*

* Selected lines are exempt, the discount cannot be used with any other offer or discount and the Partnership discount is only available to National Trust supporters signed up to Cotswold Outdoor's Explore More benefits scheme. Further details of exempt lines and full terms are available here: nationaltrust.org.uk/ cotswoldoutdoor. Offer expires on 31.12.22 or as may be extended. Up to 5% of the purchase price paid by National Trust supporters is payable to the National Trust to help look after the places you love to explore. In exceptional circumstances, up to 7% of the purchase price may be payable. The National Trust also receives 50p from each sign up to Explore More by a National Trust supporter.

Opposite: The Crowns Engine Houses cling to Botallack Cliffs between Cape Cornwall and Pendeen (see page 18).

South West

1 Porthcurno
Logan Rock Inn

A sensational 16th-century pub named after a famous local landmark, the National Trust-owned **LOGAN ROCK INN** welcomes walkers back from exploring Cornwall's beaches, secret coves and hidden history. The pretty, stone-built inn has an atmospheric, low-beamed bar, a real fire and cosy snugs where home-cooked food and Cornish ales and ciders are served. There's a patio area and a large garden, perfect for sipping drinks in the sun after a stroll on the South West Coast Path. Friendly staff happily suggest additional walks if you're thirsty for more.

Logan Rock Inn
Treen, St Levan,
Cornwall TR19 6LQ
01736 810495
www.theloganrockinn.co.uk

About this walk

- Stunning beaches
- Sealife
- The Minack theatre
- South West Coast Path
- Cornwall AONB

Start/Finish Treen village car park
Distance 4 miles (6.5km)
Time to pub 2 hours
Walking time 2 hours 15 minutes
Terrain Coastal and cliff-top trails, beach, lanes

After viewing Logan Rock, stroll past a prehistoric hill fort and along cliffs to explore secret sandy beaches, coves and historic telecomms sites around Porthcurno. Look for dolphins and visit the theatre at Minack Point before returning across farm fields to a fantastic pub.

Spring Scan the sea for dolphins, seals, basking sharks, barrel jellyfish, minke whales and (if you're *really* lucky) orca and leatherback turtles.

Summer Sedge warblers sing in flowering heather. Rock sea lavender, oxeye daisies and foxgloves attract butterflies, including silver-studded blue and small pearl-bordered fritillary.

Autumn Dartmoor ponies patrol clifftops, improving conditions for Cornwall's emblematic chough, and fields are full of finches, meadow pipits and skylarks.

Winter Atlantic waves crash into Treen Cliffs, the trails are quiet and the sea views are crisp.

A St Austell pub, the Logan Rock Inn serves the Cornish brewery's popular beers including Tribute, Proper Job IPA, Hicks and Korev lager, plus boutique-brewed Logan Rock Cornish pale ale.

Follow in the footsteps of ...

Until the early 19th century, Logan Rock topped a boulder pile at Treryn Dinas, naturally balanced so it could be wobbled, but not toppled – or so the story went. In April 1824, however, Royal Navy Lieutenant Hugh Goldsmith ill-advisedly ordered his HMS *Nimble* crew to challenge this claim. In an impressive show of strength and stupidity, the sailors successfully shifted the boulder from its lofty perch, but the community outcry was such that Goldsmith had to restore the rock to its former position, which took several months and cost £130 8s 6d (over £5,000 today).

How to Get There

By Car Take the A30 past Penzance, turning onto the B3283 at Catchall. Park in Treen village car park (TR19 6LF; not National Trust).

By Public Transport The closest train station is Penzance (8 miles/13km). Go Cornwall Bus 1 travels between Penzance and Sennen Cove/Land's End.

OS Map OS Explorer 102 (Land's End), Landranger 203 (Land's End & Isles of Scilly); grid ref (for start): SW 394/230.

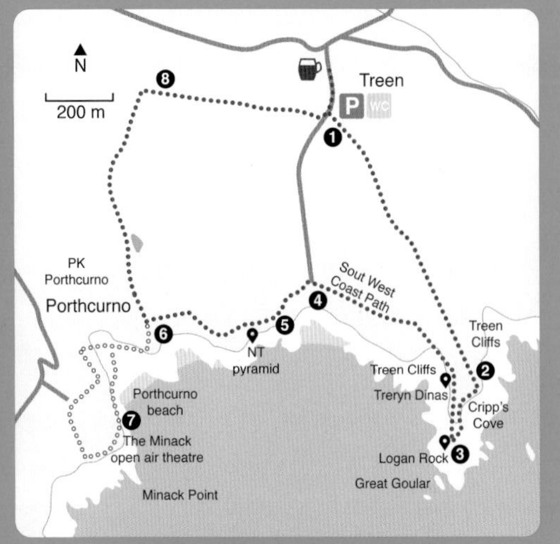

1. Leave the car park, passing the toilets and shop, and turn left by the chapel, along a footpath with a low-placed arrow pointing to Logan Rock. Go left again, up a short set of steps, walk along a track for 100 yards, then bear right through a gate. Walk diagonally across fields and over stone stiles, following Logan's Rock signs.

2. Walk through a gate to coastal cliffs, site of Treryn Dinas, an Iron Age hill fort. Iconic crags and the Atlantic Ocean lie straight ahead, and Treen Cliff stretches left and right.

3. Descend to the headland and explore the jumble of giant granite boulders topped by Logan Rock, which no longer moves as much as it once did (see opposite). Loop back and turn west (left) along the South West Coast Path (SWCP), a 630-mile/1,014-km trail between Poole in Dorset and Minehead in Somerset, via the coasts of Devon and Cornwall. Walk along Treen Cliff, looking for dolphins.

4. Go through a gate and meet a confluence of paths by a Treen Cliffs NT sign. It's possible to shortcut to the pub here, turning right along a lane past Treen campsite, or you can go straight ahead on the SWCP (a good option if you prefer easier trails), but our route bears left, along a cliff-hugging path with superb views.

5. Ignoring a second left turn towards Pedn Vounder beach (which is dangerously steep), continue past a stone pyramid, built by the National Trust to mark the spot where, in 1870, a submarine telegraph cable was landed, linking Britain to places as distant as India, via Brest in France (an event explored in the nearby PK Porthcurno museum).

6. Rejoin the SWCP, turn left and walk past a Second World War pillbox to a junction. You can go right here, but preferably carry on for 50 yards before turning left down a path to picturesque Porthcurno Beach, passing another pillbox and scoring views of Minack Point's open-air theatre.

7. After enjoying the beach, either retrace your footsteps, or, for a closer look at the extraordinary theatre, built into the granite cliff-face in the 1930s by Rowena Cade, climb steep steps up the cliff on the right of the beach. Check out the theatre, then leave through the car park. By a large exit sign, where the road bends left, turn right and follow an alleyway to the coast path. Go left, then right at the NT Porthcurno sign, walking back up the path you previously descended. At the junction, take the bridleway leading inland, along an unsealed lane.

8. Turn right at Trendrennen Farm, crossing a stile and following footpath arrows through fields to steps leading into Treen village. Turn left for the Logan Rock Inn. After the pub, walk up the road, past Treen Farm and a phone box, to the car park.

2 Cape Cornwall

The North Inn

The North Inn
Pendeen, Penzance
Cornwall TR19 7DN
01736 788417
www.thenorthinnpendeen.co.uk

About this walk

- Cornish Mining World Heritage Site
- Cornwall AONB
- South West Coast Path
- Lighthouse

Start/finish Cape Cornwall car park (National Trust)
Distance 10 miles (16km)
Time to pub 3 hours
Walking time 4 hours
Terrain Coastal paths, lanes, country roads

With Geevor and Levant mines nearby, the wood-beamed bar at **THE NORTH INN** would have once bustled with miners. A cart remains at the front, but the clientele now is a mix of locals and tourists. The mining theme runs deep, though, along with *Poldark* references (the landlord was an extra in the popular TV series). Inside features include a fire and tropical fish tank. There's a large, sunny beer garden, with pétanque pistes (boules). Pub food (including excellent curries) is served. B&B accommodation and basic camping (pitches with sea views) are available.

From the rugged cape where the English Channel meets the Atlantic Ocean, this walk traces the South West Coast Path across cliffs and through the evocative remains of Cornwall's mining history to a lonely lighthouse, before turning inland to seek solace in a friendly village inn.

Spring Gannets and fulmars nest on the Brisons Rocks. Peregrine falcons and kestrels soar round engine houses, and choughs chatter in mineworks.

Summer While Land's End teems with tourists, wildflower-flanked paths remain relatively quiet along the wild Atlantic coast between Cape Cornwall and Pendeen. You might spot dolphins, seals, sunfish, basking sharks or even minke whales.

Autumn Oceanic birds such as storm petrels, skua, shearwaters and auks (including puffins) can sometimes be seen close to the cape and around the Brisons, especially during gales.

Winter Storms send waves crashing into Cornwall's metal-veined and mineral-stained cliffs (pictured above).

A St Austell pub, The North Inn serves the Cornish brewery's best-loved beers including Tribute pale, Proper Job IPA, Mena Dhu stout and Korev lager, plus seasonal ales, and South West ciders including Healey's Cornish Cyder Farm's Rattlers.

Follow in the footsteps of ... Despite its rugged remoteness, the coastline between Cape Cornwall and Pendeen was heavily industrialised for centuries, with thousands of miners living and toiling here, burrowing under land and sea to extract tin, copper and arsenic. Abandoned shafts, adits and chimneys remain atmospherically scattered across the Tin Coast, alongside preserved mines and restored steam-driven beam engines.

How to Get There

By Car There's a car park at Cape Cornwall (TR19 7NN; National Trust), located at the end of Cape Cornwall Road from St Just.

By Public Transport The nearest train station is Penzance (5 miles/8km). Buses run between Penzance, St Just and Pendeen.

OS Map OS Explorer 102 (Land's End), Landranger 203 (Land's End & Isles of Scilly); grid ref (for start): SW 352/318.

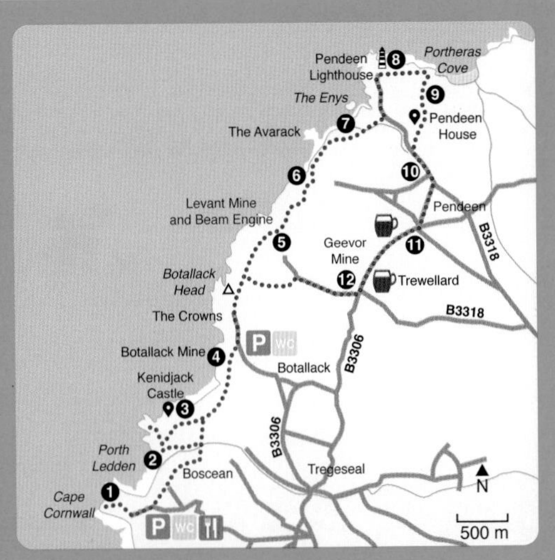

1. From the car park, explore Cape Cornwall, once believed to be mainland Britain's most westerly point until the first Ordnance Survey was conducted in 1801, when that claim (and subsequent waves of tourism) transferred to Land's End. Consequently, this stunning headland, one of the UK's two capes (where two significant bodies of water meet – the other one being Cape Wrath in Scotland), has retained a raw and rugged ambience, complemented by the ruins of the mining industry that surround it. The chimneystack atop the headland, built in 1894, was left in place after the Cape Cornwall Mine ceased working because it's a useful navigation aid for shipping travelling this rocky coastline. Look south (left) across the Brisons Rocks, bristling with birds, to Land's End, then loop back, passing the cross marking medieval St Helen's Oratory. Climb the hill, along the path beside the car park and Cape Cornwall Road, then turn left along the South West Coast Path (SWCP).

2. Ignore the first turning right, and when the path forks follow the SWCP left, descending and crossing a bridge over tumbling Tregeseal River. Bear left, then right at a Y-junction. Climb, turn left then right and cross a stone wall. To your left is the poetically named Zawn Buzz and Gen ('gully of food and song'). Walk around the site of Kenidjack Castle – ruins now stand on the promontory where an Iron-Age fort once perched.

3. Rejoin the SWCP, bear left at a T-junction and stay left. Walk past Wheal Edward and West Wheal Owles engine houses and follow the path across and above the deserted catacombs of Botallack Mine, where tin, copper and arsenic were mined in treacherous conditions, via subterranean shafts that burrow almost half a mile out to sea.

4. Near the National Trust car park, a down-and-back path leads left on a diversion to see the Crown Engine Houses desperately clinging to the cliff edge. Back on the main route, follow the SWCP as it forks left, and continue to the trig point on Botallack Head. Look out for choughs flying around the old mineworks – members of the crow family, these distinctive red-billed birds appear on Cornwall's coat of arms, but disappeared from the county for three decades until making a comeback in 2001.

5. Keep walking along the SWCP, across Roscommon Cliffs, bearing left to see the lovingly restored Levant Mine and Beam Engine, built in the 1840s and looked after by the National Trust.

6. The SWCP continues through old arsenic works below Geevor Tin Mine and crosses a footbridge over a stream at Trewellard Bottoms. Continue, past rock pools around the Avarack (some blasted by miners to create plunge pools for swimming in) up on to Pendeen Old Cliff.

Cape Cornwall's tin mine-topped peak overlooks the meeting point of the English Channel and the Atlantic.

7. The path passes above the rocky islet of Enys and meets the road. Turn left and walk down to the lighthouse, which has been shining a guiding light across Atlantic waves since 1900.

8. From the foot of the lighthouse, continue along the SWCP towards Portheras Cove, a super-secluded spot used by smugglers for centuries.

9. Before reaching the cove, turn right along a footpath that passes Pendeen House, built in 1589 and home to the Borlase family, which produced two notable archaeologists. The house has a fogou – an underground chamber connecting to the coast, reputedly haunted by a hobgoblin and almost certainly exploited by smugglers to move and hide contraband.

10. Past the house the path becomes a track, which leads to a road at Pendeen Gate. Turn left, then take the second right. When you meet the B3306, turn right and The North Inn (ironically one of Britain's most southerly pubs, but north of Pendeen' s other pub, the Radjel Inn) is 100 yards down the road, on the right.

11. Leaving the pub, turn right and walk through Pendeen and Trewellard mining villages, passing the entrance to the Geevor Tin Mine museum and heritage centre on the right. After half a mile, the Trewellard Arms appears on your left. This granite-built freehouse, once home to the owner of Geevor mine, has a wooden-beamed main bar, a snug and sunny patio; it serves several Cornish ales (Skinner's, Tintagel) and local ciders (Skreach Farm) and food.

12. Just beyond the pub, turn right on Levant Road. At the bottom of the lane, turn left along a path and go right at the second fork. On meeting the SWCP, turn left and retrace your earlier footsteps to Cape Cornwall, taking the more direct route past Kenidjack Castle.

3 Halzephron Cliffs

The Halzephron Inn

The Halzephron Inn
Helston, Cornwall
TR12 7QB
01326 240406
www.halzephron-inn.co.uk

About this walk

- South West Coast Path
- Sea cliffs
- Marine wildlife
- History

Start/finish Church Cove car park (National Trust)
Distance 8 miles (13km)
Time to pub 3 hours
Walking time 4 hours
Terrain Clifftop sections of the South West Coast Path, farmland and footpaths

THE HALZEPHRON INN is a 550-year-old sea-facing pub, steeped in history. The name Halzephron derives from 'cliffs of Hell' in Old Cornish, and this coast is renowned for storms, shipwrecks and smuggling. The pub's thick walls feature wood retrieved from local wrecks, and apparently conceal secret tunnels leading to caves and hiding places. Inside there are two traditional bars, snugs, a log fire and an eating area. Outside, picnic tables look across fields to Mount's Bay. The menu includes Cornish cheeses and mussels harvested nearby, perfect for pairing with local ales.

SOUTH WEST

Always a dramatic walk, this route is most exciting when waves are high after a storm. On calmer days, search for seals basking in bays where flotsam from many an unfortunate vessel has washed ashore along this perilous coast. Return via a rural ramble through fields and along country lanes.

Spring The cliffs explode into colour with the unfurling of white sea campion, pink thrift, blue spring squill, yellow kidney vetch and bird's-foot trefoil.

Summer Ox-eye daisies burst into bloom, along with sea carrot (a relative of the familiar orange veg, but with a woody and rather unappetising white root), followed by colourful heathers. Look out for painted lady and tortoiseshell butterflies, hovering skylarks, sunbathing seals and passing dolphins.

Autumn Keep an eye out for the delicate purple spikes of Autumn squill decorating the cliffs – a South West speciality. Migrating birds (martins, swifts and swallows) bid Britain goodbye from the country's southernmost tip, before leaving for Africa.

Winter Listen for the distinctive 'cheeoow' from Cornish choughs echoing around the cliffs. These birds, a rare red-billed member of the crow family and allegedly the reincarnation of King Arthur's spirit, returned to Cornwall in 2001 after a 30-year absence.

The Halzephron Inn serves several Cornish real ales and cider, including Skinner's Porthleven pale ale and Betty Stogs Cornish bitter.

Follow in the footsteps of ... Famous for her novels, including *Jamaica Inn* (centred on a real pub on Bodmin Moor) and *Rebecca*, Daphne du Maurier spent much of her adult life in Cornwall, including on the Lizard Peninsula, the setting for *Frenchman's Creek*.

How to Get There

By Car Take the A3083 from Helston towards Lizard Point and follow signs leading right to Gunwalloe. Continue on towards Church Cove and park in the car park on the left by Winnianton Farm.

By Public Transport Buses serve Gunwalloe from Helston (36A) and Redruth (34).

OS Map OS Explorer 103 (The Lizard), Landranger 203 (Land's End & Isles of Scilly); grid ref (for start): SW 660/208.

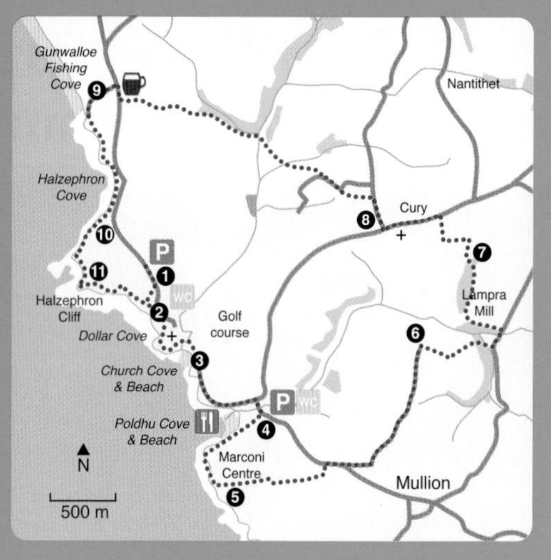

1. Leave the National Trust car park at Gunwalloe Church Cove and turn left along the lane, walking past Winnianton Farm. Descend to a Y-junction, opposite public toilets, where there's a National Trust sign for 'Gunwalloe Towans'. Take the right fork and walk down to Dollar Cove.

2. Walk with the sea on your right around the bluff overlooking Church Cove Beach. Tucked into the nape of the headland here is St Winwaloe, also known as 'The Church of the Storms'. Explore this evocative chapel, where salt-bitten gravestones and statues look out across the waves, then cross the beach, often frequented by surfers.

3. Jump the stream and pick up the South West Coast Path on the far side. Climb away from the beach, passing through a little car park and rounding the headland to drop into Poldhu Cove, a beautiful little bay cared for by the National Trust.

4. Behind the café and surf school, the path climbs briefly before dropping right (follow the South West Coast Path sign) to skirt around the Old Poldhu Hotel. This impressive pile is now a care home, but in 1901 it hosted the Italian inventor and radio pioneer Guglielmo Marconi, who made the first ever transatlantic wireless transmission from Poldhu to Newfoundland on 12 December that year. The Marconi Centre here commemorates this achievement.

5. From the Marconi monument, tear yourself away from the view of Mullion Island (a bird sanctuary), go through a gate and follow a path arrow pointing inland, towards Mullion Village. After a second gate, walk straight on (ignoring the left turn) until the path becomes a lane, snakes through a cluster of houses and meets a road. Turn right, and when the road forks, go left along Polhorman Lane.

6. Pass Newton Equestrian Centre and continue until the lane roughens into a track and ends at a gate. Follow the bridleway sign pointing right, along a zig-zag downhill route to a stream-hopping bridge. At the road, go left. Walk for about 100 yards and then, at Lampra Mill, take the footpath leading left. Pass Lampra Mill Cottage, go through the gate and walk up the hill.

7. Turn left, and after crossing a bridge follow the footpath until you encounter stepping stones leading to two gates. Go through the larger gate and climb straight up a short, steep section of single track, emerging with fields on your right. After 100 yards or so, at a crosspath, turn left and climb over a stone stile. Hug the hedgeline, cross a second stone stile, then at the end of the following field, turn right and trace the hedge to a path between two sets of houses, leading to a road. Turn left and walk into Cury village.

8. Turn right along the lane opposite the church, following signs pointing towards Milliwarne. After the graveyard, climb a stile on your left, cross a field, go through a gate and follow a lane through Sowanna Farm. The route passes through a small wood and jumps a stile into a field. Hug the hedge on your right, and continue through gates along a series of boardwalks, field paths and single track before emerging onto the road. The Halzephron Inn is just on your right.

9. Leaving the pub, take the lane opposite, walking towards the sea. At the end, turn left along the South West Coast Path and trace this trail along the cliff top as it skirts Halzephron Cove.

10. Continue along the South West Coast Path, passing Halzephron House and the National Trust sign for Halzephron Cliffs. While walking around the headland, glance right for views to Loe Bar and Porthleven. Carefully peer into Pedngwinian Cove, over the sharp-edged rocks, and you might be rewarded with a seal sighting.

11. Carry on, walking past wooden pews with sensational sea views and cliffs that plunge into secret bays where caves have provided shelter for smugglers and seals for centuries. Above Dollar Cove, branch left along a path that leads to a track. Turn left and head back to the car park.

Below: The Marconi monument at Mullion, where the Italian inventor conducted wireless experiments.

Bottom: A pew with a view along the sometimes hellish, but often heavenly, Halzephron Cliffs.

4 Godrevy

The Bucket of Blood

Originally known as the New Inn, **THE BUCKET OF BLOOD** was apparently renamed after the landlord went to draw water from the pub well one day, only to pull up a ... bucket of blood. Later the mutilated body of a murdered smuggler was found in the well. Or so the story goes. Another theory points out that water here is stained red by tin. Either way, this 18th-century, rubble-built, low-beamed pub offers a bucketload of atmosphere and character, along with great food, an open fire, painted murals, outdoor tables at the front and a raised deck at the rear.

The Bucket of Blood
14 Churchtown Road
Phillack, Hayle
Cornwall TR27 5AE
01736 697824
www.bucket-of-blood.co.uk

About this walk

- Dunes and beaches
- Coastline and surf
- Grey seals
- Lighthouse
- South West Coast Path
- St Gothian Sands Local Nature Reserve

Start/finish Godrevy car park (National Trust)
Distance 9 miles (14.5km)
Time to pub 2.5 hours
Walking time 5 hours
Terrain Sandy trails, dunes, beaches, lanes

Starting above a seal colony opposite an iconic lighthouse, stroll a sensational section of the South West Coast Path around St Ives Bay, past rockpools, through dunes and along surf-stroked sandy beaches, to a picturesque pub steeped in smuggling stories. Walk, or catch a bus back.

Spring Sand martins arrive at a specially created sandbank at St Gothian Sands Nature Reserve, also home to many waterfowl and waders. Along the cliffs, cormorants, shags and fulmars build nests. Look for skylarks in meadows, plus linnets and Cornish choughs.

Summer Wildflowers are widespread across fields fringing the coast, attracting pollen-seeking solitary bees. Scan the sea for dolphins, basking sharks and sunfish.

Autumn During storms, seabirds such as fulmar, razorbill and guillemot take shelter on Godrevy headland. Around Halloween, the pub offers 'Bucket of Blood Beer', a special-brewed spicy red ale.

Winter Grey seals use Mutton Cove all year, but in autumn and winter their numbers swell. At low tide hundreds lounge on the secluded sand, some with pups.

A St Austell's pub, The Bucket of Blood offers the Cornish brewery's beers, including Tribute, Proper Job, Hicks ale and Korev lager, plus Cornish cider, gin and rum.

Follow in the footsteps of... Virginia Woolf spent childhood holidays at St Ives and, although set in Scotland, her 1927 modernist classic *To the Lighthouse* was inspired by Godrevy lighthouse. This headland was notorious for shipwrecks, until – galvanised by a 1854 tragedy, when the SS *Nile* struck The Stones and sank with the loss of all souls – Trinity House built a lighthouse, which was first lit in March 1859.

How to Get There

By Car There's a couple of National Trust car parks at Godrevy (TR27 5ED), just off the B3301, north of Gwithian.

By Public Transport Bus 515 runs between Gwithian and Penzance and goes past The Bucket of Blood. A summer bus service (A4) connects Newquay, Perranporth, St Agnes, Portreath, Hayle and St Ives, and passes Godrevy and the North Cliffs.

OS Map OS Explorer 102 (Land's End), Landranger 203 (Land's End & Isles of Scilly, St Ives & Lizard Point); grid ref (for start): SW 582/430.

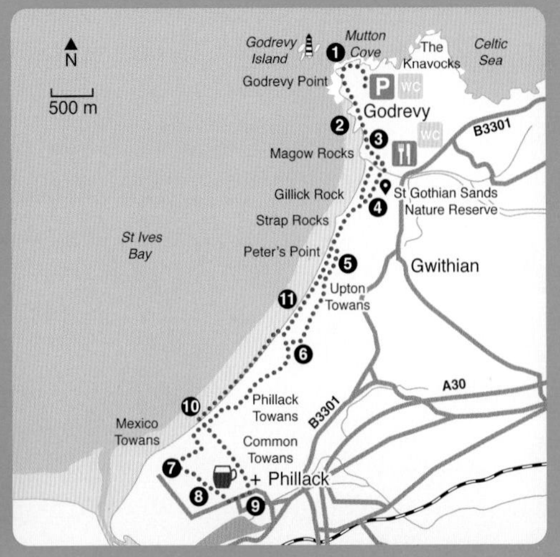

1. From the top National Trust car park nearest to Godrevy Point, walk directly up the hill, past the toilet block, to the edge of the cliffs at Mutton Cove. Grey seals can often be seen on the beach below – try and be quiet, so as not to disturb them. Turn left and walk around the headland, passing Godrevy Point and looking across The Stones to the iconic lighthouse.

2. Keep walking, watching the waves rolling into St Ives Bay. If you want to get closer, there's access to a secret beach at Godrevy Cove by The Gleeders (a group of rocks). Carry on, passing a lifeguard lookout and the slipway to Godrevy Beach.

3. Follow South West Coast Path (SWCP) acorn-emblazoned signs along a wooden walkway, skirt the edge of the lower car park and descend the steps to Red River. Bear left towards an old tin mine chimney, then turn right and cross the bridge.

4. Here you have a choice, go right and walk along the sandy beach; or bear left, initially, before going right and walking through St Gothian Sands Local Nature Reserve, with the pond – where waders and wildfowl gather – on your left.

5. Head into the dunes to pick up more SWCP waymarkers. Pass the lifeguard station and another car park on the left. Meander through the warren of Gwithian Towans (*towans* is Cornish for 'sand dunes'), past a SWCP sign pointing towards Upton

Tombstone-style waymarkers guide South West Coast Path walkers through the towans behind the beach.

Looking back across St Ives Bay to Godrevy Lighthouse.

Towans. Keep going, through Upton Towans, passing St Ives Bay Holiday Park on the left and walking past Sandy Acres café.

6. Follow a rock SWCP sign down a set of steps, bear right, then go left through a gate. Stroll along a sandy path, which leans left and comes out at a grassy open area with a SWCP sign pointing towards Mexico Towans. Follow this, ignoring several gates on the left, and keep walking through the dunes, to another SWCP sign for Mexico Towans.

7. At an obvious T-junction directly in front of a caravan park and chalets, just before you reach the Mexico Towans information sign and a World War Two pillbox, turn left, leaving the SWCP. Keep the caravan park on your right, then wander through Common Towans green space.

8. Go through a gate, walk past cottages and along Mexico Lane. Emerge on the road, turn left and go towards the church, and The Bucket of Blood is on the left.

9. It's possible to get a bus some of the way back. To walk, leave the pub, turn left and stroll through the churchyard. Go through a gate, turn right on the path, then take the next left and walk back through Common Towans to the coast.

10. Turn right and walk back the way you came, following the SWCP or strolling along the beach (please note: dogs are not permitted on the sand in summer).

11. If you choose to return along the sand, after 1 mile (1.6km) look for an exit from the beach back into the dunes, otherwise you can be cut off. Retrace your earlier footsteps through the dunes and nature reserve (or take a slightly different strand of path, which splits and rejoins, like braided hair, for a new view) all the way back to Godrevy car park.

5 Cotehele
The Tamar Inn

Cradled in the Cornish village of Calstock, **THE TAMAR INN** sits beside the river that runs between Cornwall and Devon. The 17th-century, stone-built pub was once a meeting place for smugglers and highwaymen, but now proudly supports local artists and writers, with paintings and bookshelves showcasing their work, and live music most weekends. The split-level interior features drinking snugs, woodburners, beams and a mix of wooden and flagstone flooring. The outdoor area looks across the water and up at the arches of the Tamar Valley-spanning Calstock Viaduct.

The Tamar Inn
The Quay, Calstock
Cornwall PL18 9QA
01822 832487
www.tamarinn.co.uk

About this walk
- River and valley views
- History
- Viaduct
- Gardens and woodlands
- Tamar AONB

Start/finish Cotehele Quay
Distance 4 miles (6.5km)
Time to pub 1.5 hours
Walking time 3 hours
Terrain Woodland paths and riverside roads

SOUTH WEST

From the dovecotes, orchards and gardens of a medieval mansion imbued with intriguing Tudor tales, this route rambles through Cotehele Woods into the Tamar Valley and along the river to a waterside pub beneath an iconic viaduct.

Spring The Tamar Valley has a history of daffodil growing. Cotehele's gardens glow with golden flowers, backed by blooming magnolias, azaleas, camellias, snake's-head fritillaries, rhododendrons and hydrangeas, plus blossoming cherry, apple and walnut trees.

Summer With wildflowers in the woods and Cotehele's terraces and gardens bursting with roses, geraniums and irises, bees and butterflies proliferate.

Autumn In Cotehele's orchards, juicy fruits are ready for harvesting, while the wooded valleysides are aflame with red, orange and yellow leaves. Look for little egrets around the river.

Winter Mysterious mists swirl through the valley. Avocets fossick for food around the water's edge.

The Tamar Inn serves ales from Cornish breweries including Sharps (Doom Bar, Atlantic) and Tintagel. They even tolerate 'foreign' drinks from across the river, such as Salcombe Brewery's Seahorse and Old Rosie cider.

Follow in the footsteps of ... Parts of Cotehele date to 1300, but much was built 1485–89 by Richard Edgcumbe. A Lancastrian knight and MP, Edgcumbe joined a 1483 attempt to topple Yorkist King Richard III. When the rebellion failed and soldiers came searching, he hid in Cotehele's woods and threw his cap into the river, fooling his pursuers into thinking he'd drowned. Later, Edgcumbe built Cotehele's Chapel-in-the-Wood, on the spot where he'd hidden during his narrow escape.

How to Get There

By Car Park at the lower car park at Cotehele Quay (PL12 6TA; National Trust); arrive via A388 and the villages of St Dominick and Bohetherick.

By Public Transport Calstock train station (Tamar Valley Line from Plymouth) is close to this route and can be used as an alternative start/finish point. Go Cornwall bus 79/79A between Callington and Tavistock stops at Calstock Quay.

OS Map OS Explorer 108 (Lower Tamar Valley & Plymouth), Landranger 201 (Plymouth & Launceston); grid ref (for start): SX 424/682.

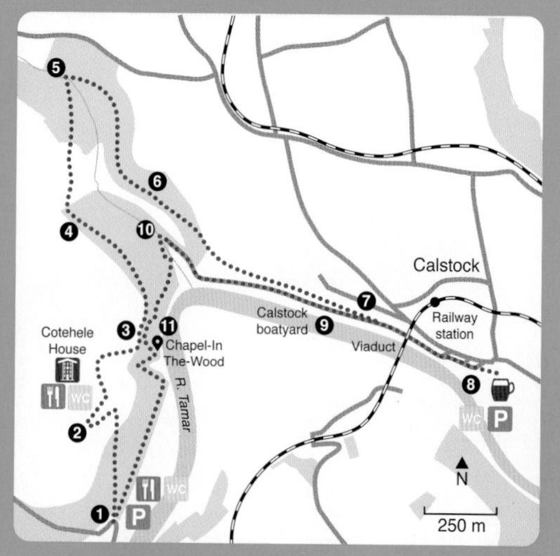

1. From Cotehele Quay, walk towards the Discovery Centre, Edgecumbe Café and Gig Club. Cotehele Mill is straight on, but our walk turns right to leave the car park just before the information board and ticket machine. Cross the lane, bear right and take the path that zig-zags up the hill, through woods. When you meet the lane, continue up to Cotehele house and gardens.

2. Keeping the green and playground on your left, follow the fingerpost pointing right, into the grounds, towards the 'Reception'. Explore the house and gardens, then leave via the footpath leading to the right of the toilets and garden centre.

3. Ignore an acute right turn, and when the path forks, go left, up the hill. Another path joins, but

keep going straight, enjoying views along the Tamar Valley to your right.

4. Ignore a path crossing your route and continue over a stream. Ignore another path joining from the left, but shortly afterwards, just after a wooden bench on the right, the path forks. Go right and descend along a path winding through trees. Cross a little wooden bridge over a bigger stream at the bottom and turn left, along a main path.

5. Walk for about 20 yards, then turn sharp right, along a path leading uphill. Ascend, passing a cottage on the left. Keep going along the main path as it flattens out. After passing three gates leading down a steep drop to huts far below on your right, the path becomes a lane.

6. Pass several wooden sheds on your left and Kelly Cottage, set away from the track on your right. Just before reaching a white cottage on the left, the lane forks – go left and ascend the path through trees. Go under a little wooden footbridge and, at the T-junction, turn right.

7. Descend to the road, turn left and walk with river on your right, passing beneath the impressive viaduct.

8. At a T-junction, go right into Calstock village and The Tamar Inn pub.

9. Leaving the pub, retrace your footsteps and go back underneath the viaduct. Stay on the road, walking past Calstock Boatyard on your left (if you have time, pop into the Honesty Box Café for cake). Continue under a small stone bridge, passing a large lime kiln on the right, Danescombe Quay on your left, and a half-boat bench on the right.

10. Pass a cottage pottery, and when the road forks go left, following the sign for Cotehele. Climb up the track, with a stream below on your left. Soon the river comes into sight.

11. At the junction you passed earlier (point 3) stay left. After an elbow in the path, check out the view over the Tamar River to the viaduct and village at Calstock lookout. Continue along the path, past the Chapel-in-the-Wood (hiding place of Richard Edgcumbe during his great escape – see 'In the footsteps of...') to reach the car park.

Opposite: A multi-storied Tudor country house with deep Medieval roots, Cotehele offers magnificent Tamar Valley views from its glorious gardens.

Below: The Tamar Inn looks up at the river-spanning viaduct that connects Cornwall and Devon.

6 Prawle Point
Pigs Nose Inn

Pigs Nose Inn
East Prawle, Kingsbridge
Devon TQ7 2BY
01548 511209
www.pigsnoseinn.co.uk

About this walk
- South West Coast Path
- Stunning coastal views
- Shipwrecks
- Marine life and migrating birds

Start/finish Prawle Point car park (National Trust)
Distance 5 miles (8km)
Time to pub 2 hours
Walking time 3 hours
Terrain Clifftop trails, footpaths and country lanes

The PIGS NOSE INN's reputation precedes it, with the high-spirited, multi-award-winning pub putting on legendary live gigs (Damon Albarn, Lee Scratch Perry, Stereo MCs, Paul Young, The Boomtown Rats) as well as providing the perfect place for South West Coast Path walkers to rest and refuel. Perched on East Prawle's village green, the old smugglers' inn has previously been a hotel and petrol station, but is now simply a brilliant pub. It serves lovely food and a range of local ales and ciders, gives campsite recommendations, and offers hot showers and laundry facilities.

Saunter around mainland Devon's southernmost point, landing place of many migrating birds, exploring secret beaches and hidden coves, spotting shipwrecks and dolphins, and visiting a legendary pub.

Spring Sea campion, thrift and wild carrot carpet clifftops. Burnet rose, mayweed and sea beet grow in crags and rare storksbill blooms at Prawle Point. Cormorants, razorbills, fulmars and little owls breed on cliffs and visiting birds include chats, warblers and pipits.

Summer Spot dolphins and search rock pools at Horseley Cove for spider crabs, strawberry anemones and starfish. Look for rare cirl buntings and butterflies, including pearl-bordered and dark green fritillaries, peacocks, red admirals, painted ladies and clouded yellows.

Autumn Purple autumn squill blooms, peregrine falcons, hobbies, ospreys, buzzards and ravens roam the sky, while oystercatchers mix with migrants including bar-tailed godwits and whimbrel on the beaches. Shearwaters and skuas seek shelter on stormy days.

Winter Waves crash around the headland. Enjoy a blustery walk around Prawle Point, a pint in the cosy Pigs Nose Inn and some beachcombing in Horseley Cove.

The Pigs Nose Inn serves ales from the South Hams Brewery (including Devon Pride and Eddystone) and Otter Brewery.

Follow in the footsteps of ... Prawle derives from the Anglo-Saxon word, 'prawhyll', meaning 'lookout hill'. Over the centuries this headland has hosted eagle-eyed observers searching for smugglers and incoming threats ranging from the Spanish Armada in 1588, to French fleets during the Napoleonic Wars and German U-boats in the 20th century.

How to Get There

By Car From Plymouth, take the A379 to Kingsbridge, Torcross and Frogmore, then head south to East Prawle where there is a small car park.

By Public Transport The nearest train station is Totnes (16 miles/26km). Buses run from Totnes and Plymouth to Kingsbridge (9 miles/14.5km). The Pig's Nose arranges special buses for events.

OS Map OS Explorer OL20 (South Devon), Landranger 202 (Torbay & South Dartmoor); grid ref (for start): SX 775/354.

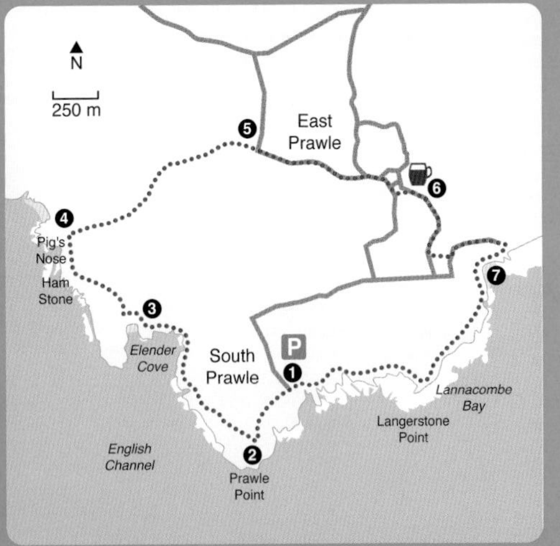

1. From the car park, head towards the sea and bear right on the South West Coast Path (SWCP), passing coastguard cottages on your right. (The SWCP is a 630-mile/1014-km trail running between Poole Harbour in Dorset and Minehead in Somerset, via the coasts of Devon and Cornwall.) During the Second World War, the grass-covered bunker near the path here housed a radar station. Walk with the cliffs on your left, uphill to the lookout.

2. Continue through a gate to Prawle Point, the southernmost part of mainland Devon, where a medieval chapel once stood, and a National Coastwatch Institution coastguard station now operates. Prawle Point, with its jagged rocks, has long been a notorious area for sailors. Scores of ships have been wrecked here, including the *Demetrios*, sunk during storms in 1992, the bones of which can still be seen. Divers tell tales of discovering gold coins and treasure scattered on the sea floor. Continue along the SWCP, climbing around the top of Elender and Maceley coves, a couple of beautiful bronze beaches that tantalise to your left. Elender is inaccessible, but there is a track leading to Maceley Cove if you want to explore.

3. Keep following the dramatic SWCP, passing ancient stone walls and going through a gate to Gammon Head. Carry on around the cliffs, past the Ham Stone and more coves, to Pig's Nose – not the pub, but the site of an old, unsuccessful iron mine, which struggled along between 1857 and 1860.

4. At the waymarker, turn right and walk inland, through a gate. Pass through a second gate and bear left along a bridleway, walking with farm fields on your right. Continue, through tree cover and past barns to emerge at the elbow of a road.

5. Carry straight on, strolling along the tarmac as the quiet country road snakes its way into East Prawle. At a T-junction, turn right and walk until you reach the village green. Turn left here, and the Pigs Nose Inn is just down on your left.

6. Leaving the front door of the pub, walk straight across the road and along the lane opposite, with the Piglet Stores and café on your right. Turn left down a cul-de-sac, descend the lane, which arcs right and segues into a bridleway, then turn left along a footpath signed to Gorah Rocks. At a T-junction, turn left, follow the path as it elbows left and descends to meet the SWCP at Lannacombe Bay. Bear right and explore Horseley Cove, which offers excellent rock-pooling opportunities.

7. Continue along the SWCP, walking up and over Sharpers Head and past Brimpool Rocks to Langerstone Point to enjoy a stunning view of Prawle Point. Carry on past Wollow, Landing and Western coves, to reach the right turn that leads back to the car park.

7 Wembury
The Odd Wheel

The Odd Wheel
Knighton Road, Wembury
Devon PL9 0JD
01752 862504
www.theoddwheel.co.uk

About this walk
- South West Coast Path
- South Devon AONB
- Erme-Plym Trail
- Marine wildlife and birds
- Beaches and rock pools

Start/finish Wembury Point car park, Spring Road (National Trust)
Distance 5½ miles (9km)
Time to pub 2 hours
Walking time 3 hours
Terrain Coast path, footpaths, fields, lanes and roads

Scenically situated above the South Devon hamlet of Wembury, **THE ODD WHEEL** is a welcoming traditional pub, frequented by friendly locals, South West Coast Path walkers and surfers. Originally a cider house, the pub dates to at least 1794, and was called The Old Inn and The Jubilee, before settling on The Odd Wheel in the 1960s. There's a terraced garden with coast and country views, and an undercover seated section. Inside you'll find a restaurant and bar, warmed by an open fire. Great food can be accompanied by regional real ales. There is regular entertainment.

Wander around wonderful Wembury Bay in the South Hams area, enjoying views across the Great Mewstone, and searching for seals and dolphins. Explore a fantastic rock-pooling beach and stroll a section of the Erme-Plym Trail to a delightful village for a local brew.

Spring Wild coastal plants such as thrift, kidney vetch and sea campion bloom. Fulmars, a relative of the albatross, begin nesting and breeding on Great Mewstone.

Summer Scan waves for grey seals, dolphins, basking sharks and porpoises. Search rock pools for porcelain crabs, St Piran's hermit crab, snakelocks sea anemones and starfish. Around trails, speckled wood butterflies flit between wildflowers including speedwell, valerian and weld flower, while lizards and adders sunbathe.

Autumn Look for lovely little cirl buntings (a very rare bird in Britain), plus Dartford warblers, stonechats and hummingbird moths. Comb beaches for cuttlebones and mermaid's purses.

Winter Watch cormorants fishing. Shags begin nesting on Great Mewstone from late February. Dartmoor ponies graze the grassy headland.

The Odd Wheel serves ales from Summerskills Brewery in Plymouth, plus Dartmoor and St Austell brewery beers. The rotating cider list includes Inches and Thatchers.

Follow in the footsteps of ...
During the Second World War, Wembury Point and Great Mewstone were commandeered by the Ministry of Defence, and holiday camps were transformed into a Naval gunnery school, HMS Cambridge. When the MOD withdrew in the early 2000s, this area was under threat of development, until the National Trust raised funds to purchase 146 acres (59ha) of the headland and began rewilding it.

How to Get There

By Car Drive towards Wembury Point and park at the end of Spring Road (PL9 0BA; National Trust).

By Public Transport The nearest train station is Plymouth (7 miles/11.3km). Plymouth City Bus 49 goes to Heybrook Bay (limited service).

OS Map Explorer OL20 (South Devon), Landranger 201 (Plymouth & Launceston); grid ref (for start): SX 503/487.

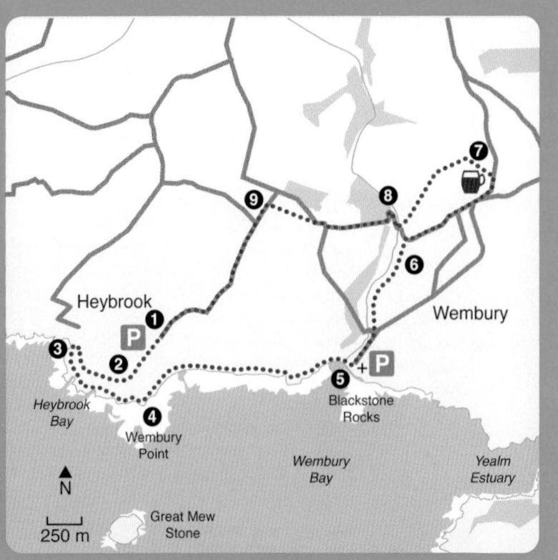

1. Leave the car park through a gate, pass the picnic area and stroll seawards, along Marine Drive – the old HMS Cambridge access road.

2. At a five-bar gate, carry straight on, walking towards Heybrook Bay, where Royal Navy ships are often silhouetted against the horizon.

3. Descend and turn sharp left, joining the South West Coast Path (SWCP) and walking with waves on your right to Wembury Point, opposite the Great Mewstone. Cared for by the National Trust, this is now an uninhabited bird sanctuary, but in 1744 a local man was convicted of a minor crime and transported to the tiny island for seven years.

4. Continue along the SWCP, enjoying spectacular views across Wembury Bay, over Blackstone Rocks and into the Yealm Estuary. This rocky foreshore is full of marine, bird and plant life, and the tidal swimming pool, the last remains of the historic Heybrook Bay Lido, is still visible.

5. At Wembury Beach, walk across the cove, past Old Mill Café to the Marine Centre. Continue, briefly, along the SWCP, then turn inland around 11th-century St Werburgh church. Bear left, then right along a path that joins the road rising from the beach. Walk up to a T-junction, go straight across, then take the fingerposted footpath, following the Erme-Plym Trail through lower Churchwood Valley.

6. At Ford Road, turn right, leaving the Erme-Plym Trail and walking up the steep, leafy lane. Pass several houses approaching West Wembury, then turn left on Church Road. This segues into Knighton Road, and The Odd Wheel is on your left, on the corner of Traine Road.

7. Leaving the pub, walk along Traine Road for 100 yards, then follow a fingerpost pointing left, through a metal gate. Walk diagonally across a field towards the top right-hand corner, pass into the next field and follow the path straight across. When the path forks at the hedge, go left and walk diagonally across two fields towards trees. Meet a hedge and walk with it on your right to a stile. Cross, ignore the path leading right, and meeting Ford Road again, turn right.

8. Follow the road across a stream and around a hairpin bend. Ignore a footpath going left through Churchwood Valley Holiday Park and continue to a T-junction. Go left, then immediately right, following a fingerpost through a farm. Walk across a field, with a fence on your right, go through a kissing gate, and turn right, then left on a lane. Go right through a gate just afterwards, taking a footpath across a field to meet Cliff Road.

9. Turn left along the road, which becomes Spring Road, and leads all the way back to the car park.

8 Castle Drogo
Fingle Bridge Inn

Fingle Bridge Inn
Drewsteignton
Devon EX6 6PW
01647 281287
www.finglebridgeinn.co.uk

About this walk
- River views
- Castle
- Sections of Two Moors Way and Dartmoor Way
- Wildlife
- Steep climb after the pub

Start/finish Castle Drogo car park (National Trust)
Distance 4½ miles (7km)
Time to pub 1.5 hours
Walking time 2.5 hours
Terrain Valley, woodland and riverside trails

Beneath an Iron-Age hill fort beside the River Teign, on the north-east edge of Dartmoor National Park, the **FINGLE BRIDGE INN** welcomes walkers for locally brewed drinks and good food. Originally called the Anglers' Rest, the pub began life as a teahouse in 1897, and you can still get a Devon cream tea (scone, cream, jam – strictly in that order – a treat apparently invented 1,000 years ago at nearby Tavistock Abbey). Garden terrace tables overlook the river and fabulous Fingle Bridge, while inside you'll find wooden beams, log fires and lots of character.

From England's youngest castle, stroll the Teign Valley's tor tops, enjoying spectacular views across Dartmoor, before plunging into trees and rambling beside the river to a charming waterside pub.

Spring Wild daffodils and bluebells enliven the woods. Look aloft to spot buzzards and kestrels. Listen for woodpeckers and spy wagtails, dippers, herons and kingfishers along the Teign.

Summer Cool your heels at paddling spots along the river, beside meadows vibrant with wildflowers and bees. Teign Gorge is home to multiple butterfly species, including silver-washed and pearl-bordered fritillaries.

Autumn Fallow deer rut in October and November, when males bellow along the valley. In Whiddon, Hannicombe and Drewston woods, oak, beech, birch, ash, larch and rowan trees sensationally change colour. Salmon and brown trout jump up weirs near Fingle Bridge when the river is in spate.

Winter As trees drop their last leaves, Teign Valley views open up. Dartmoor ponies graze on Piddledown Common below Castle Drogo. At the Fingle Bridge Inn, log fires glow.

The Fingle Bridge Inn serves several Devon-brewed real ales on rotation, with beers from Teignworthy and Dartmoor breweries usually featuring. Two local real ciders are offered too, typically Sam's Cloudy and Rosie's Pig.

Follow in the footsteps of ...
When architect Edwin Lutyens designed Castle Drogo 100 years ago, he was inspired by Dartmoor's rugged tors. Above Fingle Bridge Inn, atop Prestonbury Common, lie the prehistoric remains of a hillfort, from where the Dumnonii tribe looked out over the forests of Dartmoor 2,000 years ago, as the Romans occupied Exeter.

How to Get There

By Car There's a large car park at Castle Drogo (EX6 6PB; National Trust), signposted from the A30, between Exeter and Okehampton.

By Public Transport The nearest train station is Yeoford (8 miles/13km). Dartline Coaches number 173 serves Castle Drogo from Exeter.

OS Map OS Explorer OL28 (Dartmoor), Landranger 191 (Okehampton & North Dartmoor); grid ref (for start): SX 726/903.

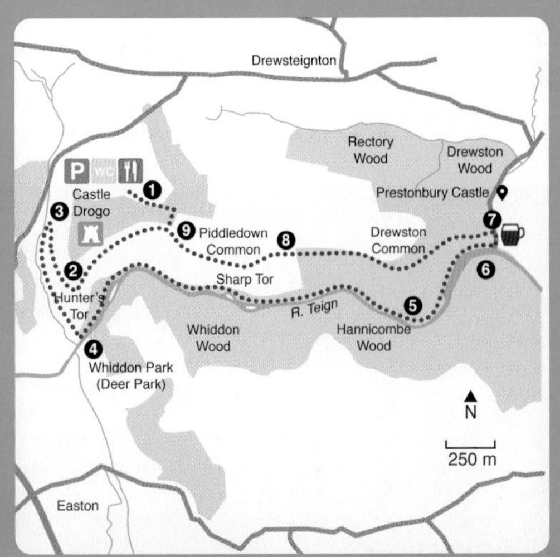

1. Follow signs for estate walks, Fingle Bridge, Teign Gorge and the river. At a fingerpost, go straight downhill towards Hunter's Path. After two sets of steps, go right on Hunters Path, following a sign for Dogmarsh Bridge. You're now on a section of the Two Moors Way, a 117-mile (188-km) coast-to-coast route, crossing Exmoor and Dartmoor. Look left across a precipitous drop and along the valley, and listen for woodpeckers.

2. Just past David's Seat you enter a small clump of trees and reach a three-directional fingerpost. From the viewpoint at Hunter's Tor, drink in the wonderful views along the Teign Valley, over the treetops of Whiddon Wood and deer park, and out across the mysterious expanse of Dartmoor. Continue along Hunter's Path and the Dartmoor Way with Drogo Castle uphill on your right.

3. Stay on the path as it descends through a gate by a National Trust sign. Go left along the lane and follow a fingerpost pointing left again to Fisherman's Path and Teign River, walking with a stream on your right. When the lane forks, go left (avoiding a private house), then left again to go around thatched Gibhouse.

4. When you reach the river, don't cross the bridge (except to look along the tumbling Teign), which leads to an old deer park, enclosed around 1560. Instead, leave the Two Moors Way and turn left along Fisherman's Path with the river on your right. Walk along the bank-hugging path, past a weir. At the base of Sharp Tor, the trail rises and becomes more rugged, before passing through a gate and sending you up and down some steps.

5. Continue, with the river racing you on the right, rushing and gushing through occasional rapids and then relaxing on wider sections. After several more sets of steps, you reach a peach of a picnic spot by babbling water, complete with a bench.

6. Continue to photogenic Fingle Bridge, the best views of which are enjoyed from the beer garden terrace at the eponymous inn.

7. Leaving the pub, head up the road, away from the bridge. After 100 yards, take the footpath leading left, following a fingerpost pointing to Castle Drogo. This steep uphill section through the oaks of Drewston Wood is part of the Dartmoor Way, a 95-mile (153-km) circular loop of the moor for hikers and bikers. A path comes in from Drewston Common on your right but keep going straight.

8. Pass through a pair of granite posts (Hunting Gate). When the Two Moors Way comes in from Drewsteignton on the right, continue straight to Sharp Tor, where another stunning vista along the Teign Valley awaits.

9. At a signpost for the castle, head right and walk back to the car park.

9 Branscombe
The Fountain Head

The Fountain Head
Branscombe, Devon
EX12 3BG
01297 680359
www.fountainheadinn.com

About this walk

- Pebble beach
- South West Coast Path
- Sea views
- Includes a steep climb, with some steps

Start/finish Branscombe Forge car park (National Trust)
Distance 3 miles (5km)
Time to pub 1.5 hours
Walking time 2 hours
Terrain Countryside, coastal and woodland footpaths, lanes, B-road

Found in a fold of the voluptuous verdant hills of East Devon, just off the South West Coast Path, **THE FOUNTAIN HEAD** is a wonderful pub (formerly a forge, cider house and smugglers' den) that dates to the 14th century. The atmospheric interior features flagstone floors, wooden panelling, thick walls and a fireplace with its own resident ghost. A freshwater spring bubbles up in the garden, which overlooks Branscombe valley. Good food, local ales and ciders are served every day except Monday (when it is typically closed).

From an old forge, this walk explores the beautiful beachfront of Branscombe before strolling a section of the South West Coast Path (part of the World Heritage-listed Jurassic Coast), to a 500-year-old pub full of stories.

Spring Pitt Coppice becomes awash with bluebells and aromatic with wild garlic, while fabulous foxgloves line the South West Coast Path. Swallows and swifts arrive from Africa, and butterflies including wood whites and Adonis blues, flit between wildflowers.

Summer Branscombe Beach is a wonderful, wave-stroked, sand-and-pebble expanse of shoreline to explore, while cormorants fish from rocks. The Fountain Head garden is a great place to relax, and there's a midsummer beer festival.

Autumn With the woods changing hue, and migratory birds coming and going, resident species such as chiffchaffs, robins, blackbirds, chaffinches, goldfinches, great and blue tits and blackcaps can be seen in the branches. As evenings draw in, look for horseshoe bats.

Winter As leaves disappear from trees, views through the valley across the Jurassic Coast are extra special on clear, cold winter days. The fire at The Fountain Head beckons.

The Fountain Head serves ales and ciders brewed by Branscombe Vale Brewery: Branoc is the regular beer, with Summa That (pale), Summa This (bitter), Golden Fiddle and Sea Cider on rotation.

Follow in the footsteps of ... The cove- and cave-indented coast around Branscombe was once a hotspot for smuggling. In 1837, local character Jack Rattenbury – nicknamed the Rob Roy of the West – published *Memoirs of a Smuggler* detailing his life as fisherman, pilot, seaman and smuggler.

How to Get There

By Car Parking is available by the Forge and Old Bakery (National Trust), the village hall (not National Trust) and Branscombe Beach (not National Trust).

By Public Transport The closest train station is Honiton (8½ miles/14km); Axe Valley bus 899 between Sidmouth and Seaton serves Branscombe, with connections to Honiton.

OS Map OS Explorer 115 (Exmouth & Sidmouth), Landranger 192 (Exeter & Sidmouth, Exmouth & Teignmouth); grid ref (for start): SY 197/887.

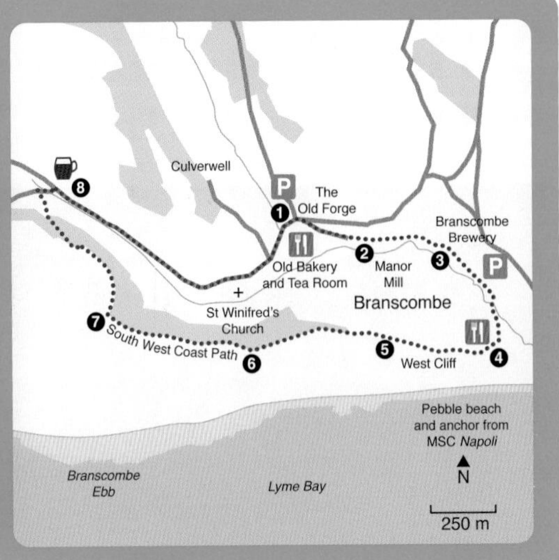

1. Before you start walking, it's worth watching the resident blacksmith working in the fascinating forge (built in 1580 and believed to be Britain's oldest thatched working forge) and exploring the offerings at the Old Bakery, Devon's last traditional bakehouse. When you're ready, leave the car park, go left along the road and then right along Mill Lane with a stream running to your right.

2. Go through a gate and pass Manor Mill on your right. This building operated as a corn mill from 1700 until 1939 and has a restored water wheel – it's now looked after by National Trust and is sometimes open to visitors. Continue along the footpath, which stays on the flat, following the flow of the stream.

3. Ignore paths leading left, which go up to the Mason's Arms (another good pub, named after the stone workers once employed in nearby Beer Caves), and continue all the way to the beach. Branscombe Vale Brewery is based in an anonymous building on the hill over to your left as you approach the beach car park, but they don't let visitors in to see where the magic happens.

4. Go past the Sea Shanty (a licensed café with a wonderful coastal view) to the pebble beach and beautiful bay where, in 2007, the MSC *Napoli* famously foundered, with her cargo washing ashore and attracting the attention of beachcombers and the world's media. The ship's enormous anchor is on display here. Explore the beach and foreshore, all looked after by the National Trust, then return towards the car park. Take the path leading left of the Sea Shanty and climb the steep hill, going through a field with a couple of Second World War pillboxes and ascending a set of steps.

5. When you reach the top of the hill, take in the view along the red and white cliffs of the Jurassic Coast, before walking along the South West Coast Path (SWCP) with West Cliffs on your left.

6. Ignore the first few paths leading right, including one with a fingerpost pointing to St Winifred's Church, and continue straight on. Go through a large gate, keeping to the SWCP.

7. After going through the humps of an old quarry, go right, following a fingerpost pointing to The Fountain Head. Ignore another right turn and continue through a kissing gate, descending through the trees and wildflowers of Pitt Coppice, along a single-track path. Pass through another gate, go left then right, to reach the pub.

8. After leaving the pub, turn right and carefully walk along the road. Continue through the pretty, elongated village of Branscombe, passing delightful cottage gardens and the beautifully positioned church of St Winifred's, until you reach the car park.

10 Heddon Valley
The Hunter's Inn

Hidden in Heddon Valley on North Devon's Exmoor coast, **THE HUNTER'S INN** is a large pub patrolled by peacocks, and popular with walkers exploring this dramatic section of the South West Coast Path. Cared for by the National Trust, the inn has a snug front bar and an open-plan area, with a fireplace and garden views. There's outdoor seating at the front, and a beautiful back garden, with dovecotes, a stream and carved wooden animals. Lovely locally sourced food is served. Accommodation is available above the pub; there's a bothy next door and a pop-up campsite nearby.

The Hunter's Inn
Heddon Valley, Exmoor
Devon EX31 4PY
01598 763230
www.thehuntersinnexmoor.co.uk

About this walk

- South West Coast Path
- Tarka Trail
- Exmoor National Park
- Dark Sky Reserve

Start/finish Heddon Valley car park (National Trust)
Distance 4½ miles (7km)
Time to pub 2–2.5 hours
Walking time 2–2.5 hours
Terrain Coastal footpath, woodland trail, lanes, roads

After an initial climb, this route rewards with a hill-hugging adventure along one of the most spectacular, yet least-trodden, sections of the South West Coast Path, where Exmoor plunges over cliffs into the Celtic Sea. Descend, then, into the cleavage of Heddon Valley to explore a secret beach and stroll beside a chattering river to a spectacular country inn.

Spring Wildflowers abound around Heddon Valley and on the hilltops. Scan the sky for peregrine falcons and buzzards, and look for signs of otters in the creek and majestic red deer on the hillsides.

Summer Scan the sea, searching for dolphins and seals. Look for butterflies, including the endangered high-brown fritillary, and enjoy the Hunter's Inn's gorgeous garden.

Autumn Walk amid purple heather and vibrant yellow gorse. Look for red deer and, from September, listen for bellowing stags during the rut.

Winter Snowdrops sprout and the river runs fast. Linger after sunset to explore the galaxy above Exmoor – Europe's first official Dark Sky Reserve.

The Hunter's Inn serves beers brewed by Exmoor Ales, including Stag, Gold and Exmoor Beast (a porter). Exmoor Cider is also available.

Follow in the footsteps of ... Romantic poets Shelley, Coleridge and Wordsworth all found inspiration on Exmoor's wild west coast. The Hunter's Inn is the product of a romantic notion harboured by eccentric Colonel Benjamin Lake, who built the pub in the style of a Swiss Chalet at the beginning of the 19th century and constructed a dramatic coastal tramway to the inn from Woody Bay. The grand design collapsed after a financial scandal, but the inn remains a lovely legacy of his dream.

How to Get There

By Car Park at the car park opposite the National Trust office, welcome centre and The Pantry (EX31 4PY; National Trust). The Hunter's Inn is signposted from the A39 between Parracombe and Lynton, or you can approach from Combe Martin along a wider road passing between Holdstone Hill and Trentishoe Down.

By Public Transport The nearest train station is Barnstaple (17 miles/27km).

OS Map OS Explorer OL9 (Exmoor), Landranger 180 (Barnstaple & Ilfracombe); grid ref (for start): SS 655/480.

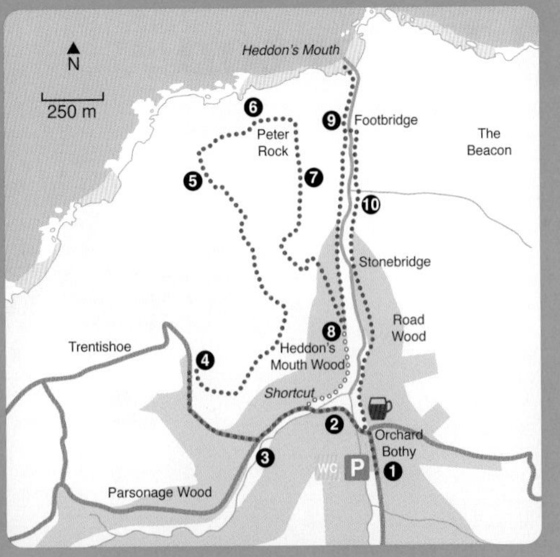

1. Exit the car park and go left, passing toilets, welcome centre, The Pantry and info boards on local flora and fauna. Walk towards the Hunter's Inn, passing a bothy on the right – one of a series of such accommodation options available to South West Coast Path (SWCP) walkers on this coast.

2. When the road forks, go left of the pub, passing a phone box and walking to Harry's Orchard. As you continue around this field, a fingerpost points right to Heddon's Mouth. Continue along the road.

Shortcut: the next section involves a stiff climb – for a less challenging walk, take the footpath right, just past Harry's Orchard, along the river to Heddon Mouth. Rejoin the main route at 8.

3. After a couple of cottages, turn right, up the steep road, following a sign for Trentishoe Church.

4. Ascend for 800 yards, then take a footpath leading right, following coast path signs. Walk around the hillside, past a seat, where spectacular valley views open up to the right, with the pub visible way below, nestled among the trees.

5. At a T-junction with a three-way fingerpost, take the path leading right, signed towards the Coast Path and Hunter's Inn. Look west (left) along the coast to Great Hangman (1,044ft/318m), the SWCP's highest point, which also boasts England's tallest sea cliff (800ft/244m). This coastline is so remote, and the bays so inaccessible, that German U-boats landed here to take on water during the Second World War, and the crews were confident enough to get out and kick footballs around.

6. Walk along a stunning path, part of both the SWCP and the Tarka Trail (a 180-mile/290-km route tracing the journey of Tarka the Otter in Henry Williamson's famous novel). Stroll round East Cleave to Peter Rock, where more amazing views open up, looking east across Heddon's Mouth, over the Valley of the Rocks and Lynton to Foreland Point and up the Bristol Channel.

7. Continue along the path, which hugs a contour line and then descends through Heddon Mouth Cleave, dropping into the trees and through a gate.

8. At a T-junction, turn left. Pass a stone bridge on the right; this leads straight back to the pub if you're in a rush, otherwise continue along the river.

9. Pass a wooden bridge and old limekilns, before meeting the rocky beach at Heddon's Mouth. After exploring, return to the wooden bridge, cross and turn right, following the path with the River Heddon running on your right.

10. Keep walking, ignoring trails leading uphill. Stay right along the path closest to the river. Follow signs leading into the Hunter's Inn garden. After leaving the pub, walk straight up to the car park.

11 Killerton

Red Lion Inn

A 16th-century pub at the heart of a pretty village seemingly suspended in time, despite being just 5 miles (8km) from Exeter, the **RED LION INN**, owned by the National Trust, attracts a friendly mix of locals and visiting walkers. Positioned by a church, mill and green, the pub has a lovely beer garden and courtyard. The interior features immense wooden beams and stone walls with deep-set fireplaces, where woodburners flicker in winter. Wonderful food is served seven days a week – booking ahead on Sundays is advisable. Accommodation is available.

Red Lion Inn
Broadclyst, Devon EX5 3EL
01392 461271
www.redlionbroadclyst.co.uk

About this walk
- Working watermill
- Woodlands and orchards
- Fantastic flower displays
- Butterflies

Start/finish Killerton car park (National Trust)
Distance 7½ miles (12km); shortcut available
Time to pub 1–1.5 hours
Walking time 3 hours; 2 hours with shortcut
Terrain Footpaths, bridleways, woodland trails, lanes, quiet roads

Stroll through orchards, fields and farms to a village of yellow thatched cottages and a 400-year-old pub, before exploring woodlands and an extraordinary country park.

Spring Fruit trees blossom in Sparrow Park and Clyston Mill orchards. Wild garlic perfumes the paths through Danes and Columbjohn woods, and magnolias, azaleas, rhododendrons and bulbs flower in Killerton's gardens. A purple haze surrounds Bluebell Gate.

Summer Songbirds serenade ancient oaks in Danes Wood, while buzzards wheel overhead. Wildflowers bloom in Columbjohn Woods and Ashclyst Forest, attracting butterflies including white admiral, silver-washed and pearl-bordered fritillary.

Autumn Apples are ripe for scrumping in orchards and squirrels squabble for chestnuts in woodlands. Killerton's views reveal a landscape ablaze, with trees flaming yellow and red. Spot horseshoe and barbastelle bats at dusk.

Winter A cyclamen carpet blooms around Killerton's chapel, while exotic winter trees and shrubs like Tibetan cherry and 'Midwinter Fire' dogwood glow. Snowdrops appear in Danes Wood and The Red Lion's woodburner blazes.

The Red Lion serves local ciders and beer, including Devon Scrumpy from Sandford Orchards and Firefly Bitter from Hanlons Brewery near Exeter.

Follow in the footsteps of ... Killerton estate near Exeter, encompasses an extinct volcano, an Iron Age hill fort, expansive woodlands and exquisite gardens. In 1944, it was passed to the National Trust by Sir Richard Acland because he believed the public should have access to the countryside. A Liberal and Labour MP, Acland was a founding member of CND.

How to Get There

By Car Park at Killerton (EX5 3LE; National Trust), just off the M5 – take J28 when travelling southbound or J29 when going northbound, and follow signs.

By Public Transport Take a train to Exeter Central or Exeter St David's (both 7 miles/11km). Stagecoach bus 1 between Exeter and Tiverton stops at Broadclyst and passes close to Killerton.

OS Map OS Explorer 114 (Exeter & the Exe Valley), Landranger 192 (Exeter & Sidmouth); grid ref (for start): SS 977/002.

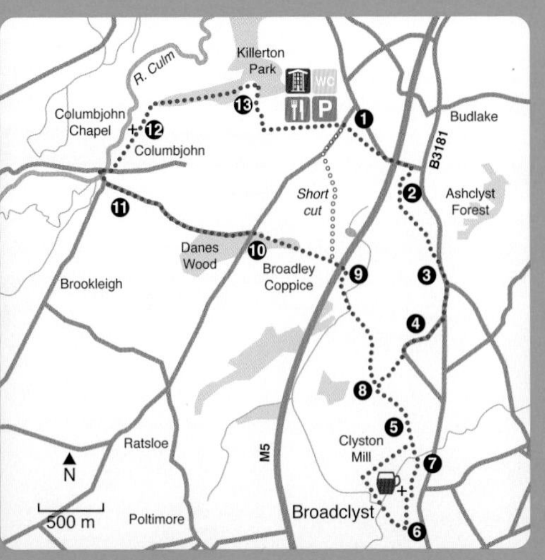

1. From Killerton car park, carefully cross the road and enter the orchard opposite, through a gate. Wend past picnic tables and apple trees, following fingerposts pointing to Budlake Old Post Office. Keep walking, through Sparrow Park, passing the delightful, thatched post office on your right, and cross a bridge over the M5.

2. Turn right and walk along the lane and bridleway, with the buzz of the motorway fading. Continue past Newhall Farm and, just before meeting the road, follow horseshoe and bike waymarkers going right.

3. Walk along a wide path running parallel to the road. At the end, turn right along a lane. Continue past a turning for Reed Cottage, and then turn right opposite a barn, still following bridleway waymarkers.

4. Pass a thatched cottage and, at a junction with a path, stay on the main bridleway as it arcs left. Go through Martinsfield Farm (where you will find a barn with a table typically laden with organic produce for sale, with an honesty box) and continue along the lane with fields on either side.

5. Go around a right-angle bend and continue, past a pylon, as the track elbows left. Cross a little bridge over the River Clyst. The turning for Clyston Mill (a working water mill cared for by the National Trust) is immediately on your left, via a little gate that takes you through an apple orchard with picnic tables.

6. If it's open, you can go across the grounds of the mill and through the church graveyard to the pub. Otherwise, follow the track to a T-junction, turn left along Wiltshier Close to Broadclyst House and Cottage, then go straight along the lane to the church and pub.

7. Leave the pub and turn left, walking along a lane between yellow thatched cottages. Continue straight along a footpath through a green tunnel of ivy-covered hazel hedgerow. Cross a bridge over the river and go through a field, turning right then left along the bridleway you walked earlier.

8. Pass through Martinsfield Farm, then leave the bridleway, going straight along a lane, following footpath arrows. Immediately turn right across a little wooden bridge. Follow footpath arrows across a field, over another little bridge, then walk diagonally across a second field to the right corner, before going through a gate, over a stile and straight across a third field. Continue, past a farmhouse, over a stile, along a path between fields, through a couple more stiles and gates.

9. Cross the footbridge back over the M5, pass through a gate and walk along a footpath between fields.

A framed view from Killerton's Bluebell Gate, looking across Devon towards Dartmoor.

Shortcut: To cut this walk short, take a footpath right here, crossing a field then turning left along a track past Francis Court Farm, and right along the road (no pavement) to Killerton.

Otherwise, continue along the permissive path, through Broadley Coppice. When the path forks, go right and wend through sycamore, holly, sweet chestnut and ash trees.

10. Reach the road by a three-way junction and turn left into Dane's Wood, where Vikings once camped. Bear right and follow the track leading along the right edge of the wonderful woods. Keep right, and when the track veers left up a hill, go right, down to the road, and turn left.

11. Walk to a junction and turn right, following a sign for Rewe. Just past the bend, go right, into the entrance for Columbjohn Farm, where there's a National Trust sign for Ellerhayes Bridge and a footpath fingerpost. Leave the lane after 100 yards and turn left on a footpath along the River Culm.

12. Go through a kissing gate, pass lovely little Columbjohn Chapel and turn left on the lane, following a fingerpost pointing towards Park Wood and Ellerhayes Bridge. After the lane snakes left then right, take the path leading through a kissing gate, uphill into the woods.

13. Go past Killerton's 'lost mansion', a massive building that was started in 1775, but never completed, signs of which lay hidden for centuries until being unearthed in 2017. Stay on the path as it leans left, then goes right, through a wooden gate into a field, following a fingerpost pointing towards The Clump. Walk uphill towards Bluebell Gate but don't go through – instead bear right and walk along a path passing a giant wooden rectangle framing the bucolic view across Dane Woods towards Dartmoor. Continue down to a wooden gate, then turn left through a kissing gate and follow a fingerpost pointing towards the Stables Café. Walk with a ha-ha wall on your left as the path takes you between the Front Park and the main house. Turn left through the gate at the end to return to the car park.

12 Lorna Doone
Rockford Inn

Rockford Inn
Brendon, Lynton
Exmoor, Devon EX35 6PT
01598 741214
www.therockfordinn.co.uk

About this walk

- Exmoor National Park
- Rivers, waterfalls, woods
- Coleridge Way
- Red deer and wild Exmoor ponies

Start/finish Lorna Doone Farm car park (EX35 6NU, National Trust)
Distance 11 miles (17.5km)
Time to pub 2 hours
Walking time 4.5 hours
Terrain Riverside and woodland trails, footpaths across open moorland, some road

The remote **ROCKFORD INN** is a picturesque pub-hotel hidden in an Exmoor valley on the Devon–Somerset border, surrounded by wonderful walking trails, woods and waterways. Located beside the East Lyn River, with a patio offering waterside tables, the 17th-century building features a low-beamed bar with stone walls and an open fire. The faces of dozens of Toby jugs grin back at you from behind a bar stocked with local ales. The inn offers good food, B&B accommodation, and even fishing permits for one of Britain's best salmon and trout rivers.

From Lorna Doone, on the Devon–Somerset border, amble along the banks of the East Lyn River, past rapids and waterfalls, exploring a storied Exmoor valley with two welcoming inns. Return across evocative open moorland, following beautiful Badgworthy Water.

Spring Wood anemone, sorrel, woodruff and bluebells bloom. Dippers bob on river bank boulders. On the moor, skylarks soar, and you may spot ring ouzels and Exmoor pony foals.

Summer Sand martins swoop along the Lyn and Badgworthy Water, where beaches beckon paddlers. Search the shallows for crayfish, chase butterflies across moorland and listen for stonechat, tree pipit, whinchat, wheatear, cuckoo and lapwing.

Autumn Salmon leap the waterfalls and bask in pools, as iridescent kingfishers flash past. Search for signs of otters and hear stags roar during the red deer rut. The wooded valley turns red and gold.

Winter Look for hunting herons and grey wagtails along the waterways, and the Dartford warbler in the gorse. Owls, merlin, buzzards, kestrels and sparrowhawks circle Exmoor's sky, which becomes star studded after dark.

The Rockford Inn offers Exmoor Ales' Stag, Gold, Cider and Wicked Wolf, gravity-poured from barrels. Exmoor-distilled gin is also available.

Follow in the footsteps of ... Doone Valley and Malmsmead were immortalised in R.D. Blackmore's 1869 novel *Lorna Doone*. The story (about a local lad's dramatic relationship with a beautiful girl brought up by a family of outlaws in the late 17th century) accurately describes Exmoor and incorporates many historical events.

How to Get There

By Car Take the A39, turn off along New Road to Oare and follow signs. Park at Lorna Doone Farm car park (EX35 6NU; National Trust).

By Public Transport The nearest train station is Barnstaple (25 miles/ 40km), from where buses go to Lynmouth, 5 miles (8km) from Lorna Doone Farm.

OS Map OS Explorer OL9 (Exmoor), Landranger 180 (Barnstaple & Ilfracombe) and 181 (Minehead & Brendon Hills); grid ref (for start): SS 791/478.

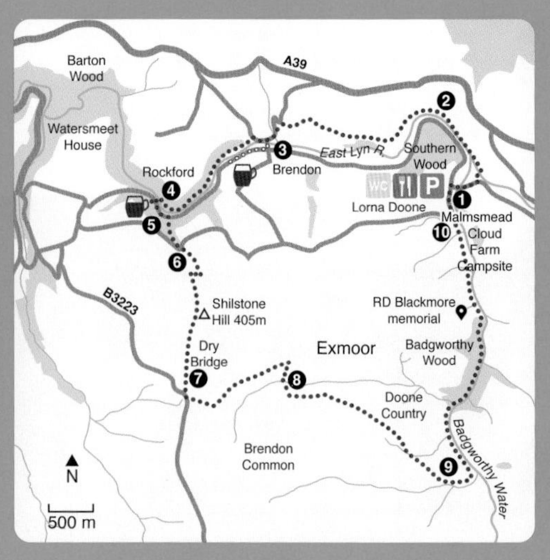

1. From Lorna Doone Farm – a historic former inn, where you will now find an excellent National Trust tea-room offering coffee, cakes, ice cream and light bites – cross the pretty stone bridge by a ford on Badgworthy Water. Walk up the hill, passing from Devon into Somerset en route, and turn left on a lane just past Parsonage Farm. Go through a gate, over a little footbridge across the East Lyn River, turn left and walk along a lovely path with the river on your left, following a fingerpost pointing towards Brendon and feather waymarkers for the Coleridge Way (a 51-mile/82-km trail though Somerset and Devon, tracing the landscape that inspired poet Samuel Taylor Coleridge).

2. Go through a gate and walk in front of a farm, passing a bridge on your left. Keep walking along the river bank, through more gates and across fields. The path becomes rocky as you pass a crag on the left and a section of little rapids – the perfect place to pause for a paddle or picnic. After a small fingerpost for Brendon, the path rises steeply away from the river, through Ashton Cleave. Keep climbing, with the ancient oak, ash and beech trees of Southern Wood cascading colourfully to your left. Go through a gate and continue walking along the Coleridge Way, which undulates through fields, with stunning valley views. After the path drops, follow a yellow arrow left, descending a bank and passing through Hall Farm.

3. When you meet the road, turn right. There's an option to cross the bridge and turn right here, a diversion taking you into Brendon Village to visit the Staghunters Inn; a pleasant pub and hotel offering Exmoor Ales, ciders and food in an atmospheric riverside setting. Otherwise, continue along the right bank of the East Lyn, following Hall Hill, then taking a lane leading left to walk along Countisbury Mill footpath. The path hugs the curves of the lively Lyn, taking you through woods and along a stunning section of riparian trail towards the National Trust tea-room at Watersmeet.

4. Before you reach Watersmeet, cross a footbridge over the river into the little village of Rockford; the inn is just on your right.

5. Leave the pub, walk back up Church Hill for 250 yards, then turn right by a building, going up steps, passing a waterwheel and ascending a steep footpath through woods, with a stream cascading to your left. Keep climbing, zig-zagging left then right to meet the road.

6. Turn left and walk to a sharp left turn in the road, where a fingerpost points straight ahead, towards Dry Bridge. Cross the stile in the elbow of the bend and walk uphill along a path, with a row of gnarled beech trees on your immediate right. Bear right and follow a little fingerpost along the path to buildings. Go past Shilstone Cottage, through a farmyard and wide wooden gate, passing Shilstone

Farmhouse into a field, then take an immediate right, following a fingerpost. Cross a stream and continue up the path as it ascends a steep hillside, snaking right then left until you emerge on open moor, with a fence on your right. Follow yellow-topped wooden stakes running parallel to the fence to a gate with a memorial. Bear left here and trace the stakes uphill (ignoring scrappy paths on the left and right) to a trig point atop Shilstone Hill. Go straight over and follow the path down to the road at Dry Bridge.

7. Cross Dry Bridge and go left on a path passing between two large boulders. When you meet a broad track, turn left and walk across Brendon Common until you reach a four-way fingerpost. Turn right here, following the arm pointing to 'Doone Country', where the infamous Doone family had their bandit base in R.D. Blackmore's popular novel.

8. Drop through a dip, ford the stream, and continue across open moorland, tracing the track. Pass through a gate and keep following blue bridleway pointers as the route starts to descend into trees.

9. The path narrows and then forks at a wooden post, just before you meet Badgworthy Water at a spot where a medieval village once stood. Go left here, passing a three-way fingerpost and continuing straight along a path that brings you out by the river. Walk with the beautifully clear water running on your right, crossing a stream, a section of rocks and a footbridge, into Badgworthy Wood. Leaving the trees, you pass a memorial to R.D. Blackmore, author of *Lorna Doone*.

10. Shortly after passing the National Trust's Cloud Farm campsite on the opposite bank (a wonderful spot to pitch a tent beside the river), bear left slightly, and follow a fingerpost pointing to Malmsmead, walking along a bridleway, through fields. When you meet a lane, continue straight ahead to Lorna Doone Farm where you can enjoy more refreshments from The Buttery, a tearoom right beside the river.

Doone Valley on Exmoor echoes with stories and legends, including tales of outlaws, many of which are inspired by historical events.

13 Lundy Island
The Marisco Tavern

The Marisco Tavern
Lundy Island
Devon EX39 2EY
01237 431831
www.lundyisland.co.uk

About this walk
- Seals
- Puffins
- Stunning coast and cliff walking
- Lighthouses and castle

Start/finish Lundy Island Harbour
Distance 10 miles (16km); shortcuts possible
Time to pub 3.5 hours
Walking time 4 hours
Terrain Coastal and clifftop paths and tracks

THE MARISCO TAVERN is Lundy's social hub, where islanders and visitors swap tales over ales in an apparent time warp (the bar clock goes backwards, literally). Famously, this pub never shuts (although alcohol isn't consumed beyond serving hours). Built in the 1860s as a store and 'refreshment room' for quarrymen, a café/restaurant sells meals on one side, and a bar with a mezzanine floor occupies the other. Boat lifebuoys adorn walls, alongside nautical and military memorabilia, flotsam, funny signage and books. There's a lovely walled beer garden outside.

Circumnavigate a unique island bobbing between the Bristol Channel and the Celtic Sea, visiting three lighthouses, a 13th-century castle, prehistoric remains and beaches bustling with seals and puffins, before pausing for a pre-ferry pint.

Spring On the island's sheltered east side, primroses, bluebells, Lundy cabbage, red campion, herb-robert and foxgloves flower. From April, breeding seabirds including puffins, guillemots, kittiwakes, shearwaters and razorbills nest on west coast cliffs.

Summer Snorkel with seals and spot puffins. The wild west coast becomes vivid with blooming stonecrop, tormentil, thrift and bell heather, attracting bees and butterflies.

Autumn Atlantic grey seals give birth to their pups on Lundy's beaches. Gorse flowers, and sika deer and Soay sheep rut, with males clashing spectacularly.

Winter In colder months, Lundy is sparsely populated, evocatively wild and beaches are busy with seal pups – visits are only possible by helicopter.

The Marisco Tavern offers regional real ales with an island twist, including St Austell Brewery's Lundy Old Light golden ale. The store sells Madrigal Brewery's Lundy Pale.

Follow in the footsteps of ... Occupied for over 3,000 years, Lundy ('puffin island' in Norse) was named by visiting Vikings and has been a base for pirates, smugglers, rogues and rebels – including the infamous de Marisco family, after whom the pub is named (in 1242, William de Marisco was hanged, drawn and quartered for treason). Later Lundy was allegedly won in a card game by two 'gentlemen', before being bought by a former slave owner. Since 1969, it's been cared for by the National Trust and the Landmark Trust.

How to Get There

By Ferry The MS *Oldenburg* ferry operates from Ilfracombe or Bideford (depending on tides) at least three times a week, April–October. It's possible to arrive by helicopter from November to March, if you're keen to do a winter stay. The 7-minute flight leaves from Hartland Point in Devon.

OS Map OS Explorer 139 (Bideford, Ilfracombe & Barnstaple), Landranger 180 (Barnstaple & Ilfracombe); grid ref (for start): SS 145/438.

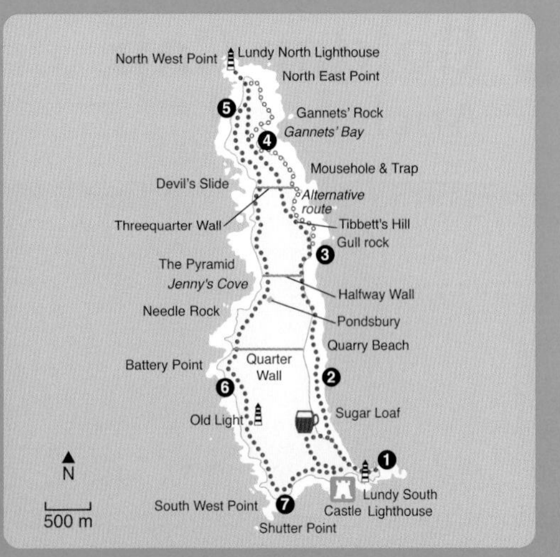

1. From the harbour, walk up the track beneath Lundy South Lighthouse, looking for seals, often seen around Landing Bay. Towards the top, before the village, turn right, walking over a stone bridge, past benches, through a gate and along a footpath above Ladies Beach. Pass through another gate, going past steps and beneath the arch of an overhanging oak, around a prominent shard of rock and the Sugar Loaf.

2. The path rises, crosses a stile at Quarter Wall, passes an old kiln above Quarry Beach and arrives at a flat open area. A path comes in from the left, and in VC Quarry you'll find a memorial to John Pennington Harman, son of millionaire Martin Coles Harman (one-time owner of Lundy Island), posthumously awarded the Victoria Cross for bravery during the Burma Campaign in 1944.

3. Where another quarry yawns left, the path forks. To hug the coastline and spot seals close-up, take the smaller, rougher path leading right, around the top of Halfway Wall Bay and Tibbett's Point to Threequarter Wall Bay, Frenchman's Landing, and Mousehole and Trap, then bear left at Gannets' Bay, returning to the main path. Or, for easier walking and better views, keep climbing along the main path, pass distinctive rocks at end of Halfway Wall, hop over a stone stile and continue to Tibbett's Hill; from the old Admiralty lookout station, take the path leading diagonally through heather to a gate and turn right along a track lined with large stones.

4. The paths meet above Gannets' Bay. Continue towards North End, site of a prehistoric settlement, where the path forks again – go right to loop and look over Gannets' Rock and North East Point, or continue straight to Lundy North Lighthouse at North West Point. Steps are hewn into the rock here, and a metal walkway leads to the lighthouse (built in 1897), beside a track that once lowered supplies. Look across the Hen and Chickens, searching for seals, then return along the path.

5. At a fork, bear right to walk along Lundy's wild and weather-beaten west coast, sculpted by waves and winds over millennia. Rock climbers flock here to clamber up sea crags including the Devil's Slide – an immense granite slab – and the rugged cliffs are seasonally home to colonies of seabirds, including Manx shearwaters. Jenny's Cove is a good place to spot puffins. Lundy ponies can often be seen around Pondsbury.

6. Continue past Battery Point to Old Light, Lundy's original lighthouse (built in 1819). Climb to the top for fantastic views, before continuing around the coast.

7. After rounding South West Point, walk with a stone wall and the island church on your left. Just before a gate, the path forks – go right, over a stile and stroll down to Marisco Castle, originally built by King Henry III around 1250. Turn acute left and walk up the lane to the Marisco Tavern.

14 Golden Cap
Anchor Inn

Anchor Inn
Seatown, Bridport
Dorset DT6 6JU
01297 489215
www.theanchorinn seatown.co.uk

About this walk
- Golden Cap peak
- Fossil hunting
- Jurassic Coast views
- South West Coast Path
- Dorset AONB

Start/finish Langdon Hill car park (National Trust)
Distance 4 miles (6.5km)
Time to pub 2 hours
Walking time 3 hours
Terrain Woodland and hillside paths, country lanes, small amount of road

Nestled beneath the peak of Golden Cap, the 160-year-old **ANCHOR INN** sits on the water's edge at Seatown, and the outside tables enjoy exceptional easterly views along Dorset's World Heritage-listed Jurassic Coast, right round Lyme Bay to the peninsula of Portland. The rustic interior has several rooms and a fire. Dorset-sourced food and drink is served, including local shellfish, with fine food sitting alongside pub grub. Accommodation is available. In the winter the pub sometimes shuts on Mondays and Tuesdays – check the website.

Stroll around Langdon Hill and St Gabriel's Wood to a ghost village and ancient chapel, then ascend Golden Cap to the South Coast's highest point, enjoying a panoramic vista along the Jurassic Coast, before dropping into a pub with stunning views.

Spring Bluebells and foxgloves enliven Langdon Hill woods. Look for lapwings, linnets and skylarks. Buzzards and ravens soar over Golden Cap.

Summer Blue butterflies flutter around Langdon Hill. From atop Golden Cap, Lyme Bay sparkles and the World Heritage-listed Jurassic Coast's multi-coloured cliffs stretch east and west.

Autumn Squirrels are busy in branches, while fungi surround trees on Langdon Hill amid a colourful carpet of leaves. Spy shy roe deer and elusive harvest mice in the brambles.

Winter Fossick for fossils along Seatown beach, where ammonites and belemnites (remains of locals who lived here during the Jurassic and Cretaceous periods) are revealed with every tide and after each storm.

The Anchor Inn stocks ales (IPA, Dorset Pale, Dorset Gold) and ciders (Orchard Gold, Haze and First Press) from Bridport's Palmers Brewery. Wines and spirits include Classic Cuveé from the Furleigh Estate in nearby Salway Ash, and Dorset-made Conker Gin.

Follow in the footsteps of ... St Gabriel's church (c. 1240) has an interesting history. According to legend, when two newlyweds escaped a stricken ship in a storm and sought shelter on the beach, praying to St Gabriel for salvation, the husband promised to build a church on the spot. Despite his wife dying, he honoured the oath. After the village was deserted, the disused chapel was used by smugglers to stash contraband.

How to Get There

By Car Park at Langdon Hill (DT6 6EP; National Trust), off the A35 between Chideock and Morcombelake.

By Public Transport The closest train stations are Axminster (5 miles/8km) and Dorchester South and West (20 miles/32km); Firstbus services X53 and X51 link Lyme Regis, Axminster, Dorchester South and Weymouth, passing Golden Cap between Charmouth and Bridport.

OS Map OS Explorer 116 (Lyme Regis & Bridport), Landranger 193 (Taunton & Lyme Regis); grid ref (for start): SY412/930.

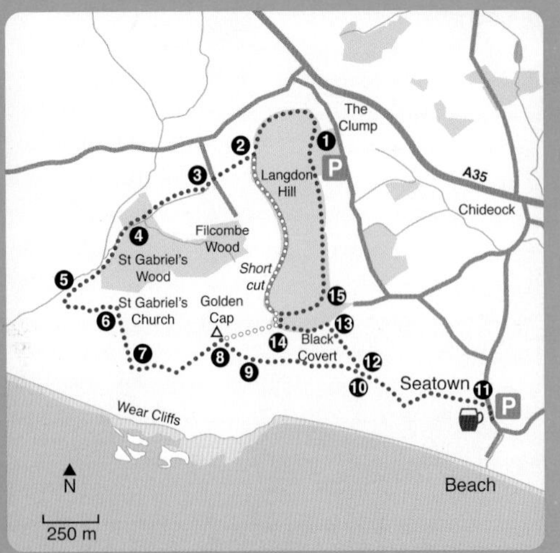

1. From Langdon Hill car park, join the main track, turn right and follow the broad trail anti-clockwise around the hill. At a signpost indicating Langdon Wood Walk, turn right.

2. At a fingerpost saying 'St Gabriel's ¾', turn right through a gate, descend across a field and cross a lane (the West Dorset National Trust office is to the left).

Shortcut: to cut 1½ miles (2.4km) from this route, and avoid some climbing, don't turn right here – continue around Langdon Hill, following signs for Golden Cap, and rejoin the main walk at point 8.

3. Follow a fingerpost for St Gabriel's, walking down a field, through a gap in the hedge and continuing into the next field. Pass through a large gate with another fingerpost pointing to St Gabriel's, and take the track going straight ahead, towards St Gabriel's Wood.

4. Pass through a small gate and take a narrow path through trees, walking beside a brook. A duckboard takes you across the stream and through a second small gate. Follow a fingerpost pointing straight on, towards St Gabriel's.

5. Go through a large gate and continue straight. Pass through another gate and turn left, into the tiny hamlet of Stanton St Gabriel, described by Sir Frederick Treves in 1906 as: 'A village which was lost and forgotten centuries ago.' It's a scenic, but very remote and exposed spot, and most of the population left in the 18th century. Now, National Trust holiday cottages offer quiet serenity.

6. Follow a fingerpost by a bench pointing to Golden Cap and Seatown. Walk up the hill, go through a large gate and pass the ruined remains of storied St Gabriel's church (see opposite). Bear right and walk uphill along the path.

7. Go through a gateway, turn left on the South West Coast Path (SWCP) and follow a fingerpost pointing up a steep, grassy field towards the summit of Golden Cap, so-named because of its orange sandstone head. Pass through a gate and keep ascending, following signs to Golden Cap and Seatown.

8. Zig-zag up to the broad, blonde, typically wind-tousled summit. Go over the brow of the hill, drinking in 360-degree views over waves and white horses to the horizon, all along the World Heritage–listed Jurassic Coast, and across the Wessex hinterland of Thomas Hardy novels. Glance west, over Lyme Regis and into Devon, and when the path forks, go right and look east across Lyme Bay's coves, which curve around to the outstretched arm of Portland peninsula. Walk around the trig point to a memorial to the Earl of Antrim, the National Trust chairman who led the

Looking east along the Jurassic Coast from the peak of Golden Gap, across Seatown and The Anchor towards the Portland peninsula.

1965 Enterprise Neptune campaign to purchase and protect sections of Britain's unspoiled coastline, such as the one you're exploring. Descend steps with rope railings on your right. At a wooden gate, go right, following a fingerpost to Seatown.

9. Pass through a wooden gate and descend across a field. Go through another two gates and cross a patchwork of fields, keeping the sea on your right.

10. Ignore a path leading sharp left, and keep following signs to Seatown, going through several more gates, a small patch of woodland, across a little boardwalk bridge and another field, and along a path.

11. Emerge onto the road and go right, past Golden Cap Holiday Park, walking towards the sea. The Anchor Inn is on the right, opposite the car park.

12. From the pub, retrace your steps up the road before taking the footpath (SWCP), fingerposted left to Golden Cap and Charmouth. Ascend, through double gates, up a steep section of steps and along the path to a wooden bench, where the path forks. Go right and follow a fingerpost pointing towards Langdon Hill, crossing a stile, hugging the fence on the right and continuing through a gate.

13. Hop over a stile at the top of the field and go left, uphill, following signs to Golden Cap and Langdon Hill.

14. At the next junction, turn right to Langdon Hill, then right again, following the fingerpost pointing to the car park. Meet the main track and keep going right, passing a Gold Nugget sculpture – created by artist Zac Greening, who used Portland stone with golden leaf detailing to mark the 50th (Golden) anniversary of the Enterprise Neptune Campaign in 2015. Walk along a lovely leafy, tree-lined track to the car park.

15 Cerne Abbas
The Giant Inn

Formerly known as The Red Lion – a name that still appears across the wonderful glass frontage of the Victorian building – **THE GIANT INN** is located right in the heart of Cerne Abbas, beneath the huge naked figure on the hill, after whom it has been renamed. The last remaining free house in the village, this character-filled pub was rebuilt in 1898 after a fire destroyed the 15th-century coaching inn – somewhat ironically, the fireplace is the only surviving original feature. The cosy bar welcomes walkers, serves food and offers a secluded beer garden for summertime visits.

The Giant Inn
24 Long Street
Cerne Abbas
Dorset DT2 7JF
01300 341441
www.thegiantcerneabbas.co.uk

About this walk

- Iconic chalk figure
- Iron Age remains
- Cerne Valley Trail

Start/finish Kettle Bridge car park
Distance 4 miles (2.5km)
Time to pub 1.5 hours
Walking time 2 hours
Terrain Footpaths, hillside trails, some road

SOUTH WEST

Walk around Britain's biggest chalk hill figure and take in wonderful Wessex views, before exploring a 1,000-year-old abbey, enjoying a drop of local ale in a delightful Dorset village, and returning via a riverside ramble.

Spring Early purple orchid, a plant associated with love and reproduction, blooms around the Giant, who has folkloric associations with fertility.

Summer Wildflowers bloom, including common spotted and pyramidal orchids. Butterflies abound – spot marsh fritillary, grizzled skippers, Duke of Burgundy, Adonis blue, dingy skipper, brimstone, peacock, orange tip and green hairstreak.

Autumn Garden spiders spin spectacular orb webs across grassland punctuated by patches of purple autumn gentian. Dippers bob along the River Cerne and buzzards, depicted on Cerne Valley Trail waymarkers, circle above the hill.

Winter Frost nips the chalk grassland. Goldfinches, thrushes, wrens, tits and robins flit between trees along the River Cerne and tawny owls silently hunt at dusk.

The Giant Inn serves ales from the local Cerne Abbas Brewery, plus Butcombe Rare Breed, Ringwood Razorback and various Wriggle Valley beers.

Follow in the footsteps of ... The Giant's origins have, until recently, been shrouded in mystery. The figure only began to be mentioned in writing from the 17th century, and experts have long argued about whether he was a pagan fertility symbol, a Roman rendition of Hercules, or even a satirical depiction of Oliver Cromwell. However, in May 2021, using high-tech equipment and analysing the remains of snails in the chalk, scientists narrowed down his birthday to somewhere between AD 700 and 1100.

How to Get There

By Car Take the A352 to Cerne Abbas and park at Kettle Bridge (DT2 7GY; not National Trust).

By Public Transport Dorchester West and Dorchester South are the closest train stations (8 miles/13km). South West Coaches bus X11 between Dorchester, Sherborne and Yeovil stops at Cerne Abbas.

OS Map OS Explorer 117 (Cerne Abbas & Bere Regis), Landranger 194 (Dorchester & Weymouth); grid ref (for start): ST 664/015.

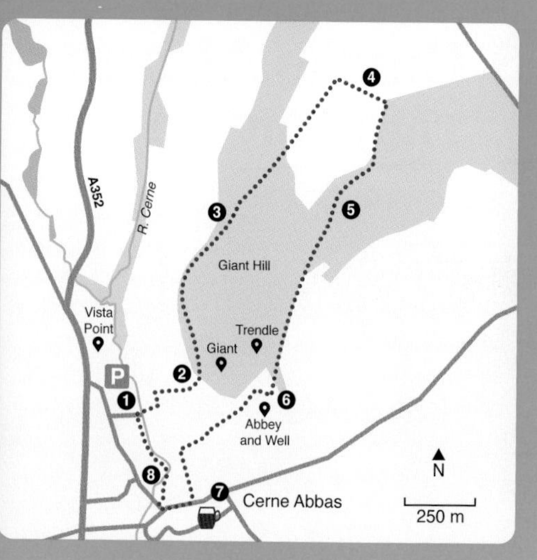

1. Before setting off, it's worth checking out the Giant from the well-signposted viewpoint on Duck Street, near the junction with the A352, because the scale of the 180ft (55m) geoglyph means you can only really appreciate it from afar. The club-wielding warrior has undergone numerous changes over the centuries, losing a cape that once draped over his left arm and gaining an extension to his impressive 36ft (11m) genitalia when a circle that once depicted his navel became incorporated into this area. When you're ready to walk, head east from the car park, along Kettle Bridge Lane towards the hill, crossing the River Cerne over a stone bridge. At a fork, turn left and follow a track around to the base of the hill, before going through a gate and bearing left along an obvious path.

2. Walk below the Giant's toes, tracing a contour line along the bottom of the hill (originally called Trendle Hill, after an Iron Age enclosure above the figure's head, which long predates the geoglyph, but is now known as Giant's Hill). To prevent damage to the delicate figure (rumours of his powers of fertility have historically encouraged couples to get far too close), the National Trust has installed a fence, which is on your right as you ramble.

3. When the path forks, keep right to maintain the higher ground, strolling across open fields with fantastic views along the Cerne Valley and the Wessex landscape of Thomas Hardy novels.

4. After passing a grove of trees on your left, turn right along a path leading uphill through farm fields, towards more woods. Go through a gate, turn right and walk along a bridleway traversing the hilltop, through the site of a prehistoric settlement.

5. The path descends the east side of the hill, passing through woodlands.

6. At a junction, the track splits several ways. Take the second right and walk towards Cerne Abbas, through the remains of Cerne Abbey, a Benedictine monastery founded by Æthelmær the Stout in AD 987 and plundered by King Cnut. Explore the elaborate three-storey Abbot's Porch, the old burial ground and St Augustine's Well, a water source with alleged curative properties.

7. Continue along Abbey Street, passing the 13th-century church of St Mary the Virgin on your left, where the cemetery includes a pirate's grave, and the carved face by the porch door used to be a working chimney, breathing smoke from its nose and mouth. Emerge on Long Street, by the Royal Oak, turn right and The Giant Inn is opposite.

8. After leaving the pub, continue along Long Street, then turn right on Duck Street, just after The New Inn. Immediately turn right again, onto Mill Lane, which leads to a lovely leafy track that traces the Cerne River to Kettle Bridge and the car park.

16 Spyway
Square and Compass

Square and Compass
Weston Road
Worth Matravers
Dorset BH19 3LF
01929 439229
www.squareandcompass
pub.co.uk

About this walk
- South West Coast Path
- Dinosaur footprints
- Cliffs and sea views
- Priest's Way

Start/finish Spyway car park, Langton Matravers (National Trust)
Distance 8 miles (13km)
Time to pub 2.5–3 hours
Walking time 4 hours
Terrain Coastal footpaths, clifftop trails, lanes

A quintessential walker's pub, run by the same family for over 100 years, the **SQUARE AND COMPASS** occupies a perfect position on the Isle of Purbeck, close to the South West Coast Path. A pub since 1776, the stone building houses a fossil-filled museum as well as two snug bars, warmed by open fires. Locally made ales, ciders, pies and pasties are served over a counter. The sprawling, sea-facing garden, scattered with Purbeck-stone benches and slab tables, is forever busy with hikers, bikers and climbers toasting their adventures. There is regular live music.

This Jurassic Coast classic traces a dramatic and storied cliffscape around the delightful (but disingenuously named) Purbeck Island, from Dancing Ledge to St Aldhelm's Head, before visiting a legendary walker's pub with outstanding views and fantastic brews. Return along the Priest's Way, via a quarry where you can see fossilised dinosaur footprints frozen in time.

Spring On Purbeck's limestone grassland, gorse and impatient wildflowers such as early gentian and spider orchids begin blooming.

Summer Skylarks sing and male meadow pipits perform a curious parachuting courtship flight. Look along cliffs and out to sea to spot guillemot, razorbills, shags and even puffins, which raft up in large groups. Milkwort, bird's-foot trefoil, eyebrights, vetches and knapweed flower, attracting butterflies including Lulworth skipper and Adonis blue.

Autumn Scan the sea for passing dolphins. The Square and Compass hosts beer and cider festivals in October and November.

Winter Watch wild waves crashing over Dancing Ledge. If you're very lucky, you might spy a white-tailed sea eagle, recently reintroduced to the nearby Isle of Wight.

The Square and Compass serves cider and ales made by Purbeck brewery Hattie Brown's, including Moonlite and Dog on the Roof, named after the manager's Irish terrier, often seen sat atop the pub's slate roof.

Follow in the footsteps of ...
Just off the Priest's Way, discover fossilised brachiosaurus tracks left by enormous, long-necked, plant-eating dinosaurs towards the end of the Jurassic period (145 million years ago). It's thought this must have been a watering hole where dinosaurs gathered to drink.

How to Get There

By Car Take the B3069 to Langton Matravers, then follow Durnford Drove and signs to Langton House and Spyway car park (BH19 3HG; National Trust).

By Public Transport Morebus service 40 runs between Poole, Wareham and Swanage, stopping at Langton Matravers.

OS Map OS Explorer OL15 (Purbeck & South Dorset), Landranger 195 (Bournemouth & Purbeck); grid ref (for start): SY 998/782.

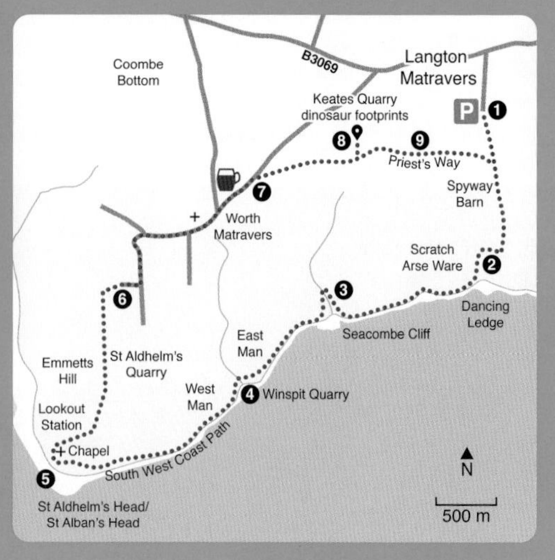

1. From the car park at Spyway, go through the gate and walk towards the coast, strolling along a gravel lane. Keep going straight, across an intersection with the Priest's Way, to the barn, where you will find information boards explaining the flora, fauna and history of the area, including stories about the smuggling that used to take place here. Pass through a gate to the left of the barn and walk along a track traversing a limestone grass-covered meadow where wildflowers bloom in spring and summer, attracting an array of butterflies. Greet a sculpture of a Limousin cow (created by artist Sarah Moore), go through a second gate and across another field.

2. After a gate, turn right, briefly, walking towards an area of gorse and limestone grassland known as Scratch Arse Ware, before bearing left and heading down the hillside to meet the World Heritage-listed Jurassic Coast at cliffs overlooking Dancing Ledge. If you have time, it's well worth descending to explore this extraordinary limestone plateau, named after an optical effect created by waves on the rising tide that appear to make the ledge dance. Formerly a Purbeck stone sea quarry, these days it's usually busy with climbers and coasteerers clambering and scrambling over the rocks. There's also a plunge pool, originally dynamited for the enjoyment of local school children, which fills with sun-warmed seawater after each high tide. Once you've explored Dancing Ledge, continue west, along the South West Coast Path (a 630-mile/1014-km trail running between Poole Harbour in Dorset and Minehead in Somerset, via the coasts of Devon and Cornwall).

3. Walk towards the distant view of Portland, passing through several gates and turning inland for a short section as the path skirts around Seacombe Cliffs. Turn left through a gate and climb some steps by a signpost for Winspit. At the top of the hill, pass through another gate, bear left and follow the coast path through more gates and down a series of steep steps.

4. While walking, see if you can make out strip lynchets (visible lines created by medieval ploughing) on the flanks of East and West Man, hills either side of Winspit Quarry. The coastal quarry, recently acquired by the National Trust, is interesting too, with strange crags and deep caves created by the historic quarrying of Purbeck stone, prized by the Romans and used extensively in the building of prominent buildings (including Westminster Abbey and Corfe Castle) during medieval times. Quarrying has long since stopped, but this unique landscape is popular with rock climbers and has been used as a film set for sci-fi shows such as *Doctor Who*. Continue walking along the South West Coast Path towards St Aldhelm's Head, passing several extraordinary wind- and rain-sculpted rock formations, and an installation by local artist Tony Viney, who has combined two radar dishes to resemble a fire basket,

commemorating the beacons that once lined this coast, which were lit to warn of the approach of the Spanish Armada in 1588.

5. At St Aldhelm's Head (also called St Alban's Head) you'll find a National Coastwatch Institution (NCI) Lookout Station, and the volunteers are usually happy to allow in visitors and answer questions. This is a great dolphin and birdwatching spot. There's also a stone seat with a wild view over the channel, and a chapel – the current building dates to the 19th century, but there has been a place of worship on the headland for over 800 years. Leave the South West Coast Path and turn right here, walking inland along a lane/bridleway.

6. Walk past St Aldhelm's Quarry, turn right at the next junction, and then left along Bonvils Road. At Weston Farm, turn right and walk along the road into Worth Matravers. Bear right on Pikes Lane, walk past the village pond, and go right again at the next junction to reach the Square and Compass, located in the middle of a large fork in the road.

7. Leave the pub and walk up the road. Pass a National Trust sign for East Man to your right, beyond which a deep valley plunges towards the coast, its sides scarred by strip lynchets. Keep walking up the road until you see a footpath sign pointing right and follow this across the corner of a field. Cross a lane and go through another two fields. When you meet a large gate, go straight through and follow a fingerpost pointing towards Langdon Matravers and Swanage. You're now walking along the Priest's Way (a 3-mile/5-km track historically used by a clergy to travel between churches in Worth Matravers and Swanage).

8. Pass a National Trust sign for Eastington on your right, but continue straight, through a gate. Look out for a gate on your left, with a sign saying 'Dinosaur Tracks'. Go through and check out the fossilised footprints just off the Priest's Way.

9. Rejoin the Priest's Way and carry on along the broad track. When you meet a crossways, follow the fingerpost pointing left towards Langton and walk down to the car park at Spyway.

Secret sea caves below Seacombe Cliff, between Dancing Ledge and Winspit Quarry.

Studland
The Bankes Arms

The Bankes Arms
Manor Road, Studland
Dorset BH19 3AU
01929 450225
www.bankesarms.com

About this walk
- Stunning coast views
- Marine wildlife and birds
- Second World War history

Start/finish Knoll Beach, Studland Bay (National Trust)
Distance 6 miles (10km)
Time to pub 2.5 hours
Walking time 3 hours
Terrain Beach, clifftop trails, footpaths, small amount of road

With a large clifftop beer garden overlooking Studland Bay, **THE BANKES ARMS** is a sensational seaside watering hole owned by the National Trust. Made from locally quarried stone, the 16th-century building has been operating as a pub for 200 years, and takes its name from the family that once owned Studland, Corfe Castle and Kingston Lacy. Two fires warm the open-plan interior, and candles burn on tables. Nine handpumps offer real ales and ciders from the Isle of Purbeck Brewery, based next door. Locally sourced food is served. Accommodation is available.

Stroll along a sandy beachscape, passing fortifications where British and US military top brass oversaw D-Day planning, and traverse a great chalky headland to Old Harry Rocks. Return across Ballard Down, before stopping at a pub with a view over stunning Studland Bay.

Spring Look out for Dartford warblers bobbing between bushes. The heathland behind the beach is home to all six British reptiles, and as the weather warms, lizards sometimes sunbathe on boardwalks.

Summer Enjoy a sea swim and search rock pools for signs of marine life. Studland Bay is a breeding site for short-snouted and spiny seahorses, which live in seagrass meadows around Redend Point. Skylarks hover over Ballard Down.

Autumn Spot sedge, willow, reed and grasshopper warblers on Ballard Down, and cormorants, black-backed gulls and peregrine falcons on the coast. Search the sea for bottlenose dolphins and seals.

Winter Brent geese eat eelgrass on Studland Bay, while sanderling play in the waves. Views from Ballard Down trig point are best on crisp, cool days.

The Bankes Arms offers Isle of Purbeck ales including Best Bitter, Studland Bay Wrecked, Purbeck IPA, Fossil Fuel and Solar Power.

Follow in the footsteps of...
On 18 April 1944, Winston Churchill, King George VI and General Dwight Eisenhower (Allied Forces Supreme Commander) watched soldiers rehearse for the Normandy invasion from Fort Henry on Redend Point. D-Day happened six weeks later. Meanwhile, The Bankes Arms was the control base for Project Fougasse, an experiment testing the use of burning oil as a defence against a German seaborne invasion.

How to Get There

By Car Drive along the B3351 from Corfe Castle and Swanage or arrive via chain ferry from Sandbanks, Poole. Park at Knoll Beach car park (National Trust).

By Public Transport Morebus service 50 from Bournemouth to Swanage stops at Studland Village.

OS Map OS Explorer OL15 (Purbeck & South Dorset), Landranger 195 (Bournemouth & Purbeck); grid ref (for start): SZ 035/833.

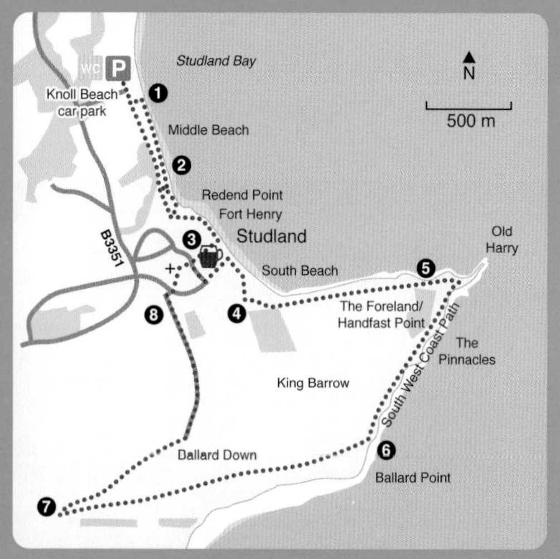

1. From the car park, walk towards the sea, past the National Trust's beach-side visitor centre, café and shop. Turn right and meander along the sand or take the boardwalk by the beach huts. Follow the sign to Middle Beach car park.

2. At Middle Beach, spot concrete 'Dragon's Teeth' anti-tank defences on your right. Walk through the car park and follow the path past Groom's Cottage (where there's a second-hand book shop). Pass an information sign about the Bankes family – who owned much of Purbeck Island, including Studland Bay and Corfe Castle, until they gifted it all to the National Trust in 1981 – and continue along the South West Coast Path (SWCP) into trees. Emerge by Fort Henry, an observation bunker overlooking Redend Point, where Allied soldiers rehearsed for D-Day (see opposite).

3. Follow the SWCP right as it turns briefly away from the sea (due to a landslip). Meet Manor Road, turn left and walk between The Bankes Arms and its glorious beer garden.

4. Continue to a bend in the road, where you can turn left to explore South Beach (at low tide it's possible to walk along the beach and rejoin the SWCP on the other side). However, our walk continues straight, briefly, following a fingerpost for Old Harry Rocks and the Coast Path, before bearing left just past the toilets. Keep following the SWCP across chalky grassland on to The Foreland.

5. The path brings you out onto a broad meadow, which eventually plunges dramatically over white cliffs into the sea at No Man's Land and St Lucas' Leap, beyond which chalk sea stacks rear out of the waves. Old Harry (a nickname for the Devil) is the largest. Once, a solid chalk ridge ran from here to the Isle of Wight (usually visible across the waves); The Needles and Old Harry Rocks are the remains of this isthmus. Continue around the headland, enjoying views of Natural Arch and the Pinnacles.

6. At a gate, turn right, leaving the SWCP and ascending Ballard Down. Walk uphill along the Purbeck Way to a trig point with fantastic views across Poole Harbour and Brownsea Island into Dorset (north), and across Swanage (south).

7. Walk along the ridge, passing a tombstone-shaped waymarker. The Purbeck Way drops left but carry on straight until you reach a large stone bench where a path crosses your way. Turn sharp right here, and walk down through the Glebeland Estate and along a lane, back into Studland.

8. When you reach the village (the inspiration for Toytown in Enid Blyton's *Noddy*) pass a tall Celtic cross, go straight up School Lane, then turn immediately right on Church Road. Walk through the church, turn right, and you're back at The Bankes Arms. After leaving the pub, reverse your footsteps to Knoll Beach car park.

18 Pamphill
The Vine Inn

The Vine Inn
Vine Hill, Pamphill
Dorset BH21 4EE
01202 882259

About this walk
- Wildflowers
- Riverside trails
- Stour Valley Way
- Birds and wildlife

Start/finish Pamphill Green car park (National Trust)
Distance 3½ miles (5.5km)
Time to pub 1.5 hours
Walking time 2 hours
Terrain Footpaths, farmland, riverside trails, meadows, country lanes

Near Kingston Lacy, surrounded by delightful Dorset countryside and owned by the National Trust, **THE VINE INN** is a former bakery-turned-pub, run by the same family for over 120 years. The current landlady, Linda, took over in 1986, continuing a tradition that began in 1900, when her grandfather opened the inn. Inside you'll find a cosy public bar where locals chat, a rear bar with interesting paraphernalia and an open fire, and a larger upstairs room. Outside there's a gravel garden and patio. Lunches are served. It's cash only, and opening times vary.

This gentle stroll through the stunning Stour Valley skirts the National Trust's Kingston Lacy estate, passes through the wildlife-rich rural landscape of Cowgrove and follows the banks of the River Stour past ancient weirs to a hidden gem of a pub.

Spring Abbott Street Copse floods with bluebells, and early blooming wildflowers, including wood anemones, pop up in copses and meadows. Common pipistrelle bats hunt midges at dusk around Rivers Edge Natural Green Space.

Summer Look out for the flash of kingfishers along the river, and search for signs of otters and water voles. Badgers are active along All Fools Lane, butterflies and bees buzz around wildflower-strewn meadows, and The Vine's garden is idyllic on sunny afternoons.

Autumn In a slow-motion display of alchemy, the oak avenue running through Pamphill turns to gold, capturing St Stephen's Church in a gilded frame. Keep your eyes peeled for treecreepers and the tiny goldcrest.

Winter Shy water rail, egret and heron hunt along the banks of the River Stour. Paths are very muddy, so wear boots.

The Vine Inn sells a rotating range of regional real ales, including Moonlight from Hattie Brown's in Swanage, and Otter Brewery's Amber Ale.

Follow in the footsteps of ...
Pamphill was once part of the sprawling estate of Kingston Lacy, owned by the Bankes family. William John Bankes filled the house and estate with art and antiquities, including a 2,000-year-old Egyptian obelisk and the sarcophagus of Amenemope, an Egyptian notable from the 13th century BC. Despite fleeing England in 1841, following a conviction for homosexuality, he continued to send *objets d'art* back.

How to Get There

By Car Take the B3082 between Blandford and Wimborne and, close to Kingston Lacy, turn off on Abbott Street or Cowgrove Road. Use Pamphill Green car park, near St Stephen's Church (BH21 4ED; National Trust).

By Public Transport The closest train station is Poole (8½ miles/14km). Buses run from Poole to Wimborne, from where a limited service runs to Kingston Lacy.

OS Map OS Explorer 118 (Shaftesbury & Cranborne Chase), Landranger 195 (Bournemouth & Purbeck); grid ref (for start): ST 990/008.

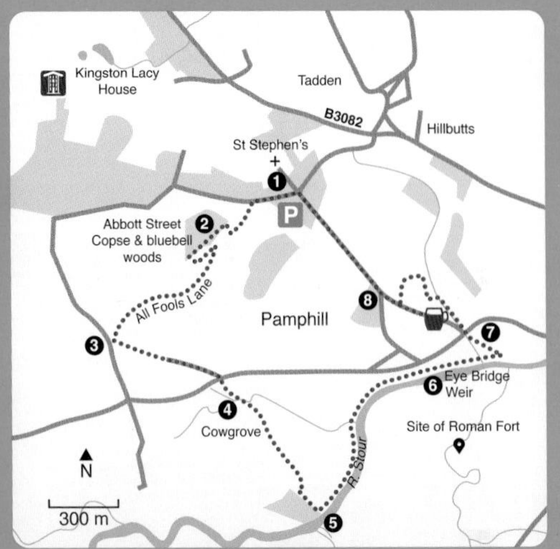

1. From the car park, walk towards St Stephen's Church, bearing left along a path. At the road, go left, and after 50 yards, left again on All Fools Lane, following arrows for Stour Valley Way (SVW), a 64-mile/103-km route through Wiltshire and Dorset.

2. On your right is Abbott Street Copse, famous for bluebells in spring. Do a little loop around this plantation, passing through young trees into ancient woods, before rejoining and turning right on All Fools Lane, which ducks under pylons and narrows as you descend.

3. Just before the road, turn left. Walk past a house and around a wooden gate. Ignoring a footpath going left, walk along a wide track, past a thatched cottage and around an S-bend. Pass Poplar Farm, cross a small road and, by thatched Drews Cottage, pick up a National Trust-signed footpath leading into Cowgrove.

4. Cross two footbridges, ignore gates leading left, and stay on the main path (which floods after rain, but a smaller, drier path runs to the left). When the path forks, stay left.

5. Meet the River Stour, wend left with the current and pass a thicket of blackthorn to a bench. Continue across a footbridge, ignore a permissive path leading left and keep walking with the river on the right and grazing fields to your left, often occupied by Red Ruby Devon cows, native to the West Country. Pass more benches and a tree-stump carving of an otter.

6. Go through a wooden gate and pass Eye Bridge, the site of an ancient ford. Stay on the left bank and follow the path through the car park. Keep walking along the river, following SVW fingerposts pointing towards Wimborne. Cross a stile, a field, a second stile and a little footbridge to reach Rivers Edge Natural Green Space. Wimborne Minster is visible through trees on the far side of the meadow, but after about 50 yards, opposite an orange life-saver ring on the river bank, turn sharp left and follow a footpath through a gap in the hedgerow. Trace the path left, through another hedge, then right to leave the field via a stile.

7. Carefully cross the road and go over a stile to the right of Vine Hill Road, following a SVW arrow. After 200 yards, cross a stile and footbridge on your left, leave the field and go through trees. Climb steps, go right over a stile and along a path. At a footbridge, turn left and follow SVW arrows up steps and along a path, bearing left beneath the legs of a pylon. When you reach the road, by a yellow thatched cottage, the Vine Inn is on your left.

8. Leave the pub and walk back up Vine Hill, past Pamphill School and along an oak-lined avenue towards St Stephen's Church. Cross the green, skirting a traditional English cricket pitch with a thatched pavilion, to the car park.

19 Corfe Castle
Bankes Arms

Named after the Royalist family that occupied Corfe Castle during the Civil War, the **BANKES ARMS** is a National Trust–owned 16th-century pub and hotel in the heart of the historic village, amid the Purbeck Hills. The beer garden has an alfresco bar, offers castle and countryside views, and trains from the nearby Swanage Steam Railway regularly puff past. Inside you will find a real fire, a traditional drinking area at the front and a restaurant at the rear, where you can enjoy quality home-cooked meals made with locally sourced ingredients. Accommodation is also available.

Bankes Arms
23 East Street, Corfe Castle
Dorset BH20 5ED
01929 288188
www.bankesarms
hotel.co.uk

About this walk

- Castle and history
- Wildflowers
- Dorset AONB
- Purbeck Way

Start/finish Castle View Visitor Centre car park (National Trust)
Distance 5 miles (8km)
Time to pub 2 hours
Walking time 2.5 hours
Terrain Countryside footpaths, castle ramparts and village streets

From the hilltop ruins of Corfe Castle, walk across wildlife-rich commons, passing a vintage steam railway and climbing Brenscombe Hill, before rambling back along the Purbeck Way ridgeline, taking in spectacular views.

Spring Skylarks shoot into the air above the commons, singing in the new season and looking for a mate to share it with.

Summer Rare electric blue southern damselflies hover around purple moor-grass by Corfe Common's slow-moving streams. Look for wild chamomile and yellow, star-like flowers of bog asphodel.

Autumn Spectacular sunsets blaze over Corfe Castle. Spot sika deer along the ridge and hear stags bellowing during the rut.

Winter Ponies roam the common, the castle ruins stand proud of winter mists, and a fire awaits in The Bankes Arms.

The Bankes Arms serves ales from Dorset's Palmers Brewery and Gritchie Brewing Company, a beer farm on the Dorset–Wiltshire border owned by film director Guy Ritchie.

Follow in the footsteps of ... Corfe's history is full of dark intrigue. King Edward the Martyr was murdered in the main square in 978 and the 11th-century castle (built by William the Conqueror) was a place of imprisonment during the reign of King John (1199–1216). In 1210, Maud de Braose, a noblewoman who offended the king, was thrown into the dungeon with her son and left to starve. During the English Civil War, the castle was robustly defended by Lady Mary Bankes during two sieges by Parliamentary forces. She was eventually betrayed by one of her own soldiers, defeated, and the castle was deliberately blown up, resulting in the ruined structure you can see today.

How to Get There

By Car There is a National Trust car park by the Castle View Visitor Centre, on the A351, opposite the castle mound on the left when approaching from Wareham.

By Public Transport The nearest train station is Wareham (5½ miles/9km). The Breezer 40 bus service (Poole to Swanage, via Wareham train station) serves Corfe.

OS Map OS Explorer OL15 (Purbeck & South Dorset), Landranger 195 (Bournemouth & Purbeck); grid ref (for start): SY 960/824.

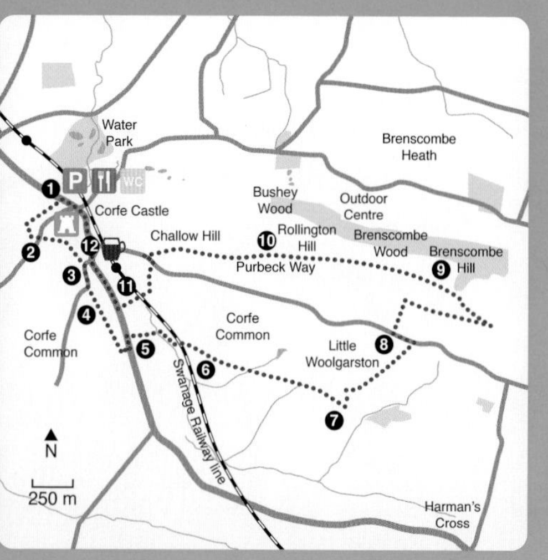

1. From the car park, cross the road via the traffic island opposite the Castle View Information Centre and café. Take the path between wooden fences, following a fingerpost pointing towards 'Castle and Village'. Walk along the wide woodland trail that skirts around the western edge of the castle mound, where the ruined battlements can be seen from all sorts of interesting angles through the trees. A river runs playfully on your left, and you can explore its banks in places.

2. At another fingerpost indicating the way to the castle and village, go left. Cross the road and walk with the fractured fortress on your left and Corfe River running to the right. Emerge onto West Street. The entrance to the castle grounds is on your left. It's a fascinating site, with a storied history, and well worth exploring if you have time, but our walk goes right.

3. Walk through the village square – where King Edward the Martyr was murdered in 978, possibly on the orders of his stepmother Ælfthryth – passing the National Trust shop on your right and a cross on the left constructed to commemorate Queen Victoria's Diamond Jubilee. The Bankes Arms is visible beyond the cross, but leave that until later and walk straight up West Street. You will soon encounter The Fox Inn on your right. This attractive 16th-century pub, which reopened in 2018 after being closed for several years, has a delightful wooden interior with lots of snugs, and a fantastic garden with great castle views and a barbecue shack. It serves several real ales, including Moonlite from Hattie Brown's Brewery in nearby Swanage.

4. As the road bends right, follow a street fingerpost sign pointing between two houses towards the Purbeck Way, Ballard Down and Chapman's Pool. When you reach the village green, follow another fingerpost indicating Kingston and Chapman's Pool, crossing the grass and entering a field through a gate. Cross this common land, known as the 'Halves' or 'Haws' and used for centuries by locals to graze ponies and cattle, bearing left along a path. Look back from the corner for great view of castle, then turn left through trees to meet East Street.

5. Exit to the road via a kissing gate. Carefully cross, turn left and walk about 50 yards, going past Calcraft Road on your right, and then turning right just before the bus stop (by a building with a set of stone steps), where you'll see a footpath arrow near a National Trust sign for Corfe Common. (A second footpath arrow goes right after the bus stop, but you want the first one.) Go through a large gate and across a stone bridge over a stream. Follow a National Trust arrow as the track narrows and becomes a nice grassy single path. Go under the railway and along a section of boardwalk, through a gate and into a wide meadow.

Ponies graze on the commons, in front of the evocative ruins of Corfe Castle.

6. Follow yellow arrows on wooden posts, sticking close to the left side of the meadow, next to the hedgerow, and walking uphill with the commons sprawling to your right. Pass through a gate next to another National Trust Corfe Common sign and go straight down the field to a gate next to a cottage.

7. Turn left on the lane, then right along a footpath going towards Little Woolgarston. Walk over a wooden bridge and cross a field, heading towards the top left corner, following a footpath arrow. Cross another two fields, hopping over stiles and going through a gate until you emerge on a lane.

8. Go left and then turn right on a bridleway. Pass through a gate by a fingerpost, ignoring a pointer for Corfe and instead going right. When you meet an obvious T-junction, go left and climb the track.

9. At a fingerpost, go left along the ridge. You are now on part of the Purbeck Way, a long-distance walking route between Wareham and the coast. Enjoy stunning views across the Isle of Purbeck (which isn't actually an island at all, but is beautiful all the same) over waves of rolling hills. Poole Harbour and Brownsea Island are across to the right, and the ruin of Corfe Castle soon looms into view, straight ahead.

10. By the mobile phone mast, bear left and descend. At the bottom of the hill, go left along the lane, then turn right across a field, following Purbeck Way signs.

11. Take the footbridge over the river and proceed up the steps to cross the railway tracks and come out by The Castle Inn, a traditional Purbeck stone-built pub with inglenook fireplaces. Turn right, walk into the village to the Bankes Arms, which is on your right.

12. Emerge from the pub and walk around the east side of the castle, either on the road, or taking the path that goes around the mound, before carefully crossing the road and returning to the Castle View visitor centre and car park.

20 Montacute
The Prince of Wales

The Prince of Wales
Ham Hill
Stoke Sub Hamdon
Somerset TA14 6RW
01935 822848
www.princeofwaleshamhill.co.uk

About this walk

- Iron Age hill fort
- Monarch's Way
- Woodlands
- Stunning views

Start/finish Montacute House car park (National Trust)
Distance 5 miles (8km)
Time to pub 2 hours
Walking time 3.5 hours
Terrain Footpaths, fields, hillsides and some road

Occupying a lovely, lofty spot in the Somerset hills, **THE PRINCE OF WALES** overlooks verdant Ham Hill Country Park, and boasts stunning views from the front terrace. Set back from the road, it has a hideaway feel and is popular with walkers. There's often live music in Amy's Garden on summer Sundays, along with barbecues, oven-baked pizza and ice cream. In colder months, a fire warms the flagstone-floored interior, where you can sip mulled cider on saddle seats built into a brick bar. The pub opens early for breakfast. The main menu features locally sourced, seasonal fare.

SOUTH WEST

Explore the grounds of Montacute House (pictured above) before ascending St Michael's Hill for a spectacular vista. Hike through Hedgecock Hill Wood to Ham Hill Country Park, where wild trails lead to Iron Age hill forts, Roman remains and a secluded country pub with sensational views.

Spring In Ham and Hedgecock Hill woods, blackthorn blossoms and a yellow carpet of lesser celandines unfurls, followed by blooming primroses, violets and wild garlic. Bluebells surround the tower on St Michael's Hill.

Summer Buzzards soar above St Michael's Hill and skylarks hover over hay meadows teeming with wildflowers, bees and butterflies. Montacute house glows in the sun.

Autumn Squirrels scamper in woodlands, where native ash, oak, beech and hazel trees turn bronze, red and gold, together with sycamores introduced by the Romans. Sloes are ripe.

Winter Robins, blackbirds and finches are busy in bare hedgerows. Spy shy roe deer and, when frosts relent, listen for woodpeckers drumming in the warmer weather.

The Prince of Wales revolves its barrels and gravity pours local-made real ales from breweries including Butcombe, Yeovil, Cheddar and Bath Ales. Somerset ciders include Ham Hill, Harry's and Burrow Hill.

Follow in the footsteps of ... Occupied by tribes since prehistoric times, Ham Hill later housed a Roman garrison. Montacute was the boyhood home of John Cowper Powys (1872–1963), author of novels invoking West Country landscapes, including *Wolf Solent*, *A Glastonbury Romance*, *Weymouth Sands* and *Maiden Castle*. Montacute House has starred in dramas including *Wolf Hall* and *Sense and Sensibility*.

How to Get There

By Car From the A303, take the A3088 towards Yeovil and follow signs. Park at Montacute House (TA15 6XP; National Trust).

By Public Transport The nearest train stations are Yeovil Pen Mill (5 miles/8km) and Yeovil Junction (7 miles/11km). Buses run from Yeovil.

OS Map OS Explorer 129 (Yeovil & Sherborne), Landranger 183 (Yeovil & Frome) and 193 (Taunton & Lyme Regis); grid ref (for start): ST 500/172.

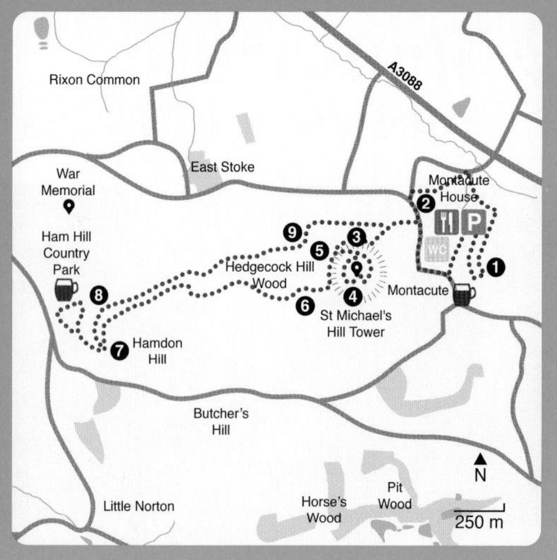

1. Pass through the welcome area, turn right towards Montacute House, then right again to walk between the house and café. Turn right at the gatehouse and follow the path through a hedge, past a twisted chestnut tree and along the cedar lawn. Continue through a picnic area, past tables and under holm oaks. From a gate in the top right corner, turn left and walk into Montacute Park. Turn left and follow fingerposts and purple arrows directing you through the park towards St Michael's Hill.

2. At the road, go left, carefully cross and walk towards a play area, before turning right, through a sports field. Go left through a gate and ascend towards the steep hill that gave Montacute its name (*mons acutus* means 'sharp hill' in Latin).

3. Pass through a kissing gate, climb to the treeline, go through another gate and follow the snaking path to the summit of St Michaels's Hill, where a lonely tower looks out across Somerset.

4. After enjoying the view, descend. At a fork, instead of returning the same way, turn right. Ignore the path dropping steeply left, and continue around the hill, gently descending to a T-junction. Turn left and walk downhill to a gate.

5. Turn left, initially following a purple arrow, then bearing right and walking diagonally across the field, beneath wires, to the top right-hand corner. Cross a stile and follow footpath arrows right, into Hedgecock Hill Wood. You're now on the Monarch's Way, a 625-mile (1,000-km) trail, tracing the escape route of King Charles II after his defeat at the Battle of Worcester in 1651.

6. At a junction, turn left and walk through a verdant collection of broadleaf ferns and colourful beech and sycamore trees. A path leads right, up Hedgecock Hill, but continue straight. At a fork, go right, and stroll along an undulating path.

7. Reaching a clear area, go through a gap to a large standing stone and sculpture. Ignoring the sharp right turn, take the gentle right and walk straight along a broad track, which bends left, passes picnic tables and emerges by Ham Hill Country Park rangers' office. Bear right to The Prince of Wales.

8. Leave the pub, return to the standing stone and follow the fingerpost pointing left to Montacute, tracing the bridleway along the bottom of Hedgecock Hill Wood.

9. The track arcs left and meets a lane. Turn right, walk to a bend, then go right, into the field, and walk below St Michael's Hill to the gate you passed through earlier. Turn right and walk up the road to Montacute village. Bear left at the 17th-century Kings Arms Inn, left again at The Phelips Arms (named after Montacute House's original owners) and walk along the drive to the car park.

21 Bath Skyline
The George Inn

The George Inn
Mill Lane, Bathampton
Somerset BA2 6TR
01225 425079
www.chefandbrewer.com/pubs/somerset/george-inn

About this walk
- Views over the historic city of Bath
- Canal towpath trails
- Woods and wildlife

Start/finish The George Inn
Distance 7½ miles (12km)
Distance to pub The pub is at the start/finish
Walking time 4–5 hours
Terrain Footpaths, towpath and some pavement

SOUTH WEST

THE GEORGE INN occupies an ivy-clad, Grade II-listed, 17th-century sandstone building on the banks of the Kennet and Avon Canal. The lovely just-off-the-towpath beer garden gets busy with boaters and walkers in summer. Inside there are snugs and real fires, and the building – some of which dates to the 1100s (when it was part of a monastery) – is allegedly haunted by the ghost of Vicomte John Baptiste Du Barre, a foreign noble, who died in the last legal duel fought in Britain. Now owned by the Chef and Brewer chain, the pub retains plenty of character and serves great food.

Starting and finishing at a wonderful waterside pub, this walk circles the hillside hovering over historic Bath, a World Heritage Site, tracing the skyline and offering amblers excellent views over the Roman spa town, before dropping down to stroll back to the pub on the Kennet and Avon Canal towpath.

Spring Parts of Claverton Down, Bathampton and Smallcombe Woods become pungent with wild garlic and bright with vibrant bluebells. Look out for dog's mercury and hart's tongue fern in Rainbow Woods.

Summer Wildflowers abound across hillside meadows, with butterflies and other pollinators buzzing between them. Green woodpeckers are active in Prior Park, while the canal and towpath bustle with boaters and bimblers.

Autumn The beech trees in Bathampton Woods become vibrant with autumn colours, and squirrels scamper between the sweet chestnut trees.

Winter After a frosty foray over the hill and along the canal, warm snugs and open fires await at The George.

The George Inn stocks standard Greene King ales and ciders, and Bibble, a highly flavoursome, premium-priced pale ale from Somerset's Wild Beer Company.

Follow in the footsteps of ... Beautiful Bath and its scenic surrounds have long inspired authors, from Jane Austen and Mary Shelley (both one-time residents) to Charles Dickens (*The Pickwick Papers* satirises Bath's social scene, and the writer apparently conceived Little Nell from *The Old Curiosity Shop* during a stay here in 1840) and Anna Sewell (*Black Beauty*).

How to Get There

By Car Parking is available at The George – you get 3 hours free, but that can be extended to 10 hours if you're a pub customer (be sure to inform bar staff that you'll be back to eat/drink).

By Public Transport Bath is well served by trains and buses. Several buses run between the city and Bathampton.

Map OS Explorer 155 (Bristol & Bath), Landranger 172 (Bristol & Bath); grid ref (for start): ST 776/665.

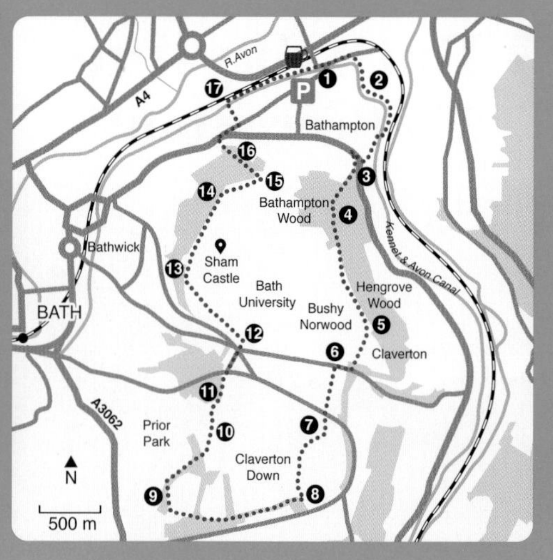

1. Walk past the pub and up the steps to the towpath. Turn left along the canal, with the water on your right. Stroll under the bridge, past picnic tables and a Bathampton information sign.

2. Cross the canal at Bathampton Swing Bridge. Ignoring the path directly opposite, turn left and walk along the bank for 20 yards, before taking the path climbing diagonally right, up through trees.

3. Pass through a gate and meet the A36. Turn right, walk along the pavement, around a bend, until you see a footpath fingerpost on the other side of the road. Carefully cross, and follow this footpath left, past a large house. When the path forks at a wooden post, go right and walk straight up the hill along a wide, sometimes stone-clad path, into Bathampton Woods.

4. At a wooden post with a Bath Skyline waymarker, go left along a rocky and root-ribbed path through beech and field maple trees, passing a curious cave. Go through a gate, past Skyline number 6 and an NT sign for Bushy Norwood. Ancient history echoes across this grassy meadow, where standing stones (claver 'key' stones) the remains of an Iron Age hillfort and Roman earthworks can be seen.

5. Go through a gate and bear right, following more Skyline waymarkers. Pass through another gate, leaning left and then right before meeting a road.

6. Follow signage through another gate into woods. An easy-to-miss waymarker immediately sends you left, over a stone stile by a footpath fingerpost. Go right, walk along Claverton Hill road for about 25 yards before turning left along a footpath beside Bath University's Limekiln sports fields.

7. At the road, cross and turn left then right, to go through a gate with Skyline number 7 on it. Walk straight along the path with farm fields to your right. Keep going through several gates.

8. Follow a waymarker pointing right, through Claverton Down woods, where an information sign features Skyline number 8. Signs lead through a wonderful woodland with holly, hawthorn and beech trees. Ignore a gate on your left and keep going past Klondike House, through a gate, across a lane and along a footpath. Arc right, around some playing fields, and follow the footpath back into the trees.

9. Just before a stile and stone wall, follow a waymarker left, down to a kissing gate bearing Skyline number 9. Enjoy the view over Prior Park – an estate looked after by the National Trust, originally designed by poet Alexander Pope and landscape gardener Capability Brown, and home to a spectacular Palladian Bridge. Follow waymarkers right, along the fenceline, past a bench with beautiful views across Bath, and up a set of steps. Ignore a metal gate leading left, and follow the

Skyline waymarker pointing straight ahead. At a T-junction, turn left along a bridleway.

10. Walk with Claverton Down on your right to a wooden post wearing the Skyline number 10. You can turn left through the kissing gate here and descend to the outskirts of Bath, following signage, but our walk leaves the Skyline route temporarily here, continuing straight and passing the Claverton Down National Trust sign.

11. Continue along a sealed path through woods. After passing buildings on the right, the track turns into a tarmac lane and emerges on Widcombe Hill. Carefully cross the road and go straight along the small road (Copseland) opposite. At the end, cross Oakley Road, go through the gap and walk along Soldier Down Lane towards Bath University.

12. Just before the main university, turn left along a lane with the South 2 building on your right. This lane becomes a gravel footpath, passes more university buildings and crosses a bridge over a road. Continue straight ahead, over a large rock, and when the path immediately forks, go right, along the larger path. Walk along the top field edge, with the trees and Bath Golf Club on your right.

13. Continue through a kissing gate, passing Sham Castle (a 1762 folly) and the golf club buildings. Go through a kissing gate and you're back on the official Skyline trail.

14. Continue past a communications tower, following Skyline waymarkers on wooden posts. When the broad grassy track forks, go left and head towards the treeline.

15. At the fence, go through a gap and follow footpath arrows leading left, down into the trees. Keep bearing left (ignoring arrows pointing right and a metal kissing gate), then go straight through a wooden gate and descend along a path through woods.

16. At the main road, carefully cross and go right along Bathampton Lane towards the village centre. At Meadow Lane, follow the footpath fingerpost left, down the sealed laneway.

17. Cross the canal, turn immediately left through a gate, left over a stone stile, and left again to walk under the bridge and along the towpath with the water on your right. Walk along this pretty stretch of canal, busy with boats, past a number of houses, to The George Inn.

Sham Castle is an ornamental folly on Claverton Down, overlooking Bath.

22 Badbury Hill
The Radnor Arms

The Radnor Arms
32 Coleshill, Coleshill
Oxfordshire SN6 7PR
01793 766667
www.theradnorarms.co.uk

About this walk
- Woodlands
- Wildflower displays
- Rural views
- Wildlife
- Historic barn

Start/finish Badbury Hill car park (National Trust)
Distance 7 miles (11.3km)
Time to pub Allow 1.5–2 hours
Walking time 3–4 hours
Terrain Woodland trails, country lanes

On the Oxfordshire/Wiltshire border, by the Vale of White Horse, **THE RADNOR ARMS** is a cosy country pub in an old stone building (a former blacksmith's forge and brewery, now owned by the National Trust), surrounded by beautiful countryside. Brought back from closure by local residents in 2019, the pub is at the heart of Coleshill village in every sense. Features include an open fire, long sofa-style seating, a split bar with walls covered in images of rural scenes, and a courtyard area for enjoying an alfresco ale. Food is available.

From a prehistoric hill fort and a forest seasonally bejewelled with bright beech trees and blooming bluebells, wander through rich Oxfordshire farmland to an extraordinary 13th-century barn, before continuing to Coleshill in Wiltshire and stepping into the embrace of The Radnor Arms.

Spring A rising tide of bluebells climbs the hill, floods the Iron Age fort and rushes around the beech trees at Badbury.

Summer Butterflies flutter in wildflower-rich meadows around Great Coxwell Barn. Swallows and house martins flit from muddy nests amid the beams, tirelessly searching for food for their chicks.

Autumn Badbury's beech trees turn a deep red before losing their leaves, while other woodland species add more vibrant shades to the blazing backdrop.

Winter Enjoy views of the Thames floodplains through the bare branches of Badbury, where a host of birdlife can be spied, including blue tits, blackbirds, woodpeckers and blackcaps.

The Radnor Arms serves regional real ales and ciders on rotation from Wiltshire, Oxfordshire and elsewhere in the country – keep an eye on the website for up-to-date details about which breweries and beers are available on tap. Wines, spirits and soft drinks are also on offer.

Follow in the footsteps of ...
Badbury Hill has been occupied since 600 BC. Music producer extraordinaire, George Martin, often referred to as the 'fifth Beatle', lived in the Grade II-listed former rectory alongside The Radnor Arms and was known to pop into the pub.

How to Get There

By Car Parking is at Badbury Hill (National Trust), part of the Buscot and Coleshill Estates, near Coleshill, Swindon SN7 7NJ; it is just off the B4019 between Coleshill and Faringdon.

By Public Transport Swindon train station is 10 miles (16km) away.

OS Map OS Explorer 170 (Vale of White Horse), Landranger 174 (Newbury & Wantage); grid ref (for start): SU 261/945.

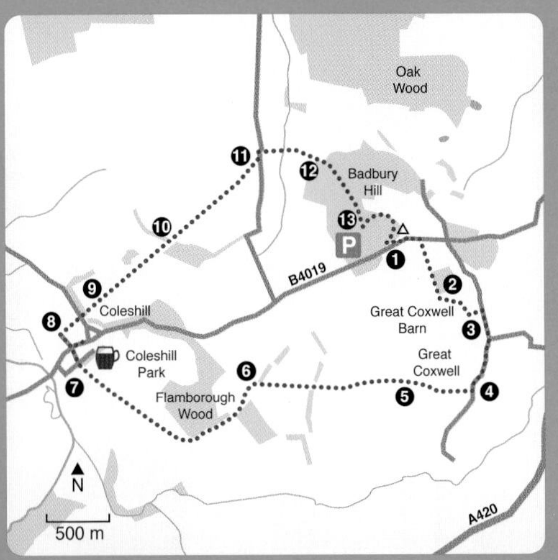

1. From Badbury Hill car park, walk towards the exit (away from the woods, which this walk explores later), and look for a fingerpost for Great Coxwell Barn. Take this path, which runs to the left of the road. After 100 yards, follow another fingerpost pointing across the road and along a footpath opposite, with more signs indicating the way towards Great Coxwell Barn.

2. Follow the broad path as it meanders through meadows, wends left and passes through a kissing gate. Keep bearing left and walk towards the impressive barn, past a lovely old thunderstruck oak with a hollow trunk. Go through a kissing gate and admire the medieval barn, complete with duck pond and dovecots. Dating to 1292, and with a stunning timber roof, it's more like a cathedral than a farm building. The barn, looked after by the National Trust, is open to the public and you can explore it at your leisure; an honesty admission fee of £1.50 is payable at a donation box.

3. Exit the barn area and turn right along the lane to the hamlet of Great Coxwell. Walk past Puddleduck Lane and down through the pretty hamlet with thatched cottages, a reading room and war memorial.

4. Pass the 12th-century church on your left and, just past Pear Tree Cottage, turn right on a footpath following a fingerpost pointing towards Coleshill. Cross a little bridge over a stream, go through a kissing gate and turn right. Ignore the gate exiting the field after 50 yards, and instead keep going with the hedge on your right. Pass through a field gate and continue through the next field, again with the hedge on your right.

5. Keep going through several fields in the same way. When the track bends left and then right, look for a footpath (indicated by a yellow arrow on a stile) leading left into trees. Cross the stile, go over a little wooden bridge and through a gate. Continue across a field, through another gate and field to Ashen Copse Farm.

6. As soon as you pass the farm buildings, turn left. Cross the lane and follow a footpath and National Trust waymarkers pointing straight ahead, through a field, walking towards wind turbines on the far hill. Keep going, past Flamborough Wood on your right. Pass through a gate and bear right, following footpath and National Trust signage though another wooden gate. Go across a field, through a metal double gate and yet another field, walking towards Coleshill church spire, visible straight ahead.

7. After passing through two more gates you will emerge in Coleshill village. Go straight towards the church, passing the Old Carpenter's Yard (National Trust), where there is a café and conservation skills area. At the main road, turn right and walk to the welcoming pub.

Built during the reign of Edward I, Great Coxwell Barn is over 720 years old.

8. After leaving the pub, walk downhill along the main road, past a phone box on the left, then turn right along lane towards the church. Pass the church and the Old Slaughterhouse (National Trust holiday accommodation), go through a gate and turn right across a field, following a footpath fingerpost and a green National Trust arrow. Stick to the right-hand side of the field and bear right to a stile. Cross the road and pick up the footpath opposite, following more arrows. Go straight into a field and walk with the hedge on your left.

9. Walk in a straight line for about two-thirds of a mile (1km), through two large fields, and when you meet the corner of second field, go straight on, through trees and over wooden bridges across a stream.

10. Emerge into a field and walk straight ahead, with the hedge on your left. At the corner of the field go straight, through a gap in the hedge and over another wooden bridge and stile. Bear left in the next field, keeping the hedge on your left. Look for a gap in the hedge after 50 yards and cross the stile into the next field. Walk diagonally towards a clump of trees, cross a stile and go through the woods, over another stile, then turn right along a lane through a farm.

11. When you emerge from the farm buildings, go straight, through a wide gate (ignore the green National Trust sign pointing right, and other arrows pointing left and right) towards the wooded hill directly ahead. At the corner of the field, cross a wooden bridge over a stream and then hug the left side of the next field until you reach Badbury Woods, announced by a National Trust sign.

12. Walk up the hill, through magical mixed woodlands of beech, hawthorn, oak, wild cherry, ash and sycamore trees. Keep climbing up the main path, ignoring cross paths and spur tracks leading left and right, and pass a wild play area. At the top, a large flat plateau is punctuated by hundreds of beech trees, a natural nirvana for children and dogs. You can walk around the summit circuit (enjoying good views over Oxfordshire and the Thames floodplains) or go straight to the car park.

23 Dinton Park

The Compasses Inn

The Compasses Inn
Lower Chicksgrove
Tisbury, Wiltshire
SP3 6NB
01722 714318
www.thecompassesinn.com

About this walk

- Woodlands
- Rural valley views
- Wildlife

Start/finish Dinton Park car park (National Trust)
Distance 7 miles (11.3km)
Time to pub 2 hours
Walking time 3.5 hours
Terrain Rural lanes, countryside footpaths, some road

A fabulous 14th-century thatched country inn surrounded by beautiful Wiltshire countryside, which warmly welcomes walkers, THE COMPASSES INN is a real destination pub. There's a lovely outside area overlooking fields and the Nadder Valley, but the interior is a particular treat, with an inglenook fireplace, thick stone walls, low, wood-beamed ceilings, gentle candle and lamp lighting, characterful furniture, antique farm machinery tastefully built into the décor, and bunches of hops around the bar. Social events are held regularly; delicious, locally sourced food and drink is served, and accommodation is available.

From the grounds of a discreet country mansion, walk across a wonderful Wiltshire landscape, passing through the wildlife-rich woodlands and delightful villages of the Nadder Valley, to reach a gorgeous hidden pub that – once discovered – is very hard to leave.

Spring Swallows swoop, hares box and spring flowers bloom – including some escaped daffodil and narcissus varieties developed by Reverend George Engleheart in his garden at Little Clarendon, next to Dinton.

Summer Grassland around Philipps House is resplendent with wildflowers and busy with bees and butterflies. Red kites and hobbies soar overhead, iridescent kingfishers dart across the lake, and barn owls hunt at dusk.

Autumn Squirrels bury their winter larder amid colourful fungi, across 230 acres (93ha) of parkland around Dinton Park. Mature beech and centuries-old sweet chestnut trees perform their spectacular and well-rehearsed costume change.

Winter Frost grips the grass across the park and views to the cathedral city of Salisbury can be enjoyed through leafless trees. Spy roe deer around the woodlands and listen for drumming woodpeckers.

The Compasses Inn has several handpumps, serving local and regional real ales and cider such as Sheep Dip from Salisbury's Plain Ales brewery, Hop 226 from Yeovil Ales, Butcombe Original and Old Rosie.

Follow in the footsteps of ...
There's an Iron Age hill fort at Wick Ball Camp, close to the grand Neo-classical Philipps House, which was built 1814–17 for the MP William Wyndham. In the Second World War Dinton Park was used by the US army.

How to Get There

By Car Head to Dinton and park in the National Trust car park (SP3 5HR) by St Mary's Church.

By Public Transport The closest train station is Tisbury (5 miles/8km from Dinton, 2 miles/3km from The Compasses Inn) or Salisbury (9 miles/14.5km). Salisbury Reds service 25 from Salisbury or Tisbury stops at Dinton.

OS Map OS Explorer 130 (Salisbury & Stonehenge), 143 (Warminster & Trowbridge), Landranger 184 (Salisbury & The Plain); grid ref (for start): SU 009/316.

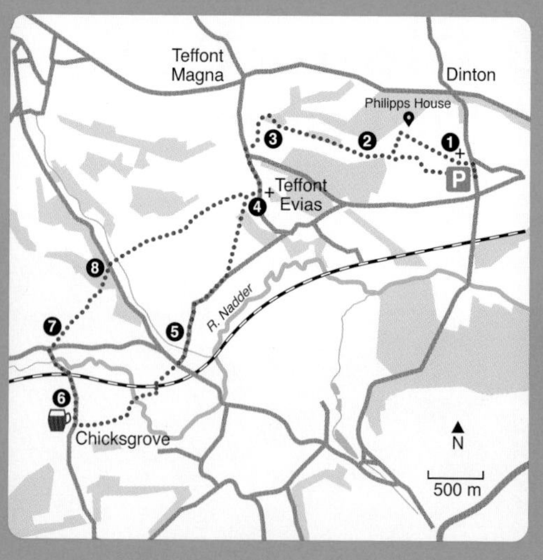

1. As you walk into Dinton Park from the car park by St Mary's Church, the restored ornamental lake is off to your left. Paths lead off in several directions, but take the one bearing right, heading past a copse of trees towards Philipps House, which is fronted by a ha-ha. This august 17th-century Neo-Grecian mansion was known as Dinton House until 1916, when it was bought by Bertram Philipps, who renamed it. Philipps gifted the property to the National Trust in 1943, and until recently it was used for art retreats, with leading contemporary artists like Tom Coates, Deborah Manifold, John Yardley, Edward Wesson and Ken Paine providing tuition. Currently, the house is off-bounds to the public, but you're free to roam the park. Just past the mansion, off to the right, is Wick Ball Camp, where the ramparts and earthworks of an Iron Age hill fort can be seen. Instead of going uphill into the woods, arc left and walk until you reach a bench. Turn right here, strolling through oaks to meet a fence with a kissing gate. Go through and continue to a second gate.

2. Walk along a path between woods (on your left) and the grassy common leading to a hill (on the right). Pass by a fishing lake on your left and follow footpath arrows into the trees. Keep going along the path, crossing a couple of tracks, and continue through mixed woods of chestnut, beech and holly.

3. At end of the woodlands, before a gate, bear left and descend through a tunnel of trees to the road. Turn left on the road and cross to walk along the pavement. Go right at the first junction, on a corner by a group of cottages, and walk towards the church spire, with a stream running on your left. Before you get to the church and village of Teffont Evias proper, turn right along a cul-de-sac, following a fingerpost.

4. Stroll up the small road and turn left at footpath arrow on a pole, climbing steps, going through a metal kissing gate and walking up the field towards the right edge of a copse of trees and through a gateway. Pass through a metal kissing gate, go across the top end of the field, through another gate and walk diagonally across a large farm field, following a footpath arrow through crops (depending on the season). Emerge through a gap in the hedge, on to the road, and turn right. Don't be tempted to take the path fingerposted left across a field after about 50 yards – this goes down to the Nadder River, but only leads to fishing spots and results in a dead end. Instead, carry on, carefully following the road around a left bend, past Ley Farm and down a hill, before rising up again and passing a prominent aerial on the left.

5. When a road comes in from the left, by a road sign for Tisbury and Fovant, go straight across and

pass through a metal gate, following bridleway arrows on a post. Walk straight across the field, go through a gateway, pass some farm buildings on your right, and then bear left. Cross the bridge over the railway line, go through a metal gate and turn right. Walk through a field, past two large standing stones, and cross a bridge over the river. Walk up a path between fields, cross a small wooden bridge, go through a metal gate and turn right, following bridleway arrows to walk diagonally across a field. Pass a wooden post, continue through a wide gate onto the road, and The Compasses Inn is just up to the left.

6. Leave the pub and turn left. Carefully walk downhill along the road, go over a hill and down the other side. Stroll across a railway bridge, follow the road around to the left and cross the nattering Nadder River over a pretty little humpback bridge. At the T-junction, turn right and walk briefly along the road signed towards Salisbury.

7. After 50 yards, look for a footpath arrow on a post, pointing left. Follow this and climb gradually along a lovely footpath, often overhung with ivy-clad trees. Pass the ruins of a large stone building and continue along a footpath that goes through a tunnel of small hazel trees between fields, before descending through a deep holloway towered over by mixed woods of fir, beech and holly.

8. Meet the road, turn left and then immediately right, following a bridleway arrow on a post to go through a gate. Walk up a bridleway (which is often muddy because it's used by cattle) between two hedges. Meet a broad farm lane and keep going straight for about three-quarters of a mile. Go past a large metal gate, walk down the lane, passing the steps you climbed earlier, until you reach Teffont Evias. From here, turn left, walk towards Teffont Magna, before cutting right along the footpath though the commons, reversing the route you took earlier, all the way back to Dinton Park. Instead of walking back via the mansion, wander directly across the grassy park towards Hyde's House and St Mary's Church, to the car park.

Originally known as Dinton House, Philipps House was renamed when it was bought by Bertram Philipps in 1916.

24 Stourhead
Spread Eagle Inn

Spread Eagle Inn
Church Lawn, Stourton
Wiltshire BA12 6QE
01747 840587
www.spreadeagleinn.com

About this walk
- Stunning landscape gardens
- Stour Valley Way
- Woodlands

Start/finish Stourhead car park (National Trust)
Distance 3 miles (5km)
Time to pub 2 hours
Walking time 2 hours
Terrain Public footpaths and estate trails

Perched in the gorgeous green grounds of the stunning Stourhead Estate, near a picturesque Palladian mansion, the **SPREAD EAGLE INN** is an attractive, brick-and-slate, one-time coaching inn that dates to 1772. On sunny days, the large walled courtyard – overlooked by a stern stone eagle crest and surrounded by former stables that now house an ice cream parlour – is the perfect place for a pint of West Country ale or cider. The spacious pub boasts an impressive wooden bar and a fireplace. Good food is served all day, from breakfast to dinner. Accommodation is available.

Embark on a micro Grand Tour, visiting Palladian and Italianate installations in a wonderful Wiltshire setting, among wildlife-rich woodlands around an ornately landscaped garden at the source of the River Stour, before relaxing in an 18th-century coaching inn.

Spring Wild daffodils and bluebells bloom in Bonham Wood, behind the Temple of Apollo. Magnolias appear, followed by rhododendron and azalea. Swallows arrive, and gaggles of ducklings and cygnets brave the lakes.

Summer Wildflowers, including several orchids, dot the grasslands. Sunbathe around the lake, buzzed over by dragonflies, or seek shade on leafy trails.

Autumn A colour display unfurls around Stourhead's lakes, with American maples the first to turn, followed by Japanese acers. Hornbeam, chestnuts and tulip trees radiate yellow, while oak and beech glow orange.

Winter Roe deer pass through frozen woods and frost grips the grass, but willows on the island near the Pantheon defiantly spark orange. Snowdrops flower from late January. Look for golden plover, plus native species including tree sparrows.

The Spread Eagle offers Wessex Brewery's Stourton Pale Ale and Kilmington Best, and Butcombe Original, plus Ashton Press and Lilley's ciders.

Follow in the footsteps of ... There's an Iron Age fort at Stourhead, where Alfred the Great rallied his troops before defeating the Danes at the Battle of Edington in 878. The Palladian house and landscaped gardens were created by several generations of the Hoare family. Henry Hoare II, 'Henry the Magnificent', is credited with most of the famous features of this 'living work of art' as the gardens were described when they opened in the 1740s.

How to Get There

By Car Follow brown signs from the A303 or the B3092 from Frome. Use Stourhead car park (BA12 6QD; National Trust).

By Public Transport Buses run from Warminster and Shaftesbury; alight at Zeals (1¼ miles/2km). The closest train station is Gillingham (6½ miles/ 10.5km)

OS Map OS Explorer 142 (Shepton Mallet & Mendip Hills East), Landranger 183 (Yeovil & Frome); grid ref (for start): ST 779/340.

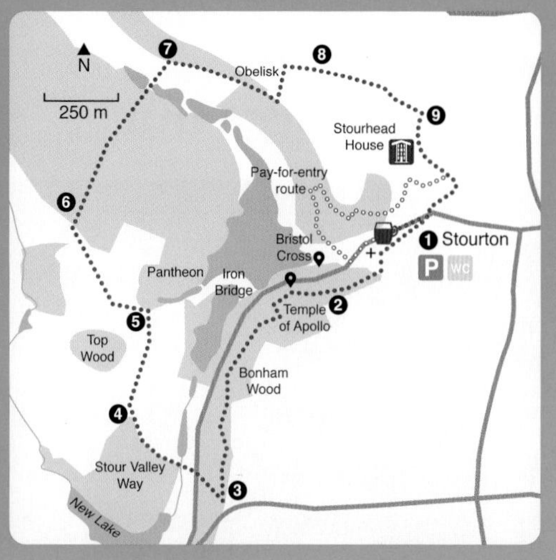

1. From the car park, go through the main entrance, turn left and zig-zag down the path towards the walled gardens. Before going over a little bridge, where the path splits into four, take a hard left along an unsealed footpath, following pink arrows. Pass pretty St Peter's Church on your right, and walk through beautiful beech woods, an absolute riot of colour in autumn.

2. Go through a green barrier and bear left when the path forks. Walk uphill, following pink arrows, then turn right at a T-junction at the top. Down to your right is the domed roof of the Temple of Apollo, and beyond that the garden lake, fringed with a variety of trees. Keep going along the path, which undulates through the beech trees and bluebells (in spring) of Bonham Woods.

3. Ignore a path joining from the right, but then, just before meeting the road, turn right and walk down a steeply descending footpath. Leaving the pink arrows behind, you are now on a section of the Stour Valley Way (SVW), a 64-mile (103-km) long-distance footpath tracing the river through Wiltshire and Dorset. Follow the SVW green arrows across a road and along Top Lane. Keep going uphill, ignoring a track joining on the left.

4. At a corner by a cottage, go right, through a gate and across a field, following SVW arrows. Stay on the high path, with Top Wood on your left and, to the right, wonderful views across Stourhead.

5. Bear right towards Beech Cottage and join the track coming up from the direction of the lakes, turning left and walking uphill.

6. Heeding SVW signage, cross a stile then bear right into woods. It's a stiff climb through chestnut trees, but keep going straight, ignoring paths crossing your way. At a seat, follow SVW arrows down a steeply descending path, with some steps, and pass between a couple of lily ponds. Hop over a stile into a field and chase arrows across another field and stile.

7. Go right and take a track with a fence on your right. Cross another stile and emerge by the Obelisk, where there are more stunning views down to the mansion. Follow blue and red arrows to pass the Obelisk and join an obvious track.

8. Turn right along the track, towards the house. Go through two kissing gates at end of the field, and keep following SVW and blue, red and orange arrows to reach the mansion, on your right.

9. Walk past the house, on your right, continue until you meet High Street, then go right to the Spread Eagle. Or, if you're a National Trust member or happy to pay for entry, turn right along a footpath just after the house, pass into the property and walk towards the lake. Bear left to the Palladian Bridge and Bristol Cross, then turn left on High Street and walk past the church to the pub.

25 Lacock
The George Inn

The George Inn
4 West Street, Lacock
Wiltshire SN15 2LH
01249 730263
www.georgeinnlacock.co.uk

About this walk
- River Avon
- History
- Famous film locations
- Medieval abbey

Start/finish Hither Way car park (National Trust)
Distance 2¼ miles (3.6km)
Time to pub 1 hour
Walking time 1.5 hours
Terrain Riverside footpaths, lanes and village streets

Built in 1361, **THE GEORGE INN** has an enormous inglenook fireplace complete with a surviving cooking spit that was once turned by a special breed of long-bodied dog called a Turnpike, which ran on a wheel to rotate the meat as it roasted. Meals (cooked by humans not hounds) are served most days (times vary, check the website) in an atmospheric main bar with big oak beams. There's a garden and a great courtyard with stocks, a wishing well and play area for children. Accommodation is available. Along with The Red Lion and The Sign of the Angel in Lacock, The George is owned by the National Trust.

Stroll along the beautiful banks of the River Avon opposite the famous 13th-century abbey, and wander through the historic Wiltshire village of Lacock, a veritable time capsule that has formed the backdrop for many films and period dramas, to an inn where locally brewed ales have been enjoyed since medieval times.

Spring There is wild garlic in the woods and tulips are in bloom around Lacock Abbey. Birds sing along the River Avon.

Summer With butterflies and bees flitting between the wildflowers, the meadows along the banks of the River Avon are perfect for picnics.

Autumn Collect conkers from the heels of the horse chestnut tree in the Pound in Lacock village, and kick through mounds of leaves on the ground around the abbey.

Winter Bright winter berries and late-flowering shrubs liven up the frost-nipped banks of the Avon and the grounds of the abbey.

The George Inn stocks real ales brewed in Wilshire by Wadworth, including Horizon, 6X, Henry's IPA, Swordfish and Burnt Orange. Real ciders are also sold, along with lagers, wines and spirits.

Follow in the footsteps of ... Lacock has a long association with film. William Henry Fox Talbot created the earliest surviving photographic negative at Lacock Abbey in 1835, and the village has been used as a shooting location for multiple movies (*Harry Potter and the Half-Blood Prince, Wolfman*) and TV series, including, *Downton Abbey, Pride and Prejudice, Cranford* and *The Hollow Crown: The Wars of the Roses*.

How to Get There

By Car Take exit 17 from the M4 and follow signs on the A350. Park in Lacock's Hither Way car park (SN15 2LG; National Trust).

By Public Transport The closest train stations are Melksham (3 miles/5km) and Chippenham (3½ miles/5.6km). Faresaver bus X34 between Chippenham and Frome (via Melksham) stops outside The George Inn in Lacock.

OS Map OS Explorer 156 (Chippenham & Bradford-on-Avon), Landranger 173 (Swindon & Devizes); grid ref (for start): ST 917/682.

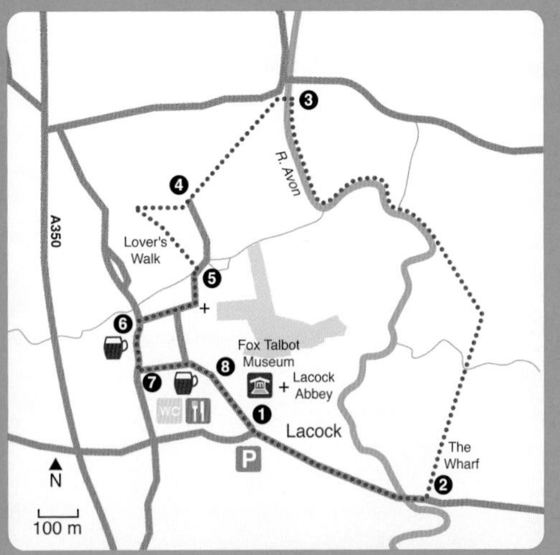

1. Exit the car park, carefully cross the road and go right along Hither Lane, past Lacock Abbey, which can be seen over the wall on your left. Walk along the raised path running parallel to the road, then cross the bridge over the River Avon.

2. Turn left over a stone stile and follow a fingerpost, walking across a riverside meadow. The footpath goes across the centre of the field, but you can wander along the banks of the Avon for good views of the river, abbey and gardens. Cross a footbridge and stile leading into the next field and follow the hedge-hugging path on the left. Pass into a third field, following footpath arrows. Cross a stile and walk with the river on your immediate left.

3. Exit the field and turn left across a beautiful four-arch bridge over the river. By thatched cottages, turn left and walk between two stone cottages along an alleyway with a cycling sign. Go through a gate into a field and follow the sealed path running across it (alternatively, you can walk along the arc of the river).

4. Go through a gate at the top of the path, walk across the turning circle at the end of a residential cul-de-sac, then go over a stile and follow a footpath sign across a field, keeping to the left. After crossing a stile, go left down Lover's Walk.

5. You emerge by a footbridge and ford. Cross the stream and enter lovely Lacock village by walking along Nethercote Hill, passing St Cyriac's Church and a pottery on your left. Bear right and walk along Church Street, passing The Carpenter's Arms on your left and a bakery on the right. Continue past the turning for East Street on your left, and the Sign of The Angel hotel on the right.

6. At the end of the road, turn left onto West Street, and you'll see The George Inn on the opposite side of the street.

7. After leaving the pub, continue along West Street, then turn left along High Street. Walk past the village store on your right, and the school on the left, and continue to The Red Lion at the end of the road on the right. This red-brick Georgian-era gastro pub also sells ales from Wadworth Brewery and boasts a beautiful beer garden at the back.

8. Turn right immediately after The Red Lion, into a parking area where there's a café, ice cream parlour and public toilets. Go through a gate and walk through a picnic area until you emerge by the main entrance to Lacock Abbey and the Fox Talbot Museum (which explores the history of photography). Turn right and walk up the High Street, with the abbey on your left, back to the car park.

26 Avebury
The Red Lion

Housed in a 17th-century thatched building, a former farmhouse converted into a pub 100 years ago, **THE RED LION** is located in the midst of the prehistoric stone circle that draws people to this fascinating site. Inside the pub is a 66ft (20m) deep well that's older than the building, dating to around 1600, which is 'the last resting place of at least one unfortunate villager', according to the inscription. Besides the historic interior, there's a delightful outside area overlooking the nearby standing stones. Food is served all day every day.

The Red Lion
High Street, Avebury
Wiltshire SN8 1RF
01672 539266
www.greeneking-pubs.co.uk/pubs/wiltshire/red-lion/

About this walk
- World Heritage site
- Rural views
- Birdlife and wildflowers

Start/finish Avebury visitor car park (National Trust)
Distance 6 miles (10km)
Time to pub 3 hours
Walking time 3–4 hours
Terrain Countryside footpaths, farm fields

Visit Avebury World Heritage Site, exploring the world's largest stone circle, where you can walk among the stones. This route takes in Silbury Hill, West Kennett Long Barrow Neolithic tomb and the Sanctuary, before returning to Avebury via a megalithic stone avenue and circle, to a thatched pub.

Spring Wildflowers bloom in the meadows around Avebury, and West Kennet Avenue turns golden with buttercups and dandelions. Wild hares and deer can be seen, while kites and buzzards soar overhead.

Summer Skylarks hover and rare plants like hybrid tuberous thistle and round-headed rampion thrive on henge banks. Purple clustered bellflowers also bloom, a flower that, with its blood-red stem, was once thought to grow from dead bodies.

Autumn Enjoy evocative moonrises above this ancient landscape, watching for owls and bats (five bat species occupy the Barn Gallery of Avebury's Alexander Keiller Museum), or come early for a luminous sunrise above the Bronze Age barrows.

Winter Corvids rule the Avebury skies in winter, with jackdaws and rooks hopping among the frosty stones and barrows. Look out for grey partridge, yellowhammer and corn bunting. Inspect the intricate patterns lichens have etched on Avebury's ancient sarsen stones.

The local elixir served at The Red Lion is Avebury Well Water. This is a Greene King pub, and other beers include the big brewery's signature IPA.

Follow in the footsteps of … During this ramble you are walking among Neolithic features and stone structures painstakingly arranged by our ancestors around 5,000 years ago.

How to Get There

By Car Avebury is 6 miles (10km) west of Marlborough on the A4361 – there's a car park on site (free for National Trust and English Heritage members).

By Public Transport The closest train stations are Pewsey (10½ miles/17km) and Swindon (11½ miles/18.5km); buses 49 (Swindon–Devizes) and 42 (Calne–Marlborough), stop opposite The Red Lion.

OS Map OS Explorer 157 (Marlborough & Savernake Forest), Landranger Active 173 (Swindon & Devizes, Marlborough & Trowbridge); grid ref (for start): SU 098/697.

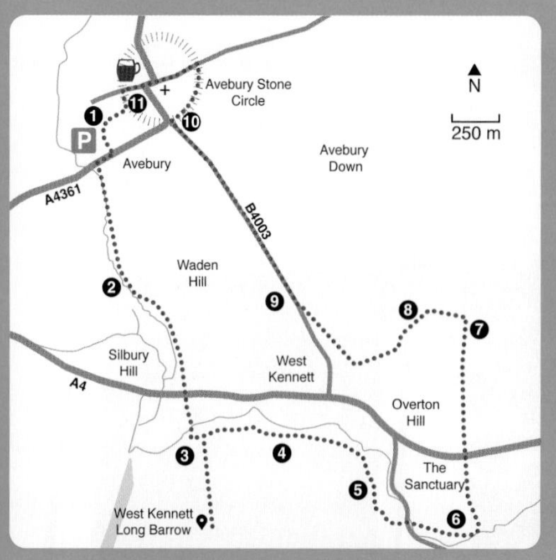

1. Leave the car park via a gap in the hedge located just west (right) of the main vehicle entrance and turn right. Carefully cross the A4361, dogleg right then left, and go through a gate. Stroll along the footpath (part of the 96-mile/154-km White Horse Trail) towards the distinctive shape of man-made Silbury Hill, which erupts from the bucolic Wiltshire landscape like a green pyramid.

2. Go through a double gate, walk past Silbury Hill, passing through another gate and continuing along the bottom of Waden Hill (left), keeping the River Kennet on your right. Carry on to Roman Road (A4). Carefully cross opposite a thatched cottage. Pick up the footpath on the other side and follow a fingerpost pointing towards the Long Barrow.

3. Go through a kissing gate and follow the footpath left. At a majestic oak tree, just 50 yards on, turn right up a broad track to visit West Kennett Long Barrow. Retrace your footsteps down the hill, turning right when you rejoin the path and continuing east.

4. Climb over a stile and cross a lane. Keep following the footpath and White Horse Trail waymarkers. Hop over another stile and walk through a woody copse.

5. At a junction with a green lane byway, turn left, leaving the White Horse Trail and continuing to the road. Cross and turn left, passing over a bridge across the River Kennet. Go past a bridleway sign and turn right into a field. Hug the field's right edge to the top right corner.

6. Turn left, up a track between hedgerows. At the road, the Sanctuary (a ceremonial stone circle dating to 2500 BC) is on your left. Cross the road, go through a car park and walk along the Ridgeway National Trail, with barrows on your right.

7. Walk up the hill, and at a junction turn left, leaving the Ridgeway and taking the byway.

8. After 150 yards, go left through a National Trust gate. A barrow with a crown of beech trees is on your immediate right (one of three tumuli). Descend the hill, go through a gate and follow the path right. Cross the road, go through the gate and follow fingerpost signs to West Kennet Avenue.

9. Go through a double gate, turn right and walk across a field, along 'West Kennet Avenue', a path between two parallel lines of standing stones.

10. Exit via a gate, cross the road and go through another gate opposite. Either walk around the impressive henge bank until you meet the lane then turn left to The Red Lion, or go straight through the henge and stone circle to the pub.

11. Leave the pub, turn right and follow signs back to the car park.

SOUTH WEST

Haresfield Beacon

Vine Tree Inn

Vine Tree Inn
The Stocks, Randwick
Gloucestershire GL6 6JA
01453 763748
www.thevinetreerandwick.co.uk

About this walk

- Stunning views
- Birds of prey
- Prehistoric barrows
- Cotswold Way
- Wildflowers
- Cotswold AONB

Start/finish Shortwood car park (National Trust)
Distance 5 miles (8km)
Time to pub 1.5 hours
Walking time 3 hours
Terrain Countryside, footpaths, lanes, small amount of road

The **VINE TREE INN** is a friendly, independent pub – a community hub for locals (the last pub in a village that once boasted seven) and welcome watering hole for walkers. Clinging to the hillside, the garden offers stunning Stroud Valley views across Rodborough and Selsley commons. Inside are three rooms, interlinked to the main bar, with snug drinking corners and a restaurant area. A wood-burning stove keeps the whole place cosy. Excellent food is served, with several Hungarian options reflecting the landlords' heritage. Opening hours may alter in winter – check the website.

Explore the Cotswold escarpment and enjoy Severn Valley vistas, before descending past prehistoric burial grounds to a character-fuelled pub offering brews with yet more views. Return along the Cotswold Way, wending through wildlife-rich Standish Wood.

Spring Bluebells bloom throughout Standish Wood. Buzzards soar and circle above the Cotswold escarpment.

Summer The escarpment's limestone grasslands come alive with orchids and butterflies.

Autumn Standish Wood glows with golden leaves and shivers with scampering squirrels. Above the grasslands, look for kestrels hovering and hunting.

Winter Views from the Topograph – over the Cotswold AONB, across Gloucestershire and along the Severn Valley towards Bristol and into Somerset and Wales – are often crispest on cold days.

A freehouse, the Vine Tree Inn offers regional real ales including Tiley's Ordinary Bitter and Ekuanot Pale Ale (made at the Salutation Inn at Ham, Gloucestershire), Merlin from Stroud Brewery, and Mad Goose from Purity in Warwickshire.

Follow in the footsteps of ... Every spring, Randwick celebrates The Wap. Dating to the Middle Ages, festivities feature a procession, with a Wap Mayor and Queen being carried through the village, while a Mop-Man clears the way and soaks onlookers with water. The Mayor is then dunked in the pond, and cheeses are rolled down the bank, before being divided and eaten.

How to Get There

By Car Shortwood Car Park (GL6 6PP; National Trust) is 3 miles (5km) north-west of Stroud, between the A419 and A46. Head towards Whiteshill, carry on north for 1 mile (1.6km), then turn left, following signposts for Haresfield.

By Public Transport The nearest train stations are Stroud (2½ miles/4km from Randwick) and Stonehouse (3 miles/5km).

OS Map OS Explorer 179 (Gloucester, Cheltenham and Stroud), Landranger 162 (Gloucester and Forest of Dean); grid ref (for start): SO 832/086.

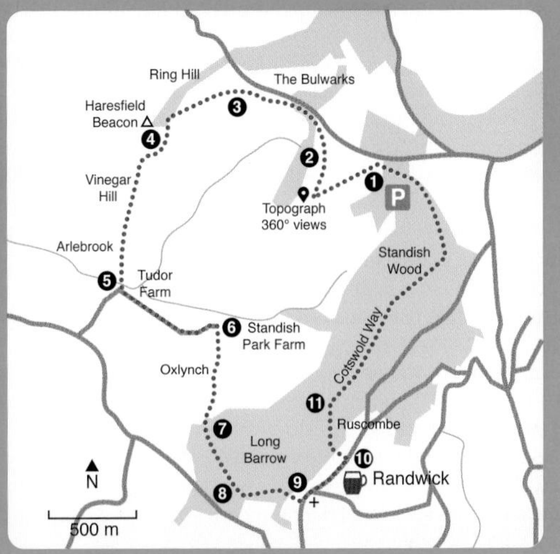

1. Leave the car park via a gate by an information sign and map, and follow orange National Trust arrows pointing directly ahead to the Topograph. This 3D orientation table explains the panoramic vista across the multiple counties you can gaze over from this vantage point, complete with compass points and distance indicators for everything you can see, including the Brecon Beacons and Black Mountains in Wales, and the Mendip Hills and Dunkery Beacon in Somerset. Closer landmarks include Ring Hill and Haresfield Beacon to your right, and the sensational Severn Vale ahead.

2. Turn around and walk back across the grassland, bearing left along the Cotswold Way (a 102-mile/164-km route across the Cotswold escarpment between Chipping Camden and Bath), which runs at a 30-degree angle to the way you approached. As you get closer to the treeline, disregard National Trust arrows and bear left, taking a footpath leading through trees. Walk along the track, enjoying valley views across plunging Bunker's Banks on your left, and go through a gate. When the path forks go right, staying high and following Cotswold Way arrows. Pass a set of steps on your right but keep going straight.

3. Go through another gate with a Cotswold Way arrow, but instead of bearing right, as it indicates, go straight on, along the edge of the escarpment with a drop-off to your left. To your right, on recently cleared Ring Hill, lie the remains of an Iron Age hill fort and a Bronze Age long barrow called Haresfield Beacon (the latter bequeathing its name to the area). Head over the little mounds and you will see the Haresfield Beacon trig point on your right. Pause for a moment to take in the panoramic views across the Cotswolds Area of Outstanding Natural Beauty (AONB).

4. From the trig point, leave the Cotswold Way, go straight on over the hill and descend, walking south, with Vinegar Hill on your right. At a junction, turn left briefly, but then zig-zag back right and keep going down. Go over a stile with a footpath arrow and keep descending with the fence on your right. Cross another stile and walk through a meadow, past a mighty oak. Hop over a further three stiles, the last of which emerges on a lane at Tudor Farm.

5. Ignore the fingerpost indicating a footpath leading left, and instead go right over a stream to meet a small road, then turn left and follow the road gently uphill. Ignore the first and second fingerpost signs pointing right, and walk on until the end of the lane, where you enter Standish Park Farm.

6. Follow a fingerpost for Standish Woods along a footpath bending right. Pass through a gate and walk along the right edge of a field, tracing footpath arrows to a wooden field gate. Go through and walk along a nice, wide, gently rising trail, shaded by

trees. Emerge onto a gravel track. Ignore a footpath leading hard left and carry on up the track.

7. Turn left at the second metal gate, then 20 yards on, turn right at a T-junction to follow a broad track through a beautiful beech treescape, the southern extent of Standish Wood. Keep on the main track.

8. The Cotswold Way crosses your path along a track known as Robber's Road – people interested in prehistoric sites might be keen to take a diversion left here to see a Neolithic long barrow (dating to 3500–2000 BC), two Bronze Age round barrows (2000–700 BC) and an Iron Age cross dyke (700–43 BC) all found in Standish Wood, but our route carries on straight on. Go down some little wooden steps and over a stile into a field. Walk downhill along the left edge of this field, enjoying amazing views ahead and right.

9. Go through a gate and keep descending until you meet the road opposite a church. Turn left and walk up the road, past a war memorial, to the Vine Tree Inn.

10. Leave the pub and continue walking up the road. After about 100 yards, take a footpath left indicated by a fingerpost. Enter Standish Wood and ascend a path leading up a hill. When you meet a major path, go right and follow signs for 'Randwick 2000 Steps', which lead you on to the Cotswold Way, where you bear right.

11. There's a bridleway version of the Cotswolds Way here (blue arrows) and a footpath version (yellow arrows). Keep following the yellow arrows, ignoring all other turns, walking through the beautiful beech trees of Standish Wood to the car park.

From the trig point atop Haresfield Beacon, on the edge of the limestone escarpment, you can enjoy views across the Cotswold Area of Natural Beauty.

28 Snowshill Manor

Snowshill Arms

Located in a 15th-century Cotswold-stone building beside historic Snowshill Manor, the **SNOWSHILL ARMS** is a very attractive and historic village inn. It offers good pub food made with locally sourced ingredients (including famous Vale of Evesham asparagus). Cradled in the arms of the Cotswold Hills, the pub is very dog- and family-friendly and welcomes walkers warmly with real ales and a proper log fire. There is a lovely garden with views across rolling green hills, a children's play area and a skittles alley.

Snowshill Arms
Snowshill, Broadway
Gloucestershire WR12 7JU
01386 852653
www.snowshillarms.co.uk

About this walk

- Woodlands
- Cotswold Way
- Winchcombe Way
- Wyche Way
- Cotswold AONB

Start/finish Snowshill Manor car park
Distance 3½ miles (5.6km)
Time to pub 1.5 hours
Walking time 2 hours
Terrain Footpaths, lanes, quiet roads

SOUTH WEST

From the gardens of a Tudor manor house, explore footpaths leading across Cotswold hills, through ancient woodlands full of wildlife and birds, with views over the Vale of Evesham, before relaxing in a wonderfully welcoming 500-year-old country pub.

Spring The manor house reopens. Around Snowshill's gardens and orchards, daffodils bloom and fruit trees blossom.

Summer Snowshill's gardens, which polymath Charles Wade designed with Arts and Crafts architect Mackay Hugh Baillie Scott, burst into bloom. Wildflowers proliferate through the woodlands and meadows.

Autumn Trees in the orchards are heavy with fruits and nuts (50 apple varieties grow here), while Littleworth Wood blazes with what the resident poet Charles Wade called the 'flaming glory' of the season.

Winter Snowshill Manor closes, but footpaths and woodlands are ripe for exploration as views open up spectacularly with trees denuded of leaves.

The Snowshill Arms offers Donnington Brewery ales made in nearby Stow-on-the-Wold, including S.B.A., B.B. and Cotswold Gold. Lagers, ciders, wines and spirits also served.

Follow in the footsteps of ...
A manor house at Snowshill was given by King Henry VIII to Catherine Parr in 1543, but the oldest part of the current building dates to c. 1550. In 1919, architect and poet Charles Wade bought the manor and filled it with an eccentric and eclectic collection of objects, including machines, bicycles, children's toys and Japanese samurai armour. Wade lived in an old cottage in the courtyard, but entertained guests including Graham Greene, John Betjeman, Virginia Woolf and J.B. Priestley in the manor. He gifted the house and its contents to the National Trust in 1951.

How to Get There

By Car Head towards Broadway and follow signposts for Snowshill from the A44. There's parking 500 yards from the manor (WR12 7JU; National Trust), and a free parish car park closeby.

By Public Transport The nearest train stations are Moreton-in-Marsh (7 miles/11.3km) and Evesham (8 miles/13km). Buses run to Broadway (2½ miles/4km)

OS Map OS Explorer OL45 (The Cotswolds), Landranger 150 (Worcester & The Malverns); grid ref (for start): SP 096/341.

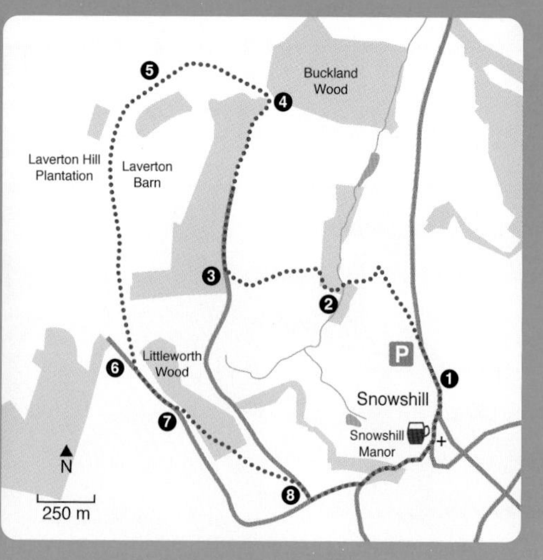

1. Go through a gate to the right of the car park entrance and take the path leading diagonally right, down the field. Trace waymarker posts through two gates, then follow an arrow pointing left, descending into woods, passing several beautiful oak trees.

2. Take the path through a gate, across a stream via a bridge and boardwalk, and around a corner in the woods, following a yellow arrow on a tree. Ignore a gate into a field, and continue along the path as it snakes upwards, along the edge of the woods. Emerge through a gate into a field and gently climb, with the fence on your left.

3. At the top, go through a gate and turn right on a wide track, following a fingerpost pointing along the Winchcombe Way (a 42-mile/67.6-km figure-of-eight trail around Winchcombe). Walk with woods on your left and, to the right, views across the Vale of Evesham to Broadway Tower, an impressive folly envisaged by landscape maestro 'Capability' Brown, designed by architect James Wyatt and built for George William, 6th Earl of Coventry in 1798 (with a nuclear bunker added during the Cold War).

4. Go through a wide gate by Buckland Wood, then immediately turn left through a small gate, still following Winchcombe Way signs. Descend diagonally across a field, going through a small gate then, immediately, a big gate. Pass (but don't cross) a stile on your right. Walk with the fence on your right to a large gate and continue along a footpath.

5. At the junction, ignore the right turn and keep going straight, following the fingerpost pointing along the Cotswold Way. Pass Laverton Barn on your left, and continue along the track, with great views of Snowshill Manor across the valley.

6. Keep going, until you see Littleworth Wood on your left and meet a junction. Go left, leaving the Cotswold Way (which goes right). You're now on part of the Wyche Way (a route linking the Cotswold Way with the Offa's Dyke Path).

7. Ignore a turning marked 'Cotswold Way Circular' to the left, and continue along the sealed lane until you see a National Trust sign for Littleworth Wood and a public footpath on the left (just before a derelict stone building). Take this down through woods, ignoring paths coming in from the left, until you reach a gate. Pass though, and descend across a field, enjoying a lovely view of the village and manor to your left.

8. Go through a gate, turn right along a lane, then immediately left along the road. Keep left at the next junction and walk into the village. The pub is on your left, opposite the church. After leaving the pub, continue up the road to the car park, passing a clutch of cottages on your right as you leave the village.

Opposite: Wildflowers on Dunstable Downs, Bedfordshire (see page 128).

South East

29 Bembridge
The Olde Village Inn

The Olde Village Inn
61 High Street, Bembridge
Isle of Wight PO35 5SF
01983 872616
www.yeoldevillageinn.co.uk

About this walk
- Beach and harbour
- Historic windmill
- Nature reserves
- Yar River Trail

Start/finish St Helens Duver car park (National Trust)
Distance 6½ miles (10.5km)
Time to pub 1 hour
Walking time 3 hours
Terrain Coastal causeway, country footpath, lanes and some road

A community-focussed pub in a building where pints have been pulled since 1787, **THE OLDE VILLAGE INN** works hard to cater for both loyal locals and visiting Isle of Wight walkers. Recently revamped and re-energised, the pub boasts an alfresco bar in a great garden, with undercover areas and lots of comfortable seating and heaters. The inside features a new eating area and a traditional pub bar. Excellent food, made with local ingredients, is served from an internationally inspired menu – and there's a pizza oven. Entertainment is regularly on offer.

From the seashore at St Helens, stroll across a tide-lapped causeway, through a historic harbour. Pause for a pint in Bembridge, before wandering around a windmill and across wildflower-covered meadows to return through a nature reserve.

Spring Myriad plant species flower in St Helens' sandy dunescape. Great spotted woodpeckers drum in Centurion's Copse, where bluebells bloom beneath coppiced hazel, and male lapwings perform for mates.

Summer Swim or go rock-pooling at St Helens. Blackcaps serenade walkers in Centurion's Copse, while warblers and yellowhammers nest. Orchids flower and butterflies flit around St Helen's Common.

Autumn Spot woodpeckers and buzzards in Centurion's Copse. Oak and ash transform colour, autumn squill flowers, while red squirrels and dormice prepare for winter.

Winter Brent geese migrate from Russia to the harbour, while linnets and other finches forage for food in Centurion's Copse, and winter heliotrope flowers in St Helen's Copse.

The Olde Village Inn stocks Ale of Wight and rotates real ales from around the country.

Follow in the footsteps of...
In the 18th century, smugglers like Dickie Dawes landed contraband including brandy, silk and tobacco at St Helens, stashing it beneath the church tombstones, before bringing it into the village via secret passages. Dickie's daughter, Sophie, born here in 1792, escaped from a life of winkle-picking and the workhouse to the French court, becoming a mistress of Duc de Bourbon, later Prince of Condé, and then marrying Baron de Fouchères.

How to Get There

By Car Take the B3330 from St Helens village and park in the car park at St Helens Duver (National Trust).

By Public Transport Regular ferries serve the Isle of Wight from Portsmouth and Southampton. Regular buses run from Ryde and Newport to St Helens Village Green.

OS Map OS Explorer OL29 (Isle of Wight), Landranger 196 (The Solent & the Isle of Wight); grid ref (for start): SZ 637/892.

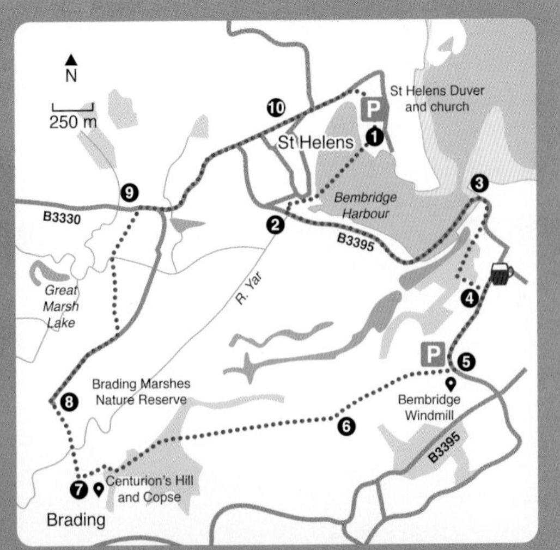

Opposite: Bembridge Windmill, near The Olde Village Inn, is over 300 years old.

Above: Bembridge's historic harbour.

1. From St Helens Duver, turn your back on the sea and head left, crossing the lane leading towards the car park and harbour, and walking along a footpath through the marsh (which was once a golf course, patronised by royalty), following coastal path arrows. Walk along the raised causeway across the harbour, which is surrounded by water at high tide. Keep following coast path signs through the harbour and out onto Latimer Road.

At high tide, the causeway path across Bembridge Harbour, allows you to walk across water.

2. Turn left on Embankment Road, cross the River Yar, walk past the marina and yacht club, and stroll along the pavement, with the harbour on your left. Continue into Bembridge, passing weird and wonderful houseboats.

3. At the Palmer Memorial, just before the Pilot Boat Inn, turn right and walk along Station Bridge Road into Church Wood, on the Yar River Trail (a 20-mile/32-km route along the island's longest river). Ignore a turning left and keep going straight, with an RSPB-managed marshland on your right. The path elbows left and climbs to meet Bembridge High Street. Turn left, and 200 yards down the road is The Olde Village Inn.

4. Exit the pub, turn left and walk along the High Street until it bends 90 degrees left – there's a footpath most of the way, on the left side of the road by houses at the top, but take care when approaching the corner.

5. At the bend, go straight ahead, along a lane to Bembridge Windmill, which was built in 1700. Turn right along a footpath behind the windmill, go through a gate and follow footpath arrows across a field, over a stile and through another field.

6. To your right sprawls the RSPB's Brading Marshes Nature Reserve. Continue through a gate, cross a field, hop over a stile and walk along a path between hedges. Go through several more gates, across a meadow and along another path into woody Centurion's Copse.

7. At a junction, turn right, following a fingerpost pointing towards Brading. Stay on this path (ignoring paths leading left), as it bends right and crosses a footbridge over the River Yar.

8. At a gate, go right, following a fingerpost for St Helens. Go through a gate on your left, along a path that runs parallel to the lane for a while, then veers left through woods. Emerge from trees, with Great Marsh Lake on your left. Turn right and walk diagonally across the field towards Carpenters Farm.

9. Pass to the right of the buildings, through a kissing gate and along a small lane, and just before the road, go right along a permissive path. When this ends, continue along the road into St Helens. Stroll through the pretty village, straight over the mini roundabout, past St Helen's Green and Common (one of England's biggest village greens) and The Vine Inn. When the main road corners left, continue straight, along Duver Road. Just before traffic lights, take the footpath leading right and follow this downhill to St Helens Duver, the church and the car park.

30 The Needles
The Highdown Inn

The Highdown Inn
Highdown Lane, Totland
Isle of Wight PO39 0HY
01983 752450
www.highdowninn.com

About this walk
- Stunning coastal views
- Wildflowers
- Military history
- Bronze Age barrow

Start/finish High Down Chalk Pit car park (National Trust)
Distance 5½ miles (9km)
Time to pub 2.5–3 hours
Walking time 3 hours
Terrain Coastal paths, headlands

SOUTH EAST

Superbly positioned between Tennyson Down and Headon Warren, near The Needles, **THE HIGHDOWN INN** is a delightful Isle of Wight gem that warmly welcomes walkers all year round. There's a large, sun-trap garden with an undercover area for enjoying alfresco ales. Inside, the pub is split into two bars, one with a big open fire and another with a little reading library. Good food is served (using fresh caught seafood and other local ingredients), B&B accommodation is available and there's camping nearby.

From the Tennyson Monument, wander along Highdown Cliffs to the western point of England's largest island, where the bright white Needles emerge from the sea. Continue around Alum Bay to explore Headon Warren, where wildflowers adorn a Bronze Age barrow, before enjoying an ale in a friendly pub.

Spring Across West High Down, the rare early gentians burst into bloom. Herring gulls, cormorants and ravens nest on the chalk cliffs around the headland. Look out for enormous white-tailed sea eagles, recently reintroduced to the Isle of Wight after a 250-year absence.

Summer Pyramid orchids, crimson clustered bellflowers, mouse-eared hawkweed, rosebay willowherb, centaury, dwarf gorse and tormentil splash colour across the rich chalk grass headland, attracting butterflies including Adonis blue, chalkhill blue and dark green fritillary.

Autumn Heather erupts, turning Headon Warren into a riot of colour. Look out for dolphins larking about around The Needles. The Highdown Inn traditionally has a beer festival in September.

Winter Flowering gorse turns the flanks of the headland gold. You may spot peregrine falcons hunting above the scrub.

The Highdown Inn has three handpumps, with rotating ales including Island Wight Gold, Ringwood Razorback and Wychwood Hobgoblin Gold. Isle of Wight lager is available too.

Follow in the footsteps of ... Originally called Highdown (hence the pub's name), Tennyson Down was rechristened in honour of the poet Alfred, Lord Tennyson. Queen Victoria's poet laureate lived in nearby Farringford House and enjoyed walks across the downs, saying that the air was worth 'sixpence a pint'.

How to Get There

By Car Take the B3322 from Yarmouth/ Totland, or the Alum Bay road from Freshwater Bay. Park at High Down Chalk Pit car park (PO39 0HY; National Trust).

By Public Transport Regular ferries serve the Isle of Wight. Southern Vectis No.7 bus service, Newport to Alum Bay, passes close and leaves half-hourly.

OS Map OS Explorer OL29 (Isle of Wight), Landranger 196 (The Solent & the Isle of Wight, Southampton & Portsmouth); grid ref (for start): SZ 325/856.

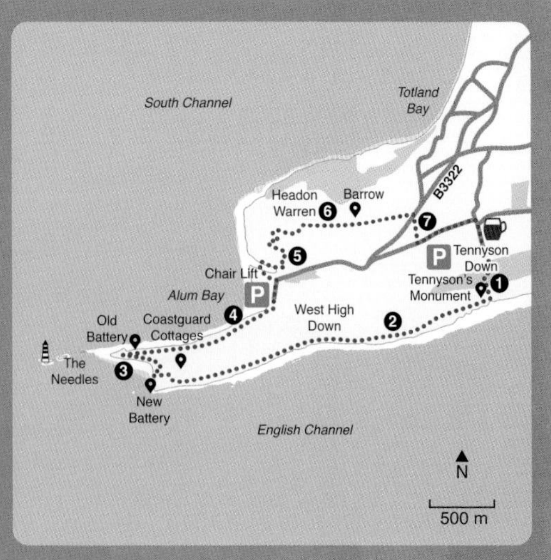

1. Standing in the car park, facing towards the quarry, turn left and walk along the path signed towards Freshwater Bay. Almost immediately (after 50 yards), turn right, following a fingerpost pointing uphill to Tennyson's Monument. Ascend through mixed woodland of ash, sycamore and oak to the Cornish granite cross, erected in memory of the poet laureate in 1897. Enjoy the panoramic views offered by this lofty spot, at 482ft (147m) above sea level, the highest point on the iconic chalk cliffs of West Wight.

2. Turn right and walk along the grass and wildflower-covered downs, looking out for pyramid orchids (the Isle of Wight's county flower), and taking in the view of the English Channel below Highdown Cliffs, and the bright white western flank of the island as you go. Several paths criss-cross the downs – including the Tennyson Trail (a 14-mile/22.5-km walk from Carisbrooke to The Needles) but aim for the aerial mast on the skyline, and don't venture too close to the precipitous cliff edge, and you can't go wrong. Crossing the stile between Tennyson Down and West High Down confirms you're on the right track. As you approach the headland, go through a gate, pass a National Trust information sign and walk to the right of the aerials. Bear left, by the corner of the Coastguard Station, and descend a concrete track to viewing platforms where you can gaze out at The Needles.

3. The Isle of Wight's westernmost point guards the entrance to the Solent and the important harbours of Poole, Bournemouth, Southampton and Portsmouth, so historically it has been very well guarded. While you're here, it's well worth exploring the buildings, which include fortifications, gun emplacements and a rocket-launching site, all with excellent views. The New Battery, which dates to the 1890s and was used as a rocket-testing site during Britain's 20th-century Space Age programme, has a great vista across Scratchell's Bay and St Anthony Rock. From here, walk through the gun buildings and descend to the viewing station closest to the Old Battery complex. This fort was commissioned by Lord Palmerston in 1862 to protect the Solent from a French invasion that never came. Beyond the Victorian lighthouse at the end of The Needles, you can see the Isle of Purbeck, protruding from the Dorset coastline on the other side of Poole Bay. When you are ready to set off again, walk along the sealed path with Alum Bay on your left and the Coastguard Cottages on your right, before picking up the chalk path that runs alongside the road.

4. Walk along the road as it arcs left and keep following blue signs for the Coastal Path through the large car park. Turn left into the busy, touristy part of Alum Bay. By the chair lift, take the footpath leading right and descend steps passing below the dangling chairs. At the bottom, you can go left to explore Alum Bay Beach (famed for its multicoloured cliffs), but our route turns right and walks up through the trees of Hatherwood.

5. When you reach a T-junction, turn left along the path (not the road), passing a National Trust sign for Headon Warren and following a fingerpost for the Coastal Path. Ascend a narrow path, passing a clearing on the left, location of another Palmerston-era gun emplacement (Hatherwood Battery), from where a very different view over The Needles can be enjoyed, with far fewer people to share it with (this is a great picnic place). Rejoin the Coastal Path and continue to climb.

6. At the top of the hill, by a fork in the trail, you reach a wooden bench (offering yet another superb view). Leave the Coastal Path here and go right, walking along a gravel footpath through Headon Warren, with a view of the Tennyson Monument in the distance, slightly off to the right. The path undulates through heather across Headon Hill and takes you past a mound on the left – this Bronze Age barrow is believed to be the burial site of a local chieftain, who presided over this area around 3,500 years ago.

7. Keep to the right, and when the path forks, go right and descend through heather and gorse, past a solar panel. Ignore a little path leading sharp right, and when you meet a wooden post shortly afterwards, continue straight, following a yellow footpath arrow through two gates to meet the B3322. Carefully cross the road, turn right very briefly, then immediately turn left along a path signed 'footpath T28 Alum Bay Old Road' and walk across a field. When you meet Alum Bay Old Road, turn left and walk up to a crossroads, where The Highdown Inn is on your right. After leaving the pub, walk straight up Highdown Lane to the car park.

High Down drops into the sea at The Needles, the famous saw-tooth of chalky rocks originally named after a distinctive 120ft (37m) needle-shaped spike, which collapsed in 1764.

31 The Seven Sisters   

The Tiger Inn

The Tiger Inn
The Green, East Dean
East Sussex BN20 0DA
01323 423209
www.beachyhead.org.uk/the-tiger-inn

About this walk

- Stunning coastal views
- Seven Sisters Country Park/South Downs National Park
- Wildflowers/butterflies

Start/finish Crowlink car park (National Trust)
Distance 6 miles (10km)
Time to pub 2 hours
Walking time 2.5 hours
Terrain Countryside, coastal and clifftop paths, lanes

A destination pub for South Downs dawdlers, crouched in the Sussex Hills, **THE TIGER INN** has been serving smugglers, soldiers, hikers and bikers since the 15th century. Overlooking a village green, there are outdoor tables for sunny days, while inside the main bar is full of character, from stone floors to wooden beams. A massive open fire crackles during colder months, with locals and walkers enjoying a convivial atmosphere encouraged by the open-plan layout. Maps adorn the walls, along with tiger-themed features. Food is served, and accommodation is available.

From a famous smuggling village, walk one of the most recognisable sections of Britain's coast, the rollercoaster route over the Seven Sisters to Birling Gap and Belle Tout Lighthouse, where you can wave at Beachy Head before heading inland across wildflower-covered meadows to an iconic pub.

Spring Skylarks soar and wheatears arrive from Africa. A carpet of buttercups and daisies rolls out across Hobb's Eares meadow, and rare salad burnet flowers from May, releasing a cucumber scent.

Summer Waves of deep purple and gold wash across Hobb's Eares, as knapweeds appear. Butterflies, including the common blue, flutter around blooming wildflowers such as bird's-foot trefoil.

Autumn House martins and swallows swoop low over cliffs, feasting on insects before flying south. Autumn gentian and devil's-bit scabious provide nectar for painted lady and red admiral butterflies preparing to migrate across the Channel. Ripe hawthorn berries, sloes and blackberries attract thrushes and foragers.

Winter Flowering gorse gilds the trails, sending off a coconut aroma. Fossick for fossils and watch sunsets before retreating to the warmth of the pub.

The Tiger Inn serves several Sussex-made ales, including beers from Harvey's, Gun, and Long Man breweries.

Follow in the footsteps of... Opposite The Tiger Inn, a cottage boasts a blue plaque claiming 'Sherlock Holmes, consulting detective and bee keeper, retired here 1903–1917'. Intriguing... especially since Holmes is a fictional character, and Arthur Conan Doyle didn't specify where he'd retired his famous sleuth. However, Holmes aficionados are adamant that this is the spot.

How to Get There

By Car Crowlink car park (BN20 0AY; National Trust) is off the A259 at Friston Pond, between Seaford and Eastbourne.

By Public Transport Travel by train to Eastbourne (6 miles/10km) or Seaford Station (5 miles/8km). Catch bus 13X (to Brighton) or 12 (to Friston Pond).

OS Map OS Explorer OL25 (Eastbourne & Beachy Head), Landranger 199 (Eastbourne & Hastings); grid ref (for start): TV 549/979.

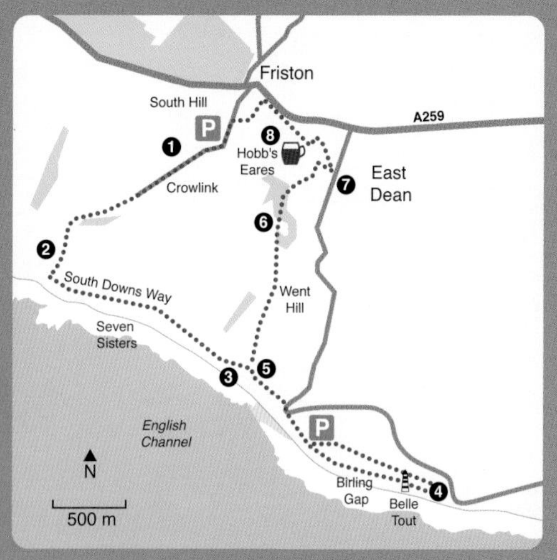

1. From Crowlink car park, stroll straight down the tarmac lane towards the coast. Pass through a gate next to a cattle grid and keep walking along a sealed track, over a second cattle grid. As you walk past several houses, the track becomes rougher. This is the hamlet of Crowlink, a village so synonymous with smuggling in the 1700s and 1800s that cheap, illegally imported 'Crowlink gin' was the drink of choice in the bars, lanes and alleyways of London, and was even marketed under the name 'Genuine Crowlink gin' for a while. Rough-and-ready smugglers (also known as 'free traders' or 'owlers'), such as the infamous Hawkhurst Gang, operated along the Sussex Coast, occasionally fighting violent pitched battles against customs officials. After the last house, go through a gate and follow bridleway arrows along the track, which becomes grassy. Walk with the fence on the right, ignoring a stile. Go through another gate and keep walking next to the fence as the track gently descends towards the sea. The path crosses a track coming in from the right, and arcs left.

2. Keep going, all the way to a gate in the fence just before the Sussex chalkland falls away over the cliffs, between the shoulders of the Seven Sisters. Pass through the gate and turn left, to walk east along the South Downs Way, a National Trail that stretches 100 miles (160km) between Winchester in Hampshire and Eastbourne in East Sussex. Pass a memorial to men lost in the First World War, then ascend the west side of Went Hill. Go through Malcolm's Gate by the National Trust sign for Went Hill, and carry on along the undulating grassy track, taking in the stunning view across Birling Gap to Belle Tout Lighthouse.

3. When you reach the fingerpost pointing right to Beachy Head or left to East Dean, a choice needs to be made: you can go left and walk straight up the hill to the pub, or you can continue through the car park to take a closer look at one of the most famous lighthouses in Britain. To continue along the coast, go up the gravel track behind the toilet block, pass through a wide wooden gate and wend right to take the path ascending to the lighthouse.

4. Originally built in 1832, following several major maritime incidents and accidents, Belle Tout was deliberately designed to be visible 20 miles (32km) out to sea, with the light disappearing if ships strayed too close to the cliffs. Decommissioned in 1902, when Beachy Head Lighthouse made it redundant, Belle Tout has been owned by various people and organisations since, including the BBC, which used it as a filming location. In 1999 the entire building was moved 56ft (17m) back from the edge of the cliff because of fears that erosion would cause it to topple over. Do a loop around the lighthouse, looking (and walking if you wish – though it will add 3 miles/5km each way) further east to another iconic beauty spot – the immense chalky headland of Beachy Head. Afterwards, head

The roller-coaster path across the Seven Sisters chalk cliffs is one of southern England's most stunning seaside walking routes.

back, either taking the same route or exploring another footpath that runs slightly inland.

5. Pass back through the car park and walk behind the toilet block. Turn right and climb uphill along a gravel track that segues into a path. Pass through a gate beside a National Trust sign for Went Hill. Ascend a broad, grassy track towards a clutch of gorse and windblown hawthorn trees, where there is a second gate. Keep the gorse bushes to your immediate right as the track becomes less distinct.

6. Go past a red-roofed barn, where a seat overlooks the stunning vista west, along the coast towards Brighton and Hove. Continue over the flat-top brow of Went Hill, keeping the hedgeline on your immediate right. At a post, take the path leading down to the right, into trees, as views of the South Downs unfold. Pass a National Trust sign for Went Way and go through a wooden gate. Descend, passing through another wooden gate, and continue straight towards some houses. Go through a wide metal gate, and along Went Way.

7. At the end of the lane you'll meet a row of white cottages. Turn right and walk across the village green to The Tiger Inn, passing a war memorial and flagpole. Look left from the flagpole to find the cottage with a blue plaque on the wall claiming that Sherlock Holmes retired there.

8. After leaving the pub, turn right and walk uphill to a lane (Upper Street), and turn left. Just before a bend, turn right up a short drive and go past a National Trust sign for Farrer Hill. Go through a wooden gate by the National Trust Hobb's Eares sign and walk up the hill. Before you reach a gate, bear left and walk along the top of the field. Go through a gate and continue straight to the car park.

32 Devil's Dyke

The Shepherd & Dog

The Shepherd & Dog
The Street, Fulking
West Sussex BN5 9LU
01273 857382
www.shepherdanddogpub.co.uk

About this walk

- South Downs National Park
- Sensational views
- Prehistoric barrows
- Mythology
- Steep climbs

Start/finish Devil's Dyke car park
Distance 5 miles (8km)
Time to pub 1.5–2 hours
Walking time 3 hours
Terrain Hills and countryside footpaths

Nestled beneath Fulking Hill, **THE SHEPHERD & DOG** is an attractive, traditional pub that welcomes South Downs walkers with a lovely patio and beer garden, complete with a stream and beautiful countryside views. Inside the 400-year-old bar, you'll find an inglenook fireplace, low beams and a wall entirely festooned with beer mats. The pub offers local real ales and craft ciders, and there's an excellent menu. Throughout the year the pub hosts beer, cider and 'gin and jazz' festivals. The Devil's Dyke pub-restaurant at the start/finish also offers ales and panoramic views.

Explore an extraordinary chalk escarpment overlooking the Sussex Weald, visiting a historic farm and donkey wheel before ascending dramatic Devil's Dyke, a grass-carpeted valley hanging amid the folds of the spectacular South Downs, resplendent with wildlife and rich in folklore. Pass the 'Devil's Graves', where the Devil and his wife are buried, according to local folklore, and loop around Fulking Hill to enjoy a drink in a classic country pub.

Spring Spy skylarks soaring and singing above the South Downs. White bursts of blossoming blackthorn can be seen on the sides of Devil's Dyke.

Summer Look out for the rare county flower, the round-headed rampion, also known as the Pride of Sussex, which blooms June–August. Butterflies, including the chalkhill blue, bring extra colour.

Autumn Trees turn russet, and wax cap fungi appear together with late blooming wildflowers such as devil's-bit scabious. Look out for long-tailed tits flitting between bare branches.

Winter Redwings arrive from colder climes, green woodpeckers drum in the branches and kestrels soar overhead.

The Shepherd & Dog stocks ales from Downlands Brewery, based just up the road, including Best and Bramber, with other seasonal ales on rotation.

Follow in the footsteps of ... According to local folklore, this dramatic landscape was shaped by Satan during a failed wager with St Cuthman of Steyning. The Devil boasted he could flood the Weald by digging a channel in one night, and the gouges he made became the mounds and valleys visible today. Cunning Cuthman, however, made a cock crow and fooled the Devil into thinking dawn had broken early, thereby causing him to abandon his quest.

How to Get There

By Car Devil's Dyke car park (National Trust) is 2 miles (3.2km) north of the A27 Brighton ring road, and just off the A281.

By Public Transport The closest train station is Brighton (6 miles/10km), from which bus 77 travels to Devil's Dyke on weekends and bank holidays.

OS Map OS Explorer OL11 (Brighton & Hove), Landranger 198 (Brighton & Lewes); grid ref (for start): TQ 258/110.

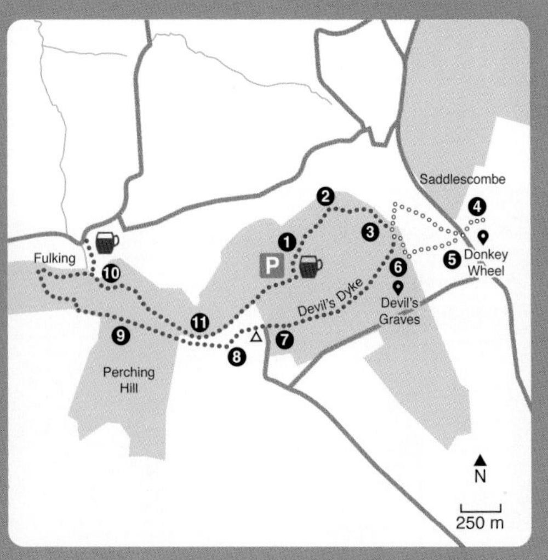

1. Standing with your back to The Devil's Dyke (pub), with the view unfolding in front of you, turn right and walk east through the car park, with buildings on your right and the edge of the escarpment plunging away on your left. Keep going, past stone benches on your left and a copse of trees to your right, through a gravel overflow car park, past a metal gate and along a path. After about 150 yards, bear left, leave the plateau and go through a kissing gate. Carefully descend the steep, narrow path. A funicular railway once ran here, ferrying sightseers up and down from the village of Poynings, visible down below, through gaps in the greenery.

2. When you reach a kissing gate, bear right and follow the path through woods. At a crossways, go straight across and continue to a T-junction.

3. Here, you can either visit Saddlescombe Farm and the Donkey Wheel or skip straight to Devil's Dyke valley. To shortcut, turn right and jump to point 6, otherwise bear left, and walk up a steep footpath. Take the next path leading right, which runs along the edge of a field by a line of telegraph poles, leading on to a tarmac track running to a gate. Carefully cross the road and enter Saddlescombe Farm, passing a pond on the right.

4. Cared for by the National Trust, Saddlescombe Farm is a hidden hamlet with a rich history stretching back over a millennium; in the 13th century it was controlled by the Knights Templar, who used it to finance crusading knights heading to the Holy Lands. Here you can visit the Wildflour Café and see the Donkey Wheel, one of only four such contraptions surviving in Britain, which was once turned by a donkey to bring up drinking water from the ground. After exploring, go back across the road and through the gate.

5. Turn immediately left, passing a trough, and then go right above the fence. Follow a ditch briefly (for about 50 yards), then leave it and stride straight up the field, looking up through Devil's Dyke valley, directly ahead. Cross a stile at the top, continue along the path for 100 yards, then take a sharp right. Follow the path as it wends left, then, by a junction you passed through earlier, take a sharp left.

6. Begin the long ascent up through Devil's Dyke, looking out for the Devil's Graves (two humps in the ground said to be the burial place of the Devil and his wife) to the left. As you get higher, peer up the side of the slopes to spot concrete footings from the Great Cableway that once ran across the chasm – built in 1894, this was Britain's first cable car.

7. At the top, dogleg right then left, go through a gate and carefully cross the road. Hop over a stile and step lightly along the embankment of an Iron Age hill fort to the trig point. Drop down from the bank and bear left.

8. When you hit a well-defined path (after about 50 yards), turn right. Pass through a gate and follow a fingerpost indicating you're now on the South Downs Way (SDW), a 100-mile (160-km) path from Winchester (Hampshire) to Eastbourne (East Sussex). Walk along the SDW until you reach a gate and the start of a chalk track.

9. Turn right and take the path snaking downhill. Keep the fence on your left, passing (but not crossing) a stile. Continue, around a right-hand bend and along the path, until you reach a junction by a National Trust sign. Turn left and walk down a path that goes right past The Shepherd & Dog beer garden.

10. Leaving the pub, go back up the footpath by the beer garden, onto the downs. At the National Trust sign, turn left and climb the steep hill, taking in superb views across the village and over West Sussex. When you reach a knot of footpaths and bridleways on a ridge, where a collection of fingerposts point excitedly in every direction, cross straight over and follow the bridleway up the chalky incline. Go through a gate and pass a National Trust sign for Fulking Escarpment.

11. Continue to another fingerpost, go straight over and follow the path as it bears left and rises towards a nest of buildings visible atop the hill. The first structure you pass is a mysterious, virtually windowless, derelict brick barn, which dates from the Second World War – this may just be a farm building, but Devil's Dyke has been used for various activities over the years, including military tests and an acoustic experiment known as 'the Howling Terror', which projected an amplified human voice through the valley and scared locals stiff when it was first conducted without warning in July 1900. Continue on, hopping over the hummocks of a pre-historic hill fort constructed by Iron Age Britons on this lofty ridge, to reach the car park.

Devil's Dyke is a dry valley in the South Downs that echoes with folklore and offers fabulous footpaths leading to wonderful walker-friendly watering holes.

33 Bodiam Castle

The Castle Inn & The Salehurst Halt

The Castle Inn
Main Road, Bodiam
East Sussex TN32 5UB
01580 830330
www.castleinnbodiam.co.uk

About this walk

- Medieval castle
- Riverside and woodland
- Wildlife

Start/finish Bodiam Castle car park (National Trust)
Distance 6½ miles (10.5km)
Time to pub 1.5 hours to Salehurst Halt; 3 hours to the Castle Inn
Walking time 3 hours
Terrain Woodland and riverside paths, some lanes

THE CASTLE INN, positioned directly opposite Bodiam Castle and by the River Rother, is a National Trust-owned, food-orientated pub, which welcomes walkers with a wonderful garden and an atmospheric, open-plan interior warmed by an open fire. THE SALEHURST HALT is a classic country pub dating to 1867, with a fantastic garden (created and maintained by a local landscape gardener) overlooking the Rother Valley's hop fields. This warm pub has an open fire, a bar covered in pennies and lined with bunches of hops, and a menu flavoured with locally sourced seasonal produce.

Meander from the moat of a spectacular 14th-century fortress, past iconic oast houses and through the hop fields and orchards of the rural Rother Valley on the seam of Sussex and Kent, to a vintage village pub, before returning along a riparian route to an inn with a castle view.

Spring Oaks around Bodiam burst forth with verdant foliage, while fruit trees in orchards all through the Rother Valley come into flower.

Summer Bodiam Castle is home to five bat species and boasts Britain's biggest Daubenton's bat maternity roost. Bat pups are born in early summer.

Autumn Hops in the fields along the Rother Valley are harvested, while trees around Bodiam Castle and grounds transform in colour.

Winter Mist drifts across the castle moat, cloaking the reflected curtain walls. Open fires await winter walkers at the Salehurst Halt and Castle Inn.

The Castle Inn is a Shepherd Neame pub, serving the Kent brewery's Whitstable Bay pale ale and Spitfire bitter. The Salehurst Halt is a free house offering real ale from several local breweries including Harveys, Cellar Head, Old Dairy, Three Legs and Gun.

Follow in the footsteps of ... Built in 1385 to protect the area from French invasion during the Hundred Years' War, Bodiam Castle was partially demolished by Parliamentarian forces in the English Civil War. The castle was saved from demolition in 1828 by MP John 'Mad Jack' Fuller, who bought it at auction with wealth earned from sugar harvested by slaves in Jamaica. It's been looked after by The National Trust since 1925.

How to Get There

By Car Parking is available at Bodiam Castle (TN32 5UA), 3 miles (5km) east of the A21 at the southern end of Hurst Green village, halfway between Tunbridge Wells and Hastings.

By Public Transport A seasonal steam train operated by Kent & East Sussex Railway runs from Tenterden town to Bodiam Station; the nearest mainline railway stations are at Robertsbridge (5 miles/8km) and Battle (10 miles/16km).

OS Map OS Explorer 136 (High Weald), Landranger 199 (Eastbourne & Hastings); grid ref (for start): TQ 784/254.

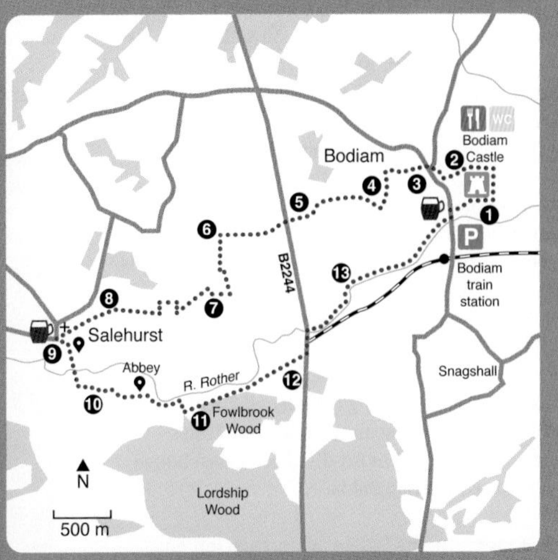

1. From the car park, walk past the information board and turn right along the trail towards the castle, bearing right and passing to the left of a Second World War pillbox. When the track splits, go to the right of the castle – a fabulous fortification with castellated battlements, a portcullis and tall towers accessed by spiral staircases, all surrounded by a broad moat, patrolled by ducks and large carp. Keep going around the moat until you reach the entrance, accessed by a bridge. Cross and explore the interior, and then head up to the Castle View building, where there's an excellent information display, a café and toilets.

2. Instead of rounding the castle, keep going, past the toilets (on your right) and through a gate into the National Trust staff car park, then follow the lane around to the right.

3. Carefully cross the main road, turn right along the pavement and then immediately take a footpath going left, walking with vineyards on your right. Go left through a metal gate and follow arrows leading through buildings until you reach a T-junction, then go left down the sealed lane.

4. Keep going, past Four Boys Farm and New House to a T-junction, where you turn right along an unsealed lane. Go through a wooden gate and pass several buildings, then take a footpath going left, across a footbridge to a pond with picnic benches. Bear right of the pond and take the path to a stile; cross and follow footpath arrows right. Cross another stile and walk to the road (B2244).

5. Cross carefully, go over a stile on the other side and follow a footpath arrow left, up the grassy hill, before bearing right and tracing the fence and tree line along a clearly marked path. Cross a stile and footbridge, and walk across a field, bearing slightly right and passing little copse of trees. Keep walking until you meet a stile in the hedge, but don't cross.

6. Turn left and walk down the field with the trees and fence on your right. After about 400 yards go right, through a gap in the hedge, which leads across a footbridge and along a lovely path through beech woods.

7. When the path forks (easy to miss, but it soon becomes obvious if you've gone too far), go left, over a stile into a field, and walk with trees on your left. Cross another stile and follow footpath arrows left through orchards at Moat Farm, heeding signs for Salehurst. Go past Moat Farm, over a stile and across a field. Cross another stile and field, go left at the end and follow a path leading around to the right.

8. Cross a little lane and keep going straight, towards the square church tower in Salehurst. Go through a kissing gate into the graveyard, walk around the church and emerge opposite The Salehurst Halt pub.

9. Exit the pub, turn right and walk along a bridleway with the church on your left. Bear right and keep going downhill, ignoring paths left and right until you cross a footbridge over the river. Keep going straight, until you meet a T-junction with a tarmac lane/bridleway. Turn left here.

10. Pass the remains of an old abbey on your left and walk around the bend to a wooden gate where several paths are signed. Go straight through this gate, then over a stile, across a field and over another stile, still following footpath arrows.

11. Walk along the riverside path when possible (taking field paths along the edge of Fowlbrook Wood when flooding dictates, as sometimes happens), looking out for distinctive oast house roofs across the hop fields.

12. Emerge on the B2244 again, turn left and carefully walk along the road, past Udiam Farm on your right and over the bridge across the river, then immediately turn right through a metal gate.

13. Keep walking along the riverside path, with the water on your right. Pass a weir and Oastbrook Vineyard, until you see The Castle Inn up on the left. From here the castle and car park are just across the road.

Below: Sussex breweries such as Harveys use locally grown hops.

Bottom: The 14th-century Bodiam Castle is one of Britain's best-preserved medieval fortifications.

34 Harting Down
The Three Horseshoes

The Three Horseshoes
Elsted, Midhurst
West Sussex GU29 0JY
01730 825746
www.3hs.co.uk

About this walk
- South Downs Way
- Stunning views
- South Downs National Park
- Wildlife watching

Start/finish Harting Down car park (National Trust)
Distance 7 miles (11.3km)
Time to pub 1–1.5 hours
Walking time 3 hours
Terrain Grassy hillside footpaths, woodland trails, bridleways, lanes

A hidden gem of a gathering place on the western edge of the Sussex Weald, **THE THREE HORSESHOES** at Elsted is everything you look for in a traditional countryside pub. An enormous grassy garden, patrolled by free-ranging chickens and happy hikers, offers sensational views of the South Downs. Inside, hand-carved walking sticks are sold in a tile-floored, low-beamed bar, warmed by a woodburner. There are several rooms, including one for eating, and lovely food is served inside and out, along with a wide range of local ales.

Stroll a section of the South Downs Way to hilltops offering fantastic views across the fields and woodlands of the Weald, passing the site of a Napoleonic War beacon and pausing for a pint in a beautiful beer garden, before looping back via Kill Devil Copse.

Spring Swallows swoop through the South Downs, catching insects on the wing. Other migrant birds pass by, some resting and nesting in the scrub – spot wheatears, meadow pipits, blackcaps, willow warblers and yellowhammers.

Summer Roe deer rut and skylarks serenade walkers. Pollinators buzzing around wildflowers on the chalk grassland include blue carpenter bees, brown hairstreak and grizzled skipper butterflies, and six-spot burnet moths.

Autumn Listen for the deep guttural calls of rutting fallow deer. Look for cheese snails, a speciality mollusc of the South Downs with a wheel-of-cheese shaped shell.

Winter Flocks of greenfinch whirl, while redwings and fieldfares fly in to feast on the last juniper berries. Spot short-eared owls, kestrels, sparrowhawks and buzzards.

The Three Horseshoes offers up to five real ales, all gravity poured from the barrel. Regulars include Sussex-brewed Flower Pots Bitter and Langham Hip Hop.

Follow in the footsteps of ...
Just east stands Uppark, a National Trust–maintained 17th-century mansion where H.G. Wells' mother worked as a housekeeper. In winter 1887–88, 20-year-old Wells convalesced here, observing the social inequality that influenced his writing. It's also where he first used a telescope; peering at planets perhaps planted the seeds of his science fiction stories, such as *The War of the Worlds*.

How to Get There

By Car There's parking (National Trust) below Harting Down, on Harting Hill off the B2141, near South Harting.

By Public Transport The nearest train station is Petersfield (5½ miles/8.8km), on the London–Portsmouth line. Stagecoach bus 91 runs between Petersfield and Midhurst, stopping at Elsted (opposite the pub), and the 54 goes between Petersfield and Chichester, stopping at South Harting.

OS Map OS Explorer OL8 (Chichester), Landranger 197 (Chichester & The South Downs); grid ref (for start): SU 791/181.

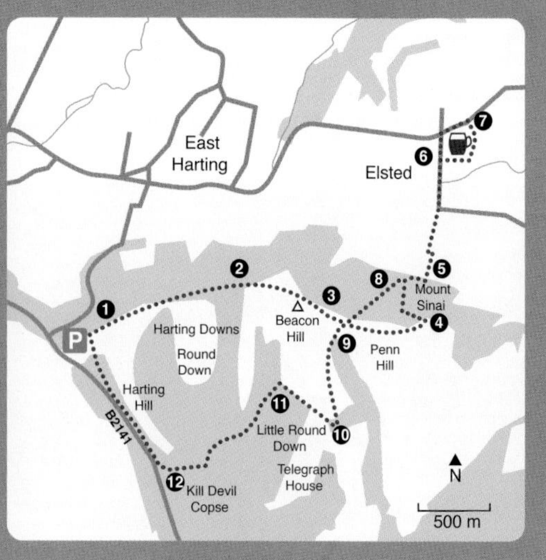

1. From the car park, walk straight up the grassy hill and go through a wooden gate. Bear slightly left, following two National Trust walk indicator arrows (for the Harting Walk and the Short Walk), and joining a path coming in from the left – the South Downs Way (SDW), a 100-mile (160-km) National Trail tracing the South Downs' chalk escarpment between Winchester and Eastbourne. Go past a wooden fingerpost and continue heading straight along the SDW, past the National Trust sign for Harting Downs. Glance back in the direction of the car park and Uppark for a glimpse of the ruined Vandalian tower, an 18th-century folly on Tower Hill commemorating the short-lived British colony of Vandalia in West Virginia.

2. Descend the far side of Harting Hill, going through a wide gate to reach a five-way fingerpost at Bramshott Bottom. The left arm indicates the way to East Harting, while two fingers point right, one along a footpath and the other along the SDW. Ignore all of these and instead carry straight on, ascending the steep flanks of Beacon Hill. Go through a wooden gate and reach the summit, one-time location of a prehistoric hill fort (inhabited in both the Bronze and Iron ages), an Anglo-Saxon burial mound and a Napoleonic Wars-era telegraph station. Now you'll find both a beacon marker and a trig point. Enjoy superb views across Sussex, Hampshire and Surrey, before descending the other side, passing another Harting Downs National Trust sign.

3. Ignore tracks leading left and right, and instead follow a SDW fingerpost pointing straight up Pen Hill, the peak of which delivers more great views across the South Downs National Park and the Weald.

4. Continue along the SDW and through a gate next to a cattle grid, ignoring the first footpath turning left. At a fingerpost, take the footpath leading left following the SDW markers and descend a hillside (Mount Sinai), which is quite steep in places (take care – when wet, chalk surfaces can be very slippery). When the path meets a bridleway turn right and keep descending through the trees, following the bridleway to the right.

5. By a three-way fingerpost at the bottom of a clearing, turn left then right along a restricted byway and then keep going straight, ignoring footpaths left and right, until you find yourself on a sealed road. Follow the road to the left.

6. Walk to a crossroads, turn right and follow a road sign to Midhurst and Iping. Just past Elsted Village Hall (on the left) is The Three Horseshoes (on your right). Go past the car park turning and Spitfire Cottage, and you will see the pub sign. Look out for free range chickens and check out the magnificent views from the garden, up to the hills you have just walked across.

7. Leave the pub from the end of the garden, turning right along a footpath that traces the top edge of a field, with South Downs' views to your left. Pass through the hedge into the next field, then follow a fingerpost pointing right. Follow the path around the edge of the field. Go down some small steps, and when you reach the road you walked up earlier, turn left and stroll downhill, reversing your previous steps. When the sealed road elbows left, leave it and go straight ahead, following a fingerpost pointing along a restricted byway. Keep to the middle path (the same one you walked in the opposite direction previously) and climb gently as you retrace your steps.

8. At the T-junction with a three-way fingerpost, turn right, up through the trees along the bridleway. After 100 yards, when the lane forks, go left and walk uphill, following a bridleway fingerpost. After about 150 yards, a fingerpost indicates the footpath leading left (which you emerged from earlier) but ignore this and keep climbing up the bridleway.

9. At the top of the climb go through the gate. When you meet a crosspaths in the saddle between Pen Hill (on your left) and Beacon Hill (on your right), there's a National Trust sign for Harting Down. Take the path going straight ahead, keeping the National Trust sign to your right. Follow the SDW along the bottom of Beacon Hill, walking with a fence on your left, beyond which there are fantastic views across Millpond Bottom to Philliswood Down.

10. When you meet a T-junction near Telegraph House, turn right – again following signage for the SDW – continue along the path and pass through a gate.

11. At a three-way fingerpost, leave the SDW and turn left along a bridleway that skirts Little Round Down. When you reach a crosspaths, by a round, fenced-off pond, go straight over, picking up a footpath that goes alongside the enigmatically named Kill Devil Copse.

12. At the next T-junction turn right and follow the footpath or the bridleway (they run parallel) up the southern flank of Harting Hill to the car park.

The large garden at The Three Horseshoes offers uninterrupted views of the South Downs.

35 Hinton Ampner

The Flower Pots Inn

The Flower Pots Inn
Brandy Mount, Cheriton
Hampshire SO24 0QQ
01962 771318
www.theflowerpots.co.uk

About this walk

- Battle site
- Itchen Way
- South Downs views
- Wayfarers Walk

Start/finish Hinton Ampner (National Trust)
Distance 7½ miles (12km)
Time to pub 2 hours
Walking time 3 hours
Terrain Countryside and farmland footpaths, bridleways, lanes, some road

Hidden in the Hampshire Hills, amid the South Downs, **THE FLOWER POTS INN** is a superb pub and brewery, owned by three locals, which warmly welcomes walkers. The Georgian-era, brick-built former farmhouse remains divided into three rooms: the public bar, with a large open fire and a well; the saloon, where locals chat by a small fire; and the back bar, warmed by a potbelly stove. There's a separate restaurant/function area. The original landlord was a gardener (hence the name), and the large garden remains a star attraction. Accommodation is available.

From Hinton Ampner estate, explore a Civil War battle site, walking through fields on the western edge of the South Downs National Park to a village where the River Itchen rises and chalk-filtered water is transformed into award-winning beer at a picturesque pub and microbrewery.

Spring Waves of bluebells and wood anemones flood Hinton Ampner, where cherry trees blossom, and magnolias flower. House martins and swallows swoop, and hares streak across fields where the Battle of Cheriton is occasionally re-enacted.

Summer Rutting roe deer stags battle and bellow. Wildflowers line lanes and Hinton Ampner's gardens are abloom, attracting bees and butterflies. The pub hosts a beer festival in August.

Autumn Beech, ancient oaks and maple trees stage a kaleidoscopic colour show. Badgers, deer, squirrels, foxes and barbastelle bats are active around the woodlands.

Winter Hinton Ampner's lily pond may ice over, sweet box and snowdrops flower, and the South Downs' views are crisp.

The Flower Pots brews and serves Pots Bitter, Goodens Gold, Perridge Pale, Flower Pots IPA, Cheriton Porter and Buster's Best (named after a much-loved pub dog), plus locally made Meon Valley cider.

Follow in the footsteps of ... This walk traverses the site of the Battle of Cheriton, fought on 29 March 1644. During the bloody engagement, Sir William Waller's Roundhead Army of the Southern Association defeated Royalist forces, jointly commanded by the Earl of Forth and Sir Ralph Hopton. The Parliamentarian victory scuppered Royalist hopes of retaking south-east England, influencing the outcome of the English Civil War.

How to Get There

By Car Take the M3, use exit 9, drive towards to Petersfield on the A272 and look for property signs. Park at Hinton Ampner (SO24 0LA; National Trust).

By Public Transport The closest train stations are Winchester (9 miles/14.5km) and Petersfield (10 miles/16km). Bus 67 serves Cheriton and Hinton Ampner from both.

OS Map OS Explorer OL32 (Winchester), Landranger 185 (Winchester & Basingstoke); grid ref (for start): SU 597/279.

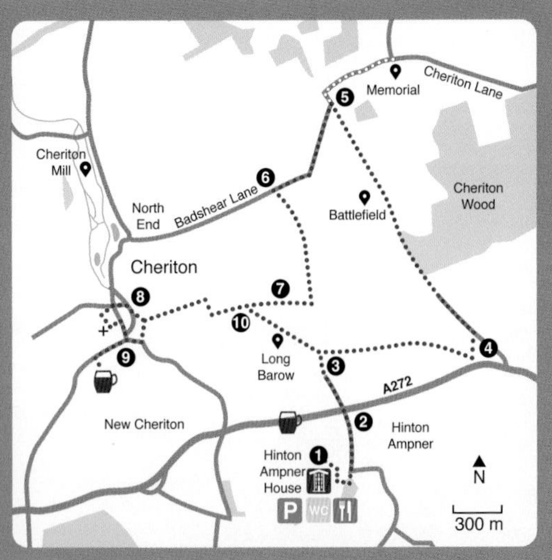

1. From the car park, stroll through Hinton Ampner gardens and around the church. Walk past Church Cottage, on your right, go through the grand gate and follow the lane as it goes downhill, passing a thatched cottage and meeting the A272.

2. Carefully cross the road to the lane opposite. You will see a Cheriton Battlefield Walk information board on your left – pause and have a read, before continuing up the lane, which turns into a track.

3. Go under a tall metal forestry gate, and turn right along Cheriton Lane, an unsealed track that passes across the lower section of the battlefield.

4. Just before you meet the road, turn left into a field, following a footpath arrow, and walk with the hedge on your right. The path bends left and then cuts through the hedge to meet a lane. Turn left along this track and walk uphill. Ignore footpaths leading right and left, and continue walking along the undulating track, with the battlefield over the hedge on your left. It's a gently folding farm field today, but much blood was spilt on this soil on 29 March 1644, when a 10,000-strong Parliamentarian army violently clashed with Royalist forces numbering around 7,000. Cheriton Wood, on your right, was a key strategic area, too, and the scene of hot fighting as control of this vantage point changed hands.

5. When you meet the road, you can either turn left straight away, along Badshear Lane, or follow Cheriton Lane as it bends right and walk about 500 yards to the junction with Scrubbs Lane, where a memorial to the hundreds of men who lost their lives in the battle poignantly overlooks Cheriton Wood. After seeing the memorial and taking in the view of the woodlands and South Downs, return to the junction, do a dogleg and walk along Badshear Lane.

6. When you pass a large barn, turn left and walk along a track (Broad Lane). Ignore a path coming in from the left, but shortly afterwards, at a crossways, turn right along the Wayfarers Walk, a 71-mile (114-km) walking route between Walbury Hill in Berkshire and Emsworth in Hampshire, which both follows an ancient drovers' path and traces the first flightpath of aviation pioneer Geoffrey de Havilland.

7. At a confluence of paths, our route is joined from the left by the Itchen Way, a 32-mile (51.5-km) footpath following the route of the River Itchen from its source (Hinton Ampner) to its mouth at Woolston. Do a little dogleg to continue going straight, along both the Wayfarers Walk and the Itchen Way. Walk between a fence and a hedge and keep following the path on a zig-zag route, until you meet a long narrow section that descends between two fences and emerges by a stream and school in Cheriton.

The farm fields around Cheriton look bucolic now, but this was the scene of a bloody battle during the English Civil War.

8. Cross the little bridge into the village. Turn right, walk across the road and stroll with the stream on your right. Bear left and follow a fingerpost for the Wayfarers Walk. Cross the road and go along Hill Houses Lane. Turn immediately left through a gate, walk across a field and go through a second gate into the church graveyard. Walk to the left of the church, and when you meet the road, go right. Emerge opposite a green and houses, turn right and walk past a war memorial (on your left). At the junction, turn right and carefully walk up the road to The Flower Pots Inn, which is on your left.

9. Leave the pub, turn right and walk back along road. Bear right at the end, cross the stream, continue to another stream, then turn left along a footpath with a fingerpost, and walk with the water on your left. At the end of this path, turn right and walk back up the footpath between fences that you walked down earlier.

10. Reverse your earlier footsteps along the zig-zag path to the junction where the Itchen Way and the Wayfarers Walk meet. Here, briefly go right on the Itchen Way, then take an immediate left to walk diagonally right along a footpath across a farm field. You will pass a raised long barrow to your right. Keep going to the bottom right corner of the field, where you will join the track you walked along earlier, taking you across the A272 road and back into Hinton Ampner.

36 Hindhead

The Three Horseshoes

A freehouse saved from closure by locals in 2004, and community owned and run ever since, **THE THREE HORSESHOES** is situated in the leafy embrace of the Surrey Hills, in a historic village named after the god of thunder, between the Devil's Punch Bowl and Hindhead and Thursley commons. Popular with walkers and cyclists, the pub has a large outside area, with shelter. Inside there's a cosy front bar, a real fire and a more formal restaurant area at the back. Fantastic food is served from a varied menu.

The Three Horseshoes
Dye House Road, Thursley
Surrey GU8 6QD
01252 703900
www.threehorseshoes thursley.com

About this walk

- Historic murder mystery
- Greensands Way
- Surrey Hills AONB
- Birds and butterflies

Start/finish Devil's Punch Bowl car park (National Trust)
Distance 7½ miles (12km)
Time to pub 1.5–2 hours
Walking time 3.5 hours
Terrain Footpaths, woodland track, lanes

SOUTH EAST

From the Devil's Punch Bowl – an inverted hill, brimful with wildlife – trace the tragic tale of a murdered sailor from the scene of the crime, across commons to the churchyard where he's buried, via the spot where his assailants were placed in gibbets and the village where he had his last, fateful drink. Return through the middle of a natural amphitheatre.

Spring Nightjars nest, while wildflowers bloom on Hindhead Common. Dragonflies, damselflies and mayflies arise from the bog asphodel and marsh orchids across Thursley Common.

Summer Flowering heather attracts bees and butterflies, including purple emperors and silver-studded blues. The rare heath tiger beetle is active.

Autumn Listen for green, great and lesser-spotted woodpeckers and woodlarks in increasingly colourful beech woodlands. Ponies and deer graze grassland.

Winter Stonechats scuffle in scrub, and buzzards and kestrels soar, searching for shrews and mice. The Devil's Punch Bowl's streams run fast.

The Three Horseshoes offers ales from the Crafty Brewing Company based in nearby Dunsfold, Shere Drop from Surrey Hills Brewery, and Hog's Back Brewery's TEA.

Follow in the footsteps of ...
On 24 September 1786, an unknown sailor stopped at the now-closed Red Lion at Thursley, en route to Portsmouth. He bought drinks for three men, who subsequently robbed and murdered him in the Devil's Punch Bowl. Quickly caught (at Rake's Sun Inn) they were tried, executed and displayed on Gibbet Hill. Charles Dickens mentions this crime in *Nicholas Nickleby*. The sailor is buried in Thursley. A memorial stone stands near the scene of the crime.

How to Get There

By Car There's a large car park by the Devil's Punch Bowl (GU26 6AB; National Trust), signed from the A3.

By Public Transport The nearest train station is Haslemere (3 miles/5km); Stagecoach buses 18A, 18 and 19 stop at Hindhead Crossroads.

OS Map OS Explorer OL33 (Haslemere & Petersfield), Landranger 186 (Aldershot & Guildford); grid ref (for start): SU 890/357.

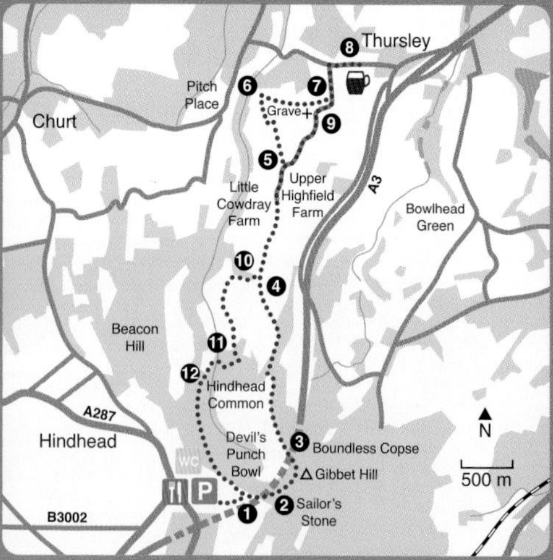

1. Leave the car park and walk with the Devil's Punch Bowl and eponymous café off to your left. According to legend, during a battle between Satan and Thor (after whom Thursley is named), the devil scooped up a great clod of earth and threw it at the god of thunder – the depression left behind is the Devil's Punch Bowl. The more prosaic explanation is that it was created by erosion caused by underground springs, but either way, the natural amphitheatre is a tree-lined haven for wildlife and walkers. Take the top path, following waymarkers for the 'Sailor's Stroll', along a broad track through mixed woodlands. You're walking across ground where the cacophonous A3 road once ran like an angry scar across the commons, until it was banished underground. The Hindhead Tunnel opened in 2011, and the land above was returned to nature, with spectacularly serene results.

2. Go left on a sealed lane and walk to the Sailor's Stone, which marks the spot where an unknown sailor was brutally killed in 1786. Just beyond this, turn right onto Gibbet Hill, where the sailor's murderers were displayed in gibbets after being hanged. At 892ft (272m), this is the Surrey Hills' second highest point, offering fantastic views across Surrey (all the way to London) and the Sussex Weald. There's a trig point, information board and a Celtic cross erected to combat fears the place is haunted. Keep going, and when the lane forks, bear left and walk downhill.

3. When you meet a broad track (the old Portsmouth Road), turn right and walk around the rim of the Punch Bowl. You're now on a section of the Greensand Way (a 108-mile/174-km path tracing the greensand ridge running through Surrey, Hampshire and Kent). When the main track forks, go left. Cross a cattlegrid and keep walking.

4. Descend along the Greensand Way, and at a crosspaths with a four-way fingerpost, keep going straight, following the arrow pointing to Thursley. Continue straight, passing a National Trust sign and walking along a sunken track (holloway) fringed by beautiful beech trees that often arch over to form a verdant tunnel. Keep walking until you meet houses. Go straight on the sealed lane, following a Greensand Way sign, past Little Cowdray Farm.

5. At Hedge Farm, just before Kestrel Wood Stables, turn left and take the narrow footpath that zig-zags through fields, turning left and then right along a lane by buildings.

6. At Smallbrook, opposite a large house, turn right, go through a gate and walk along the path to the church of St Michael and All Angels. Here, if you search the small cemetery, you can find the gravestone of the Unknown Sailor, which features a graphic depiction of his murder.

7. Exit the church grounds, turn left on The Street and follow this road into Thursley. The village name derives from the Old English word for place ('lee') of Thunor (Thor), and it's thought the god of thunder was worshipped here.

8. At the green, where a village sign celebrates the link with Thor, turn right. The Three Horseshoes is up Dyehouse Road, on the right.

9. Leave the pub and reverse your earlier route along Dyehouse Road, turning left on The Street and this time continuing past the church. Bear right along Highfield Lane, ignoring footpaths going straight ahead and left, and walk past Little Cowdray Farm, all the way to Upper Highfield Farm, where the road segues into a path (the Greensand Way).

10. At a crosspaths, turn right, leaving the Greensand Way and walking around Highcombe Bottom, crossing a cattlegrid and passing a National Trust sign for the Devil's Punch Bowl. Stay on the main track, ignoring paths going off either side, as it arcs left. The terrain opens up as you enter the bowl, and you'll pass a fingerpost confirming you're heading towards the café.

11. Stay on the main track, going past a bench, crossing a cattlegrid and passing Gnome Cottage (which dates to 1730 and is cared for by the National Trust). At a T-junction, turn right, following the fingerpost pointing towards the café. Pass Prices Cottage and keep going along the single-track path. Descend, cross a stream over a footbridge and climb up the path on the other side. Go through a gate and turn left along a wide path, following the fingerpost for the café. Views open up through beech trees, looking right up to the bowl-top path you walked along earlier.

12. When the track forks, stay left, taking the lower path, passing a National Trust information sign about the woodlands and going through a gate. Climb steadily, past another information board, which explains the geology and mythology behind the Devil's Punch Bowl. Ignore paths leading right and left, and keep ascending all the way to the top, then turn right and walk back to the car park.

The Sailor's Stone marks the point where an unknown sailor was robbed and murdered by three assailants in 1786.

Wey Navigation

The Star

Shining bright in the heart of historic Godalming, a short walk from both the River Wey and the train station, THE STAR is a welcoming, award-winning pub. The building dates to the 1700s, and there's been a tavern here since 1832. The main bar has an intimate feel, with locals and visitors mingling beneath a beamed ceiling entirely covered in pub clips from hundreds of beers. Side rooms seat larger groups; there's a back room with sofas and a bar billiards table, and a plant-filled outside area. Good food is on offer.

The Star
17 Church Street
Godalming, Surrey
GU7 1EL
01483 417717
www.starinngodalming.co.uk

About this walk
- River bank rambling
- Birds
- Wildflowers

Start Guildford train station
Finish Godalming train station
Distance 6 miles (10km)
Time to pub 2.5 hours
Walking time 2.5 hours
Terrain Towpath, riverside trails, road

On this stroll along a historic, navigable section of the River Wey, between Guildford and Godalming, you'll pass wildflower-filled flood meadows, Second World War pillboxes and pretty locks to arrive at an award-winning pub.

Spring Lady's-smock blooms pink along the river bank, and wildflowers like meadow saxifrage, black knapweed and meadow barley enliven the Lammas Lands. Reed and sedge warblers arrive. Mallards control broods of ducklings and mute swans mind their cygnets.

Summer Wild swimmers, kayakers, stand-up paddle-boarders and dragonflies are all out on the water. Creamy white meadowsweet flowers become aromatic, hemp-agrimony, orange balsam and tall purple loosestrife flower, attracting pollinators including brimstone butterflies, red-tailed bumblebees and elephant hawk-moths.

Autumn Stay alert for the iridescent flash of a passing kingfisher. Willows drop golden leaves into the river. Traditionally the Wey River Festival takes place at Dapdune Wharf in Guildford.

Winter Sparrowhawks patrol the skies, snipe sneak around Lammas Lands and statuesque herons hunt along the river bank, where, towards the end of the season, weeping willows produce yellow catkins.

Winner of Surrey Cider Pub of the Year on numerous occasions, The Star stocks a wide revolving range of local real ale, cider, perry and mead.

Follow in the footsteps of ... Godalming's Phillips Memorial Park is dedicated to John (Jack) Phillips, a local man who was Chief Wireless Telegraphist on the *Titanic* and bravely remained at his post, broadcasting an SOS signal, as the ship sank on 15 April 1912.

How to Get There

By Car Parking is available at the Farnham Road car park next to Guildford train station.

By Public Transport Guildford and Godalming are on the London Waterloo–Portsmouth railway line.

OS Map OS Explorer 145 (Guildford & Farnham), Landranger 186 (Aldershot & Guildford); grid ref (for start): SU 992/496.

1. From Guildford train station, follow signs for 'Town Centre via Riverside Walk', using the underpass, going around Wey House and down steps to the river. Turn right under the road bridge and walk through a car park with the river on your left – note the statue of a river worker on the opposite bank. Head towards St Nicholas Church, pass the bridge and turn left by The White House pub to walk along the river bank. Pass a sculpted scene from *Alice's Adventures in Wonderland* and continue past The Britannia (a good pub to finish in, if you walk back or do this route in reverse).

2. A short section of the river bank is currently closed, so our route crosses the navigation at Millmead Lock, skirts around the Yvonne Arnaud Theatre and turns right along the busy A281/ Shalford Road. Walk to The Weyside Inn, turn right over a footbridge across the river, and walk across a meadow with Guildford Rowing Club on your left. Cross the weir and continue.

3. As you approach another footbridge, pause at a stone bench by a stream to read an inscribed poem dedicated to the waterway. Walk beneath the bridge, pass the orange sand of St Catherine's Hill, to your right, and stroll on, around the serpentine curves of the river, passing an old turning circle. Go past St Catherine's Lock and under a railway bridge. Look for a Second World War pillbox by a National Trust sign, where the Railway Walk splinters right, along an old embankment.

4. Carefully cross the road at Broadford Bridge and amble along a lovely section of path between the river and flood meadows, often full of wildflowers and dragonflies. Pass beneath a footbridge and go over a little wooden bridge across a spur in the navigation to reach Unstead Lock.

5. Cross another road, rejoin the river and go past a second pillbox, hidden in the undergrowth. Pass the Farncombe Beefeater beer garden on your right, then Trowers Footbridge on your left.

6. After Farncombe Boat House, where fleets of narrowboats are moored, cross the road and go past Catteshall Lock. To your right lie the Lammas Lands, grassy floodplain meadows full of flowers, invertebrates and birds.

7. The path becomes sandy as the river enters Godalming Wharf. Turn left across Town Bridge, then immediately cross the road and take the path leading right, into Phillips Memorial Park. Trace Riverside Walk through the park, following fingerposts to the bandstand and train station. Head towards the church spire and walk through the graveyard. Emerge into Deanery Place, turn left along Church Street and The Star is on the right.

8. From the pub, walk back towards the church and follow signs for the train station.

38 Leith Hill
The Plough Inn

The Plough Inn
Coldharbour
Surrey RH5 6HD
01306 711793
www.ploughinn.com

About this walk
- Tower
- Greensand Way
- Woodlands
- Stunning views
- Surrey AONB

Start/finish
Rhododendron Wood car park (National Trust)
Distance 7 miles (11.3km)
Time to pub 2 hours
Walking time 4 hours
Terrain Countryside footpaths, bridleways, sandy tracks, heath, lanes

THE PLOUGH is a sensational 17th-century inn with its own brewery, scenically situated amid the Surrey Hills Area of Outstanding Beauty. There's a large garden, usually thronging with ramblers and riders exchanging tales from nearby trails while sipping Leith Hill Brewery ales, made on site. Inside you will find a relaxing bar area warmed by a woodburner, and plenty of room for drinkers and diners. Top-quality food is offered, made from locally sourced, seasonal ingredients. Boutique accommodation is also available, and there's a lovely, old-school village shop attached.

Climb through woods to Leith Hill, where an iconic tower crowns South East England's tallest point, offering views across 13 counties. Continue through an ancient treescape to a spectacular pub and brewery, before returning across wildlife-rich commons and heathland.

Spring Inhale the fragrance of rhododendrons and walk among primroses and foxgloves under newly coppiced hazel.

Summer See woodcock roding and hear nightjars churring on Duke's Warren, where golden-ringed dragonflies hover above the heath. Butterflies abound; white admirals and silver-washed fritillaries flutter through Dingwall Woods.

Autumn Flowering heather sets the heath ablaze, while beech leaves turn and burn above trails tiptoeing through sunken lanes. Migrating birds use the tower to navigate, and raptors soar over commons.

Winter Views from Leith Hill are crystal clear on cold, crisp days, through leafless trees. Overwintering birds including redwings, redpolls and crossbills can be seen, along with roe deer.

The Plough serves Leith Hill Brewery beers including Crooked Furrow (bitter), Smiler's Happiness (pale) and Surrey Puma (stout), and supports other local breweries (Firebird, Tillingbourne, Hogsback), vineyards (Denbies, Biddenden) and Silent Pool Distillery.

Follow in the footsteps of ...
Leith Hill Place – once owned by the Wedgwoods – was the childhood home of English composer Ralph Vaughan Williams (whose well-known works include 'The Lark Ascending'). Charles Darwin, whose sister married into the Wedgwood family, visited regularly, conducting research on Leith Hill with his nieces.

How to Get There

By Car Approach via the A29 and B2126, and park at Rhododendron Wood car park (RH5 6LU; National Trust).

By Public Transport The closest train station is Holmwood (2½ miles/4km).

OS Map OS Explorer 146 (Dorking, Box Hill & Reigate); Landranger 187 (Dorking & Reigate); grid ref (for start): TQ 131/428.

1. Leave the car park on the lower path, walking to the right of the fingerpost for Leith Hill Place (which leads directly to the house, open to visitors Fridays and Sundays in summer) and descending steps. Turn right and then left, picking up orange arrows for the Woodland Trail (one of several waymarked routes the National Trust has laid out around Leith Hill). Keep following orange arrows, through rhododendrons on Leith Hill's southern slopes (a riot of colour in spring and early summer, thanks to Caroline Wedgwood, who planted the shrubs in 1900) into Dingwall Woods. The Etherley Farm Loop branches off to the right, but keep left.

2. Go through a kissing gate into a meadow, walking with Leith Hill Place uphill on your left. Built around 1600, this mansion was purchased by Josiah Wedgwood (grandson of the famous potter) in 1847 and donated to the National Trust in 1944. While crossing the field, look out for one of Charles Darwin's slowly sinking 'wormstones' (an ongoing experiment by the evolutionary scientist to show how objects are undermined by earthworms over time, and end up buried). Keep walking, past a ha-ha wall on the left, with fantastic views spilling to your right. Dogleg (left then right) across a road, picking up orange arrows and posts on the other side, and walking along a path into Leith Hill Place Woods.

3. Go over a little wooden bridge across a stream and pass a walled garden on your left. Continue past a turning for Hartshurst Farm and a track where the Etherley Farm Loop rejoins the route, and follow the timber sign for the Woodland Trail. Keep going straight, up through Leith Hill Place Wood, still following orange arrows.

4. Dogleg (left then right) across Abinger Road and go through Windy Gap car park. Follow orange arrows up steps and along the footpath towards the tower, bearing right at the top of the climb.

5. Built in 1765 by Richard Hull of Leith Hill Place, Leith Hill Tower stands 965ft (317m) above sea level and offers astonishing views that stretch to London (looking north) and the English Channel (south). Climb to the top if it's open. After exploring the tower, take the path leading east, walking directly away from the café hatch, and going downhill. (You're no longer on the Woodland Trail, so disregard orange waymarkers.)

6. At the bottom of the hill, where there's a confluence of footpaths and mountain-bike tracks, take the second right, ascending along a broad track with Summer Lightning mountain-bike waymarkers. As the route arcs left, pick up green arrows (waymarkers for the Heathland Trail), which leave the main track and amble along a lovely winding footpath through woods, passing the site where three American Dakota aircraft tragically crashed into the hillside in the winter of 1944, with no survivors.

7. When you emerge at Coldharbour Common cricket pitch, turn right along a public byway. Descend along this deep lane, overhung by trees, until you emerge opposite The Plough.

8. Leave the pub, go past the red phone box and stroll up Wolverns Lane, immediately opposite the pub. Pass a fingerpost and go straight along the bridleway, keeping left and burrowing along beneath ancient boundary banks topped by towering layered beech hedges that overhang the deep holloway.

9. When the lane opens up and you reach a three-way fingerpost, turn left along a bridleway and pass a National Trust sign for Coldharbour Common. The path forks but stay right and keep walking along the main track. At a major junction, go straight on, staying on the bridleway. Pass through a wooden gate into the Duke's Warren (where dogs need to be kept on leads to protect ground-nesting birds such as skylarks). Go past a little fenced off pond and, at a crosspaths, continue straight across, ignoring the National Trust arrows going left and right.

10. As you descend the path frays, but all strands meet back up so keep walking until you meet a wooden gate with a National Trust sign for Duke's Warren (seen from the back as you approach). Go through, cross a wooden bridge over a stream and then, at a crosspaths, turn left along a stretch of the Greensand Way (a 108-mile/174km path along the Greensand Ridge between Haslemere in Surrey and Hamstreet in Kent).

11. Walk along the gently undulating track until you reach a gate and the major junction you met earlier. Turn right and ascend the short, steep climb to the top of Leith Hill. Walk directly past the tower and keep going straight along the Greensand Way, following signs towards Starveall Corner car park.

12. When path forks, go left and follow orange arrows to descend, sometimes steeply, back to Rhododendron Wood car park.

The extraordinary views from Leith Hill tower extend all the way to London and the coast on a clear day.

39 Chiddingstone
The Castle Inn

The Castle Inn
Chiddingstone
Kent TN8 7AH
01892 870371
www.castleinnchiddingstone.co.uk

About this walk
- Castles and history
- Woodlands
- Eden Valley Walk
- High Weald AONB

Start Hever train station
Finish Penshurst train station
Distance 5 miles (8km)
Time to pub 1–1.5 hours
Walking time 2.5 hours
Terrain Countryside and woodland footpaths and bridleways, lanes, some road

Sitting pretty in the heart of the historic and beguilingly attractive Tudor village of Chiddingstone, **THE CASTLE INN** has been hosting wayfarers since the early 15th century. Surrounded by trails (hiking and biking routes are suggested on the website) the pub welcomes walkers and cyclists warmly. There is a sunny courtyard and large rear garden, and inside the higgledy-piggledy, Grade II-listed building you will find fireplaces, tiled floors and oak panelling. Good food is served, with a focus on local produce. Opening hours may change seasonally, check the website.

Do part of the Eden Valley Walk (a 15-mile/24-km route along the rivers Eden and Medway) through historic villages and woodlands on the edge of the High Weald AONB, passing two castles, a 12th-century church, a much-storied stone and a magnificent old pub.

Spring Explore the gardens, orangery and fish-filled lake at Chiddingstone Castle (entry free; go through a gate by the pub) and enjoy the annual literary festival. Listen for nightingales serenading the setting sun in Tangle Wood.

Summer Spy butterflies (including speckled wood, painted lady, peacock, orange tip, tortoiseshell, red admiral, common meadow brown) in woods around Hever Castle, where the extraordinary hummingbird hawkmoth can sometimes be seen.

Autumn See long-eared and pipistrelle bats embarking on hunting sprees as evenings draw in. Produce from local orchards fills The Tulip Tree in Chiddingstone, believed to be Britain's oldest working shop, dating to 1453.

Winter Great spotted woodpeckers, short-eared owls, robins and blue tits are active in Tangle and Park woods.

The Castle Inn serves Kentish real ales from Chiddingstone's Larkins Brewery (Traditional Bitter, Pale, Best and Porter).

Follow in the footsteps of ...
Cared for by the National Trust and surrounded by buildings central to the ill-fated story of Henry VIII and Anne Boleyn, Chiddingstone is Britain's best-preserved Tudor village. Its name derives from the curious Chiding Stone where, according to folklore, nagging wives and suspected witches were dragged to be chided by an assembly of villagers in medieval times. Other stories claim it was used by druids.

How to Get There

By Car Parking is available at Chiddingstone Castle (TN8 7AD; not National Trust; £3 donation).

By Public Transport This walk starts at Hever train station and finishes at Penshurst station.

OS Map OS Explorer 147 (Sevenoaks & Tonbridge), Landranger 188 (Maidstone & Royal Tunbridge Wells); grid ref (for start): TQ 465/445.

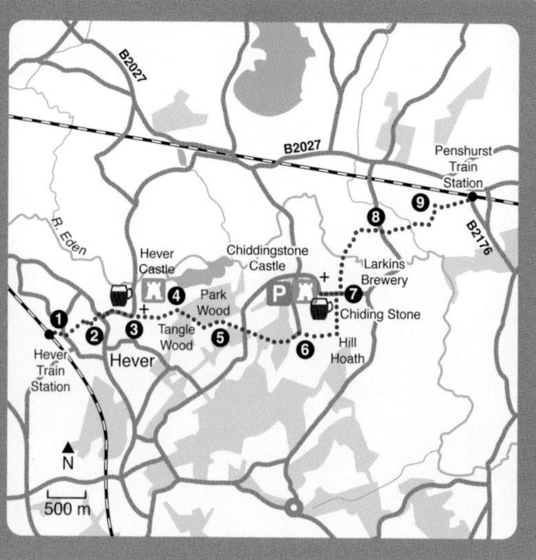

1. Leave Hever station, turn right on Chippings Lane, then left along a footpath between fields. Go through a gate and cross a field, following red arrows for Hever Castle. Pass through more gates and bear right across a field.

2. At a junction, turn left on the Eden Valley Walk (EVW). Meet the road, turn right then left, following Hever Castle signs. Walk up the road to The King Henry VIII pub, which dates to 1597.

3. Cross the road and enter 12th-century St Peter's Church, where Sir Thomas Boleyn (Anne Boleyn's father and Queen Elizabeth I's grandfather) is buried. Walk right of the church, exit the graveyard and cross a stream. Continue around the grounds of Hever Castle, once the Boleyn family home, where Henry VIII courted Anne.

4. Bear right, along an unsealed lane between Park and Tangle woods, overhung with oak, sycamore and chestnut trees. Pass a wide gate and follow EVW arrows right, along a path beside Bothy Cottage (by a post box).

5. At the road, cross and go through a kissing gate opposite. Pass through another gate, cross a footbridge and climb steps into beech woods. Cross a track and continue through a kissing gate. Meet a bridleway, turn left and walk along a holloway scything through sandstone, to a cluster of cottages at Hill Hoath.

6. Follow an EVW arrow right, then take the lane leading left, through a large gate. Pass through a kissing gate, and when the path forks, go left (straight), leaving the EVW. At the next junction, go left and walk to the road. Turn left and, just past Chiddingstone's village sign, divert left along a path to see the Chiding Stone. Return to the road and go left to explore the village, pub and castle.

7. Leaving the pub, turn right. Just past the Chiding Stone turn-off, cross and go left, along a footpath. After crossing a bridge over the River Eden, immediately go right through a gate. Bear left and walk with the hedge on your right, through a gap. Pass a stile by a tree, turn right and walk through two fields to reach the road.

8. Cross and follow a footpath fingerpost pointing past Sandholes Farm. Cross a stile, bear left and walk across a field to a gap. Turn right and walk with the hedge on your right. Pass a post with footpath arrows, bear left and cross a footbridge. Go straight across a field, hugging the fence when it appears from the right.

9. Go through a gate, turn left, thread a gap and cross a field with the hedge on your left. Climb a stile and turn right. Go through a gateway, bear left then follow the path diagonally across a field to a gate just to the right of a pylon. Cross the next field to a gate, and you're at Penshurst station.

40 Ankerwycke

The Perseverance

The Perseverance
2 High Street, Wraysbury
Berkshire TW19 5DB
01784 482375
www.the-perseverance.co.uk

About this walk
- River views
- Historical interest
- Ancient trees
- Wildflower meadows

Start/finish Wraysbury train station
Distance 4½ miles (7km)
Time to pub Allow 2.5 hours
Walking time 3 hours
Terrain Riverside and rural footpaths and lanes, some streetside pavements

SOUTH EAST

A CAMRA award-winning, Cask Marque-accredited pub, **THE PERSEVERANCE**'s distinctive sign features a solitary snail making a valiant effort to reach Noah's Ark. Inside the Grade II-listed building you'll find a comfortable, convivial front room boasting bookshelves, an inglenook fireplace (complete with a real fire), sofas and a piano. Other rooms have table seating, and there's a large, attractive garden with beer barrels and plenty of tables under trees. Food is served daily (lunch and dinner) and there are regular 'Buskers' Nights' with music.

This Thames-side stroll explores the river's northern bank, opposite Runnymede (where the Magna Carta was sealed in 1215), visiting the National Trust's oldest tree, the remains of a 12th-century Benedictine nunnery and a welcoming pub. Despite close proximity to London and the M25, this is a quiet and relaxing route.

Spring Ducklings bob on the river, while around Ankerwycke snowdrops give way to bluebells, lesser celandines, dog's mercury and wood anemones.

Summer Wildflower-festooned river meadows attract 19 species of butterflies, including brimstone, peacock, tortoiseshell, red admiral, orange tip, common blue and meadow brown. Emerald and large red dragonflies dart between the ponds.

Autumn The Ankerwycke Yew is, of course, evergreen, but many trees around it are deciduous, and the woods go through a spectrum of colour changes as the leaves turn and fall. Listen for the rat-a-tat of green woodpeckers.

Winter With trees denuded of leaves, views of the Thames are best in winter. Look for kingfishers in the bare branches along the banks. At the pub, a fire will be roaring in the inglenook fireplace.

Otter Ale is The Perseverance's regular beer, while three guest ales – sourced from local and national breweries, including Windsor & Eton – are served on rotation.

Follow in the footsteps of ... Visit the ancient Ankerwycke Yew, beneath the branches of which King Henry VIII apparently courted Anne Boleyn. The area has been drawn by J.M.W. Turner and provided inspiration for the poem 'The Reeds of Runnymede' by Rudyard Kipling.

How to Get There

By Car There is a very small car park at Ankerwycke (better to visit by public transport if possible), and the pub has a car park too.

By Public Transport The route starts at Wraysbury train station, which is on the Windsor Line and has regular daily services to and from London Waterloo.

OS Map OS Explorer 160 (Windsor, Weybridge & Bracknell), Landranger 176 (West London); grid ref (for start): TQ 013/743.

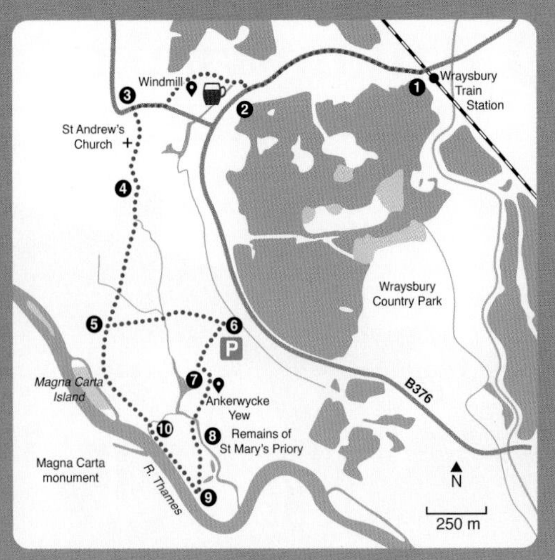

1. From Wraysbury train station, walk west along Station Road using the pavement on the left.

2. Turn right into The Green by The Perseverance. Walk along the lane, which elbows left, passing an eccentric wooden windmill between the bowls club and Baptist church. Continue past tennis courts, a cricket club and playground until you emerge on Windsor Road, with The George on your right and a distinctive, half-timbered building opposite.

3. Carefully cross the road and turn right. Take a left into St Andrew's Close and walk to St Andrew's church. Cross the stile over the wall (or go through gate) into the churchyard. Do a dogleg through the graveyard, then pick up the path going between fields, with the stream on your left.

4. Go through two gates, past the National Trust sign for Ankerwycke, into a wide water meadow. Cross a little bridge over a stream and go through a gate to reach Magna Carta Lane, which leads to Magna Carta Island on the Thames to the right, but access to the river is blocked by private properties.

5. Turn left and walk along the lane to the small National Trust car park, where there's an information board with a map and details about Ankerwycke and Runnymede.

6. Bear right and walk towards the woods, following a path across a meadow with the hedgerow on your immediate left. Pass through a gate and keep going towards a group of trees.

7. At the trees, turn left through a gate with a National Trust arrow and wooden sign. After 50 yards, go through another gate, and turn right, to walk through a lovely avenue of poplar trees leading to the ancient Ankerwycke Yew, believed to be 2,500 years old.

8. Take in the tree, a silent witness to events over two and half millennia, and then continue on to the remains of St Mary's Priory – a Benedictine nunnery built in the 12th century. Keep going, through mixed woodland of hawthorn, sycamore and beech, until you reach a gate. Turn right, then take another right through a second gate.

9. Walk, with the River Thames immediately to your left and a widening meadow to your right, passing beneath mighty sycamore and oak trees, with massive arms spread wide.

10. Pass a wooden bench, go through a gate and cross a bridge, which leads into another vast riverside plain. On the opposite bank is the Magna Carta Memorial, amid meadows where King John is supposed to have set his seal on the famous charter on 15 June 1215. Continue across the middle of the meadow until you reach a gate leading back onto Magna Carta Lane. Cross the lane and retrace your steps back to The Perseverance.

41 Thames Loop

The George

The George
77 Borough High Street
London SE1 1NH
020 7407 2056
www.nationaltrust.org.uk/george-inn

About this walk
- Historic inn
- River views
- Multiple London landmarks

Start/finish London Waterloo train station
Distance 5 miles (8km)
Time to pub Allow 2 hours
Walking time Allow 3–4 hours
Terrain City streets, alleyways, Thames Path

SOUTH EAST

London's last surviving galleried inn, THE GEORGE is a Grade I-listed, National Trust-owned building dating to 1677. An inn has occupied this spot since 1542 (after surviving the 1666 Great Fire, the original George & Dragon burned down a decade later). Stepping beneath the oak beams from modern city streets is like entering a time capsule. Ancient wooden floors sag and drinks are served via a hatch in the Parliament Bar. The upstairs Gallery Bar was once sleeping accommodation, and the cobbled courtyard, a legacy of the coaching inn, is a beer garden. Food is served.

Starting under the clock at Waterloo Station, as many adventures do, this walk wanders along London's South Bank – past theatres, galleries, pubs, prisons and world-famous landmarks, and though centuries of history – to a storied inn, before crossing the river and returning via the Thames Path.

Spring Sand artists sculpt extraordinary works of ephemeral art on river beaches, before the tide wipes the slate clean, and buskers fill the fresh air with optimism.

Summer The South Bank shimmers with life as the denizens of London enjoy riverside strolls and alfresco liaisons. At The George, the cobbled courtyard offers an oasis from gritty city streets.

Autumn The famous market and narrow alleyways around Borough dish up a sensory smorgasbord of colour, aroma and fantastic flavours.

Winter London's lights twinkle in the Thames at dusk, street vendors hawk aromatic roasting chestnuts and hearty pints of porter are poured in The George's cosy Parliament Bar.

Now a Greene King pub, selling the brewery's signature beers, The George also serves a range of revolving guest ales, porters and lagers from national and London-based breweries (including Southwark Brewing and Camden Town).

Follow in the footsteps of ... Shakespeare frequented the original George & Dragon, where plays were staged in Elizabethan times. Dickens, whose father was imprisoned for debt in Marshalsea on Borough High Street when the author was a child, knew the inn well, and The George features in *Little Dorrit*. Chaucer's pilgrims in *The Canterbury Tales* set off from a pub nearby (the long-gone Tabard).

How to Get There

By Car Not recommended; take a black cab if necessary.

By Public Transport London Waterloo is on myriad bus routes, plus the Northern, Bakerloo and Jubilee underground lines; mainline trains coming into the overground station are operated by South West Trains.

OS Map OS Explorer 161 (London South), Landranger 176 (West London); grid ref (for start): TQ 310/799.

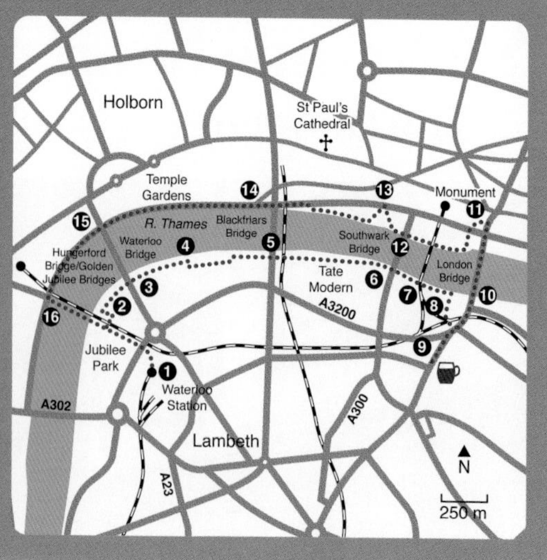

1. Leave Waterloo Station by the main exit/ entrance, descend the well-worn steps to Cab Road (take a second to glance back at the impressive station building, which opened in 1848). Turn left, walk to the traffic lights and cross York Road. Go straight ahead, on Sutton Walk, then bear left along Concert Hall Approach and walk towards Royal Festival Hall.

2. Go up the steps, with the Royal Festival Hall and the Southbank Centre on your right, past the bust of Nelson Mandela. Continue, then turn right and descend steps to the riverside path.

3. Walk past the graffiti-emblazoned underground skate park, the British Film Institute (BFI) building and the National Theatre; the statue outside depicts Laurence Olivier as Hamlet. Go underneath Waterloo Bridge and pause to peruse the second-hand and antiquarian book market before continuing along Queen's Walk.

4. If the tide is out, look down to the riverbed at Gabriel's Wharf, where artists may be busy transforming the exposed silt and sand into golden sculptures. Continue on, past the Oxo Tower.

5. Go beneath Blackfriar's Bridge and past the Tate Modern. The pedestrian Millennium Bridge spans the Thames here, and the dome of St Paul's Cathedral is visible on the opposite bank. Stay south of the river, however, and at Cardinals Wharf you pass a blue-plaqued house (on your right) where Christopher Wren lived while creating elements of London's cityscape that still define the city today.

6. Carry on, past Shakespeare's Globe, a stylistically authentic recreation of the Bard's theatre. Originally built by Shakespeare's acting company The Lord Chamberlain's Men in 1599, plays were performed here to standing audiences of up 3,000 people from all sections of Elizabethan society, with Shakespeare himself occasionally acting as well as writing the scripts. His brother was also an actor, and it is believed they both drank at The George & Dragon (as it was then named) on occasion. Climb the steps and cross the street at Southwark Bridge, then descend again to the river and keep walking, with the Shard straight ahead.

7. Amble past The Anchor riverside pub at Bankend (a lovely spot for a cold drink on a summer's day) and go under the colourful arches of Cannon Street Bridge, passing the Shakespeare mural.

8. The alleyways on this section take you past The Clink (the site of a prison dating back to 1144, whose unfortunate inhabitants included some of the Puritans who later sailed to the Americas, settled in Massachusetts and became known as the Pilgrim Fathers), and the *Golden Hinde*, an astonishingly small – but accurately scaled –

recreation of the ship in which Francis Drake circumnavigated the globe between 1577 and 1580.

9. Stroll around the grounds of Southwark Cathedral, a place of worship for over 1,000 years, and wander through Borough Market – where all sorts of artisanal and street food and drink can be sampled – to emerge on London Bridge road. Turn right, cross the road at the traffic lights and, when the street forks, go left along Borough High Street. The George is up on the left, through an entrance that takes you down below modern street level and into another time altogether.

10. Leave the pub, turn right and walk across the Thames over London Bridge. Look east (right), over the bow of HMS *Belfast* to Tower Bridge.

11. Walk up King William Street. The Monument marking the epicentre of the Great Fire of London is just off to the right here, on Pudding Lane; divert to see it, or turn left along Arthur Street and then Swan Lane to reach the river's north bank, and turn right along Oystergate Walk.

12. Walk west on the Thames Path, along Hanseatic Walk and up Allhallows Lane, before turning left through Steelyard Passage and going beneath the tracks of Cannon Street. Pass The Banker pub and keep following the Thames Path to Southwark Bridge, and along Queenhithe.

13. Go beneath Millennium Bridge and walk to Blackfriars Bridge, before leaving the river views to travel along Victoria Embankment. Look out for J. Seward Johnson Jr's statue *Taxi!* on the corner of John Carpenter Street; this businessman has been trying to hail a cab since 2014.

14. Continue along Victoria Embankment, going past Temple Gardens and the Inns of Court, London's legal centre and location of Temple Church, English headquarters of the Knights Templar since 1185. Pass Somerset House, where the National Trust maintains the Strand Lane Baths, a historic water feature often referred to as 'Roman', but actually dating from 1612.

15. Go under the arches of Waterloo Bridge and past Cleopatra's Needle (one of a pair of ancient obelisks dating to 1450 BC, which once graced the Egyptian city of Heliopolis but now stand far apart, one here and the other in New York's Central Park), before exploring the greenery of Victoria Embankment Gardens.

16. At Embankment Station, cross Hungerford Bridge and walk back to Waterloo Station.

A local London-brewed ale on handpump in the main bar at The George.

My kingdom for a pint… it's believed Shakespeare drank and potentially acted in plays at the pub.

42 Cookham Commons & Cock Marsh

The Bounty

The Bounty
Cock Marsh, Cookham
Berkshire SL8 5RG
01628 520056
www.facebook.com/thebounty1

About this walk

- Thames Path
- Chiltern Way
- Red kites
- Winter Hill

Start/finish Cookham Moor car park (National Trust)
Distance 5 miles (8km)
Time to pub 1.5 hours
Walking time 2.5 hours
Terrain Countryside footpaths, marshland, riverside trails, some road

Scenically grounded on the banks of the River Thames, in front of Winter Hill, **THE BOUNTY** is a unique pub, full of character, enhanced by the fact you can only reach it on foot or by boat. Run by the same landlord, Damian, for over 35 years, the pub has a fantastically ramshackle, riverhut feel, with a bar built out of a boat, and flags, maritime and pop culture memorabilia scattered everywhere. There's an open fire in colder months, and in summer an outdoor bar and ice-cream shack operates. Good pub grub and regular entertainment is offered. Opening hours vary.

Climb over Winter Hill, enjoying excellent views along the Thames Valley and great red kite-spotting opportunities, before passing Bronze Age burial mounds on Cock Marsh to reach a unique riverside pub. Return along the banks of the Thames, via historic Cookham.

Spring Blackthorn blossoms and wildflowers, including custard-coloured rock-roses and various orchids, begin to bloom on the chalk grassland of Cock Marsh and across Winter Hill, attracting bumblebees and other pollinators.

Summer Wild thyme and the rare brown galingale flower. Cock Marsh and Winter Hill are busy with butterflies – try to spy green hairstreak, chalkhill blue, brown argus, meadow brown, ringlet, marbled white, brimstone and clouded yellow.

Autumn Red kites soar on updrafts above Winter Hill, moving effortlessly with huge wings spread wide. Blackthorn trees are heavy with sloes.

Winter Along the River Thames, elegant great crested grebes dive and hunt. Also look out for dark-bellied brent geese, mute swans and coastal visitors like dunlin and knot.

The Bounty serves ales from Rebellion Brewery, including IPA, Smuggler, and a specially rebadged brew called Mutiny at the Bounty.

Follow in the footsteps of ...
Kenneth Grahame grew up in a riverside house in Cookham, which inspired the setting for *The Wind in the Willows*. Another notable local was artist Stanley Spencer (1891–1959).

How to Get There

By Car Drive to Cookham via the A4094, and park in Cookham Moor car park (National Trust).

By Public Transport Cookham train station is a 10-minute walk from the start. Bourne End train station is a short walk from The Bounty, via the footpath over the railway bridge.

OS Map OS Explorer 172 (Chiltern Hills East), Landranger 175 (Reading & Windsor); grid ref (for start): SU 893/854.

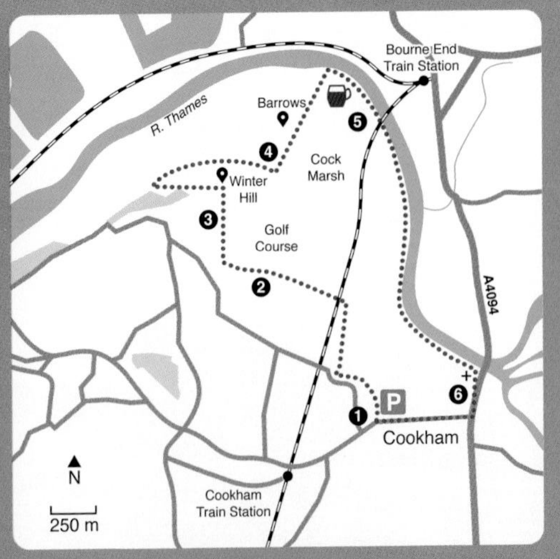

1. Walk through the car park, along the short gravel lane, turning left before you meet the field. Follow footpath fingerposts over a little wooden bridge, through a gate and past Pound Farm. Just before the pond, turn left through a gate and walk up a footpath. At the top, turn right and head towards a little group of trees. Dogleg left then right and walk with the railway track on your left. After 200 yards, turn left across the bridge over the railway, then follow the footpath straight across the driving range (watch out for flying balls).

2. Keep going, past blackthorn trees on your left, to a kissing gate with a fingerpost for the Chiltern Way (a 125-mile/200-km circular route around the Area of Outstanding Natural Beauty). Go through, turn right and walk between a field (on your left) and the golf course (right) towards trees on top of Winter Hill.

3. Pass through a gate and turn left. Walk past a bench and descend along a wide path, with Thames Valley views to your right. When you reach a junction, go sharp right and walk along the bottom of the hill. When another path comes in from the left, keep going straight, until Cock Marsh opens up on your left.

4. Turn left and walk along a wooden boardwalk crossing an old channel of the River Thames. Stroll straight across the meadow, passing to the right of a large mound – one of several Bronze Age burial barrows here. Head towards a row of riverside cottages, and when you reach them, turn right, through a gate. Amble along the bank of the Thames, with the water on your left, until you reach The Bounty.

5. After leaving the pub, continue walking with the river on your left, passing beneath Bourne End railway bridge, originally built in wood by Isambard Kingdom Brunel. From here you're walking along a section of the Thames Path, a 180-mile (290-km) trail that traces the river from its source to the Thames Barrier. Stroll along a lovely wide section of the river, rounding a left bend and passing the Cookham Reach Sailing Club on your right. Before you reach Cookham Bridge, bear right through a gate, walking away from the river, following the Thames Path past Holy Trinity Church.

6. Emerge on Church Gate and follow the road around to Ferry Lane. Across the road, to your left, is the Tarry Stone, a sarsen stone that's been used for various purposes over many centuries. Turn right on High Street, opposite the Stanley Spencer gallery. Walk past the Bel & the Dragon on your right, and the 17th-century Kings Arms on your left, and continue along the road. As you leave the village, passing the war memorial and The Crown, walk on the left to trace an old causeway. Just before the Fleet Bridge, turn right and cross the B4447 to the car park.

43 West Wycombe
The George & Dragon

THE GEORGE & DRAGON dates to 1720 and retains the look of a classic coaching inn, with a large archway leading to a cobbled courtyard. There's a welcoming front bar, thronging with locals and hikers. Good food is on offer and accommodation is available. The Plough, opposite, is another atmospheric pub with an open fire, and The Swan (down the road) is an 18th-century tavern with a homely bar. All three are owned by the National Trust.

The George & Dragon
High Street, West Wycombe
Buckinghamshire
HP14 3AB
01494 535340
www.georgeanddragon hotel.co.uk

About this walk

- Historical interest
- Country park
- Woodlands

Start/finish Church Lane car park, West Wycombe Hill (National Trust)
Distance 4 miles (6.5km)
Time to pub 1.5 hours
Walking time 2 hours
Terrain Countryside footpaths, lanes, some road

From West Wycombe Hill, on the edge of the Chilterns, explore the expansive surrounds of a Palladian mansion that has starred in dozens of period dramas, before visiting a historic village with three picturesque pubs. Return via the infamous Hellfire Caves and Dashwood Mausoleum.

Spring West Wycombe Park opens in April. Flowering bluebells flood Sands Bank Local Nature Reserve, and red kites circle above West Wycombe Hill.

Summer Explore West Wycombe Park. Wildflowers, including orchids, bloom across West Wycombe Hill, attracting bees and butterflies such as green hairstreak and chalkhill blue.

Autumn Woodlands around West Wycombe blaze through a range of colours. Squirrels busily prepare for winter, and red kites and muntjac deer can be spotted.

Winter Enjoy evocative views across the mist-shrouded Chiltern Hills as frost grips the chalk grassland. Snowdrops begin blooming in January.

The George & Dragon, The Plough and The Swan all offer real ales from nearby Marlow Brewery, including the perennially popular Rebellion IPA.

Follow in the footsteps of ...
In the 18th century, Sir Francis Dashwood formed a high-society Hellfire Club called The Knights of St Francis, which engaged in wild orgiastic parties in the Hellfire Caves beneath the Mausoleum on West Wycombe Hill. Dashwood paid villagers to tunnel into the chalk hill, forming caverns 850ft (260m) long, and a banqueting hall where notoriously lavish and lascivious bacchanalian bashes were held. Members included the Earl of Sandwich, Benjamin Franklin and the poet Paul Whitehead, who was club steward and whose heart now lies in an urn in the Mausoleum.

How to Get There

By Car Head to West Wycombe and park in Church Lane car park on West Wycombe Hill.

By Public Transport The closest station is High Wycombe (2½ miles/4km), from where several buses serve West Wycombe.

OS Map OS Explorer 172 (Chiltern Hills East), Landranger 175 (Reading & Windsor); grid ref (for start): SU 827/950.

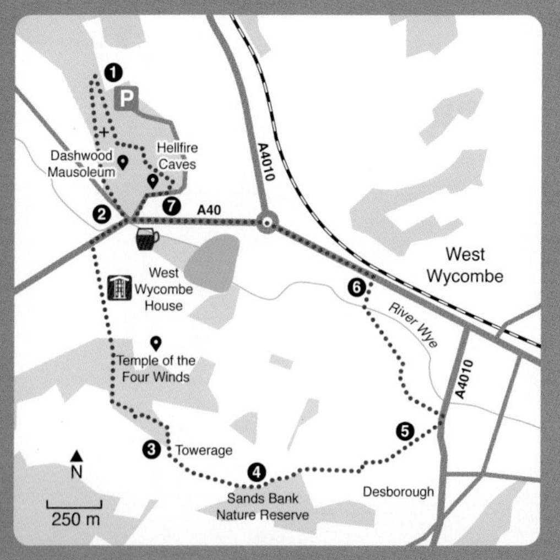

1. From the car park, walk away from St Lawrence Church and bear left. The path splits by a bench, but carry straight on, into woods. Meeting the main path, turn left and walk downhill through a tunnel of trees. Another path joins from the right, but keep going straight, following a National Trust fingerpost pointing to 'West Wycombe Park & Village'. When you emerge from the trees the path forks; go right (virtually straight), and straight again at the next crossways, continuing to Chorley Road. Turn left and walk to the main road.

2. Between April and August you can cross here, go through the gates opposite and explore West Wycombe Park and mansion. However, our all-year route goes right, along Oxford Road for 150 yards, before crossing and turning left up Toweridge Lane. Walk up this narrow lane, into tree cover, and follow it around to the left.

3. Go through gateposts into the outskirts of West Wycombe estate. At a fork, follow a bridleway sign left. Look for the Equestrian Statue on your left, past which a view of the theatrical Italianate mansion is revealed through a gap in the trees. This effigy of a Roman emperor on horseback is actually a fibreglass film prop, bought from Pinewood Studios for the price of a crate of champagne.

4. Ignore turnings left and right, and continue straight, past Druid's Hut. At a farm gate, take the footpath leading left and descend along a lovely section of trail, through hawthorn, hazel and holly trees, with Sands Bank Local Nature Reserve on your right. At a gate, ignore the path going right and carry straight on, along Toweridge Lane. A wooden bench on your left offers stunning views over the Chiltern Hills. Pass a house and walk with a fence on your right to reach a small pylon and two gates.

5. Turn left down a lane, leading to a road. Go left and then left again, following a bridleway towards Park Farm. By a circular stone gatehouse at Park Farm, bear right, then right again through gate, and walk across a little footbridge with lovely views of the house to the left. Follow the path left, through a gate and across a stone bridge over a stream. Walk along the tarmac, and at the main road, turn left.

6. At the roundabout, bear left and walk into West Wycombe, where you'll find The George & Dragon and The Swan on the left, and The Plough on the right.

7. Exit the pub and continue along High Street. Turn right at a National Trust sign for West Wycombe Hill and ascend a lane, past a school. Cut up onto the hill and follow the path running parallel to the lane to the Hellfire Caves. Explore the caves (entry fee; not National Trust), then head up the hill to the extraordinary Dashwood Mausoleum, built in 1765 by John Bastard the Younger of Blandford. Continue past St Lawrence Church to the car park.

44 Coombe Hill
The Russell Arms

The Russell Arms
2 Chalkshire Road
Butlers Cross
Buckinghamshire
HP17 0TS
01296 624411
www.therussellarms.co.uk

About this walk

- Red kites
- Butterflies/wildflowers
- Chilterns AONB
- Ridgeway National Trail

Start/finish Coombe Hill car park (National Trust)
Distance 5½ miles (9km)
Time to pub 1 hour
Walking time 2.5 hours
Terrain Countryside, woodland, farm footpaths, some road

Found in a fold in the Chiltern Hills, THE RUSSELL ARMS welcomes walkers and the occasional prime minister, being the local for Chequers (the Russell family resided in the nearby estate – now used by British PMs for R&R – when the pub was built, hence the name). Dating to 1763 and community-owned since 2012, The Russell blends heritage with modern style. A quiet garden offers bucolic views in summer, and a real fire roars in winter. The excellent food offering combines pub classics with ever-changing seasonal à la carte specials.

From a hilltop with awe-inspiring Aylesbury Vale views, circled by majestic kites, wander through wildflowers and box woodland, across acid heath and chalk grass, to a community owned village pub, where prime ministers have been known to pop in for a pint while staying at nearby Chequers.

Spring Red kites (reintroduced to the Chilterns in the 1990s) nest in March. Look for their broad-winged, forked-tail profile, and listen for mewing.

Summer Wildflowers, such as pyramid orchid, marjoram, basil, thyme and rock rose, bloom across the chalklands, and butterflies (chalkhill blue, ringlet, small heath and meadow brown) thrive on Coombe Hill.

Autumn Famed for beech woods, the Chiltern Escarpment turns russet in fall. Colourful fungi decorate the ground, while wayfaring trees and buckthorn burst into berry around Bacombe Hill.

Winter Mist hangs in Aylesbury Valley, shrouding the shoulders of Chequers and Ellesborough church, while frost nips and grips the chalk grassland across Coombe Hill.

The Russell Arms serves local real ales, including The Session and Fudgel, created for the pub by nearby Chiltern Brewery.

Follow in the footsteps of … Coombe Hill and surrounds were once part of the Chequers estate, now a country retreat for British prime ministers (some of whom have been known to visit the Russell Arms), where world leaders are hosted. Built in 1565, the mansion – once a place of confinement for Lady Jane Grey's sister, and home to Cromwell family members, including John Russell, Oliver Cromwell's grandson – was gifted to the government in 1921, while Coombe Hill was donated to the National Trust.

How to Get There

By Car There is a car park at Coombe Hill (HP17 0UR; National Trust), between Wendover and Princes Risborough.

By Public Transport This walk passes very close to Wendover railway station, on the Chiltern line; to use this as an alternative start/finish point, follow directions from point 9.

OS Map OS Explorer 181 (Chiltern Hills North), Landranger 165 (Aylesbury & Leighton Buzzard); grid ref (for start): SP 851/062.

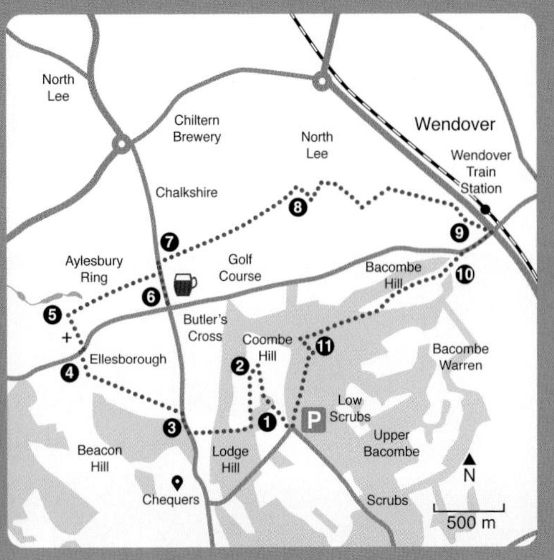

1. Go through a gate near the car park entrance, passing a National Trust sign, and walk straight ahead on the footpath. Wander through a group of trees, bear right and head across the grass to the Boer War monument, which stands atop the highest point in the Chilterns. Views across the Oxford Plain take in Wendover to the right, and the Chiltern Escarpment beyond stretches to Aston Hill and Ivinghoe Beacon. Ahead are Stoke Mandeville and Aylesbury. Left is Beacon Hill.

2. From the monument, turn left, walking along the Ridgeway, before taking a smaller path down to the right. Go past the National Trust track, then follow the main steep path down. At the bottom, cross a path and go through a gate to the road.

3. Carefully cross. Chequers is up to the left, but our route turns right and then left on a footpath leading across a large field, towards Ellesborough church, with tree-topped Beacon Hill on your left.

4. At the end of the field, briefly turn right on the lane and stroll down to the church, part of which dates to the 15th century. Go through a kissing gate and walk across a field.

5. Go through a farm gate and immediately turn right on the waymarked Aylesbury Ring (a 32-mile/51.5-km circular walk). Pass through a kissing gate and along a lane with pretty cottages. Cross a lane and continue straight across a field.

6. Meet Chalkshire Road, turn right and walk up to The Russell Arms, on your left at Butler's Cross.

7. Leaving the pub, retrace your footsteps until a footpath leads right. Take this, going through metal gates, following a fingerpost and Aylesbury Ring waymarkers, and crossing several stiles.

8. Wend around Wellwick Farm, walking through buildings and following Aylesbury Ring waymarkers along a grass path between fields. Go through a gate and turn left along the fenceline. After several more gates the path forks – go right, following Aylesbury Ring waymarkers and ignoring paths leading left and right until you meet the road.

9. The train station is left, but we go right. Walk up the road and, at the corner, carefully cross and follow a fingerpost for the Ridgeway National Trail.

10. When the path forks, stay right, following Ridgeway waymarkers and passing through a gate. Go through another gate and keep straight, ignoring a footpath forking right. Ridgeway signs lead over Bacombe Hill, where Bronze-Age barrows lay hidden among hazel, hawthorn, birch, ash, beech and juniper trees.

11. At a crosspaths, just after a gate, leave the Ridgeway and go left along a bridleway to Coombe Hill car park.

45 Dunstable Downs & the Tree Cathedral

The Farmer's Boy

The Farmer's Boy
216 Common Road
Kensworth
Bedfordshire LU6 2PJ
01582 872207
www.farmersboy
kensworth.co.uk

About this walk

- Chilterns AONB
- Red kites
- Icknield Way
- Chiltern Way

Start/finish Chilterns Gateway Centre car park (National Trust)
Distance 6 miles (10km)
Time to pub 1.5–2 hours
Walking time 3–3.5 hours
Terrain Footpaths

THE FARMER'S BOY is a 19th-century village pub now owned by Fuller's, with a lovely, large garden overlooking the Bedfordshire countryside and Chiltern Hills Area of Outstanding Natural Beauty. It's very dog- and family-friendly, with a play area for children. Inside you will find open fires, period features and good food being served from a varied menu, with vegetarian and gluten free options. Currently closed on Mondays – check the website.

From the chalky hills of Dunstable Downs, where red kites circle above prehistoric burial mounds and medieval rabbit warrens, walk to wonderful Whipsnade Tree Cathedral, before crossing heathland for a brew with a view.

Spring Red kites, successfully reintroduced in 1989, breed in April. Their distinctive silhouette is regularly seen soaring over the downs and Tree Cathedral.

Summer Picnic on Dunstable Downs with views across the Chiltern Hills. The Tree Cathedral offers cool shade and quiet contemplation amid myriad plant and tree species.

Autumn Foxes, badgers and squirrels busily prepare for winter, collecting food and building cosy dens. The rapidly revolving colours in the lofty reaches of the Tree Cathedral rival any stained glass window.

Winter Frost covers the grass across Dunstable Downs, between the modern Windcatcher and ancient, enigmatic burial mounds.

Fuller's favourites – including ESB, London Pride and Frontier lager – are available at The Farmer's Boy, alongside other ales (such as Hophead from Sussex's Dark Star Brewery) lagers and ciders.

Follow in the footsteps of... For two centuries, starting in the mid-18th century, people gathered on Dunstable Downs on Good Friday to throw, roll and chase oranges down the steep slopes to Pascombe Pit. Participants were either 'pelters' or 'pelted', with the former throwing fruit and the latter wearing things like top hats to make themselves bigger targets. Sadly the tradition stuttered during wartime food shortages and ended in 1968.

How to Get There

By Car Park on Dunstable Downs at the Chilterns Gateway Centre on the B4541 between Whipsnade and Dunstable (National Trust).

By Public Transport The closest train station is Luton (7 miles/11.3km). Centrebus routes 40 and 40A serve Dunstable Downs from Dunstable.

OS Map OS Explorer 181 (Chiltern Hills North) and 193 (Luton & Stevenage), Landranger 166 (Luton, Hertford, Hitchin & St Albans); grid ref (for start): TL 008/198.

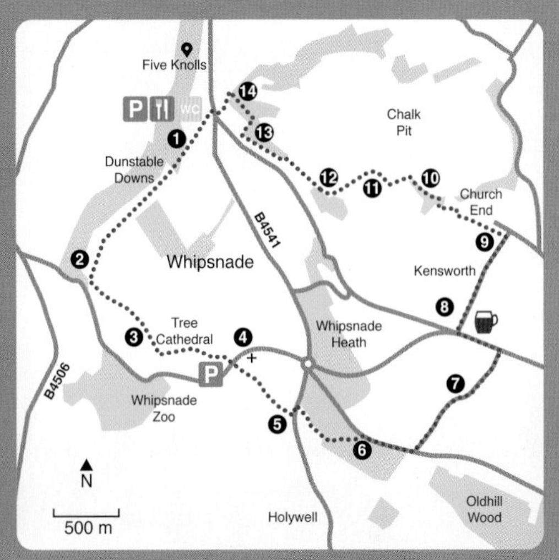

1. From the Chilterns Gateway Centre, walk towards the view and the Windcatcher (an installation which cleverly captures air and delivers it to the visitor centre via an underground duct). Turn left, following purple arrows and waymarkers for the Chiltern Way (a 134-mile/216-km route around the region) and the Icknield Way (a 170-mile/274-km trail along an ancient road across the chalk escarpment, in use since prehistoric times). Dunstable Downs has an interesting and often dark history. Barrows at Five Knolls were originally thought to be resting places for kings and chiefs, but excavations have revealed some Saxon-era skeletons of people who'd been executed and buried with their hands tied behind their backs. In medieval times the barrows were linked to alleged witchcraft and public hangings took place here. Walk with the hedge on your left, as gliders swoop silently through the vale, which plunges to your right. Go through a metal gate and follow the path through beech trees. Dogleg around Sallowspring Wood. The Chiltern Way branches off left but keep walking with the woods on your left and views cascading to the right.

2. Pass through a metal gate, following Icknield Way indicators and a fingerpost pointing towards the Tree Cathedral, and stay on the path as it wends left. Pass a cottage on the left, then take the turning left signed 'Tree Cathedral ¼ mile', going through a metal gate.

3. Go past a National Trust Whipsnade sign, cross a field and go through a gate into the Tree Cathedral (on your left). A place of quiet reflection, this is a unique church-shaped plantation of trees, shrubs and plants created after the First World War by returned soldier Edmund Blyth in the spirit of 'faith, hope and reconciliation', and to commemorate his fallen friends. The cathedral historically held regular ecumenical services, and an annual service still takes place there. It's open daily and entry is free.

4. Exit via an avenue of hornbeam trees to the car park. Go left around the green towards Whipsnade church. Cross the road and bear left across the grass towards the church, with houses on your right. Turn right into the churchyard, now following Chiltern Way indicators and footpath signs, and pass to the right of the church.

5. Go through a wooden kissing gate and cross a field with the hedge on your left. At the end of the field the Chiltern Way goes right, but our route continues straight on, along a footpath with the hedge now on your right. Go through a gate, cross the lane and dogleg (left then right) to pick up a path running around the edge of a field, keeping the hedge on your left.

6. Exit the field along an alleyway between houses. When you meet the road, turn left and walk around a bend. Follow a public footpath sign left, down

The ingenious Windcatcher atop Dunstable Downs presides over a stunning Chilterns valley view and keeps the visitor centre cool.

another alleyway, which bends right and leads to a lovely footpath running parallel to Buckwood Lane. When the path forks, go left to emerge at a road. Turn right, carefully cross and then go left, up Dovehouse Lane.

7. Ignore footpaths leading left and right and keep walking along Dovehouse Lane to the road. Cross, go left, and The Farmer's Boy is up on the right.

8. Leave the pub, walk up the road and turn right on Hollick's Lane. After 100 yards, a path runs parallel to the lane, initially alongside houses and then along the right edge of a large field, with a rolling rural landscape unfolding to the left.

9. The track rejoins the lane, and then a footpath leads left, taking you through a field with the hedge on your right.

10. Follow footpath arrows through fields and around mixed woodland of beech and hawthorn, until you meet T-junction at a quarry fence. Go left through a gate and walk with the quarry on your right.

11. Go down steps, ignore a gate and footpath on the left and carry on along a path through woods. Keep following footpath signs to arc around the edge of a large field with a hedge on your left.

12. At a sign, ignore the footpath going left and carry on around the field, with a good view of the massive chalk quarry on your right.

13. The path eventually wends left into woods, and then goes right again so you're walking with trees on your right and fields on the left. Emerge at the road going down to the quarry. Go right, then left when you see steps leading to a track through woods.

14. At a yellow post, go left, and left again at a second yellow post. Emerge at the road opposite the National Trust overspill car park. Go left and walk towards the beacon and Chilterns Gateway Centre.

Opposite: A historic working windpump at Wicken Fen in Cambridgeshire (see page 132).

East Anglia

Wicken Fen

The Maids Head

The Maids Head
12 High Street, Wicken
Cambridgeshire CB7 5XR
01353 720727
www.themaidshead wicken.com

About this walk

- Wicken Fen Nature Reserve
- Wind pumps
- Wildflowers and birdlife
- River Cam
- Lodes Way

Start/finish Wicken Fen Nature Reserve car park (National Trust)
Distance 7½ miles (12km)
Time to pub 2.5–3 hours
Walking time 4 hours
Terrain Fen-side paths

THE MAIDS HEAD is a thatched country inn, located on Wicken's village green, where there's been a pub of the same name since the 18th century. Tables spread across the grass outside, with views of one the Fenland's famous windmills. It caters for a friendly mix of locals and walkers. Good food is available, and there's a separate eating area. In colder months an open fire warms the main bar. Opening days/hours are reduced in winter. This walk also takes in the **FIVE MILES FROM ANYWHERE NO HURRY INN**, a modern bar-restaurant with a garden overlooking the River Cam.

Wander through a watery terrain of fens, rivers, rushes and meadows, where wildlife abounds and windmills dot the landscape. Visit a beer garden on the River Cam, before ambling across Burwell Fen to a thatched pub in Wicken, for a relaxing drink looking out over windmill sails and a wide fenland horizon.

Spring When brimstone butterflies alight on fen flowers, it's a sign the weather is warming. Listen for drumming snipes and the booming of bitterns, and look out for cranes and marsh harriers.

Summer Water lilies, yellow flag iris and arrowheads flower. Konik ponies and Highland cattle graze meadows, while kingfishers flash along waterways, and enormous emperor dragonflies hover, dwarfing numerous damselflies.

Autumn Search for roe deer antlers around Adventurers' Fen. Keep an eye out for lapwing and redshank as russet-coloured sedge and reeds gently sway in the breeze.

Winter Look out for dabbling ducks including wigeon, teal and shoveler, as well as short-eared owls. If you're really lucky, you may spy a hen harrier (Britain's rarest bird of prey) soaring over the sedge at dusk.

The Maids Head offers ales and ciders from Greene King and Mole Trap from Mauldons, both breweries based just across the border in Suffolk.

Follow in the footsteps of ...
Home to over 9,000 species of plants and animals, Wicken Fen has long been associated with natural history. Charles Darwin collected beetles here in the 1820s, and a century later the Cambridge botanists Sir Arthur Tansley and Sir Harry Godwin (fathers of modern ecology and conservation) did field work here, including an ongoing project called the Godwin Plots, one of the world's longest-running scientific experiments.

How to Get There

By Car Wicken Fen is 17 miles (27km) north-east of Cambridge, via the A10. There's a car park on Lode Lane (CB7 5XP; National Trust).

By Public Transport The closest train stations are Ely (9 miles/14.5km) and Soham (5 miles/8km). Taxis are available from Ely or Soham – no buses serve Wicken.

OS Map OS Explorer 226 (Ely & Newmarket), Landranger 154 (Cambridge & Newmarket); grid ref (for start): TL 565/706.

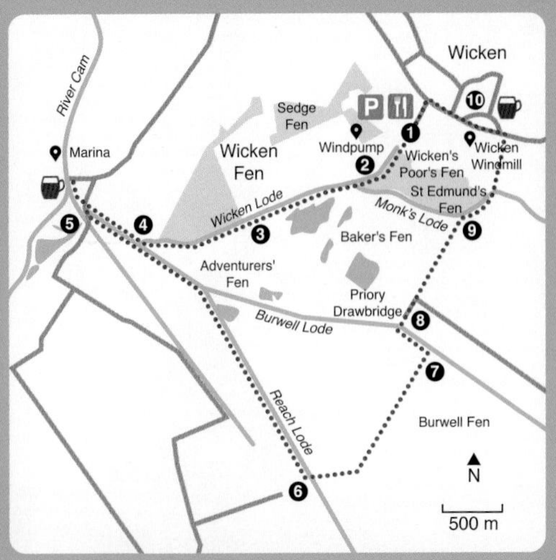

1. From the car park, walk down the lane to the National Trust hut and continue to the visitor centre and Docky Hut Café. Have a stroll around the restored wooden windpump (relocated here from Adventurers' Fen, where it was used to drain peat pits in the 19th century) and, if time permits, wander around the Boardwalk Trail to see Sedge Fen, the ancient, undrained fen. Our main walk explores the wider fens, however, so from the wind pump, loop back, cross the footbridge, and then turn right.

2. Pass an information board with a trail map and follow the waymarkers for the Adventurers' Trail along the bank of Wicken Lode, with the water on your right. To your left lies Wicken Poors' Fen, where, traditionally, local villagers had the right to harvest sedge and peat. As you pass a modern metal windmill on the right, Wicken Fen opens up. Bear left, cross Norman's Bridge over Monk's Lode and then turn right to keep walking along Wicken Lode, with water on your right, fringed with tall reeds on the opposite bank.

3. Continue, passing the lofty Old Tower Hide on the right bank. Go past the turning for West Mere Hide on your left, and carry on along Wicken Lode, passing reed beds on your left, and the more open Verrall's Fen on the opposite bank.

4. Pass the National Trust sign for Wicken Fen and turn right to cross the tall footbridge. Walk along the banks of Reach Lode, with the water on your left, usually busy with river boats. At Reach Lode Lock, where you meet the road by Far Away Farm, dogleg right then left to walk around the Lock Marina. Cross Upware Road and follow the fingerpost pointing along the Fen Rivers Way (a 48-mile/77-km route between Cambridge and King's Lynn, along the Rivers Cam and Great Ouse). Where the Cam comes in to join the waterway you'll find a riverside pub: the Five Miles From Anywhere No Hurry Inn (as it's officially called). This modern, brick-built bar and restaurant occupies a site that once housed a classic old pub, but it's welcoming to walkers and has a beautiful beer garden where you can enjoy a cold (or hot) drink under the trailing limbs of weeping willows, and watch the swans, ducks, coots, moorhens and narrowboats go by. There's also an undercover area, an atmospheric wooden shelter called the Cam Shack, where you can sit if it's drizzling – and they offer several real ales, plus local cider from Pickled Pig and Spinney Abbey.

5. Retrace your footsteps to the lock, cross the bridge and walk back along the opposite side of Reach Lode, with the water now on your left. The waterway forks, with Burwell Lode disappearing left. Continue along Reach Lode, crossing Adventurers' Fen, keeping the water on your immediate left and looking out for roe deer. Straight ahead you will see Reach Lode Bridge in the distance.

At the outset of this walk you pass the last working wooden windpump in the Fens.

6. After almost a mile, cross the bridge leading left, passing some metal statues and an information sign about Burwell Fen. From the bridge, walk straight ahead, before bearing slightly left, passing a National Trust sign for Burwell Fen and following a fingerpost for Wicken via the Lodes Way (a 17-mile/27-km cycling and rambling route from Ely to Bottisham, via Wicken Fen).

7. At a junction with a signpost for Burwell pointing right, keep going straight, crossing an open landscape of grassland crisscrossed by drainage channels, and following fingerposts for Wicken. Look out for Konik ponies and wide-horned Highland cattle grazing the nature reserve here. Cross a cattle grid, go through another set of gates with a cattle grid and bear left. Pass a National Trust sign for Burwell Fen, turn right and walk over a footbridge by Priory Drawbridge, crossing Burwell Lode.

8. Continue straight, past a picnic area, ignoring a bridleway going left. Walk up a lane, past a farm on your left and Factory Road on the right, following fingerposts for the Lodes Way route to Wicken. The gravel lane turns into a bridleway, with the sails of the windmill at Wicken visible across the treetops of St Edmund's Fen.

9. Go through a double set of gates with cattle grids, and when the track splits, with the bridleway shooting off left, walk right, going along the footpath with St Edmund's Fen woods and the water of Monk's Lode on your immediate left. By the National Trust sign for Adventurers' Fen, cross the bridge to the left and walk up the path, taking in great views of the windmill. At the end of the path, go straight ahead, along a lane between houses, until you emerge at a green. On the opposite side of the road is The Maids Head.

10. Leave the pub, turn right and walk to end of the green, before crossing the road opposite the windmill. Turn right and then left along the next lane, walking in between houses, and then go right along Back Lane. When you reach a fingerpost pointing along Wicken Way, go left and walk back to the car park.

47 Brancaster
The Jolly Sailors

The Jolly Sailors
Main Road
Brancaster Staithe
Norfolk PE31 8BJ
01485 210314
www.jollysailors brancaster.co.uk

About this walk

- Roman fort
- Norfolk Coast Path
- Peddars Way
- Norfolk Coast AONB
- Birdlife

Start/finish Jolly Sailors
Distance 4½ miles (7km)
Time to pub 2 hours
Walking time 2 hours
Terrain Coastal and countryside paths, some road sections

EAST ANGLIA

THE JOLLY SAILORS is a family-friendly pub bouncing with character, boutique ales and buoyant nautical themes. The beach-style garden features a shack serving ice cream in summer, and there's a vine-enveloped covered area. The 300-year-old whitewashed stone building splits into several rooms – a main bar with a large woodburner, two drinking snugs and a restaurant. Meal options from a seafood-heavy menu include freshly steamed, locally harvested mussels and stone-baked pizzas. Nearby The White Horse is managed by the same company.

Wander the Norfolk Coast Path, passing crab shacks and saltmarshes buzzing with birdlife, then head inland through an Area of Outstanding Natural Beauty to cross a common and explore the site of an old Roman fort, before finishing in a seaside pub.

Spring Migrating birds arrive and depart across the marshes. The botanically rich area around Barrow Common blooms, with foxgloves, meadow saxifrage, scarlet pimpernel, pearlwort, poppies, red bartsia, harebell, meadowsweet and lady's bedstraw. Look out for birds like firecrest, marsh harrier and turtle dove.

Summer Butterflies flutter and skylarks soar in the blue air above the site of Branodunum fort and Barrow Common, and The Jolly Sailors' beer garden sings a siren's song.

Autumn The gorse and bracken scrub of Barrow Common blazes a burnt orange colour, migrating birds fly across the salt marshes, and The Jolly Sailors typically stages a cider festival in September.

Winter Gaggles of pink-footed geese arrive from Iceland and Greenland to overwinter in Norfolk, while resident redshanks and oystercatchers stalk the salt marshes.

The Jolly Sailors serves several beers bubbled to the pub's own recipes by Brancaster Brewery, including Oyster Catcher, The Wreck, Lucky Lobster Pale Ale and Brancaster Best. Unsurprisingly, there's also a large rum menu.

Follow in the footsteps of ...
Nelson learned to sail in the creeks around Brancaster, which takes its name from the Roman fort Branodvnvm (meaning 'fort of the raven' in a local Celtic language), built in the 3rd century and abandoned between AD 383 and 400.

How to Get There

By Car Parking is available (for customers only) at the pub, but please be considerate and let staff know your plans. There is limited parking opposite The Jolly Sailors, on Harbour Way, although it is subject to tidal flooding; more public parking can be found at Brancaster Beach (not National Trust), 2 miles (3.2km) west.

By Public Transport Coasthopper buses stop outside The Jolly Sailors.

OS Map OS Explorer 250 (Norfolk Coast West), Landranger 132 (North West Norfolk); grid ref (for start): TF 794/443.

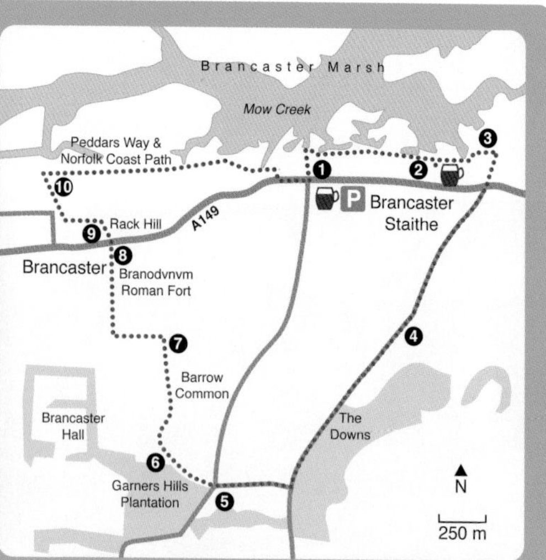

1. Walk down the lane opposite The Jolly Sailors, to meet the marshes at Mow Creek. Turn right at the fingerpost and stroll through the boat sheds, along a path with the marsh to your left.

2. Pass a row of artisan shacks by The White Horse – sister pub to The Jolly Sailors – where there's a specialist fish smoker, as well as toilet facilities.

3. At a fingerpost, turn right. Pass the National Trust sign for the Manor of Brancaster and walk up a lane to the road. Cross to the shops, turn right then left, and walk up Dalegate Lane, a quiet B-road.

4. Wander past Valley Farm, and follow the road around to the right, cutting the corner and walking beneath a gang of magnificent beech trees.

5. At a Y-junction, with Garners Hills Plantation in front of you, bear right and then turn immediately left, into Barrow Common, following the footpath fingerpost and leaving the road behind. Go straight ahead, walking along a lovely path through a mixed woodland of oak, ash, silver birch, sweet chestnut, sycamore, beech, elder, hawthorn, blackthorn, wych elm, lime, hazel and holly.

6. There are a couple of route options – both lead to the same place, but our walk goes around the left edge of the woods. After a few hundred yards the path bends right and reaches an open area with a bench, where other paths join from the right. Continue straight on, through a metal gate and past a footpath fingerpost.

7. When you meet a lane, bear left – following a blue arrow. Stay on this lane as it turns 90 degrees right and walk down to the main road. You're now approaching Branodunum, where garrisons of Roman soldiers and Dalmatian cavalry troops were once stationed.

8. At the road, a fingerpost points left for 'Circular Walk' – ignore this, and instead carefully cross and go straight ahead, through a gate with a National Trust sign, on to Rack Hill, a large enclosure where the Roman fort stood (there's nothing left now).

9. At a wooden post, bear left and walk a well-trodden path diagonally across the field to a gate. Cross the lane, pass through a kissing gate, go straight over another field and through another kissing gate to emerge by a National Trust sign for Branodunum Roman Fort.

10. Turn right and walk along the wooden duckboard. You're now back on Norfolk Coast Path and Peddars Way (a 49-mile/79km national trail along the route of an old Roman road between Suffolk and the North Norfolk coast). Walk, with the atmospheric marshes on your left, until you reach Harbour Way, where a fingerpost points right to The Jolly Sailors.

48 Horsey
The Nelson Head

The Nelson Head
The Street, Horsey
Norfolk NR29 4AD
01493 393378
www.thenelsonhead.com

About this walk
- Norfolk Broads habitat
- Windpumps
- Seals
- Sea views
- Birdlife

Start/finish Horsey Windpump car park (National Trust)
Distance 6 miles (10km)
Time to pub 2.5 hours
Walking time 3 hours
Terrain Footpaths, coastal trail, some road

The award-winning **NELSON HEAD** welcomes walkers, boaters and locals. Within a brick building owned by the National Trust, the bar has a huge fireplace and Lord Nelson paraphernalia adorns the walls (paintings of Trafalgar and other naval battles, plus various antique weapons, telescopes and nautical trinkets), along with traditional tools used by marshmen working the Broads. There's a dining area, and a beer garden. Food is available. Horsey Barns (National Trust-managed accommodation) is next door.

From the sails of an iconic windpump, walk the beautiful banks of Horsey Mere in the Norfolk Broads, to see seals on a North Sea beach, before visiting an atmospheric pub serving dozens of local ales and ciders.

Spring Horsey Windpump reopens to visitors at weekends. Migrating bird species fly overhead and, around Horsey Gap, Atlantic grey seals haul themselves onto the beaches to moult.

Summer Dragonflies and butterflies – including the rare swallowtail – hover and flutter amid reed beds around Horsey Mere.

Autumn The soft light across Horsey Mere is spectacular, with the sun setting through the windpump sails. Along the coast, migrating birds arrive, including pink-footed geese.

Winter Between November and January, female Atlantic grey seals seek shelter on the beaches around Horsey Gap to give birth, and thousands of pups can be seen on the sand. (Note: obey signs and keep dogs on leads.)

Woodforde's Nelson's Revenge and Wherry are always on handpump at The Nelson Head, alongside guest beers such as Moon Gazer's Pintail pale ale. Many more real ales are gravity poured from barrels, and the real cider menu runs into double figures.

Follow in the footsteps of ...
The Nelson Head celebrates Norfolk's famous son in name and content (the pub is crammed with memorabilia about the Royal Navy's most lauded officer). Horatio Nelson was born in Burnham Thorpe, but he learned to sail on the Broads and the whole county claims him. Arriving in nearby Great Yarmouth after the Battle of the Nile, Nelson famously declared: 'I am a Norfolk man and glory in being so.'

How to Get There

By Car There is a National Trust car park at Horsey Windpump (NR29 4EE), south of Horsey village, along the B1159.

By Public Transport Horsey is not an easy place to reach by public transport. The nearest train station is Great Yarmouth (12 miles/19.3km), from where you can get a First Bus as far as Winterton-on-Sea (3½ miles/5.6km south of Horsey)

OS Map OS Explorer OL40 (The Broads), Landranger 134 (Norwich & The Broads); grid ref (for start): TG 457/223.

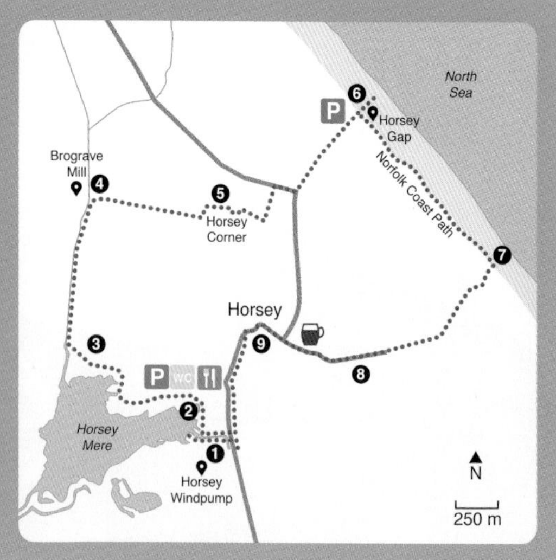

1. Before setting off on the walk proper, it's well worth exploring Horsey's famous windpump (it closes in winter – check the website). From the car park, walk along the track towards the iconic four-sailed building, going past the National Trust shop and tearoom on your left, and with the water channel on your right. There's been a drainage mill at Horsey for 400 years, but the current structure, built in 1912, is the youngest windpump on the Broads. It's had an eventful life, surviving floods, lightning strikes and long periods of disrepair, but in 2019 the National Trust opened it to the public, and between March and November you can explore the interior and enjoy the view from the cap. The path continues for a few hundred yards beyond the windpump to offer stunning views across the still water of Horsey Mere. After drinking this in, head back towards the car park.

2. Pass the car park on your right and continue to walk around the northern bank of the mere, along a lovely section of path, fringed by reeds and rushes on the left, and English oaks on the right, where there is a narrow waterway.

3. The path meets Waxham New Cut waterway, which feeds into Horsey Mere, and turns right. Walk with the water on your left and a floating meadow on the right. Brograve windpump soon looms into view. Dating to 1771, this historic building is an enigmatic and rather mournful sight, with its sails broken and drooping, looking like it's lost a fight with Don Quixote. Legend has it that the one-time owner of this mill, the infamous Sir Berney Brograve (1726–97), hid within its walls after losing a bet with the devil.

4. The path elbows right here, by Brograve Mill, and then, at Horsey Corner, turns left, crosses a footbridge and lurches right.

5. Keep walking until you meet a lane. Turn right then left, walk along a path through houses and then in between fields to a T-junction. Turn left and walk across the field to a road. Turn right, carefully walk along the pathless road for about 100 yards. Cross and, as the road corners, turn left up the lane to Horsey Gap car park.

6. Check out the beach, but obey signs, and if you're walking with dogs, it's crucial to keep them on leads here to protect seals, especially in winter when there are pups around. Turn right and walk along the path behind the dunes, passing a Second World War pillbox on the left. After about two-thirds of a mile (1km) you will reach a shipping container and an information sign about Atlantic grey seals.

7. Follow the fingerpost pointing right to The Nelson Head. Walk along the indicated route, passing between fields, going through a gate and continuing along a lane.

8. At the junction with Crinkle Hill, turn right and follow the quiet B-road to the pub, which is on your right.

9. Leave the pub, turn right and walk down the road. At the junction, bear left and walk along the permissive path on the field side of the hedge. At the end of the field, cross a little footbridge (signed to Horsey Mill car park), turn left and walk along the path beside the road. When the path runs out, dip left into the field running alongside the road, where a permissive path leads back to the car park.

Opposite: Horsey Windpump has been braving (and harnessing) the elements for over 100 years.

Below: The Nelson Head's interior could almost be mistaken for the armoury room of a naval garrison.

49 Blickling
The Bucks Arms

The Bucks Arms
Blickling
Norfolk NR11 6NF
01263 732133
www.bucksarms.co.uk

About this walk
- History
- Section of the Weaver's Way
- Spring flowers
- Woodland
- Wildlife

Start/finish Fisherman's Car Park, Park Farm
Distance 5 miles (8km)
Time to pub Allow 1.5 hours
Walking time 2 hours
Terrain Woodland, lakeside, country footpaths

Formerly The Buckinghamshire Arms, **THE BUCKS ARMS** began life as a 17th-century coaching inn. Adjacent to historic Blickling Hall, the pub sits within a sprawling, heavily wooded estate, popular with walkers. With an air of elegance, it offers B&B accommodation and quality food served in two eating areas, (one dog-friendly, one dog-free), with a small snug in the middle typically reserved for non-dining drinkers. A real fire roars in colder months, while a big garden beckons in summer. The Bucks usually closes to non-residents by 8.30pm.

From the banks of a mirror-like lake (shown above), wander through the wonderful woods of a historic country estate, past a mysterious mausoleum, an enigmatic tower and a Jacobean-era mansion, before popping in for a pint in a 400-year-old pub.

Spring Daffodils turn the Temple's grassy banks gold, magnolia explodes into pink-and-white blooms at the Hall, and a wave of bluebells washes around the feet of beech trees in the Great Wood and past the Mausoleum and Tower.

Summer Enjoy picnics around the lake, lounging on the grass in Tower Park, or sheltering in the dappled shade of the woods. Roe deer are rutting, and the Bucks Arms' beer garden beckons.

Autumn Flame-coloured trees reflect in the still water of the lake. Pumpkins and squashes grow in the walled gardens opposite The Bucks Arms and fruit ripens in Blickling's gardens.

Winter Observe barn owls hunting in the pale light above the frost-gripped grass of Tower Park, where roe and muntjac deer congregate. Spot robins, blue tits and goldfinches flitting between the frozen fingers of leafless trees in Great Wood.

The Bucks Arms has three handpumps serving real ales from Norfolk breweries such as Moon Gazer (Pintail pale/Jumper amber/Nibbler ruby), Panther (Beast of the East IPA), Grain (ThreeOneSix) and Woodforde's (Wherry/Nelson's Revenge).

Follow in the footsteps of ... The current Blickling Hall was built between 1620 and 1627, but from 1499 to 1505 the estate was home to Thomas and Elizabeth Boleyn. All three of their children were born here, including Anne, the ill-fated second wife of Henry VIII and mother of Elizabeth I.

How to Get There

By Car Park at Fisherman's Car Park (National Trust), by Park Farm NR11 6PU, near the main estate on Blickling Road, signposted off the A140 between Norwich and Cromer.

By Public Transport Catch a train on the Bure Valley Railway (heritage railway) from Hoveton & Wroxham (Great Anglia main line) to Aylsham, 2 miles (3.2km) from Blickling Estate (walkable along the Weaver's Way).

OS Map OS Explorer 252 (Norfolk Coast East), Landranger 133 (North East Norfolk); grid ref (for start): TG 180/296.

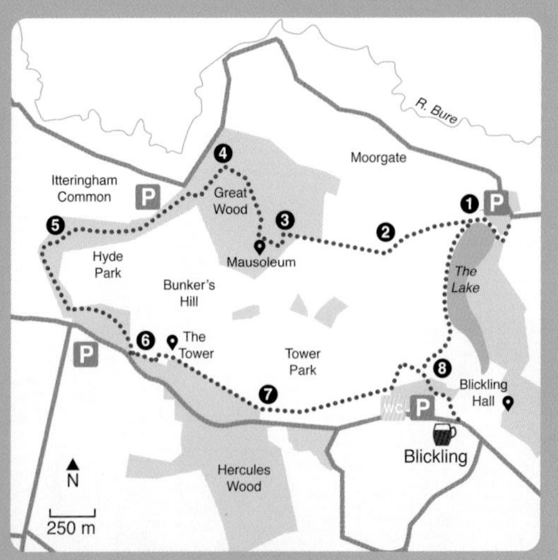

1. From Fisherman's Car Park, walk through the wooden gateway to the right of the information board and map, following the arrow and waymarker for the Weaver's Way (a 61-mile/98km trail between Cromer and Great Yarmouth). Stroll through beech, holly and oak trees, and when you reach the lake turn right and walk with the water on your left. Just after a bench the track forks – bear right and leave the lake behind, following orange NT arrows beneath sweet chestnut trees.

2. At a fingerpost the Weaver's Way turns left, while our walk continues straight, still following red arrows. Big skies and expansive views across the rural fieldscape of Norfolk open up to your right, before you enter the embrace of Great Wood.

3. At a Y-junction, go left then right, along a corridor of sombre yew trees, to view the 200-year-old Mausoleum, built to entomb the remains of John Hobart, 2nd Earl of Buckingham (1723–93) and his two wives. Continue past the Mausoleum and bear right, along a track leading back into Great Wood. Keep going until the track forks, then go left and – ignoring the first path leading left – continue until you meet the main trail at a T-junction.

4. Turn left and walk beneath beech, oak and sweet chestnut trees to Woodgate Car Park. Skirt around the car park, then go straight ahead, ignoring two other paths leading left.

5. Walk through woods that horseshoe around Hyde Park. Pass Buck's Common Car Park and continue along the path. The Blickling Tower soon becomes visible through the trees on your left.

6. Go through the gate on your left just before reaching the tower, into the wide open plain of Tower Park, and walk around the front of this eccentric edifice. The Blickling Tower (now offered as holiday accommodation by the National Trust) was built in 1773 as the Earl of Buckinghamshire's grandstand, overlooking a horse track to the south. Keep walking through the park, with the fence on your right and a group of oaks on the left. Go through a gate and continue along the right edge of the park.

7. When you meet a track, turn left. Then, at the T-junction, go right. Follow pink arrows on a route that arcs left, taking a tarmac lane to The Bucks Arms, opposite Blickling Hall. The pub is open to all, while entry to the house and gardens is free for National Trust members.

8. Leave the pub by the front door, turn left and retrace your steps along the lane. Go through the gate by the National Trust sign for the park, and then turn right – following blue arrows through another gate and along a path to the lake. Turn left and walk along the bank, with the trees reflected in the water on your right, back to the car park.

50 Blakeney
The Stiffkey Red Lion

The Stiffkey Red Lion
44 Wells Road, Stiffkey
Norfolk NR23 1AJ
01328 830552
https://stiffkey.com

About this walk
- Norfolk Coast Path
- Peddars Way
- Norfolk Coast AONB
- Estuary and salt marshes
- Seals and birdlife

Start/finish Morston Quay car park (National Trust)
Distance 7 miles (11km)
Time to pub 1.5 hours
Walking time 3 hours
Terrain Coastal trail (sometimes muddy), footpaths, some road

Dating to 1670, the atmospheric **STIFFKEY RED LION** was rescued and reopened as a pub in 1990, having been a private residence for 20 years. A large place with several rooms, it thrives as a gastro eatery serving great food, but retains the feel of a proper pub, buzzing with villagers and visitors. A stone floor, wooden beams, four fireplaces, framed local tales (including the extraordinary story of Harold Davidson – see below) and hop-entwined oars above the bar, all add charm. A garden has cool, covered pods for alfresco enjoyment. Accommodation is available.

Wander with wildlife along Norfolk's coastal wetlands between Blakeney and Stiffkey (pronounced '*stoo*-key'). Waterfowl and seabirds are ever-present, clouds of migrating birds darken spring and autumn skies, and seal sounds often fill the salty air.

Spring Terns, chiffchaffs, sand martins, blackcaps, wheatears and willow warblers arrive in March. Swallows, house martins, whitethroats and garden warblers follow in April. In May, swifts swoop in. Listen for the boom of the rare male bittern.

Summer Wetlands between Blakeney and Stiffkey are an important breeding area for terns. Oystercatchers, spoonbills, egrets and turnstones patrol the muddy marshes.

Autumn Swifts, swallows and sand martins head south, and winter visitors (including brent geese, sanderling, knot, godwits, dunlin and grey plovers) return.

Winter Blakeney's grey seal colonies are England's largest, and in November–December thousands of pups are born on the sandbanks off the spit. It's also breeding season. They're not visible, but you can hear the cacophonous seals from the coastal path.

The Stiffkey Red Lion serves Norfolk-brewed real ales, including Woodforde Wherry and Nelson's Revenge, and Stewkey Blews (named after the local cockles). Norfolk-distilled gin is available.

Follow in the footsteps of ...
In the early 20th century, somnambulant Stiffkey was shaken awake by shenanigans concerning local rector, Harold Davidson. Protesting his defrocking after accusations of immoral behaviour, Davidson staged several publicity stunts, which culminated with him being mauled to death by a lion (not a red one). Framed news cuttings in the pub tell the tale.

How to Get There

By Car Park at Morston Quay (NR25 7BH; National Trust), between Blakeney and Stiffkey on the A149 (Blakeney Road).

By Public Transport The nearest train station is Sheringham (8 miles/13km); Sanders Coaches CH1 bus runs between Sheringham Blakeney and Stiffkey.

OS Map OS Explorer 251 (Norfolk Coast Central), Landranger 133 (North East Norfolk) and 132 (North West Norfolk); grid ref (for start): TG 006/442.

The marshes at Blakeney National Nature Reserve are alive with birdlife all year round.

1. From Morston Quay car park, follow a fingerpost pointing along the coast path to Stiffkey. As you leave the car park area, walk along a raised path and aim for the wooden steps. When the path forks by a National Trust sign for Morston Marshes, bear right and walk along the Norfolk Coast Path, with the saltwater marshes on your right.

2. Cross the marsh, following the oft-muddy path as it bears left and traces the bank of Freshes Creek.

Pointing the way to the pub, along the mysterious Muckledyke Way.

Walk with a lake on the left, and the creek and marsh on your right, going past an information board about birds at North Fen. Listen for seals in winter. Note: you can't walk to see the seals on Blakeney Point (the tidal salt marshes are dangerous, and baby seals need space), but boat trips are available.

3. Ignore a fingerpost pointing left, for 'Stiffkey Stores and Barn', and continue walking along the Norfolk Coast Path, with Stiffkey Salt Marshes on your right. This is also a section of the Peddars Way, a 49-mile (79km) national trail along the route of an old Roman road between Knettishall Heath Country Park in Suffolk and Holme-next-the-Sea on the north Norfolk coast.

4. When you reach the small National Trust car park at Stiffkey Saltmarshes, turn left and walk up the lane (Green Way), past High Sand Creek campsite and a Maritime Heritage Centre.

5. At the road, carefully cross and follow a waymarker pointing left, towards the shop and pub, along a permissive path and part of the Muckledyke Way. Follow this path, which runs between the road and the River Stiffkey, until you emerge by a bench, right opposite The Stiffkey Red Lion – one of three pubs that used to serve this pretty village, and the only one still open.

6. Leave the pub, turn left and walk along Wells Road – there's a pavement on the right at first, but once you pass a property with a replica of Dr Who's TARDIS in the driveway, you have to walk along a short section of this quiet road.

7. Just after a red phone box, turn left, following a public footpath fingerpost along Hollow Lane. Keep going, past a long stone wall with various beer and cider bottles embedded in it, until the lane becomes a double track path and passes between farm fields. When the track arcs left, keep going straight on, and when you meet the Norfolk Coast Path, turn right and retrace your earlier steps back to the car park.

Opposite: A stream runs off the Long Mynd and cuts across the path in Carding Mill Valley (see page 151).

Midlands

51 Dover's Hill
The Fleece Inn

The Fleece Inn
The Cross, Bretforton
Worcestershire WR11 7JE
01386 831173
www.thefleeceinn.co.uk

About this walk
- Wildflowers
- Birdlife
- Cotswold views and villages
- Vale of Evesham

Start/finish Dover's Hill car park (National Trust)
Distance 10 miles (16km)
Time to pub 2 hours
Walking time 4 hours
Terrain Countryside footpaths, lanes and some road

A genuine destination pub, the 500-year-old FLEECE INN oozes character. After opening in the 15th century, the pub remained in the same family until 1977, when it was bequeathed to the National Trust. On the cusp of the Cotswolds, circled by walking trails, the low-beamed bar is warmed by an open fire and is full of interesting antiquities. Outside there's a large patio and award-winning orchard garden, complete with heated horseboxes for shelter. The inn boasts a medieval barn and a valuable collection of 17th-century pewter. Good food and accommodation are available.

From a historic hill, home to a uniquely English iteration of the Olympic Games and site of a Roman vineyard, walk across a wildflower-covered corner of the Cotswolds, through villages and along waterways, to a 15th-century pub frozen in time.

Spring Early purple orchids and wood anemones bloom, and bluebells cover Dover's Hill, where you can catch the eccentric Cotswold Olimpicks. Blackthorn trees flower, followed by hawthorn, while goat willow produces catkins and 'lamb's tails' appear on hazel trees. Enjoy locally grown asparagus at The Fleece Inn.

Summer Wildflowers proliferate across hills and alongside streams, attracting myriad butterflies.

Autumn Sweet chestnut cases litter the woods, evidence of squirrels busily stocking up for winter. Spotted flycatchers pause on Dover's Hill, feeding up before their long flight to Africa.

Winter Larch needles carpet the floor. Hunting buzzards float on thermals above Dover's Hill, while redwings and fieldfares flit over the escarpment. Views across the Cotswolds are exceptional through the bare trees. Look out for stoats, foxes, roe and muntjac deer.

The Fleece Inn has seven handpumps, offering rotating regional real ales including Mad Goose from Purity Brewing Co., Battledown Brewery's pale and Pigs Ear from Uley.

Follow in the footsteps of ... Dover's Hill is where the original English Olympic Games began, 400 years ago. A local lawyer, Robert Dover, initiated the games with the approval of King James. The tradition continues, and the hill still hosts the annual Cotswold Olimpicks on the Friday after Spring Bank Holiday, with events including shin-kicking contests, morris dancing and tug-of-war.

How to Get There

By Car The NT car park at Dover's Hill is 1 mile north-west of Chipping Campden on the B4035 between Evesham and Shipston-on-Stour.

By Public Transport Catch a train to Moreton-in-Marsh (5 miles/8km). Johnsons Coaches 1 and 2 travel between Moreton-in-Marsh and Stratford-upon-Avon, via Chipping Camden.

OS Map OS Explorer OL45 (The Cotswolds)/205 (Stratford-upon-Avon & Evesham). Landranger 151 (Stratford-upon-Avon) and 150 (Worcester & The Malverns); grid ref (for start): SP 137/395.

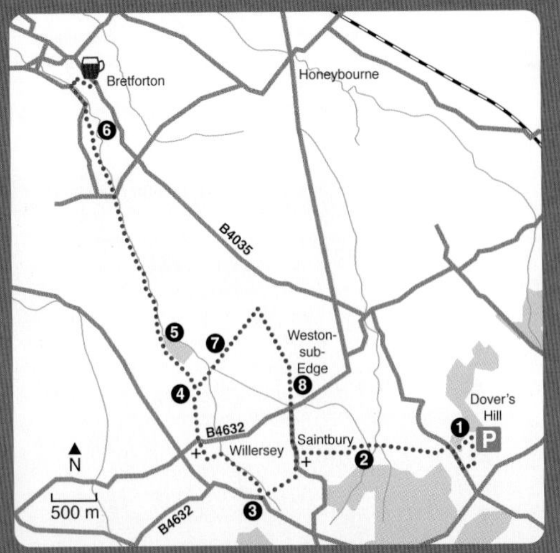

1. From the car park, walk up Dover's Hill to enjoy views north over Lynches Wood, east across Chipping Camden, south through the Cotswolds Area of Outstanding Natural Beauty, and west through the Vale of Evesham. Facing forwards, from the direction you approached, descend left and go through a gate with a National Trust sign, onto the road. Turn right, and after about 150 yards, go left through a gate. Follow a footpath across several fields, crossing a track and another path, and continuing straight ahead.

2. Cross a second track and a stream, among trees, and continue straight, walking around the bottom of a hill. When the path forks, bear left and stroll towards Saintbury's church spire. Emerge on Buckle Street, turn right, then after 50 yards, go left up a lane. Walk on the path to the left of the lane, past 13th-century St Nicholas' Church. Continue along the footpath, ignoring paths leading left and right, and walking until you almost meet Campden Road.

3. At a gate by the road, follow a footpath fingerpost pointing right and walk downhill, across fields, towards Willersey. At a junction, bear left and head towards square-topped St Peter's church. Go through the grounds, bear right along a footpath and descend through a field. Cross the B4631 and continue through more fields until a steep bank transects your path.

4. Follow the path through a gate and straight over this raised ridge, along which a Great Western Railway track once ran. On the other side the footpath immediately splits – take the left fork, walking through fields and crossing a stile to reach a plantation of tall trees on your right.

5. Go along a little gravel track, crossing a stream and keeping the trees on your right. Continue along the footpath, walking with a solar farm on your left, and a brook on your right. Keep following this stream, crossing over Stoneford Lane by buildings, and continuing along the path, through fields.

6. Approaching Bretforton, cross a footbridge, go through a gate and walk along Back Lane. Turn right, up Bridge Street, passing stone cottages. At the church, turn right for The Fleece Inn.

7. Leaving the pub, reverse the route along the stream, until you reach the old railway line. Turn left and walk along this track for about half a mile, until you see buildings, then turn right and follow a track towards Saintbury's distinctive church spire, which stabs the sky straight ahead.

8. Cross the B4632 by an antiques yard and standing cross, and continue straight up the street opposite, into Saintbury. Go along Buckle Street, pass the turning for the church, then go left along the footpath you walked earlier, and retrace your footsteps to Dover's Hill.

52 Wenlock Edge

The George & Dragon Inn

The George & Dragon Inn
2 High Street
Much Wenlock
Shropshire TF13 6AA
01952 727009
www.thebestpubintheworld.com

About this walk

- Shropshire Way
- Wildflowers
- Cross Britain Way
- Jack Mytton Way

Start/finish Much Wenlock car park (1/2 mile/1km west of the town, National Trust)
Distance 8 miles (13km)
Time to pub 2.5 hours
Walking time 3.5 hours
Terrain Country paths, fields, lanes, some road

Located in the heart of historic Much Wenlock, where the seed that grew into the modern Olympics was germinated, THE GEORGE & DRAGON INN is a traditional pub that welcomes walkers with warm hospitality, local ales and great food. Dating to at least 1714, there are two bars, both with open fires and wooden beams. In the front bar, where the ceiling is hung with whisky water jugs, the initials of family members that ran the pub between 1835 and 1958 are carved into the beam above the fireplace. Sometimes closed during the day on winter weekdays.

Explore a wildflower-covered, wooded, limestone escarpment, home to wonderful wildlife and the scene of a great escape story, before descending to a traditional pub in a historic market town that played a notable role in the creation of the modern Olympic Games.

Spring Blackcaps, swallows, chiffchaffs and willow warblers arrive. Around Blakeway Hollow, wild garlic perfumes trails where bluebells, wood anemones, violets, primroses, herb Paris and early purple orchid begin to bloom.

Summer Pyramidal orchids emerge across the limestone grassland, attracting meadow brown, little skipper, marbled white and ringlet butterflies, while enchanter's nightshade blooms beneath coppiced hazel, and flowering honeysuckle and tutsan adorn the trails. Young swifts perform aerobatics overhead.

Autumn Native field maple burns bright red. Hazel dormice munch on nuts to plump up for winter, but you are more likely to see squirrels stocking their larders.

Winter With trees denuded of leaves, spot nuthatches, great tits and blue tits, and enjoy stunning views across Shropshire from vantage points like Major's Leap.

The George & Dragon offers five rotating real ales, including locally brewed Hobsons Town Crier and Shropshire Gold, plus stouts in winter.

Follow in the footsteps of ... During the English Civil War, Major Thomas Smallman, a Royalist from Wilderhope Manor, famously leapt over a terrifyingly steep drop to escape Roundheads pursuing him across Wenlock Edge. His horse was killed at the spot now known as Major's Leap, but Smallman survived to fight another day.

How to Get There

By Car Drive towards Much Wenlock (postcode TF13 6DH); the National Trust car park is ½ mile (1km) west of the town.

By Public Transport The closest train stations are Bridgnorth (8 miles/13km) and Shrewsbury (13 miles/21km); bus 436 runs to Much Wenlock from both.

OS Map OS Explorer 217 (The Long Mynd & Wenlock Edge), Landranger 138 (Kidderminster & Wyre Forest); grid ref (for start): SO 612/996.

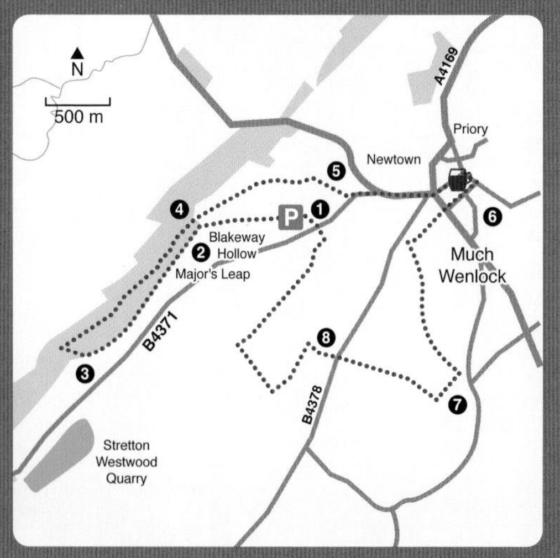

1. Leave the car park by the National Trust information sign. Turn left on a rocky track and walk uphill, ignoring a turning right and following a bridleway signed 'Major's Leap Walk'. Ascend along Blakeway Hollow, an old packhorse route between Much Wenlock and Shrewsbury in use since medieval times. Continue until you meet woods, then turn left into fields and trace the top of the limestone ridge, looking for fossilised sea creatures that unexpectedly cover this Midlands escarpment, a legacy of when this was a submerged coral reef, 425 million years ago (please leave fossils in place). Walk along a section of the Cross Britain Way (a 280-mile/450-km trail across England and Wales, between Boston and Barmouth) with the tree-covered slopes of Wenlock Edge on your right, and Lea Quarry dropping left.

2. Follow Major's Leap signs to a precipitous point where the view opens up and the hill plunges away to reveal the Severn Valley in the north. This is the site of Major Smallman's daring escape (see opposite). Continue along the path, to another viewpoint, offering a vista of The Wrekin, a distinctive hill to the north.

3. Continue along the edge of the quarry, ignoring the first broad path on the right, then bearing right when the path forks. After a short descent, go hard right along a broad track which forms a section of the Jack Mytton Way (a 100-mile/160-km trail across Shropshire celebrating another notable historical horseman) and cutting back towards Blakeway Coppice. Stroll along this undulating trail beneath Major's Leap for about 1½ miles, ignoring tracks and paths leading downhill to the left and continuing until you emerge at the junction close to where Blakeway Hollow Track leads right, back to the car park.

4. Instead of turning right, continue straight, going through a gate and walking along the arrowed Shropshire Way (a 200-mile/320-km walking route across this beautiful county). Follow a hedge (on your left) to a gate, bear diagonally across a field to a gateway and walk through Stoke Barns car park, passing through another gate to the right of a stone barn. At a kissing gate with multiple waymarking arrows, follow Shropshire Way pointers, pass through a large gate and descend a steep, stony path. Go through another wide gate, turn immediately right, still following Shropshire Way arrows, and wend through woods on a serpentine path to emerge on a tarmac lane.

5. Turn left, following a Shropshire Way fingerpost. Cross Stretton Road and go left again, along a path. At the main road (Victoria Road) go right, passing Much Wenlock town sign, and crossing the road to stay on the footpath. Walk along the raised path and continue, crossing Smithfield Road opposite The Gaskell Arms Hotel, and going straight ahead, on High Street, following signs pointing to Wenlock Abbey Ruins. Walk along this attractive town

Spanning 18 miles between Craven Arms and Ironbridge, Wenlock Edge is a fossil-rich limestone escarpment.

street, past The Talbot Hotel and beautiful timber-beamed buildings to The George & Dragon Inn, on the right.

6. Leave the pub and continue to a T-junction at the end of High Street. Left, along Wilmore Street, lie the remains of an Anglo-Saxon monastery founded around 680 by King Merewalh of Mercia, whose daughter, Milburge, became the abbess and later a saint. If you divert to check out the priory (recommended), look out for a blue plaque near Church Green marking the birthplace of Dr William Penny Brookes, a social pioneer who initiated the Wenlock Olympian Games in 1850, a series of sporting events for working class people that still takes place around Much Wenlock annually, and which was a forerunner of the modern Olympic Games. Our walk, however, turns right at the T-junction, passing along Barrow Street and going right again along St Mary's Road. At the end, cross Bridgenorth Road, go through the gate opposite and continue along a bridleway track, crossing a field with a fence on your right. Go through a kissing gate at end of the field and turn left along a footpath. Emerge into a field and follow arrows on wooden posts pointing straight on. Walk along a small section of path, then go across large field, heeding more directional arrows.

7. At a crossways, just before a stile (don't cross), turn right and trace the field edge along a waymarked path. Follow the track as it leaves the hedge and bends around to the right, going past an old barn, a ruined cottage and alongside a coppice of trees. Cross another field and go past a modern building on your left to emerge on the B4378 road.

8. Cross, turn left and carefully walk along the road for 50 yards, before turning right along the track for Bourton Westwood Farm, following footpath arrows. At the farm, bear left and walk along a track. Meeting a lane, go right, then right again along a footpath leading to Lower Farm, enjoying wonderful views of Wenlock Edge escarpment, which appears straight ahead. Pass farm buildings and go right again, following another footpath for almost a mile, until it passes Cuan Wildlife Rescue (on your right) and arcs left to meet Stretton Road. Turn right here, and carefully walk 100 yards down to the car park, which is on your left.

53 The Long Mynd

The Green Dragon & The Kings Arms

The Green Dragon
Ludlow Road
Little Stretton
Shropshire SY6 6RE
01694 722925
thegreendragonpub.co.uk

About this walk
- Shropshire Hills AONB
- Waterfalls and moorland
- Stunning views

Start/finish Carding Mill car park (National Trust)
Distance 9 miles (14.5km)
Time to pub 1 Allow 3 hours
Time to pub 2 3–4 hours
Walking time 4–5 hours
Terrain Moorland paths, country lanes, some pavements

THE GREEN DRAGON in lovely Little Stretton, midway around the route, is a friendly and attractive pub with an L-shaped bar and a beer garden set amid the Shropshire Hills Area of Outstanding Natural Beauty. **THE KINGS ARMS** in Church Stretton, near the end, is a Joule's Brewery pub in a historic building – complete with original beams, a woodburner and a snug – which warmly welcomes walkers and cyclists and features a map on the wall with local hiking and biking routes. Good food is served in both.

MIDLANDS

Trace streams and waterfalls onto a magical moorland plateau and explore the Long Mynd, a spectacular landscape with echoes of the Swiss Alps.

Spring Pollinators, including rare bilberry bumblebees, get busy as shepherd's cress, sheep's sorrel and heath bedstraw flower. Look for stonechat and snipe, and listen for red grouse. Migrating birds arrive, starting with wheatears.

Summer Bilberries fruit and heather bursts into purple flower. Dragonflies hover and haunt waterways, while butterflies – small heaths, graylings, green-veined whites and dark green fritillaries – flutter across the moor.

Autumn Dandy crimson, orange, yellow, white and pink waxcap fungi decorate grasslands. Dying bracken bronzes the Long Mynd, while flowering gorse adds a golden glow.

Winter The Long Mynd offers wonderful stargazing conditions – Shooting Box is a Dark Sky Discovery Site. Look for overwintering birds, including redwings, fieldfares and golden plovers.

The Green Dragon rotates regional real ales (including Ludlow Gold) and offers ciders like Hogan's Hazy Daisy. The Kings Arms pulls Joule's Pale Ale, Pure Blonde, Slumbering Monk and seasonal beers such as Moon Madness.

Follow in the footsteps of ...
The Jack Mytton Way, a long-distance bridleway/walk is named after 'Mad Jack' Mytton (1796–1834), an eccentric local squire, skilled horseman, outrageous rake and (very fleetingly) MP, whose infamous antics included stripping naked during hunts, feeding his favourite dogs steak and champagne, and performing numerous hair-raising horse stunts.

How to Get There

By Car Head to Church Stretton along the A49 and park in Carding Mill car park (National Trust).

By Public Transport Church Stretton train station is close to the trailhead.

OS Map OS Explorer 217 (The Long Mynd & Wenlock Edge), Landranger 137 (Church Stretton & Ludlow); grid ref (for start): SO 446/944.

Shooting Box
Lightspout waterfall
Carding Mill Valley and the Long Mynd
Pole Bank
The Long Mynd
Church Stretton station & village
Round Hill
Grindle
B5477
Ragleth Wood
Little Stretton
A49
N
500 m

Joule's Brewery restored the 16th-century Kings Arms in 2018, revealing original oak beams and enhancing the beer garden.

1. Walk up through the long car park at the bottom of Carding Mill Valley, passing the ice cream parlour, tearoom and toilets. At the end, go right, cross the bridge and amble along the footpath/bridleway, part of the Jack Mytton Way (see Follow in the footsteps of...) with the stream on your left. Continue past a signed turning for a reservoir.

2. When you reach a fingerpost pointing towards Lightspout Waterfall, turn left. Go along a raised path with a stream chuckling away on your right, to the attractive cascade.

3. Climb the rough stone steps to the right of the waterfall and follow the streamside path up the hill, over the heath and across the ancient Portway, a ridgeway route that's been trodden for 5,000 years, originally by Neolithic traders.

4. You meet up again with the Jack Mytton Way at Shooting Box, where the rare remains of a Neolithic bell barrow survive (albeit having been converted into a shooting box by Victorian sportsmen). Bear left, go through the small car park and cross the quiet road. Keep walking straight along the undulating path for about two-thirds of a mile (1km) until you reach the trig and spectacular viewpoint at Pole Bank (1,693ft/516m), Long Mynd's true summit (Mynd comes from the Welsh word 'mynydd', meaning 'mountain'). With good luck and clear weather, you can see as far as the Brecon Beacons and the Malvern Hills.

5. Continue along the Jack Mytton Way, turning soft right when you meet the road and walking past Pole Cottage to a small car park. Take the faint footpath leading diagonally left across the heath here and follow it until a wider path comes in from the right. Turn left along this broad, furrowed track.

6. When the track forks, beneath the brow of Round Hill (on your right), bear left along a slightly narrower path. The terrain plunges away into the impressive valley of Ashes Hollow on your left, and then drops dramatically into Callow Hollow on your right as you traverse the Long Mynd plateau and cross Barrister's Plain, passing the rising flanks of Grindle (1,506ft/459m) on your left.

7. The drop-off switches back to your left as the path wends between Callow (1,348ft/411m) and Nills (1,401ft/427m) before descending into trees.

8. A gate brings you out by a cottage. Go through another gate and walk down the lane, past the campsite entrance, crossing a bridge by a ford. To visit the pub in Little Stretton, keep following the stream along the lane, passing the village hall and emerging on the main road – The Green Dragon is on your right. Retrace your footsteps after leaving the pub. Cross the stile by the ford, following the footpath fingerpost, and climb a set of steps. Go through a kissing gate and up a steep (but mercifully short) hill.

9. Walk with the fence to the right and a steep drop to your left, where oak trees cling onto the bank for dear life. Cross a stile and take the footpath across a field, following a fingerpost and waymarked posts. Go along a narrow section, between trees and a fence, with a steep drop on the far side of the fence on your right. The path eventually dips to the right, goes over a stile, descends some more and brings you right down to the road at Cross Bank.

10. Turn left and look for a path immediately veering left, quickly leaving the road behind again. The route then runs behind houses and under trees, before emerging on a residential lane.

11. If you want to tackle more hills, you can take the footpath immediately leading left, but our walk follows the road up and around a hairpin bend, along Cunnery Road and into the lovely town of Church Stretton. Walk along the High Street and the Joule's Kings Arms is on the right.

12. After leaving the pub, keep going in the same direction, straight on at the roundabout by The Buck's Head (or go right if you're heading for the train station). Stroll along Shrewsbury Road for several hundred yards, before turning left up the Carding Mill Valley, back to the car park.

The Long Mynd is a plateau in the Shropshire Hills characterised by stunning vistas and steep valleys.

54 Shugborough
The Clifford Arms

The Clifford Arms
Main Road, Great Haywood
Staffordshire ST18 0SR
01889 881321
www.cliffordarms.co.uk

About this walk
- River Trent
- Staffordshire Way
- Way for the Millennium
- Woodlands
- Wildlife

Start/finish
Shugborough
Distance 6 miles (10km)
Time to pub 2.5 hours
Walking time 3 hours
Terrain Country and riverside footpaths, bridleways, lanes

Positioned on the Trent and Mersey Canal, the Staffordshire Way and Way for the Millennium, beside Shugborough Estate and close to Cannock Chase, **THE CLIFFORD ARMS** attracts boaters, bikers, hikers, towpath amblers and ramblers, who rub shoulders with locals in this traditional village pub. Named after the Clifford family from nearby Tixall, it was rebuilt by Bass in 1930, but there's been a pub here since 1818 and the original building was a gatehouse to the Anson estates at Shugborough. It boasts a big beer garden, classic pub furnishings and an open fire. Food is available.

From a Staffordshire country estate, full of follies and enigmatic monuments, explore the leafy outskirts of Cannock Chase, before returning along a waterside section of the Way for the Millennium, through the Trent Valley, to a traditional pub.

Spring Daffodils bloom and bluebells flood the grounds of Shugborough. Spot green hairstreak and the threatened small pearl-bordered fritillary butterfly, which breeds in Sherbrook Valley, and listen for the drumming of the lesser spotted woodpecker. Shugborough's seven bat species awake from hibernation.

Summer Lime trees blossom, wisteria turns Shugborough's clock tower purple, wildflowers proliferate, attracting bees and butterflies, and the unique Cannock Chase berry (a bilberry hybrid) fruits. In woodlands, spot willow and wood warblers, whitethroat, chiffchaff, blackcap, redstart and spotted flycatcher.

Autumn Cannock Chase's fallow deer rut in October. Shugborough's lime, oak and tulip trees turn red and orange.

Winter Migrant siskin and redpoll arrive around Cannock Chase. Flocks of fieldfares and redwings swoop on fields, while kestrels and buzzards soar.

The Clifford Arms offers rotating real ales including Old Speckled Hen, Doombar, Timothy Taylor Landlord and Wainwrights golden beer.

Follow in the footsteps of ... Shugborough's story is a tale of two brothers: George (1697–1762) and Thomas Anson (1695–1773). Regarded as the father of the British Navy, George went to sea at 14 and rose to become First Lord of the Admiralty. The second Englishman (after Drake) to circumnavigate the globe, he amassed a fortune capturing a Spanish galleon, and spent it, with Thomas, turning Shugborough into a 'paradise'.

How to Get There

By Car Signposted from M6 exit 13, Shugborough is 6 miles (10km) east of Stafford on the A513. Use the Milford entrance. Park in Shugborough Park (National Trust).

By Public Transport The 828 bus from Stafford train station (6 miles/ 10km) passes the park and stops by The Clifford Arms.

OS Map OS Explorer 244 (Cannock Chase & Chasewater), Landranger 127 (Stafford & Telford)/128 (Derby & Burton upon Trent); grid ref (for start): SJ 990/216.

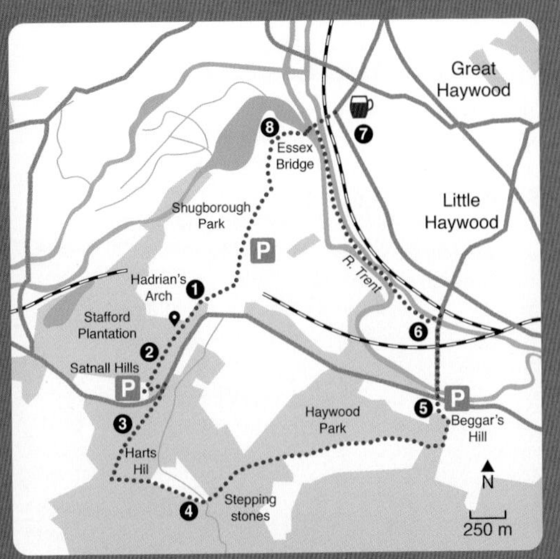

1. Leave the car park the way you drove in and walk uphill to the right of a coppice of trees, heading towards Hadrian's Arch. Thomas Anson transformed this monument, inspired by the antiquities of Athens, into a memorial when his younger brother died in 1762, and from its heights, a bust of George Anson faces Shugborough Hall. Continue across the grass towards the trees of Stafford Plantation, go through a gate, follow a fingerpost pointing left (to 'car park'), and walk along a trail with the fence on your left. Before you reach the road, by an orange waymarker, turn right along a path.

2. Keep walking along an undulating path, part of the Staffordshire Way (a 92-mile/148-km trail traversing the county), which runs parallel to the road. Ignore paths coming in from the right, go through a gate and across a track and small car park. Continue until you reach the larger Satnall Hills car parking area. Walk through this open area, bear left to the road and carefully cross to Punchbowl car park on the other side.

3. Bear right and walk along a track through the trees, staying left when the path forks. When you reach a major meeting of paths, bear left and walk around the base of Harts Hill.

4. Keep going until you meet a definite turning left, and descend to a clearing by Devil's Dumble, with stepping stones leading across Sher Brook. Hop over these and go straight ahead, along the old Sherbrook Trail, watching out for mountain bikes. Walk along the bottom of Haywood Warren, through a treescape on the northern edge of Cannock Chase, until you reach another tangle of paths at Beggar's Hill. Bear left, walk through the picnic area to the road and carefully cross.

5. Walk over Weetman's Bridge, crossing the River Trent, and go along Meadow Lane, passing beneath a railway bridge. When you meet the Trent and Mersey Canal, turn left along the towpath, to walk a section of the Way for the Millennium (a 40-mile/ 65-km east–west route across Staffordshire).

6. Stroll along the towpath, with the water on your right. As you pass a hill on the opposite bank, the ribbon of land between the canal and the river narrows. At a T-junction, go right, cross a humpback bridge over the canal and walk beneath a railway bridge and up Trent Lane to find The Clifford Arms on the left.

7. After leaving the pub, go beneath the railway and back over the humpback bridge. This time continue over beautiful Essex Bridge, a 17th-century stone structure with parapets and ornate coping.

8. Continue into Shugborough and explore the estate, or walk straight along the path – part of the Staffordshire Way – to the car park.

55 Dovedale

The Watts Russell Arms

Hidden in the heart of a tiny hillside hamlet, **THE WATTS RUSSELL ARMS** is a charming, ivy-clad, 18th-century, stone-built inn. The name derives from the Watts-Russell family, one-time owners of nearby Ilam Hall and Park, an interesting estate with cottages in the style of Swiss chalets, now looked after by the National Trust. The warm and welcoming pub has two open fires. Good hearty food is served, including an impressive evening tapas menu. Opening hours/days vary (usually closed Wednesdays) – check the website. Children under ten aren't allowed in the bar.

The Watts Russell Arms
Hopedale, Alstonefield
Staffordshire DE6 2GD
01335 310126
www.wattsrussell.co.uk

About this walk

- Peak District views
- Riverside paths
- Caves and rock features
- Stepping stones
- Small summit climb

Start/finish Dovedale car park (National Trust)
Distance 9½ miles (15km)
Time to pub 2.5 hours
Walking time 4–5 hours
Terrain Rural and riverside footpaths, small section of B-road

Trace the River Dove along the Staffordshire–Derbyshire border, via Thorpe Cloud, the famous Stepping Stones (above), curious caves and limestone crags, before heading through the Dovedale hills to a picturesque Peak District pub.

Spring The grazing fields around Hall Dale are full of little bleating lambs in springtime, while the Dovedale woodlands are aromatic with wild garlic.

Summer Splash your way across the Stepping Stones and enjoy a riparian ramble along the banks of the Dove, looking for kingfishers and woodland wildflowers.

Autumn The tree-covered flanks of Dovedale are a riot of colour in autumn. Look out for dippers on the river, and robins, chaffinches and wrens in the woods.

Winter Views from Thorpe Cloud are especially clear in the crisp, cool air. Rock formations are more distinct with trees denuded of leaves, paths are quieter and, in the pub, fires blaze.

The Watts Russell Arms is a freehouse serving real ales, craft lagers and ciders brewed within a 25-mile (40km) radius of the pub. The regular tap ales are from Bakewell-based Thornbridge Brewery, and include Jaipur (a strong IPA), AM:PM (a session IPA) and Lord Marples (a classic bitter).

Follow in the footsteps of... Delightful Dovedale has been inspiring walkers, writers and artists for centuries – Tennyson, Ruskin, Byron and Jane Austen all waxed lyrical about its beauty. The river features prominently in the 17th-century book *The Compleat Angler* by Izaak Walton, and several places along this route are named after this seminal work.

How to Get There

By Car Park in Dovedale car park (National Trust), Ilam, Ashbourne DE6 2AY.

By Public Transport The nearest train stations are Matlock (11 miles/17.7km), Uttoxeter (11 miles/17.7km), Buxton (15 miles/27.4km) and Derby (16 miles/25.7km). Bus services run from Buxton train station.

OS Map OS Explorer 24 (The White Peak Area: Buxton, Bakewell, Matlock & Dove Dale), Landranger 119 (Buxton & Matlock); grid ref (for start): SK 146/509.

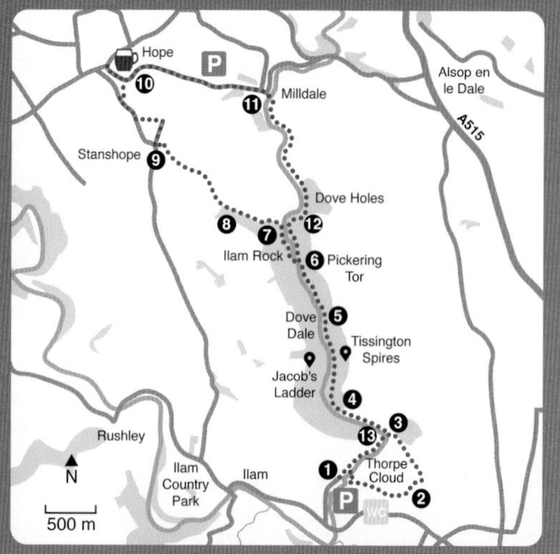

1. From the car park, walk to the river, passing the toilets and information board. Go past the Izaak Walton Gauging Station and National Trust sign for Dovedale Peak District. Cross the bridge over the river on your right, and walk around the base of Thorpe Cloud, a distinctive, dome-shaped reef knoll that gets its name from the Anglo-Saxon word for a hill, 'clud'.

2. Blue-topped posts mark the way around Thorpe Cloud and up to the summit, which offers outstanding views along the dale. If you choose to climb up to the top (and it's worth the effort) please come down the same way, to avoid eroding the surface. Continue around the base, through a fabulous fold in the landscape, between Thorpe Cloud and Hamston Hill.

3. When you reach the Stepping Stones (which you'll cross on the return route), bear right. Follow the fingerpost pointing to Milldale and go through a gap in two rocks. Walk with the River Dove on your left.

4. Ascend a fairly steep and long set of stone steps – look down and you will see many are covered in fossils of crinoids (millennia-old denizens of the dale, sometimes known as 'Derbyshire screws'). At the top of the climb there is a stony lookout point on your left known as 'Lovers Leap'. Ignore the path going right and continue straight on, back down another set of steps to the river bank. Go through a gate. The scenery opens up here, with rock formations erupting on either side of the river, including Jacob's Ladder (to the left) and Tissington Spires (to the right).

5. Stroll along a couple of sections of wooden boardwalk, the second of which ends with a little cave on the immediate right. Dovedale Wood is to the left on the opposite bank. A rock arch and more caves can be explored off to the right (with some scrambling involved). Ancient coins have been discovered here, dating back to Roman times, and one of the caverns – Reynard's Cave – was once used as a hideout by a local highwayman. The twin edifices of Pickering Tor and Ilam Rock soon come into view, glowering at one another across the river.

6. Pass Pickering Tor, taking a moment to explore the cave at its base, then turn left and cross the footbridge over the river to Ilam Rock, where a low mysterious mouth opens up in the ground just past the shard of limestone. Continue along the path with the river now on your right. Go past a fingerpost, ignoring the left turn to Ilam and following the sign to Stanshope.

7. Cross a stone stile and follow the fingerpost pointing left to Stanshope, walking up a steep rubble path that climbs through Hall Dale, a dramatic cleft between Raven's Tor and Hurt's

Wood. After a wooden stile, the path levels and continues through the steep-sided dale, going through a tiny gate by the National Trust sign for Hall Dale.

8. Pass the National Trust sign for Allen Banks. Ignore the footpath leading left, climb over a stone stile and go straight ahead, across a grazing field. After negotiating several more gates and stiles, you will emerge on an unmade lane. Go left into Stanshope.

9. At the village, turn right, cross the bottom of a triangle of roads and walk up a cul-de-sac with Stanshope Hall on your left. Pass Church Farm holiday cottages and, opposite Grove Farm (National Trust), go left through a gate and follow a footpath fingerpost across the field. Exit the field through a large gate and turn right along the road. After 200 yards, take the footpath leading right, which goes down through a field and twists to the left to meet a road. Go left, and The Watts Russell Arms is just up on your right.

10. Leave the pub, turn left and walk down the road until you reach the river again at Milldale, where you will find toilets, a shop and a National Trust Information Barn.

11. Cross historic Viator's Bridge (named after a reference in Izaak Walton's *The Compleat Angler* – see In the footsteps of...) turn right and follow the path south along the river bank, around the base of Baley Hill and the edge of The Nabs.

12. This sensational section of trail goes via Dove Holes, a couple of great gaping echo chambers that yawn wide in the limestone cliff face. Explore these shallow caverns (the larger of which is known to local climbers as the Bat Cave) and then continue along the edge of Upper Taylor's Wood until you meet the bridge at Ilam Rock. Keep the river on your right and retrace your earlier footsteps, going in reverse.

13. At the base of Thorpe's Cloud, turn right, leap across the Stepping Stones and walk back to the car park with the river on your left.

Below left: The Watts Russell Arms lies at the epicentre of a web of walking trails through Dovedale.

Below: Tiny gates lead to big adventures in Hall Dale.

56 Hardwick Park
The Hardwick Inn

The Hardwick Inn
Hardwick Park
Doe Lea, Chesterfield
Derbyshire S44 5QJ
01246 850 245
www.hardwickinn.co.uk

About this walk
- Rural footpaths
- Lakes
- Wildlife

Start/finish Hardwick car park (National Trust)
Distance 4½ miles (7.2km)
Time to pub 2 hours
Walking time 3 hours
Terrain Relatively flat rural, lakeside and woodland footpaths

Situated by the south gate of Hardwick Hall, an Elizabethan estate, historic HARDWICK INN dates to the 1500s. Impressively grand, but still comfortable, this National Trust-owned sandstone pub welcomes walkers, although a sign politely requests muddy boots be left in the entrance hallway to protect the antique carpet. Meals are served, while drinkers relax in the front bar and Stable Bar, the latter adjacent to the front courtyard. Two lovely large beer gardens (front and back) overlook the leafy estate. In winter, fires keep the heritage-heavy interior beautifully warm.

Explore 400-year-old Hardwick Hall Estate, strolling past ponds and through wonderful woodlands once reserved for the formidable Bess of Hardwick and her descendants, the Dukes of Devonshire, before enjoying a libation in a sun-catching pub courtyard.

Spring Bluebells carpet Lady Spencer's and Lodge woods, and fields are full of newborn lambs. In the gardens, crocus and daffodils bloom and irises crown the lush green ferns in the stumpery. Magnolia flowers erupt on the South Lawn and blizzards of blossom swirl through the orchards.

Summer Spot blue and long-tailed tits, wrens, nuthatches, treecreepers and goldcrests in Lady Spencer's Wood. On the ponds spy mute swans, coots, moorhens, goosanders, tufted ducks and kingfishers.

Autumn Woods go through a spectacular spectrum of colours. Conkers and sweet chestnuts festoon the floor and squirrels bounce between boughs.

Winter Enjoy evocative views of the hall through morning mist and leafless trees. Crab apples, snowdrops, aconites, narcissus, cyclamen and hellebores keep the gardens and orchards colourful.

The Hardwick offers four regular real ales, all from the local area – Black Sheep Best Bitter, Peak Ales Chatsworth Gold, Theakston Old Peculier and Theakston XB – plus a rotating guest ale.

Follow in the footsteps of ...
Hardwick was built in the 16th century by Elizabeth Cavendish. Known as 'Bess of Hardwick', she was the Elizabethan era's second richest woman (after the queen). Political philosopher Thomas Hobbes was a regular visitor, and actually died here in the hall in 1676. More recently, the mansion was used as Malfoy Manor in the filming of *Harry Potter and the Deathly Hallows*.

How to Get There

By Car Park in Hardwick Park National Trust car park (8 miles/13km south-east of Chesterfield, via A6175; leave M1 exit 29 and follow brown signs).

By Public Transport The nearest train station is Chesterfield (8½ miles/13.7km). Bus services run from Chesterfield Coach Station.

OS Map OS Explorer 269 (Chesterfield & Alfreton), Landranger 120 (Mansfield & Worksop, Sherwood Forest); grid ref (for start): SK 453/639.

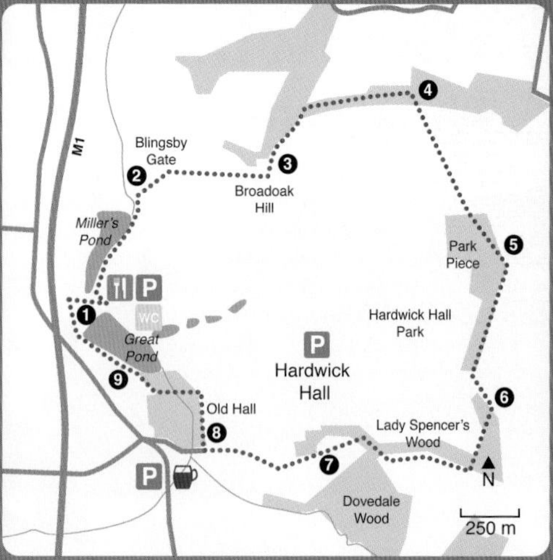

1. From the car park, walk past the shop and toilets (on your right) and enter Lower Wood, passing over a little bridge with Miller's Pond on your left. Turn left and go along part of the Sculpture Walk, passing through a gate and walking with the pond on your left. The lower path hugs the banks of the pond, but the upper path is where you'll find several sculptures, plus seats and picnic tables.

2. Just before a second gate, bear right along a distinct path, leaving Miller's Pond and Sculpture Walk behind. You are now on part of the Welly Walk. Stroll along a nice path, which gently ascends through a mixed woodland of birch, hawthorn and oak trees. Go through a gate, cross a tarmac lane by Blingsby Gate (a one-time entrance to the manor) and walk straight up the grassy hill towards the top-left corner, where several lovely large hornbeam trees stand proud. Emerge at top of The Grange, with a cottage on your left. To the right, there's a magnificent view of Hardwick Hall through the treetops.

3. Turn left through a large gate and walk along the lane. Go through a wide gate and turn immediately right, following a waymarker for the Welly Walk. Wander along a wonderful path, increasingly lined with horse chestnut, beech and sycamore trees, into thicker woods.

4. Look for a knee-high wooden post with an Oak Walk waymarker on it. Turn right here, go through a gate and across a wide meadow, passing through a line of oak trees, going straight across a tarmac lane and through another gate. Walk up the grassy hill to Park Piece woods. Wend through this woodland, beneath a canopy of sweet chestnut, horse chestnut, beech and sycamore trees.

5. Go through a gate into a field and turn right to walk with the fence on your immediate right. Go through a gate, across a footbridge and through another gate into a meadow dotted with oaks. Pass through another gate, cross the lane and go straight through two parallel-planted parades of beech trees to reach yet another gate.

6. Enter the top end of Lady Spencer's Woods, cross a stream and walk on, beneath the boughs of yew trees. At a T-junction, turn right and ascend some broad steps, passing a picnic table and going under a series of towering sycamore and beech trees.

7. Go past the National Trust woodlands play trail, but stay on the broad path. When you meet the car park for the main house and the path forks, go left, descending a little bit. Walk with a fence on your left, through a gate and across a meadow, with beautiful bucolic views across the Derbyshire countryside unfolding to your left. Go through a gate, meet the road and walk down and around an S-bend, through a gate beside a cattlegrid, to The Hardwick Inn, which is on the left.

8. Exit the pub, go back through the gate you came in via, then turn immediately left to walk along the bottom of the field – along another section of the Sculpture Walk – with oak woods on your left and Hardwick Hall up the hill on your right.

9. At the wooden post, turn left to go through woods. When you meet a small pond turn right, walk around the bank, cross the footbridge and look for the sculpted wooden waterfowl, which marks the spot where a duck decoy once lured these birds in. The path follows a section of wooden duckboard, and the Great Pond emerges on your right. Enjoy some excellent views across the water to Hardwick Hall, before continuing on to meet the top car park.

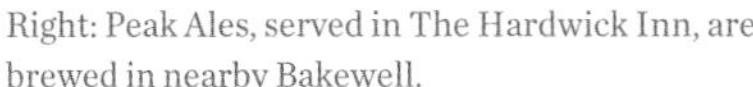

Right: Peak Ales, served in The Hardwick Inn, are brewed in nearby Bakewell.

Below: Hardwick Hall, viewed across the Great Pond, towers above the treetops.

57 Kinder Scout
The Old Nag's Head

The Old Nag's Head
Grindsbrook Booth
Edale, Derbyshire S33 7ZD
01433 670291
www.the-old-nags-head.co.uk

About this walk

- Peak District National Park
- Waterfalls
- Pennine Way
- Steep climbs

Start/finish Edale railway station
Distance 8½ miles (13.7km)
Time to pub 4 hours
Walking time 4.5 hours
Terrain Exposed trails with some rocky sections

Sitting pretty in the Vale of Edale, between Kinder Scout and Mam Tor, THE OLD NAG'S HEAD is the starting point for the Pennine Way (and myriad other routes) and the Hiker's Bar is legendary among hillwalkers. Dating to 1577, the atmospheric stone-built pub has huge fireplaces, tankards hanging from wooden beams, several rooms and snugs, and a garden. Filthy boots, wet dogs, rowdy ramblers and footsore families are all welcome. Hearty food is sold from noon, and there's an all-you-can-eat breakfast from 9am on Sundays. Opening hours vary in winter (check ahead).

This circular adventure to the roof of the Peak District, via boulder fields and waterfalls, is a sensational Derbyshire day out, ending in one of Britain's best walkers' pubs.

Spring Robins, stonechats, cuckoos and redstarts flit around lower paths. Swallows arrive, while overwintering species including waxwings and redwings start to depart.

Summer A crimson tide of flowering heather floods the moor. Wildflowers bloom around paths from Edale Valley up Jacob's Ladder. Listen to curlews and spot butterflies and bilberry bumblebees.

Autumn Mountain hares change camouflage from brown to white. Waterfalls cascade. Birch bracket mushrooms and horse's hoof fungus sprout.

Winter Conditions can be challenging, with ice- and snow-covered paths, but Kinder looks lovely in white; waterfalls are bearded by icicles and open fires warm The Old Nag's Head.

The Old Nag's Head has its own ale, Nags 1577, commemorating the year the pub opened. Beers from local breweries are also offered, including Sheffield's Bradfield and Masham's Black Sheep.

Follow in the footsteps of ...
On 24 April 1932, a disparate ensemble of around 400 demonstrators, ranging from ramblers groups to British Communist Party members, staged the 'Mass Trespass' on Kinder Scout, protesting about walkers being excluded from huge swathes of the English countryside. They were violently attacked by gamekeepers, and several were arrested, but ultimately this act of civil disobedience contributed to the creation of national parks, the establishment of national trails (starting with the Pennine Way) and the beginning of Countryside Right of Way (CROW) legislation.

How to Get There

By Car Park by the train station at Edale (S33 7ZN; not National Trust).

By Public Transport This walk begins from Edale train station.

OS Map OS Explorer OL1 (Dark Peak Area), Landranger 110 (Sheffield & Huddersfield); grid ref (for start): SK 123/853.

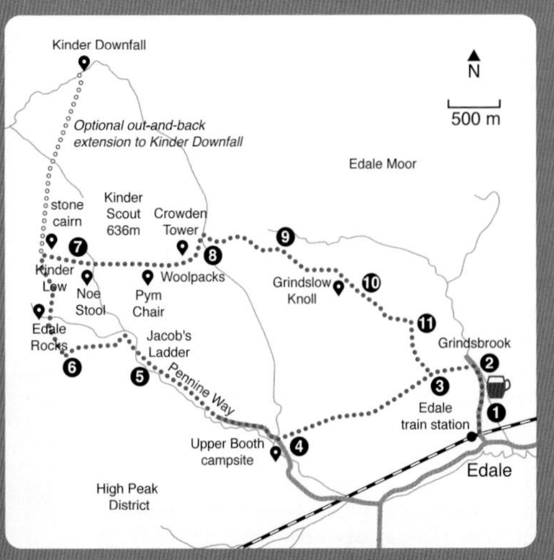

1. From Edale train station, walk north, up Marys Lane to Grindsbrook, passing The Rambler Inn on your left.

2. A footpath goes sharp left just before the entrance to Newfold Farm – ignore this and continue almost to the door of The Old Nag's Head, where a wooden fingerpost points left for the Pennine Way. You are at the southern trailhead of England's first National Trail, opened in 1965, which runs for 268 miles (431km) across the Peak District, Yorkshire Dales and Northumberland National Park to Kirk Yetholm, just across the Scottish border. Walk along this illustrious path, following signs for Booth Campsite. Go through a gate and past a sign indicating the official start of the national trail, strolling with a stream on your right.

3. Ignoring a fingerpost for Grindslow Knoll, turn left through a gate, staying on the Pennine Way. Walk along a slabbed track, through several gates, enjoying great views of Mam Tor off to your left. When the path forks at a wooden post, stay left.

4. The path undulates across hillocks, passing through several more fields and gates. Keep following signs, which eventually take you through a gate and along a track that doglegs around Upper Booth campsite (a spectacular place to pitch a tent, managed by the National Trust). By the phone box, follow a Pennine Way fingerpost pointing right. Walk along a lane and cross a bridge over Crowden Brook. Stay on the lane (ignoring the footpath going right immediately after the bridge) and walk past a Lee Farm National Trust sign. Go through a wide gate at end of Lee Farm and start ascending a broad stony track, crossing a couple of stiles.

5. Cross a lovely stone bridge with waterfalls to the right, and reach a National Trust sign for Jacob's Ladder, a set of steep stone steps you need to climb. As you pass a stone cairn, a bridleway comes in from the left. Bear right and keep ascending.

6. When the path forks, go right, along the slab path. Ascend and pass Swine's Back rocks and several cairns. Tracks scrawl right towards a distinctive rock formation known as Noe Stool but stay on the main path to reach the picturesque pile of boulders that is Edale Rocks, and then the trig point at Kinder Low, which stands 2,076ft (633m) above sea level. While Kinder Scout is the Peak District's highest point, the actual 2,086ft (636m) summit is unmarked and surprisingly hard to locate – it's somewhere over to your right

Extension: from here you can do an out-and-back extension to this walk, tracing the ridge and crossing Red Brook to reach the magnificent waterfall at Kinder Downfall, where the wind roaring up from Mermaid's Pool (reputed to be home to a mythical creature) often howls hard enough to outgun gravity and blow the water straight back up and into the sky. The return route is 2½ miles (4km). (The OS map indicates a possible circuit route, cutting back across Edale Moor along the creek to reach Crowden Tower, but the second section is extremely vague and very hard to follow across challenging terrain.)

7. From the trig, walk east along a rough trail to Noe Stool, then carry on to Pym Chair, another iconic rock formation from where the fantastic fold of the valley drops away to the right. Continue, negotiating the maze of mud and boulders that is the Woolpacks, an area crowned by Crowden Tower. The trail is nebulous here, but occasional slab sections reassure you that you're going the right way.

8. Keep walking east and descend to Crowden Brook. Cross the stream and take the path leading uphill to the right, along a well-defined trail.

9. When the path forks, by a cluster of boulders, go right and walk along a good track, initially re-enforced with slabs, which wends left and scales 1,971ft (601m) Grindslow Knoll.

10. As you drop down the far side, a path comes in from the left. Join this and keep descending, passing through a gate and walking down a rubble path, which is quite steep in places.

11. Go through a gate, cross the field then turn left along a footpath to reach the fingerpost pointing back to Grindslow Knoll that you passed earlier. Walk back along the path to emerge opposite The Old Nag's Head. When you leave the pub, walk back down the road to the train station.

Below: The Hiker's Bar at The Old Nag's Head is where many walkers start or finish the Pennine Way.

Bottom: From atop Kinder Scout plateau, the peaks and dales of Derbyshire unfold to the horizon.

58 Lantern Pike
Lantern Pike Inn

Lantern Pike Inn
45 Glossop Road
Little Hayfield
Derbyshire SK22 2NG
01663 747590
lanternpikeinn.co.uk

About this walk
- Stunning views
- Dark Peak summit
- Pennine Bridleway
- Sett Valley trail
- Steep climb

Start/finish Car park in Hayfield
Distance 4½ miles (7km)
Time to pub 1.5 hours
Walking time 2 hours
Terrain Countryside footpaths, hillside tracks, lanes and quiet roads

Located at the base of the distinctive peak with which it shares a name, the **LANTERN PIKE INN** is a classic local pub, which has been a community hub for Little Hayfield since 1851, and makes the perfect place for visiting walkers to enjoy a drink and a meal after scaling the hill. Views of the pike and surrounding Dark Peak summits can be enjoyed from the rear patio, while inside the friendly pub you'll find a comfortable lounge bar with an open fire and local ales. Meals are served every day except Monday (check the website). B&B accommodation is available.

From historic Hayfield, stroll along the Sett Valley Trail, before climbing to Lantern Pike's summit and drinking in superb views across the High Peak to the Kinder Scout plateau, Brown Knoll and Mount Famine. Wander back past woods to Little Hayfield village, and a wonderfully warm local pub.

Spring Bluebells, butterbur, wild garlic and wood anemones emerge beneath the new green leaves of ash, sycamore, beech and oak along the Sett Valley.

Summer Wildflowers line footpaths climbing from Birch Vale to Lantern Pike. Green hairstreak butterflies fly here, and views from both the summit and the beer garden below are stunning.

Autumn Guelder roses (dogberry) produce bright red berries, attracting mistle thrushes and bullfinches, while heather lights up the hilltops that dominate the view from the pike.

Winter Finches, tits and even elusive siskins flit between branches along the Sett, while mallards, goosanders and great crested grebes settle on the Birch Vale reservoir. From the pike, the snow-dusted peaks of Kinder Plateau are visible.

The Lantern Pike Inn has two handpumps selling real ales – Timothy Taylor's Landlord is a regular, while rotating guests include Sheffield's Abbeydale Brewery's Moonshine pale ale.

Follow in the footsteps of ... The first episodes of *Coronation Street* were written by the fireside in the Lantern Pike Inn by the show's creator, Tony Warren. The 1932 Great Trespass on Kinder Scout began from Hayfield. Before being gifted to the National Trust, Lantern Pike was purchased by friends of Edwin Royce, access campaigner and president of the Manchester Ramblers, and dedicated to his memory.

How to Get There

By Car Find paid parking (not National Trust) in Hayfield, on the A624 between Glossop and Chapel-en-le-Frith.

By Public Transport The nearest train stations are New Mills (3 miles/5km) and Chapel-en-le-Frith (4½ miles/7km), on the Hope Valley Line between Manchester Piccadilly and Sheffield. Buses including the 61 (Glossop–Buxton) serve Hayfield.

OS Map OS Explorer OL1 (The Peak District – Dark Peak Area Map), Landranger 110 (Sheffield & Huddersfield); grid ref (for start): SK 036/869.

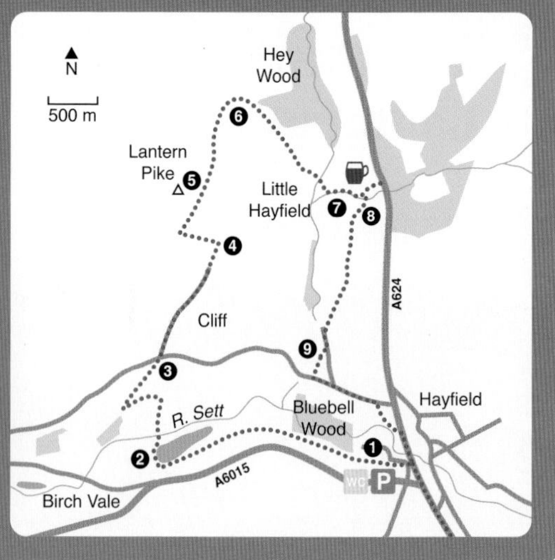

1. From the car park, stroll along the Sett Valley Trail, a 2½-mile (4km) track for walkers and riders, tracing an extinct railway line between Hayfield and Birch Vale, and part of the Pennine Bridleway National Trail. Diversions are possible to explore the River Sett and Bluebell Wood, where wildflowers bloom beneath ash, sycamore, beech and oak trees.

2. As you approach Birch Vale, pass the reservoir and follow a fingerpost right. Leave the Sett Valley Trail, walking over a bridge into a field. Go through a gap in a wall and take a path between fields.

3. Cross a stile over a stone wall and go left, up a lane. Meet the Pennine Bridleway and turn sharp right, walking up the lane. Cross a little road at Hegginbottom Farm, dogleg (right then left) and follow a fingerpost pointing up a cul-de-sac.

4. The lane segues into a stony track. Continue through a gate and, by the National Trust sign, turn left and climb a steep path by a wall. At the top, turn right and walk along the ridge.

5. Lantern Pike is so-called because a beacon once blazed on its prominent 1,223ft (373m) summit. Now a circular stone post occupies the top, inscribed with compass points and the names of features visible in the incredible 360-degree view across the High Peak. This marker is dedicated to Edwin Royce, one-time Manchester Ramblers' president, 'in memory of his labour in securing the freedom of the hills'. Continue and descend, passing another National Trust sign.

6. As you come down off the peak, bear sightly right and go straight across the field to a stile. Turn right and descend along a path with Hey Wood to your left, and Lantern Pike's steep flanks on the right. Climb another stile and go past a stile on the left.

7. At a house, turn left, pass through a tiny gate, descend a steep field and stroll along a stone-slab path to emerge by a mill and stream. Turn left, walk across two footbridges, and when you meet a lane, go left. Continue over a small stone stile, through a field and then over a little bridge. Climb over a wall via a tall stone stile, go right and the Lantern Pike Inn is at the junction with the main road.

8. Leave the pub and return over the stile, walking back across the bridge and field. At the lane, go right, then immediately left on a path, following a fingerpost pointing towards Hayfield.

9. Emerging onto a road, turn left then right along a footpath. Meet the road, turn left, and then go right along a footpath, walking across an old school field, and then bearing left along the river bank. Go right over the bridge, then turn left and follow the road around to the car park.

Opposite: Looking from Pen y Fan (see page 181) across to the summit of Corn Du.

Wales

59 Pennard, Pwlldu & Bishopston Valley
The Gower Inn & The Beaufort Arms

The Beaufort Arms
18 Pennard Rd, Kittle
Swansea SA3 3JG
01792 234447
www.sabrain.com

About this walk
- Castle
- Coast, woods and valley
- Gower AONB

Start/finish Pennard car park (National Trust)
Distance 11 miles (17.5km)
Time to pub 1.5 hours (to The Gower Inn)/3 hours (to The Beaufort Arms)
Walking time 5 hours
Terrain Coastal and country paths, lanes

Nestled between the coast and the countryside, close to wonderful trails and historic landmarks, THE GOWER INN welcomes walkers with a fantastic garden, local ales, fine fare and immaculate facilities. A food-orientated pub, the open-plan interior boasts three bars and eating areas. A mural highlights the real ales of Wales. Our walk also passes THE BEAUFORT ARMS in Kittle (pictured above). Dating to 1460, this is the oldest pub in Gower and features beamed ceilings, snug areas and woodburners.

Hike around the glorious Gower Peninsula, along cliffs to castles, coves, caves and beaches where smugglers once operated, into verdant woodlands and a valley, via two great country inns.

Spring Dainty yellow whitlow grass, unique to the Gower, blooms on cliffs and in stone walls, alongside thrift and spring squill. Flowering gorse adds a golden glow and many species of butterfly flit by.

Summer Lizards bask on hot sand in Three Cliffs Bay, while razorbills breed on cliffs. Enjoy a paddle on Pobbles Beach and search for seals and dolphins. Stonechats, whitethroats and rock pipits flit around quarries, and rock sea-lavender blooms.

Autumn Spot choughs and Dartford warblers among rocks, storm petrels and Manx shearwaters on the wing, kingfishers along Ilston Cwm and horseshoe bats in Bishopston Valley.

Winter Black- and red-throated divers fish close to the coast, among sea ducks like scoter and eider. Water thunders through the river in Bishopston Valley, making Guzzle Hole gargle.

The Gower Inn serves Gower Gold as the regular beer and rotates other real ales from Wales. The Beaufort Arms serves Brains Brewery beers.

Follow in the footsteps of ... Remote Pwlldu Bay was once a landing location for smugglers, who could hide contraband in the valley's caves. This was also the scene of a major maritime tragedy when the *Caesar* was wrecked in 1760. The navy vessel was full of press-ganged men who were trapped beneath the decks. They were buried in a mass grave at Graves End.

How to Get There

By Car From Swansea, follow the B4436 to Pennard, then signposts for Southgate and car park (SA3 2DH; National Trust).

By Public Transport Train to Swansea (8 miles/13km), then bus 14 to Pennard.

OS Map OS Explorer 164 (Gower & Llanelli), Landranger 159 (Swansea & Gower); grid ref (for start): SS 554/874.

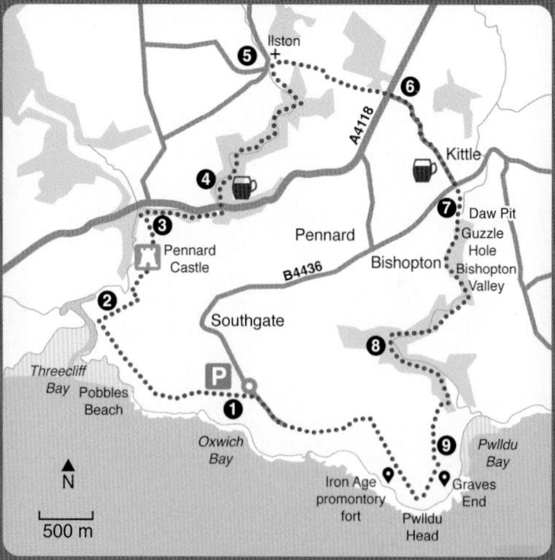

1. Head towards the sea and turn right along West Cliff and the Wales Coast Path, following signs for Pobbles Beach. Take the broad path or follow a narrower track through gorse for views of the stunning coastline, across cliffs plummeting into the waves of Oxwich Bay. At Pobbles Beach, follow a fingerpost pointing towards Pennard Castle and Three Cliffs Bay. Pass a wooden post, ascend steps, then go left, along the coast path. Go past a wooden sculpture and continue along a sandy path through dunes.

2. At a T-junction, bear right for Pennard Castle and Three Cliffs Bay. Walk inland a little, enjoying views of the medieval castle, which was built in the 12th century and bolstered with stone 200 years later, but still lost its war against encroaching sand. Behind the evocative ruin, Pennard Pill snakes towards the sea. At the next fingerpost, go straight, uphill to the castle, leaving the coast path. Circle the ruins, with the remains of an old church on your right, on the golf course. Follow green arrows along a permissive bridleway/path, and white-painted stones around the edge of the golf course, past the 6th tee. At a wooden post, the footpath forks right, but keep going straight, along the bridleway, following blue arrows.

3. Descend a path through beech, holly, hawthorn and sycamore trees, until the path coming up from Three Cliffs Bay intersects, by a fingerpost. Turn right here and walk with the river on your left. Pass a bridge (don't cross) and ascend. Continue through woods until you reach steps on your left. Descend these to a lane, cross a footbridge, turn right on the road and carefully (there's no footpath) walk past the church and across a bridge to The Gower Inn, on your left.

4. Leaving the pub, go to the end of the car park and join a footpath running alongside Ilston Cwm, with the water on your left. Cross a bridge and continue through wonderful woods, over a second bridge and past the remains of a little chapel – Wales' first Baptist church, founded in 1649 by John Myles. Follow footpath arrows across a third bridge, then turn right and walk with the river on your right. The path threads through trees, crossing another two bridges, before bearing left to follow the re-emergent river. Keep tracing the water, crossing more bridges.

5. Reaching 13th-century St Illtyd's Church in Ilston (which houses a 6th-century monastic cell), walk through the graveyard, across a river bridge, and turn right along a small road. Cross the river again, and at T-junction, go right. Follow a footpath arrow on a telegraph pole pointing along a lane, up a small hill. Before the next house, turn sharp left, following footpath arrows through a wooden gate and along a deep, tunnel-like holloway. Cross a stile and zig-zag past Courthouse Farm, to a ford. Cross, go up the hill and over another stile to meet the main road.

Looking across Pobbles Beach, Three Cliffs Bay and the Gower Peninsula from the Wales Coast Path.

6. Carefully cross and walk straight along the B-road opposite, following road signs for Kittle, snaking around Kittle Hill Farm (no pavement), before going through a metal gate and along a path running parallel to the road. Walk through a gate and field into the village. The Beaufort Arms is on your right.

7. From the pub, cross the road and follow fingerposts for Bishopston Valley and Pwlldu Bay. Pass the Bishopston Valley National Trust sign, and Great Kittle Farm (on your right), and walk along a gravel lane. At a fork, turn left and descend steps to a fence, and a big chasm called Daw Pit, a collapse caused by the river that runs underground here. Continue to the bottom and cross the stream, walking with the water on your right for 200 yards before crossing back over. Listen for strange sounds at Guzzle Hole – this is the voice of the subterranean river running below. Pass Long Ash Mine – where lead and silver were once extracted, but which is now home to horseshoe bats – and cross the water again. Climb steps and stay left when another path joins from the right. From here, keep following fingerposts for Pwlldu, walking with the river on your left, passing two bridges and several junctions.

8. Eventually a junction and fingerpost offer an option to shortcut right, to Southgate and the car park. Take this or keep going straight along our route towards Pwlldu. When the path next forks, go right, rising away from river. At the National Trust sign, stay right and ascend until you meet the Wales Coast Path – join this and keep climbing. At a junction, turn left along a broad track, following coast path arrows. At the top, pass left of some houses, and go through a metal gate.

9. Walk through a field, passing the sombre site of Graves End (see Follow in the footsteps of...). Go through a gate, descend and turn right, rounding Pwlldu Head. Climb past the site of an Iron Age fort and follow the coast path across cliffs around Deep Slade. At the road, bear left and walk along the grassy path running parallel to the tarmac, around High Tor, and back to the car park.

60 The Kymin

The Boat Inn

The Boat Inn
Lone Lane, Penallt
Monmouthshire NP25 4AJ
01600 712615
www.theboatpenallt.co.uk

About this walk

- Roundhouse with amazing views
- River walking
- Offa's Dyke Path
- Wye Valley Way

Start/finish Monmouth town centre
Distance 7 miles (11.3km)
Time to pub 2 hours
Walking time 3 hours
Terrain Streets, hillside paths and riverbank trails

Perched on the banks of the River Wye, on the Wales–England border, **THE BOAT INN** is a wonderful watering hole. Built from local stone in 1650, there are two bars, both boasting woodburners and full of character. But this pub really shines on sun-drenched days, when locals, hikers, bikers, canoeists and kayakers spill out onto the riverside patio and terraced garden that climbs the hill and features a grotto and a rockface waterfall. Excellent food is served, along with local ciders and ales. Opening hours change in winter – check ahead. Limited accommodation available.

WALES

From Monmouth, climb to an eccentric roundhouse and Naval Temple with sensational views, before strolling a section of Offa's Dyke Path, along the Wales–England border, to a unique riverside pub, and returning along the River Wye.

Spring Daffodils and wildflowers bloom around the Kymin. Sand martins arrive from Africa and nest along the River Wye, and great spotted woodpeckers begin drumming in the woods.

Summer Spy dippers and kingfishers along the Wye. If you're out in the early evening, look out for cavorting badger cubs, plus pipistrelle and soprano bats, and tawny owls.

Autumn Spot buzzards and peregrine falcons soaring over the Kymin. Beech, oak and sycamore trees blush, and bright red rowan berries attract thrushes and redwings.

Winter Along the river, look out for grey herons, mute swans, cormorants and goosanders. It's mating season for the Wye Valley's wild boars – a native species reintroduced to the Forest of Dean – which occasionally visit the Kymin.

A large, rotating range of real ales and ciders are served from the cask at the Boat Inn, including Wye Valley Butty Bach and Kingstone Gold.

Follow in the footsteps of ...
The Round House was built in the 1790s, by a group of wealthy Monmouth gentlemen who'd taken to picnicking on the Kymin each Tuesday and wanted a shelter. The Kymin Club erected the Naval Temple in 1800, commemorating the second anniversary of the Battle of the Nile. It lists 16 of the Royal Navy's most notable admirals, including Nelson, who toured the site in 1802 with his mistress, Lady Hamilton, and her husband.

How to Get There

By Car Drive to Monmouth and park in Glendower Street Car Park (not National Trust).

By Public Transport The closest train stations are Chepstow (16.5 miles/ 26.5km) and Abergavenny (17 miles/ 27.5km). Buses run from both to Monmouth.

OS Map OS Explorer OL14 (Wye Valley & Forest of Dean), Landranger 162 (Gloucester & Forest of Dean); grid ref (for start): SO 509/128.

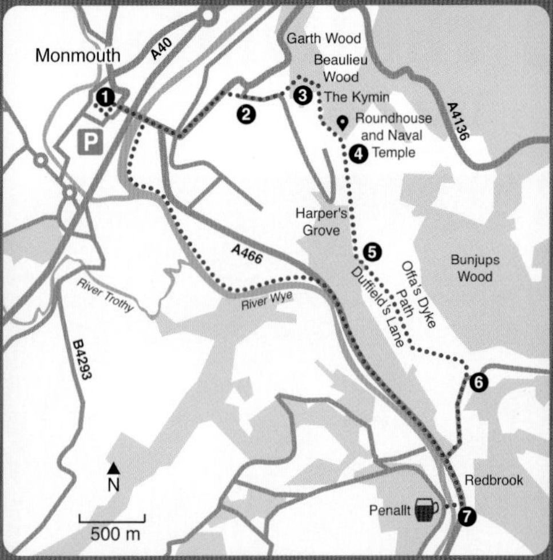

1. From the car park, turn left and walk along Almshouse Street. Opposite The Queens Head, turn right down Wyebridge Street. Cross the road via an underpass, where you'll see Offa's Dyke Path signage, confirming you're joining the 177-mile (285-km) trail along the border between Wales and England. While crossing Wye Bridge, look up to see the Round House high on the hill ahead. Continue straight, passing playing fields and the Mayfield Hotel. As the road arcs left, use the right-hand pavement, which soon peels away from the road.

2. The path climbs past an orchard and vineyard, then joins a section of the Kymin Road. When the road bends right, continue straight up the path, ascending through Garth Wood.

3. After a stiff climb, go through a gate, following waymarkers for Offa's Dyke Path and the Wye Valley Walk (a 136-mile/219-km riverside trail). Go through another gate and along a narrow path. Emerge on a lane, turn left and walk uphill, following fingerposts into Beaulieu Woods. The path climbs straight up then doglegs along a deep holloway, flanked by strange beech-topped boulders, including one bearing a National Trust Kymin sign. Explore the summit, Round House and Naval Temple, and enjoy spectacular Wye Valley views, across the borderlands of Wales and England, and west to the Black Mountains and Brecon Beacons.

4. Walk left of the Naval Temple and descend along a broad track. Bear right on a narrow path, cross the car park and go through a kissing gate. Descend along Offa's Dyke Path, with Harper's Grove woods on your right.

5. Go through a kissing gate, walk down the right edge of a field, through a wooden gate and along a narrow path. Follow arrows through several more gates and fields, until directed out past a farmhouse, and along Duffield's Lane.

6. Follow the lane around a 90-degree right turn (ignore a path continuing straight). Meet and walk down a road, and just before a bridge, follow an Offa's Dyke fingerpost pointing left. Continue to the main road, turn left and walk into Redbrook village (in England). Cross the road by the village store and turn right into a public park, following footpath arrows. Bear right, through a car park and, after 150 yards, take the path leading left towards the river. Cross a footbridge next to an old railway bridge to arrive back in Wales, by The Boat Inn.

7. Leaving the pub, cross back over the bridge and turn left along the path you were walking along previously. Almost immediately, the Wye Valley Walk drops to the left; take this all the way back to Monmouth. It briefly skirts the main road, with a very small pavement, so caution is required, but mainly it's a grassy riverside trail, passing woodlands and a stunning old railway bridge.

61 Clytha Estate

The Clytha Arms

The Clytha Arms
Groesonen Road, Clytha
Monmouthshire NP7 9BW
01873 840206
www.clytha-arms.com

About this walk

- Usk Valley Walk
- Iron Age hill fort
- Great views
- Wildflowers

Start/finish Clytha riverside car park (National Trust)
Distance 8 miles (13km)
Time to pub 2–2.5 hours
Walking time 3–3.5 hours
Terrain Country and riverside footpaths, tracks, lanes and some road

A multi-award-winning pub offering restaurant-quality meals, **THE CLYTHA ARMS** welcomes walkers with a double-sided sign: one face featuring a lion, the other a swan – the latter a nod to the original name of an older pub that fell into the river. The current building opened as a pub in the 1990s. It boasts a bar with a huge fireplace and traditional games, plus a lounge and dining room with wall-mounted Welsh poems. Pétanque can be played in the enormous garden, which hosts seasonal food-and-drink festivals. Boutique accommodation is available. Camping can be arranged.

Amble through the Usk Valley, through Clytha Park and along the riverbank to Bettws Newydd, before exploring Coed y Bwnydd, Monmouthshire's best preserved Iron Age hillfort. Continue past Clytha Castle, a classic castellated folly, to an award-winning pub with a picturesque garden.

Spring Bluebells, primroses, orchids and red campion carpet the ground around Coed y Bwnydd. Look out for otters, dippers, sand martins and kingfishers along the river.

Summer Along the banks of the Usk, wildflowers grow, while goosanders, mallard and swans shepherd their young. In the Clytha Arms' garden, walkers sample Welsh cider, local ales and great food.

Autumn Squirrels collect nuts amid yellow, red and gold leaves in the woods around Clytha Estate, where around 100 veteran trees stand among younger beech, sweet chestnut and oaks.

Winter From Clytha Castle, views of the Black Mountains – including Sugar Loaf and the Skirrid – can be seen through leafless trees. At The Clytha Arms, a festival of winter ales and dumplings happens in January.

A free house, The Clytha Arms supports and celebrates local and regional real ales and ciders. Regular beers include Whoosh pale ale and UPA from Monmouthshire's Untapped Brewing Company.

Follow in the footsteps of ... The Iron Age hillfort of Coed y Bwnydd has a history of human occupation going back over two millennia. A much more modern edifice is Clytha Castle, an 18th-century folly, known as 'the Taj Mahal of Wales', built by estate-owner William Jones and dedicated to his late wife.

How to Get There

By Car Take the A40 to Raglan and follow signs. Park at Clytha riverside car park (NP7 9BW; National Trust).

By Public Transport The nearest train station is Abergavenny (5 miles/8km). Bus 83 between Abergavenny and Monmouth stops at The Clytha Arms.

OS Map OS Explorer OL13 (Brecon Beacons National Park – Eastern Area), Landranger 161 (The Black Mountains); grid ref (for start): SO 361/085.

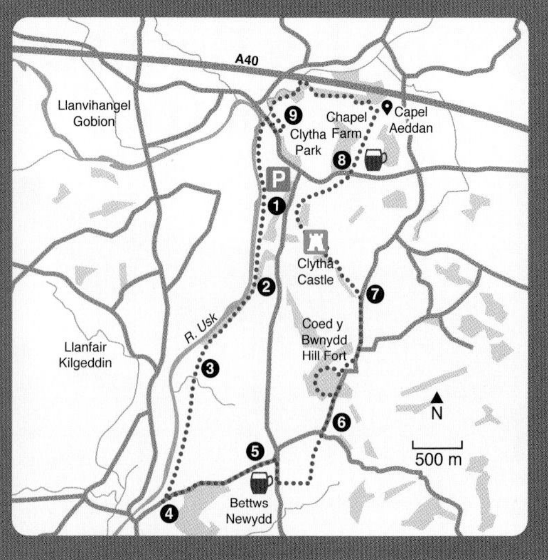

1. From the car park, walk past a map and information sign, along a path. Turn left through a kissing gate and stroll a section of the Usk Valley Walk. The river is hidden initially, but after passing a wooden bridge, it appears on your right.

2. Continue across a meadow, over a second wooden bridge. The route rises away from the river, crosses several stiles and skirts a field. Follow footpath signs across a track to meander through meadows and trees.

3. Go through a gate and cross the top of the meadow. Continue through a gate to walk along the bottom of a hill, beside a fence. Follow the footpath around the fringe of Caltan Coppice – mixed woodlands of beech, ash, oak and sycamore.

4. A gate and path lead through trees to steps. Turn left on the road and walk uphill to Bettws Newydd, passing Priory Wood on your right.

5. Turn right at the crossroads, passing The Black Bear (a 17th-century inn/restaurant) and continue up the road. Turn left, following a fingerpost along a lane into a churchyard. Pass a gnarled old yew, ignore a stile on the right and walk through the graveyard to another stile in the far corner. Cross and follow a footpath arrow along a field top. Turn left through a gate and walk uphill with a hedge on your right. At the top corner, cross a stile, turn right and walk through fields to a road.

6. Cross and walk up the road opposite, to explore Coed y Bwnydd pre-historic hill fort. A stile on the fort's north-east edge leads to a permissive path across a field, passing a barn and rejoining the road. Go left, ignoring an incoming lane and the first two footpaths leading left.

7. Turn left through a wooden gate, following a fingerpost. Climb two stiles, walk diagonally across a field with woods on your left, to another stile. Follow a signed permissive path, circling Clytha Castle. At a fingerpost pointing left, descend a steep bank. At the bottom, turn right along a path, following signs to steps that descend and abruptly meet the busy road (be very cautious here). Carefully cross to The Clytha Arms.

8. Leave the pub, turn right on a footpath, hop over a stile and go diagonally across a field. Cross a stile and follow blue arrows to an ancient oak tree in the field corner; left is medieval Chapel Farm, and right are the remains of 12th-century Capel Aeddan. Keep following arrows, across a track and left along a footpath, walking through trees almost as far as the cacophonous A40.

9. A path leads away from the din, through Twyn y Cregan woods. Emerge from the trees and follow arrows around a field with good castle views. At the road, cross and dogleg right then left. Follow a footpath to the river, turn left and stroll along the bank back to the car park.

62 Ysgyryd Fawr
The Skirrid Inn

The Skirrid Inn
Hereford Road
Llanfihangel-Crucorney
Monmouthshire NP7 8DH
01873 890258
www.skirridmountain inn.co.uk

About this walk
- Mountain peak
- Beacons Way
- Stunning views
- Steep climb

Start/finish Skirrid car park (National Trust)
Distance 8 miles (13km)
Time to pub 2 hours
Walking time 4 hours
Terrain Mountain and countryside paths, lanes, small amount of road

Reputedly Wales's oldest and most haunted pub, THE SKIRRID INN's history stretches to 1110, but the stone building is mostly 17th century. Formerly a courthouse and place of execution, 182 people were hanged in the stairwell, where marks are visible on a beam and a noose dangles as a macabre reminder. There's a great garden and the flagstone-floored interior has a huge fireplace, above which you'll see the Pwcca Cup, a tankard the landlord nightly fills with ale and places by the door to appease the devil. Food is offered and accommodation is available (if you dare).

Explore the split summit of one of South Wales' most recognisable and storied mountains, Ysgyryd Fawr, located on the eastern edge of the Black Mountains and Brecon Beacons, and topped by the remains of a medieval church and Iron Age hill fort. Descend through farm fields to a historic pub, haunted by hikers and restless spectres. Stroll back through woodlands and the gap in 'the hill that shivered'.

Spring In Caer and Pant Skirrid woods, bluebells bloom, along with wild garlic, red campion, yellow archangel and bugles. Listen for cuckoos and woodpeckers.

Summer Wildflowers fill farm fields and meadows along the Beacons Way, their blooms attracting bees and butterflies, including peacock, brimstone and white-letter hairstreak.

Autumn In woodlands, ash, hawthorn, hornbeam, beech and maple transform colour, while on the mountain, fronds of ferns burn gold and orange. Buzzards, kestrels and peregrine falcons hover and hunt.

Winter Summit views are breathtaking on crisp, cold days. Dark evenings lend themselves perfectly to ghost stories around The Skirrid Inn's fire.

The Skirrid Inn serves Wye Valley Brewery ales, including the popular Butty Batch, beside other beers including Doom Bar, plus ciders, lagers and wine. Fittingly, Wales's most haunted pub also sells an excellent range of spirits.

Follow in the footsteps of ... 'Ysgyryd' (Anglicised to Skirrid) means 'shivered' or 'shattered'. Also known as the Holy Mountain or Sacred Hill, local legend says the mountain split when Jesus was crucified. Another tale claims the rift was caused during a contest between a local giant (or wizard), Jack O'Kent, and the devil.

How to Get There

By Car Park at the Skirrid car park (NP7 8AP; National Trust) near the Copper Kettle Tea Room, found on the B4521, just off the A465 near Abergavenny.

By Public Transport The nearest train station is Abergavenny (3 miles/5km). Buses including Stagecoach X3 travel between Abergavenny and The Skirrid Inn.

OS Map OS Explorer OL13 (Brecon Beacons National Park – Eastern Area), Landranger 161 (The Black Mountains); grid ref (for start): SO 328/164.

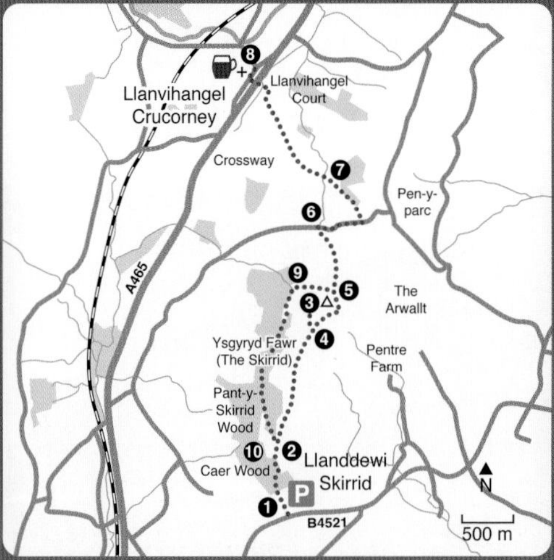

1. Leave the car park along the path, going to the left of a National Trust map and information sign. Follow the obvious trail, passing through a gate, and when the path forks, stay right. A track intersects your route, but continue on the main footpath, and repeat this when a second track crosses.

2. Ascend through the ash, maple, hawthorn and beech trees of Caer Wood, and climb some broad steps. Go past a bench, through a gate and then, at a junction, turn right and then left along the Beacons Way (a 99-mile/160-km linear trail through Brecon Beacons National Park). Keep ascending up a well-made stone path, which narrows and snakes right then left to bring you out onto open hillside with panoramic views – the distinctive peak of nearby Sugar Loaf is especially prominent in the west (to your left). Walk along the rocky ridgeline and look for a rock formation known as the Devil's Table on the left.

3. Head to the trig point on the 1,594ft (486m) summit of Ysgyryd Fawr, where you can see the remains of St Michael's Church – a medieval Roman Catholic chapel used during the 17th century as a secret place to hold mass during a period of religious persecution. Evidence of an Iron Age hill fort has also been found close to the summit. The 360-degree views from here are stunning, soaring over Sugar Loaf and across the Black Mountains and Brecon Beacons to the west; stretching to Herefordshire and the Malvern Hills to the north; gazing across Ysgyryd Fach ('Little Skirrid') through the Usk Valley into Somerset looking south; and taking in Gloucestershire and the Forest of Dean to the east.

4. After drinking all this in, turn around and walk back about 200 yards to a series of bumps and depressions and a cluster of rocks in a slight dip. Look for a path leading sharp left and follow this to descend below the peak you've just been standing on. Ignore a path coming in from the right and keep going straight. When the path forks, go right.

5. Descend to the fenceline, turn left and walk to a gate in the corner of the field. Go through and follow the Beacons Way indicator arrow down through a field, keeping the hedge on your left, to reach a stile in the bottom left corner of the field. Cross and walk through next field, again keeping the hedge on your left. Cross another stile in the left corner of the field and follow Beacons Way arrows across the corner of the field, over another stile by a farm. Trace arrows and an obvious path downhill, around to the left and out onto a lane.

6. Turn right along the lane and walk through Pant-y-tyle until you see an obvious footpath sign, Beacons Way arrow and a fingerpost pointing left towards Crucorney. Descend through a field, following arrows and passing through a gate.

7. Keep following Beacons Way and footpath arrows through a gate. Walk through a little wooded area, go over a bridge, through another gate and straight across a field, ascending and bearing left slightly to a gate on the other side. Keep going through another four gates. Bear to the right of some barns, pass through a gate and then go left along a sycamore-shaded path, following a Beacons Way arrow. The path turns into a lane and takes you past Llanvihangel Court – a Tudor-era country house with an amazing barn and peacocks – out to the road.

8. Carefully cross the road and walk straight ahead to the church at Crucorney. Turn right along the road, and The Skirrid Inn is just down on the left. After leaving the pub, retrace your footsteps along the Beacons Way, enjoying excellent views of the split in the mountain caused by Ice Age landslips.

9. When you go through the gate at the foot of the mountain, turn right and start to walk around its base. Pass a marker post indicating a very steep route to the summit of Ysgyryd Fawr on your left, but ignore that and keep going along a path, with the smaller peak of the split mountain on your right. Scattered, shattered boulders and the remains of a violent rockfall cover the ground. Keep following the lovely path through mixed woods of oak, beech, ash, holly and hawthorn. For a while, a moss-covered stone wall runs to your right. Just after leaving this wall behind, stroll along a boardwalk to a gate. Turn right here and walk back to the car park.

Below: The distinctive split summit of Ysgyryd Fawr, or 'The Skirrid', is the last peak in the Black Mountains.

63 Sugar Loaf

The Dragons Head

The Dragons Head
Llangenny
Powys NP8 1HD
01873 810350
https://en-gb.facebook.com/thedragonshead/

About this walk

- High peak
- Riverside walking
- Wild horses
- Birdlife

Start/finish Llanwenarth car park (National Trust)
Distance 10 miles (16km)
Time to pub 3 hours
Walking time 4.5 hours
Terrain Mountain trails, riverside footpaths, lanes, some road

A friendly, family owned, traditional pub on the banks of Grwyne Fawr, beneath Sugar Loaf (pictured above), **THE DRAGONS HEAD** has been run by the same couple for 30 years. An oft-overgrown entrance gives the place a hidden feel, as if you've stumbled across a secret oasis, and from the back garden you can hear the river. The interior is split into several rooms, with the welcoming main bar featuring comfy sofas and a woodburner. There's a dining area and side room, dominated by memorabilia relating to racehorses and Brecon army regiments. Lovely home-cooked food is served.

Hike to the conical peak of a hill that's just a few feet shy of being a mountain, to enjoy sensational views across the Brecon Beacons and Black Mountains, before descending to wander beside the water of Grwyne Fawr to a lovely, unspoilt pub.

Spring Lambs gambol, house martins and swallows swoop, skylarks sing as they soar above Mynydd Llanwenarth ridge, meadow pipits chatter in bracken and dippers bob on rocks along Grwyne Fawr.

Summer Red grouse stalk through flowering heather, wheatears hop along trails and cuckoos call. Bilberries ('whinberries' as they're locally known), fruit on the upland slopes. Encounter groups of wild horses, often with foals.

Autumn Look up to spot buzzards and occasional red kites circling overhead. Oak woodlands in the valleys below begin to blush, and across the flanks of the hill's three ridges – Llanwenarth, Rholben and Deri – ferns turn bronze.

Winter It might not be an official mountain, but the summit of Sugar Loaf is exposed, and the ascent can be tricky in icy weather. If you're experienced, properly equipped and confident in such conditions, the snow-dusted peak is picturesque.

The Dragons Head has a couple of handpumps and serves Welsh-brewed real ales on rotation, including Rhymney Hobby Horse and Double Dragon from Felinfoel.

Follow in the footsteps of ... The gardening writer and author Anna Pavord grew up in the shadow of the Sugar Loaf, and the peak played a formative role in her thought processes when she wrote *Landskipping*, a genre-defying book about our deep relationship with the landscapes we live within.

How to Get There

By Car Drive the A40 between Abergavenny and Crickhowell and take the turn-off leading up to the vineyard and Llanwenarth car park (National Trust).

By public transport There's a train station in Abergavenny (3 miles/5km).

OS Map OS Explorer OL13 (Brecon Beacons National Park – Eastern Area), Landranger 161 (The Black Mountains); grid ref (for start): SO 268/167.

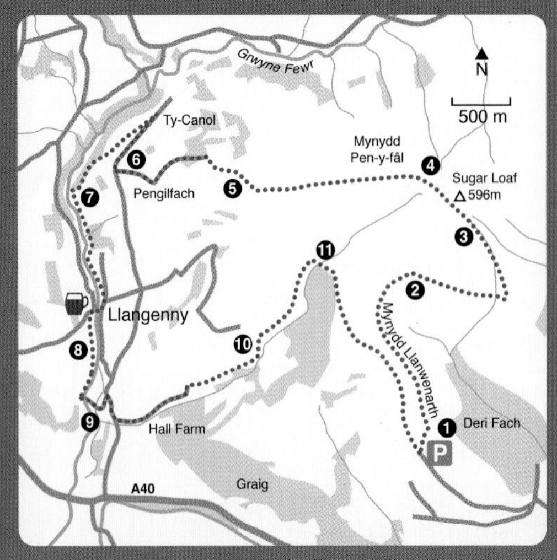

1. Leave the car park on the path passing left of the National Trust information sign. Follow the main, very obvious track along the ridge of Mynydd Llanwenarth, which arcs right, towards the distinctive conical peak of Sugar Loaf, with St Mary's Vale plunging on your right, into the greenery of Deri Fach (Welsh for 'small oak woodland'). Keep following the wide track, maintaining your height, and when you meet a distinct fork, bear right along a trail that undulates slightly, but doesn't drop.

2. Walk with the peak on your left. At a crosspaths, directly in front of the summit, avoid the temptation of taking a route 1 approach to the top and continue straight, walking along a flat path and tracing a contour line, until you cross a stream. About 200 yards further on, you meet a distinct crosspaths; turn left here and the route to the top is revealed. Start climbing, and when the path forks, stay left. Cross back over the little stream you encountered below, and soldier on towards the summit – it's a steep ascent, and rough in places, but the views are worth all the effort.

3. Standing 1,955ft (596m), Sugar Loaf (Y Fâl) is just 45ft (14m) under the height requirement to be considered a true mountain (according to the British definition), but its volcano-like profile and rugged summit approach make the ascent feel like a proper peak-bagging experience. From the top, take in panoramic views: to the north, the Black Mountains rise, while the Brecon Beacons roll away to the west – Sugar Loaf sits right in the sweet spot between these two ranges. Comparatively close by, to the east, you can clearly see the enigmatic Skirrid (Ysgyryd Fawr), and due south, across the Bristol Channel, lie the counties of south-west England.

4. Walk past the trig point, along the rocky ridge, then scramble down rocks (or take the path running to the left of them), and descend along the broad, grassy track leading west. The peak of Pen Cerrig-calch is visible straight ahead, on the other side of Grwyne Fawr valley.

5. When the path forks, stay right and keep descending. At a crosspaths, go straight over and continue down to the woods, where you'll find a metal gate. Go through and follow the path as it bears right and then curls around to pass through another gate, onto a track that leads to a lane at Pengilfach. Turn right and walk to a T-junction.

6. Turn right and walk along the road to Ty-Canol Farm, where a fingerpost points you left. Go through the yard, over a stile in the corner and follow the path as it wends left and hops over a stile. When the path forks, stay right, cross a stile and follow the path as it traces a fence on your right. Emerge into a meadow, turn right and descend steeply to a stile and bridge (don't cross).

The slopes of Sugar Loaf are an excellent place to spot wild Welsh horses.

7. Turn left and walk along the edge of a meadow, with the water of Grwyne Fawr on your right. Go through a gate, continue over a couple of stiles and along a gravel path. Keep going, past a private footbridge, to a steep stone step stile over a wall. Climb this, turn right, cross the bridge and you're at The Dragons Head.

8. Leave the pub via the beer garden and look for a footpath arrow. Cross a stile and follow the path along Grwyne Fawr, running on your left. Wander through a campsite and past a weir. Go over a stile and through woods, walking beneath magnificent beech and chestnut trees, along the riverbank.

9. Go over a stile by an enormous sweet chestnut tree and cross a stone bridge. Walk up the lane to a T-junction then turn right. Take the next left and stroll up the lane towards Hall Farm. At end of the lane, bear right, following a fingerpost through a gate and walk past a cottage. Keep going along the lane, through a wide gate, with Sugar Loaf dominating the skyline. The track veers to the right of another field, towards a ravine with a river flowing below. A bridleway fingerpost points to a left fork, and a sign saying 'way to the hill' confirms your direction.

10. Go over a stile, walk up through the field to a fence, then follow a bridleway fingerpost pointing right and walk straight towards Sugar Loaf, with the fence on your right. Enjoy lovely views, as the valley plunges to the right and the peak rises straight ahead. Go through a gate and keep hiking uphill.

11. The track wends right and dips through a creek bed. Walk up the other side and take the main path with a stone wall on your immediate right. Ramble with Sugar Loaf now on your left, and when the path forks, stay right. When the stone wall falls away to the right, carry straight on along the main path to reach the car park.

64 Pen y Fan
The Tai'r Bull Inn

The Tai'r Bull Inn
Libanus
Powys LD3 8EL
01874 622600
www.thetairbullinn.co.uk

About this walk

- Brecon Beacons National Park
- Taff Trail
- Summit views

Start/finish Cwm Gwdi car park (National Trust)
Distance 9½ miles (15km)
Time to pub 3–3.5 hours
Walking time 4–5 hours
Terrain Steep footpaths, open mountainside, lanes and some roads

WALES

A classic country pub with stunning views of Pen y Fan peak (pictured above), THE TAI'R BULL INN was revitalised and reopened in 2021. Landlady Katie warmly welcomes walkers to a refurbished bar, which retains its traditional look and links to a rich rural history, with wooden beams, low lighting and a pair of enormous bull horns in pride of place over the big open fireplace. Good food is served, alongside Welsh real ales, and bed and breakfast accommodation is available.

Summit southern Britain's two highest peaks – picturesque Pen y Fan and adjacent Corn Du – and enjoy extraordinary views, before descending past a mountain lake and walking along rushing rivers to a classic country inn. Return via a section of the Taff Trail.

Spring Prickly gorse bushes bloom bright yellow and perfume Pen y Fan's paths with a coconut-like aroma. Newborn lambs play in the fields.

Summer Llyn Cwm Llwch reflects the blue of the sky and foxgloves fill the valleys, nodding in the breeze. Spy wheatear, whinchat and ring ouzel in among the gorse.

Autumn Bronze bracken adorns the flanks of Allt Ddu, Cribyn, Pen y Fan and Corn Du. Overhead, look out for circling peregrine falcons, merlins, red kites, sparrowhawks and buzzards.

Winter Snow dusts the summits of the Brecon Beacons and views are crystal clear on sunny days, but this is a challenging and potentially hazardous walk when paths are icy and obscured, and daylight hours are short. Be prepared.

The Tai'r Bull Inn offers a couple of real ales, including the ever-popular Butty Bach (Welsh for 'little friend') from Wye Valley Brewery.

Follow in the footsteps of … According to legend, there's an invisible island on Llyn Cwm Llwch (the floating lake on the flanks of Pen y Fan and Corn Du). Each May Day, a passageway to the island would appear, allowing people to pass along it and discover an enchanted isle inhabited by songbirds and fairies, who would present them with fruit and flowers. It was forbidden to remove anything, however, and when a visitor smuggled a flower off the island, the passageway disappeared forever.

How to Get There

By Car Approach from the west end of Brecon, along Newgate Street. Park at Cwm Gwdi (National Trust).

By Public Transport The X43 bus between Cardiff and Abergavenny passes through Brecon. The nearest train station is Merthyr Tydfil (20 miles/32km).

OS Map Explorer OL12 (Brecon Beacons National Park – Western Area), Landranger 160 (Brecon Beacons); grid ref (for start): SO 025/249.

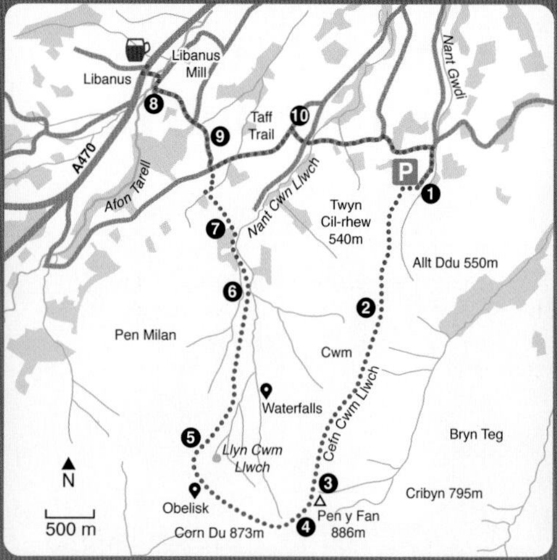

1. From the car park, walk uphill, past the information sign, and continue along a sealed lane, through a gate. Take the path running alongside the gravel track, formerly used by quarry ponies, before bearing left and walking up to a stile. Follow a National Trust arrow and continue up the slope, picking up the rocky path that wends to the left of the large, heather-cloaked hill ahead. To your left soar the flanks of Allt Ddu, once used for target practice by the army, and on the right is Twyn Cil-rhew.

2. The path climbs steadily until you reach Cefn Cwm Llwch. Walk along this ridge, with the prominent peak of Cribyn on your left and views through the valley on your right, down into Libanus, where the pub awaits.

3. A final scramble takes you up to Pen y Fan's summit plateau, crowned with a National Trust plaque and trig point, from where panoramic views unfold in each direction. To the east lie the Black Mountains, while looking south you can gaze across the Severn Estuary into south-west England. Turn west to skim over the Gower to Pembrokeshire, and look north to spy the Cambrian Mountains.

4. Descend the other side, bear slightly right and climb the stone path beside a wooden fence to the top of Corn Du (2,864ft/873m). From the broad stone cairn, descend to the right, following a clear stone path with a steep drop-off to the right. When the main track goes left, continue straight, walking along the ridgeline with Llyn Cwm Llwch down to your right. Pass the obelisk, which bears a memorial to a young boy, Tommy Jones, who tragically perished here in 1900.

5. Keep descending along the obvious path, passing a collapsed cairn by a track leading right to Llyn Cwm Llwch. This glacial lake is well worth exploring on sunny days (it's popular with wild swimmers), but our route continues straight.

6. Pass a National Trust sign for Cwm Llwch and climb over a stile. Glance back to see waterfalls tumbling down the flanks of Pen y Fan, then follow the path through an avenue of downy birch. Go left over a stile by a cottage, turn right and cross a second stile, then walk over grassy grazing land with water running audibly on your left. Join a track coming in from your right, alongside Cwm Llwch, and cross a footbridge at the confluence of the rivers. Keep going along the stony lane, with the river rushing on your right.

7. When the track forks, go left, walking away from the river. Keep bearing left, crossing a meadow, a stile and another two fields. Pass a farmhouse, cross a stile and go downhill, following footpath arrows through more fields and over several stiles until you cross a stream and emerge on a grassy lane by a farm, where another path comes in from the left.

Turn right and walk along the lane. At the road, turn right then immediate left. Walk along the tarmac, past a right turn, to a T-junction.

8. Go right, then left at Libanus Mill, crossing the bridge over Afon Tarell. Walk around the bend, then look for a footpath fingerpost pointing right. Hop over the stile and walk diagonally across the field to emerge opposite The Tai'r Bull Inn.

9. After leaving the pub, reverse the last part of the route. Turn left at the T-junction with a fingerpost for Taff Trail (a 55-mile/89-km hiking and biking route between Cardiff Bay and Brecon). Walk along the quiet road, continuing past a fingerpost where the Taff Trail departs left.

10. At a crossroads, follow the road around to the right. Continue for about a mile – going straight through another crossroads, over a bridge and past a turning left – until you meet a T-junction. Turn right, cross a cattlegrid and walk up the lane to the car park.

Below: The Tai'r Bull Inn offers great views of Pen y Fan's peak from the front garden.

Bottom: Looking back along the approach route, while ascending to the summit of Pen y Fan.

65 Talley
The Cwmdu Inn

The community-run CWMDU INN shares a National Trust-owned building with a post office and traditional grocery shop. The friendly pub has a cosy front bar, full of photos and dedications to much-loved locals, and a side room with an enormous fireplace, dartboard and pub games, where social events (including music sessions) happen. A stream runs past, with steps to a plunge pool historically used for baptisms. The beer garden opposite features a long-drop toilet so ancient it's a listed building. Open Wednesday–Saturday; food is served on Saturday evenings (check ahead).

The Cwmdu Inn
Cwmdu, Carmarthenshire
SA19 7DY
01558 685156
www.cwmdu.org

About this walk
- Valley views
- Wildflowers
- Woodlands
- Ancient abbey

Start/finish Cwmdu Inn
Distance 6 miles (10km)
Time to pub The pub is at the start/finish of the walk
Walking time Allow 2.5 hours
Terrain Countryside footpaths, hillsides, lanes and quiet roads

From a truly unique pub, climb the side of 1,079ft (329m) Mynydd Cynros, passing through woodlands and high open ground with views across Carmarthenshire, before descending to the lakeside valley village of Talley, and a 12th-century abbey.

Spring Lambs cavort in fields and flowering gorse illuminates the hills with a golden hue. Look for red kites soaring above meadows, woods and Talley Abbey.

Summer Woodlands and hillside meadows above Talley are resplendent with wildflowers, including elegant foxgloves. Great crested grebes and mute swans look after chicks on the Talley Lakes.

Autumn Bracken-covered hillsides turn biscuit brown, and the Talley Woodlands arboretum, where deciduous oak and ash grow alongside evergreen pine and spruce trees, revolves through a kaleidoscope of colours.

Winter Vistas from the viewpoint on Mynydd Cynros are spectacular on crisp winter days. Pochard, goldeneye, goosander and tufted ducks are winter visitors to Talley Lakes.

The Cwmdu Inn's ales, gravity-poured from the barrel, include Cwrw (the Welsh word for beer, pronounced 'ku ru') from Llandeilo-based Evan Evans Brewery. Drinks are sold at refreshing not-for-profit prices.

Follow in the footsteps of ... Talley Abbey was founded in the 1180s by Rhys ap Gruffydd, 'The Lord Rhys', medieval ruler of the South Wales kingdom of Deheubarth. It was home to a religious order of Premonstratensians, called the White Canons (because of their habits), until it was dissolved and destroyed by Henry VIII.

How to Get There

By Car There is a car park at the pub (SA19 7DY; not National Trust), off the B4302, between Llandeilo and Talley. (Note: there's another Cwmdu, near Crickhowell – don't go there by mistake.)

By Public Transport There is a train station at Llandeilo (6 miles/10km), from where occasional buses serve Talley.

OS Map OS Explorer 186 (Llandeilo & Brechfa Forest); Landranger 146 (Lampeter & Llandovery); grid ref (for start): SN 636/302.

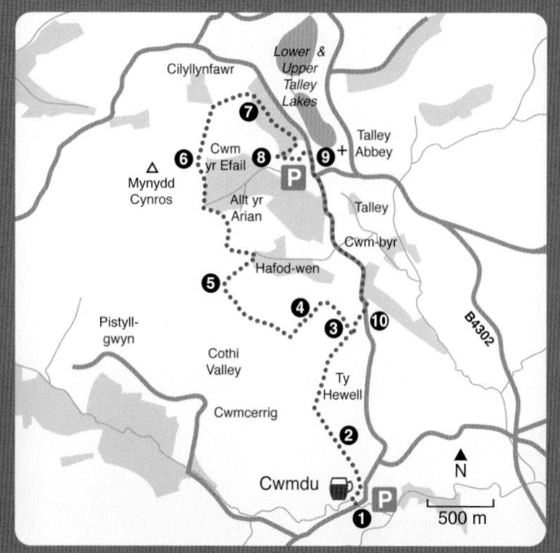

1. Walk past the pub and chapel, and turn right up a footpath, which snakes around a cottage and through a farm. Follow the footpath left up a field, with trees to your right. Go through three gates, cross a stream and through another gate to a lane.

2. Go left, walk uphill for 100 yards, turn right through a gate and left through a second gate. Keep the hedge on your left, then walk diagonally to a gate in the top right corner. Bear right, along an unsealed lane to a footpath through trees. Emerge through a gate at Penybrn farm, turn right and follow the lane past Ty Hewell.

3. At the junction, turn left and walk past Penrhiwgeingen farmhouse. Pass through a gate and continue up the lane, looking over Carmarthenshire's hills.

4. Go through a gate, down a dip, turn left via a gate and follow footpath arrows along the bottom of two fields, with a hedge on your left. At the end of the second, bear right, remaining in the same field, ascending with a fence on your left. Go through a gate and continue, enjoying Cothi Valley views.

5. At a T-junction, go right and walk to a crosspaths by Allt Hafod-wen woods. Go left and walk uphill, following the path as it arcs right and meets another woodland, Allt yr Arian, with the rising slope of Mynydd Cynros to your left. Follow the path around the top edge of the woods.

6. You can't reach the trig point atop Mynydd Cynros from here, but continue to a lookout offering cross-valley views towards the Brecon Beacons and Black Mountains. Descend along a track with red and blue waymarkers through the Talley Woodlands, where trails are managed by Natural Resources Wales.

7. Keep following blue waymarkers (for the Cwm yr Efail walk), as the track descends, circles around and follows a contour line, with the trees of Allt y Plas permitting occasional lake and village views.

8. Ignore the yellow waymarked Big Trees Walk leading right to the arboretum. At a confluence of tracks, bear left and descend to Talley.

9. Walk through Talley Woodlands car park, turn right along the road, passing St Michael and All Saints Church, and take in the Talley Abbey ruins. Follow the road around, and when it forks, go right. Walk up this quiet road for about a mile, passing houses in Cwm-byr.

10. Just after an S-bend, climb over a stile on the right. Ignore a second stile on your immediate right and walk up through the field, keeping the fence on your right, following footpath arrows to the junction by Penrhiwgeingen. Reverse your earlier route, passing Ty Hewell and Penybrn, and descending through fields to the pub.

66 St Davids Peninsula
The Farmers Arms

The Farmers Arms
14–16 Goat Street, St Davids
Pembrokeshire SA62 6RF
01437 721666
www.farmersstdavids.co.uk

About this walk
- Pembrokeshire Coast National Park
- Wales Coast Path
- Seals and birdlife

Start/finish Porth Clais Harbour (National Trust)
Distance 10½ miles (17km)
Time to pub 3–3.5 hours
Walking time 4 hours
Terrain Coastal trails, countryside paths, lanes

Popular with walkers, **THE FARMERS ARMS** is a stone-built pub in the heart of St Davids. Food is usually served in the Top Bar, while the Glue Pot Bar is where drinkers mingle around the open fire. There's also a little games room. A sunny patio with an alfresco bar and views of the cathedral is a lovely spot to sit and sip cold drinks in summer. Serving hours alter in winter, and the pub typically shuts Sunday evenings and Mondays – check the website.

Spot seals and explore bays, beaches and cliff tops while strolling along a sensational section of the Wales and Pembrokeshire Coast Path around Treginnis Peninsula, before heading inland to view a stunning cathedral and visit a traditional pub in the heart of Britain's smallest city.

Spring Cowslips bloom along the coast path, and from May the pink flowers of thrift (sea pink) decorate stone walls and hedgebanks. Wheatears arrive, butterflies begin gathering nectar and lizards sun themselves on rocks.

Summer Wander wildflower-strewn cliffs, looking for sunbathing seals and listening to linnets twittering in the gorse bushes. Cool off with a swim in the Irish Sea and enjoy a cold drink on the pub patio.

Autumn Sit amongst the golden gorse and purple heather on the coast, watching gannets plunging into the sea to catch fish for their chicks, and red-legged choughs performing aerobatics.

Winter Peregrines and ravens soar over cliffs, while kestrels hover and hunt above farm fields and waves whip the coast.

The Farmers Arms sells Welsh ales such as Felinfoel's Double Dragon, Whitesands Pale Ale from St Davids Beer Company, and Warrior from Evan Evans Brewery.

Follow in the footsteps of ... Wales' patron saint, St David, was born in 500 AD in an area now named after his mother (who was canonised as St Non). Baptised in Porth Clais (pictured above), the walk's start/finish point, David founded a monastery where the 12th-century cathedral dedicated to him now stands, and his remains are buried there.

How to Get There

By Car The A487 is the main access road to St Davids from Haverfordwest and Fishguard. Park at Porth Clais Harbour (SA62 6RR; National Trust).

By Public Transport The nearest train stations are Haverfordwest (20 miles/32km) and Fishguard (19 miles/30.5km). Regular buses serve St Davids.

OS Map OS Explorer OL35 (North Pembrokeshire), Landranger 157 (St David's & Haverfordwest); grid ref (for start): SM 740/242.

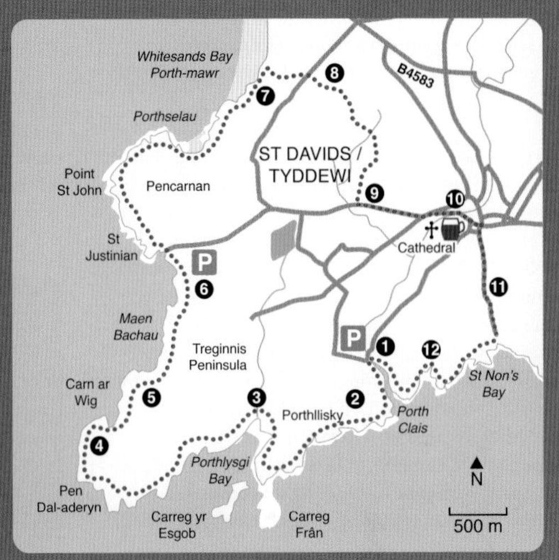

1. Turn left out of Porth Clais car park and walk to the River Alun. Pick up the Pembrokeshire Coast Path leading right, signed towards St Justinian, and walk past the top of two old limekilns. When the path forks, go right, following a National Trust arrow pointing up the side of the hill, and walking with a lovely view down to the harbour on your left.

2. Go through a gate, follow an NT arrow along the coast path with the sea on your left, looking across rock pools to the little lonely islet of Carreg Frân.

3. Pass through a couple of gates and round a bend to drop into Porthlysgi Bay, right down onto the pebbles. Enjoy the cove, then leave via the path immediately to the right, climbing steps, passing through a gate, going left and following a pink National Trust arrow. Climb steadily, looking left to see a slot in the middle island of Carreg yr Esgob. Note Grassholm Island in the distance, with its flanks stained by the birds. Some 39,000 pairs of gannets flock to the island to breed each year.

4. Go through a gate next to a National Trust sign for Lower Treginnis, scrambling over a rocky section of path. At a fingerpost, ignore the path going right and continue straight, passing a ruined building and walking up the hill. Stroll around the headland, past a stone cairn, taking in views of Ramsey Island (a bird sanctuary managed by the RSPB) off to the left, and the famous RNLI boat houses at St Justinian straight ahead.

5. Continue along the coast path and, as you pass above Ogof Felen, look for seals in the bay below. Go through a gate with a National Trust sign for the coastal farmland of Treheinif, a good place to spot linnets and goldfinches.

6. Keep walking to St Justinian – named after a monk and contemporary of St David, who was beheaded and whose skull was said to possess magical powers. Go past the lifeboat sheds and launch ramps. Keep left, following yellow arrows indicating the coast path, passing to the left of a wooden shed, and walking around Point St John to the gorgeous cove and beach at Porthselau.

7. As you approach the sandy beach at Whitesands Bay, the path goes through a hedgerow and emerges on a gravel lane. Take a sharp right here, leaving the coast path and following a footpath fingerpost pointing up the lane.

8. At the top of the lane, go straight ahead, through a gate with a four-way fingerpost and across a meadow. At the end of the field, bear right along a lane and then, after 200 yards, take a left through a metal gate, following footpath arrows along a grassy lane. Stay on this path as it wends across fields and emerges onto a road.

9. Turn left and carefully walk along the road towards St Davids, ignoring the road coming in from the right and the turning left (for

Whitesands). Keep heading for the distinctive square-topped cathedral. Go past a car park on your right and check out the ruins of the medieval Bishop's Palace on the left.

10. Cross a little bridge over the River Alun. Turn left into the main cathedral grounds, then bear right around the impressive building and walk up a set of steps, before turning right through Porth-y-Tŵr, an arched gateway in the stone wall. Immediately turn sharp right along Tower Hill Lane, passing a couple of stone cottages. An entrance to The Farmers Arms beer garden is on your left, just before you meet the road. When you leave the pub, turn left on Goat Street, then immediately right on Mitre Lane, and then right again to walk along Bryn Road. When the road goes left, carry straight on along the footpath. At a T-junction, turn right and then left along the road.

11. At a sign for 'St Nons and Well', turn right along the footpath and descend through fields. At a stile, go straight ahead, keeping the hedge on your right and passing close to St Nons Chapel (founded near the birthplace of St David), and the Holy Well that's said to have sprung when he was born. Go through a gate at the bottom of the field, turn right over a stile and walk along the coast path.

12. Go past the National Trust sign for Porth Clais, and the lovely, lively harbour soon appears below, on your left. Ignore the first path going down to the left and carry on until the path forks again. Go left here and descend to the harbour and car park.

Below: St David's Cathedral, which dates to 1181, suffered earthquake damage in the 13th century.

Above: The Farmers Arms offers views of the cathedral from its back garden.

67 Dolaucothi
Dolaucothi Arms

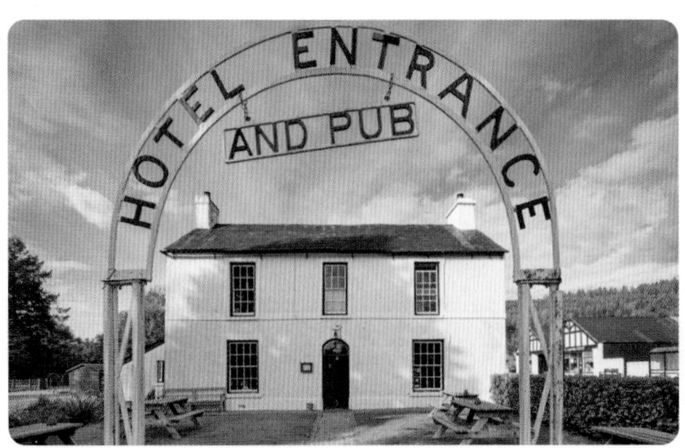

Located in the Cambrian Mountain village of Pumsaint, near ancient gold mines, the **DOLAUCOTHI ARMS** has been quenching the thirst of fortune seekers and travellers for five centuries. The stone building began life as the Inn of the Pum Saint (Five Saints), named after a local legend. Now owned by the National Trust, the pub retains traditional features, including an open fire. The beer garden, voted one of the country's best, offers excellent views over the valley and the rivers Cothi and Twrch. Accommodation is available and food is served. Opening hours change seasonally.

Dolaucothi Arms
Pumsaint
Carmarthenshire
SA19 8UW
01558 650237
www.dolaucothiarms.co.uk

About this walk
- Valley views
- History
- Bats, birds and wildlife
- Wildflowers

Start/finish Dolaucothi Gold Mine car park (National Trust)
Distance 5½ miles (9km)
Time to pub 2 hours
Walking time 2.5 hours
Terrain Footpaths, fields, woods and lanes

WALES

From the edge of gold mines burrowed by the Romans, walk through gilt-edged Cothi Valley, tracing streams, crossing woodlands, fields, meadows and hillsides to an award-winning 16th-century pub.

Spring Swallows arrive in April. Nuthatches, wagtails, long-tailed tits, treecreepers and pied flycatchers flit about, while buzzards, red kites and goshawks hover above. Bluebells flood Dolaucothi from May.

Summer Several bat species (common pipistrelle, Daubenton's, Brandt's, natterer's, long-eared, whiskered, greater and lesser horseshoe) live in Dolaucothi mines and can sometimes be seen on summer evenings. Look for otters, sand martins, kingfishers and herons along Afon Cothi's beaches and in its gin-clear water.

Autumn Look for red squirrels. The upland oak woodland around Dolaucothi Mine, 'Britain's temperate rainforest', supports rare lichens, mosses and ferns.

Winter Notoriously shy pine martens live in the Cothi Valley; winter's minimal leaf cover might help you spot them.

The Dolaucothi Arms serves Welsh real ales from Gower Brewery and Evan Evans (including Cwrw, which is Welsh for 'beer'), traditional ciders from award-winning Gwynt y Ddraig, and several lagers. It stocks Celtic Wines and has a huge gin menu.

Follow in the footsteps of ... Dolaucothi is Britain's only Roman-era gold mine. Mystery surrounds what happened to most of the treasure extracted, but in 1797, a local farmer discovered a cache of decorative items, including part of a Roman serpent-headed bracelet now in the British Museum.

How to Get There

By Car There's a car park at Dolaucothi Gold Mine (SA19 8US; National Trust). Take the A40 to Llanwrda, then A482 to Pumsaint.

By Public Transport Bwcabus 689 serves Pumsaint from Lampeter.

OS Map OS Explorer 186 (Llandeilo & Brechfa Forest), Landranger 146 (Lampeter & Llandovery); grid ref (for start): SN 663/403.

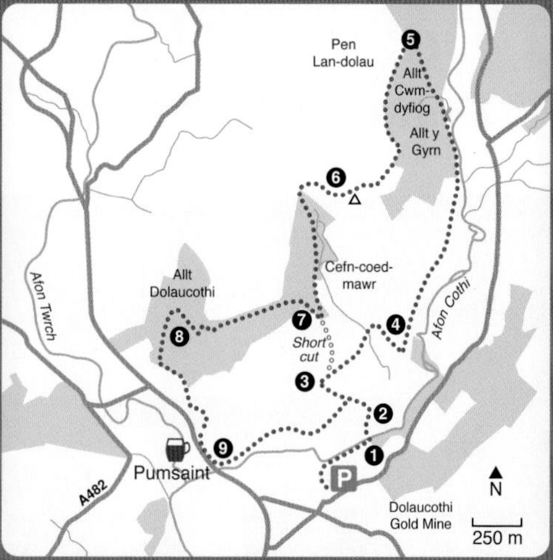

1. From the gold mine car park, follow 'Estate Trail' red arrows through mixed woodlands of oak, beech, hazel and sycamore, between the river and a caravan park. Climb a stile and turn left. Cross the bridge, turn right and walk along the river.

2. After 100 yards, turn left, go through two gates and walk with a stone wall on your right. Go through a kissing gate, cross a field to another gate and go along a wooden platform (note a sycamore tree on the right, that seems to have grown over an old kiln). Ignore a left turn and ascend some steps. Turn left along a track, following red arrows to a T-junction by Dolaucothi Farm NT sign.

3. Turn right along the lane, past the farm. (Note: while the following section is part of the Estate Trail, our route travels in the opposite direction to the information board/website description.)

Shortcut: To miss the 2½-mile (4-km) adventure to the trig point, go through the gate opposite the T-junction, walk diagonally right up the field, pass through a gate and skip to 7.

4. After 400 yards, turn right through a gate and follow the hedge down the field. At the bottom, turn left and walk with the hedge on your right. Go through a couple of gates and stiles and walk along a rough path, with the river running to your right. At a T-junction, turn left and climb a steep stone track.

5. At the lane, go left, then right on a broad path, then bear left, following red arrows along a narrow path. Walk through gorse to a gate, and continue to the trig point, enjoying Cothi Valley views.

6. Retrace your footsteps for 50 yards, go through a gate into the next field, turn left and walk with the hedge on your left. Go through a gate and follow arrows down a field to a stile. Continue through a field to a gate, then take a pretty path through woods, beside a stream.

7. At the T-junction, disregard the red arrow (you're leaving the Estate Trail) and turn right. Walk through fir trees, now following 'Dolaucothi Woodland Trail' blue arrows. When the track forks, bear right along the higher path.

8. Ignore tracks leading left. At a junction with several blue arrows, go right, uphill. Just before a wide gate, turn left on a path that passes picnic benches and wends wonderfully through mixed woodland. Descend steps to a lane. Cross, go through a gate and follow a path across fields and stiles to Pumsaint car park. The pub is opposite.

9. Leave the pub, cross to the car park, then go right, following a blue arrow. At the lane, ignore the blue arrow, go left, walk 100 yards then follow a yellow arrow right. When the path forks, bear left and trace yellow arrows through woodlands. At the T-junction, turn right and return to the car park.

68 Dinas Oleu

The Last Inn

The Last Inn
Church Street, Barmouth
Gwynedd LL42 1EL
01341 280530
www.lastinn-barmouth.co.uk

About this walk

- Sea, estuary and mountain views
- Historical points of interest
- Birdlife
- Includes a steep climb

Start/finish Barmouth train station
Distance 3 miles (5km)
Time to pub 1.5–2 hours
Walking time 2–3 hours
Terrain Hilltop footpaths, alleyways, lanes, street pavements

Beneath Dinas Oleu, just before Barmouth Bridge, the 15th-century LAST INN is so low lit and full of repurposed boat beams, snugs and nautical references it's like being aboard a sailing ship. Features include fireplaces, a wall-to-wall mural depicting the history of the harbour, an RNLI flag signed by generations of lifeboat crewmembers, and a 'well', where the rockface forms part of the pub wall and spring water collects. The beer garden across the road overlooks Barmouth Harbour, and is the start point for the Three Peaks Yacht Race. Food, with local ingredients, is served.

Climb from Barmouth town centre to the hilltop heights of Dinas Oleu ('Citadel of Light' in Welsh) – the first piece of land donated to the National Trust – passing through a ghost village and returning to the historic harbour and a charismatic pub.

Spring Like a floral sunrise, the gorse covering Dinas Oleu bursts into bloom, attracting butterflies and pollinating insects. Migratory birds including pied flycatchers pass en route to oak woods at nearby Dolmelynllyn.

Summer Beyond Barmouth's golden beaches, the restless waters of Cardigan Bay sparkle in the sun, and views across the Llŷn Peninsula can be enjoyed.

Autumn The gruff gorse- and bracken-bearded hillside around Dinas Oleu and Cae-Fadog continues its colour show, giving the site a golden glow.

Winter The white-capped peak of Cadair Idris is visible above Barmouth bridge, looking along Mawddach Estuary.

The Last Inn offers Reverend James ales (from Welsh brewery Brains) and Wainwright's on tap. Next door, Myrddins Brewery and Distillery is a specialist real ale micro pub with a large menu.

Follow in the footsteps of...
Dinas Oleu was the National Trust's first piece of land. It was gifted to the newly formed charity in 1895 by philanthropist Fanny Talbot, who lived in Ty'n Ffynnon. She also donated several houses along this route to the Guild of St George, a project founded by Victorian polymath, writer and anti-capitalist social commentator John Ruskin. One was home to Parisian political activist and horticulturalist Auguste Guyard, who is buried in Frenchman's Grave.

How to Get There

By Car Take the A496 to Barmouth. There is plenty of parking in the town, near the station (not National Trust).

By Public Transport Barmouth train station is on the Cambrian Coast Railway line that runs between Porthmadog, Aberystwyth and Shrewsbury. Our walk starts from the station.

OS Map OS Explorer OL23 (Cadair Idris & Bala Lake) and OL18 (Harlech, Porthmadog & Y Bala), Landranger 124 (Porthmadog & Dolgellau); grid ref (for start): SH 612/158.

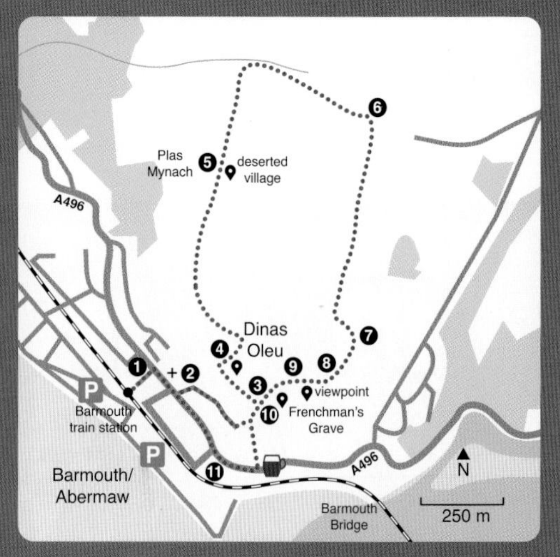

1. Leave the station and walk towards St John's Church on the hill. Turn right on High Street, passing Tal y Don Hotel. Carefully cross and turn left up Dinas Oleu Road, following a National Trust fingerpost for Dinas Oleu.

2. Cross Water Street and bear right up a steep lane. Keep climbing to a lookout with an information board.

3. Turn left and walk past the National Trust Dinas Oleu sign. When the path forks, go left. Pass the rock 'Sitting Room' and follow the path uphill as it zigs right and then zags left. Continue into a dip beneath oak and holly trees.

4. Turn right and ascend steps. The path arcs right, to the National Trust centenary structure. Go through a gate above the monument and bear left, passing through another gate and walking around the headland, enjoying views across Cardigan Bay to the Llŷn Peninsula. The path descends and forks. Go right, uphill, pass through a metal gate and continue along the Taith Ardudwy Way (a 24-mile/39-km hiking trail between Barmouth and Llandecwyn). Follow posts through abandoned stone houses in the deserted village of Gellfechan, and keep ascending.

5. Walk with a stone wall on your left, ignoring a path going right. At a wooden post, follow the arrow pointing right, indicating the Cylchdaith Circular Route, and stroll along a pretty path with rocks on your right and a stream to the left. Go through a metal gate and continue straight, now ignoring the arrow for the Circular Route and following footpath arrows.

6. Go over a ladder stile and meet a semi-sealed track. Turn right and follow this downhill for about 500yds, before turning right on a path by a metal fingerpost.

7. Go through a metal gate and along a rocky descent, following yellow-topped stakes. At a stake with footpath arrows, go right, passing through a gate in a stone wall.

8. Pass a junction by a bench, and go through a gate on the left by a National Trust sign for Cae-Fadog. Follow the arrow pointing right to a bench with stunning views over the Mawddach Estuary and Barmouth Bridge. Return to the main path.

9. Go left to reach a gate leading left to 'Frenchman's Grave only' – a short out-and-back track to Auguste Guyard's last resting place. After coming to Wales with his daughter in 1871, fleeing the siege of Paris during the Franco-Prussian war, Auguste Guyard – communist, pioneer horticulturalist and friend of Alexander Dumas and Victor Hugo – spent the remainder of his life at Dinas Oleu, growing vegetables, herbs and medicinal plants that he shared with the poor.

From the grave, return to the main path, turn left and go through a gate with a Dinas Oleu National Trust sign. Descend to the viewpoint you passed earlier.

10. Turn left and walk down the lane opposite the path you first ascended, passing Fanny Talbot's Ty'n Ffynnon (House of the Spring). A warren of steep paths and alleyways spills down through the cottages of Barmouth Old Town. You can take various routes, but keep bearing left to pass the Ruskin cottages donated by Fanny, and emerge beside The Last Inn.

11. Leave the pub, turn right, walk along High Street to Station Road leading to the train station.

Above and right: Trails around Dinas Oleu ('fortress of light') – the first piece of land donated to the National Trust, given by Fanny Talbot, so the poor people of the town would have 'a beautiful sitting room in which to take pleasure and delight'.

69 Porthdinllaen
The Tŷ Coch Inn

The Tŷ Coch Inn
Porthdinllaen
Gwynedd LL53 6DB
01758 720498
www.tycoch.co.uk

About this walk
- Beach and rocky headland
- Wales Coast Path
- Marine wildlife
- Great views

Start/Finish Morfa Nefyn car park (National Trust)
Distance 2½ miles (4km)
Time to pub 30 minutes
Walking time 1.5 hours
Terrain Beach, coastal path, golf course, lanes

A legendary seaside pub with a rocking beach bar, THE TŶ COCH INN sits on the sand at Porthdinllaen, looking out across Caernarfon Bay and the Irish Sea. Access is by foot only, bestowing on the pub a unique atmosphere and making it popular with Wales Coast Path walkers. Built in 1823, it began life as a vicarage and was transformed into a pub in 1842 to serve local shipbuilders and fishermen. Inside there's a woodburner, and storm lanterns dangle from the ceiling. Food is served. In summer, the beach bar is massively popular. Winter opening hours differ – check ahead.

Stroll around a dramatic offshoot of the Llŷn Peninsula, exploring a sensational sandy bay and a bouncing beach-side pub with views across Caernarfon Bay to the peaks of Yr Eifl (The Rivals), before rounding a headland, discovering the site of a prehistoric hill fort and returning across a scenic seaside golf course.

Spring Sand martins begin arriving from Africa in mid-March, nesting in burrows and banks around the Llŷn Peninsula. Join volunteers at Porthdinllaen lookout station and search the sea for resident seals, passing porpoises and dolphins, and a variety of seabirds.

Summer Stop for a swim on sandy Porthdinllaen cove, explore the rock pools around the headland, search for sunbathing seals and enjoy a cold drink from the Tŷ Coch Inn's beach bar.

Autumn Between fishing forays among vast seagrass meadows, cormorants stand atop rocks, stretching their wings to the sun, while oystercatchers fossick for food on the exposed sand.

Winter Look for newborn seal pups, watch the waves roll in from the Irish Sea, and clouds gathering over The Rivals.

The Tŷ Coch Inn offers its own cider, plus three rotating hand-pulled guest ales (often local), such as Sgwarnog Gwyn pale from Caernarfon, Cwrw Llŷn Brenin Bitter and Nokota by Wild Horse Brewing Co (Llandudno).

Follow in the footsteps of ... Pre-historic humans enjoyed the same view of Yr Eifl that we drink in today, from an Iron Age hill fort located where the course at Nefyn Golf Club now sprawls. Archaeologists have dated the remains of Trwyn Dinllaen to 200–100 BC.

How to Get There

By Car Drive towards Morfa Nefyn, where there's parking (LL53 6DA; National Trust).

By Public Transport Buses run via Morfa Nefyn from Pwllheli and Tudweiliog.

OS Map OS Explorer 253 (Lleyn Peninsula West), Landranger 123 (Lleyn Peninsula); grid ref (for start): SH 281/406.

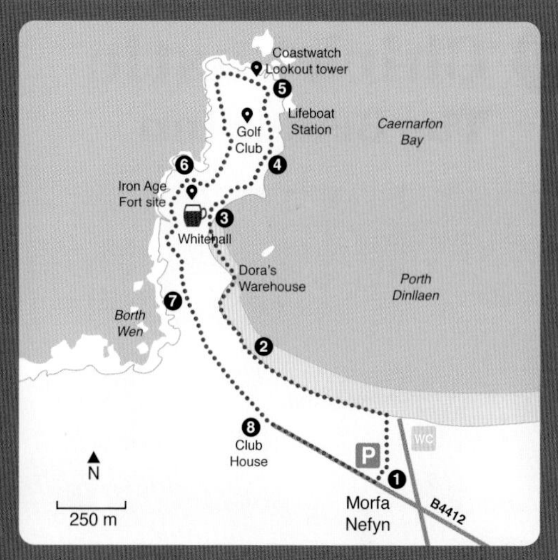

1. From the seaside end of the car park, follow a fingerpost right, going down a path, turning left on a lane and passing the public conveniences to reach the beach. Turn left and walk along the sand.

2. Walk in front of a house and around the back of stilted Dora's Warehouse, a former shipbuilding site, to reach the second cove. Pass Whitehall (a hotel built when this headland was being considered as the main ferry port for Ireland before Holyhead was eventually chosen) and the pub lies straight ahead. Tŷ Coch means 'red house' and besides being a vicarage, the inn (built, it's believed, from Dutch red bricks previously used as ballast in a ship) doubled as a school for girls in the late 19th century. Nowadays it throngs with walkers, enjoying locally brewed beverages on the beach and in the bar.

3. Leaving the pub, continue around the rocky headland. After passing several coastal cottages on the left, the footpath follows the base of the cliff above a rocky, stony section of beach. The path passes close to a double-storey house, then drops to a great little rock-pooling beach.

4. The trail undulates around the water's edge with some steps and a few rocky scrambles. Pass a wooden hut and enjoy a sandy beach by the launch ramp at Porthdinllaen Lifeboat Station. Meet Nefyn golf course at the 6th tee, cross the buggy lane and continue around the shoreline, following a fingerpost for the Wales Coast Path (a 870-mile/ 1,400-km trail launched in 2012, when it was declared the world's first dedicated path to span the entirety of a country's coastline).

5. Quickly you find yourself on a wild, craggy part of the peninsula, with the Irish Sea swirling around you, and lots of rocks to explore. Various routes can be followed here, but head towards the National Coastwatch tower, following posts with Wales Coast Path waymarkers. When it's occupied, volunteers at the lookout station will invite you in and share information about seals, dolphins, porpoises and birdlife. From the tower (which appears to have its own tee) keep following posts along the dramatic coastline.

6. At the 4th tee, take the laneway left to get a great view over the top of the pub, and read an information board about the Iron Age fort that occupied this hill in 200 BC. Continue along the lane or take the coast-hugging path on the right (staying alert to flying golf balls.)

7. At the 9th hole, walk past the three-way fingerpost for the Wales Coast Path, going straight ahead towards the clubhouse. Continue past the tee for the 1st hole, going through a kissing gate by the bar and restaurant, and the club car park.

8. Walk past the lifeboat house on the right, and along the lane to the National Trust car park.

70 Chirk Castle
The Bridge Inn

The Bridge Inn
Chirk Bank
Shropshire LL14 5BU
01691 773213

About this walk

- Castle and battlefield
- Aqueduct crossing
- Tunnel walk-through (bring a torch)
- Border hopping

Start/finish Home Farm (National Trust)
Distance 5½ miles (9km) Apr–Sep/6½ miles (10.5km) Oct–Mar
Time to pub 1.5–2 hours
Walking time 3–4 hours
Terrain Footpaths, lanes, riverside, woodland towpath, some road

Also known as The Trap, THE BRIDGE INN boasts stunning views over Chirk's aqueduct and viaduct, twin structures spanning the River Ceiriog on the seam of England and Wales. Back when alcohol couldn't be sold in Wales on Sundays, this canny inn capitalised on its position as the first/last pub in England to attract a roaring, cross-border trade at weekends. It's a classic, old-fashioned, snug pub with wooden beams, thick walls and an open fire in the main bar. A second room has a pool table, and the outside deck delivers the vista. Food is served daily.

From a 13th-century castle in Wales, walk through a battlefield, cross Offa's Dyke and follow riverside paths over the border to a perfectly positioned pub in England. Return along a canal, crossing an amazing aqueduct and going through a long tunnel.

Spring Swifts and swallows perform aerobatics around Chirk Castle's portcullis and flit in and out of murder holes in the Adam Tower. A wave of bluebells washes through the woods.

Summer Wildflowers bloom in woodlands and meadows beside the banks of the River Ceiriog and Llangollen Canal, attracting thousands of butterflies and bees. Scan the sky for buzzards, red kites and peregrine falcons.

Autumn House martins gather in Chirk Castle courtyard before flying south. Ceiriog Valley woodlands go from green to yellow, brown and blood red around the Oak at the Gateway of the Dead.

Winter The River Ceiriog runs fast, and a crackling fire awaits at The Bridge Inn. From February, snowdrops carpet the ground around Chirk Castle and surrounding woods.

Banks's Bitter is the Bridge Inn's regular beer, but the pub pours other regional ales on rotation, from breweries including Shrewsbury's Salopian and Porthmadog's Purple Moose.

Follow in the footsteps of ... In 1165, King Henry II amassed 30,000 soldiers and attempted to subdue the Welsh who were gathering in council near Corwen, with Owain, King of Gwynedd. But below Chirk Castle, where Offa's Dyke meets the River Ceiriog, his vanguard was ambushed by Welsh archers and fighters, and at the Gap of the Graves, near the Oak at the Gates of the Dead, the river ran red with blood. (Or so the story goes. Historical debates continue.)

How to Get There

By Car Head towards Chirk on the A5, follow signs for Chirk Castle and park at Home Farm (National Trust), where this route starts.

By Public Transport You can also start this walk from Chirk train station (begin at number 8), which is on the Shrewsbury to Chester line.

OS Map OS Explorer 240 (Oswestry/ Croesoswallt), Landranger 126 (Shrewsbury & Oswestry); grid ref (for start): SJ 267/383.

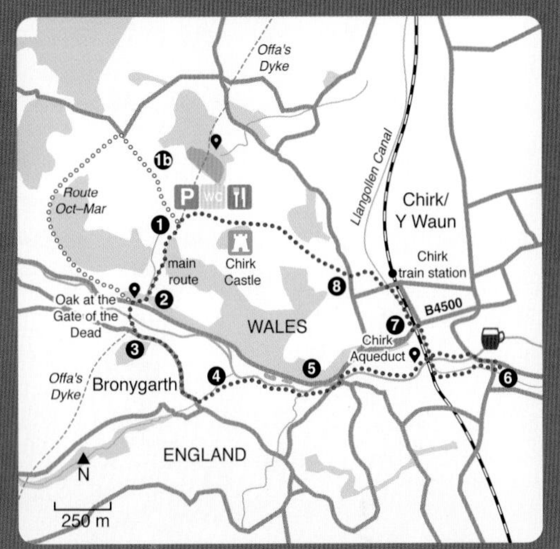

April–September

1. From the car park at Home Farm, walk towards the castle along the main visitor path. Bear right, following signs for Offa's Dyke, along the orange waymarked Castle Mill Walk, going down a lane and through mixed woods of ash, sweet chestnut, sycamore, beech, pine and hawthorn trees. You're following the route of Offa's Dyke here – an ancient earthwork construction built between AD 757 and 796 by Offa, the Anglo-Saxon king of Mercia, which roughly runs along the current Wales–England border. Just before a wide gate marked 'Private', turn right, go through a wooden gate and descend straight down through a field, which is actually one of the old castle deer parks. Go through a gate at the bottom and follow a winding path, descending through woods to the Oak at the Gate of the Dead. Information signs here tell the story of the Battle of Crogen that took place on the site in 1165 (see opposite). Continue and pass through a stone archway to meet the road (B4500).

October–March

1b. During autumn and winter, the path mentioned above is closed and you'll need to take this alternative route. From the main entrance, follow red arrows for the Old Golf Walk, up through fields. Go through two gates and walk around Rose Cottage and through a kissing gate. Walk straight up the lane for about 50 yards, then turn left through another kissing gate, following a footpath fingerpost indicating Offa's Dyke Path. Keep following Offa's Dyke waymarkers through fields, with views of the castle to your left. Go through a gate and descend into a valley. Pass through a kissing gate and go left along a lane, still following fingerposts for Offa's Dyke Path. Pass some pretty cottages, and at a T-junction turn left. Meet the road by a footpath entrance to Chirk Castle on the left (along which you can sneak for a peek of the Oak at the Gate of the Dead).

2. Carefully cross the road at Castle Mill and follow the acorn arrow up a quiet lane and over a bridge across the River Ceiriog. Walk up the steep hill, imperceptibly passing from Wales into England. At the T-junction turn left, leaving Offa's Dyke path and following a fingerpost for the Maelor Way (another long-distance footpath).

3. At the time of writing, the section of the Maelor Way that follows a riverside path by Hafod had been destroyed by floodwater, and there was uncertainty about whether it would reopen, so our route continues up the road to the footpath that turns left into Pentre Wood.

4. Descend a set of steps and walk down a path to the right of a gurgling stream, through beech, hawthorn and sycamore trees, until you meet the river. Go right, over a stile, cross a meadow and climb another stile at the far end. Go straight along the road and, at a T-junction, turn left and cross the bridge, back into Wales.

5. Go through a gate on the right and walk through grazing fields with the river immediately to your right, and a great view of the Chirk Aqueduct and railway viaduct straight ahead. Pass beneath both of these, veering back into England in the process. Meet the road, turn right and walk over the river to The Bridge Inn.

6. Leave the inn, turn right, go past the outdoor toilets and pub car park, and walk up Chirk Bank to the canal. Turn right and walk along the towpath with the water on your left, all the way across the Thomas Telford-designed aqueduct, re-entering Wales in style.

7. Continue straight and walk through Chirk Tunnel, which is long and dark – there's a handrail to stop surprise swims, but it's nice to have a torch (if you're not comfortable doing this, you can walk along Station Road instead). Emerge from the tunnel, turn right and walk up the ramp to Station Avenue. Follow the arrow for Chirk Castle along the footpath, across the top of the tunnel mouth and up some steps, before turning right into woods. The path runs parallel to the river, then elbows left through a kissing gate and field. Exit through a gate and dogleg across the road, turning right then left, following a fingerpost pointing to Chirk Castle.

8. Go through a gate and follow National Trust green arrows up through fields, bearing right then left through a couple of gates, passing woods and the castle on your left. Keep going, across the field, through a large metal gate and along a lane to the car park.

Above: The original Bridge Inn sign, attracting border-skipping Sunday drinkers.

Top: The Chirk Aquaduct and railway viaduct span the Shropshire Union Canal and Wales-England border.

71 Aberglaslyn

The Prince Llewelyn Hotel

The Prince Llewelyn Hotel
Smith Street
Beddgelert, Caernarfon
Gwynedd LL55 4LT
01766 890242
www.robinsonsbrewery.com/pubs/prince-llewelyn-beddgelert

About this walk

- Stunning mountain views
- Includes steep climb and exposed path above water

Start/finish Nantmor car park (National Trust)
Distance 4½ miles (7km)
Time to pub 2 hours
Walking time 3–4 hours
Terrain Woodland, rural and riverside paths

Housed in a Grade II-listed building by a bridge at the confluence of the rivers Colwyn and Glaslyn, in the historic hamlet of Beddgelert in scenic Snowdonia, THE PRINCE LLEWELYN is named after a Welsh ruler forever associated with a poignant local legend (see below). The pub is very welcoming to walkers, offering inside and outside seating with views across the river to the peaks either side of Nant Gwynant, a stunning valley. Food is served all day, including from a dedicated pie menu. At busy times, The Tanronnen Inn, opposite, is another good option.

This walk goes through gorgeous Nant Gwynant, traversing the wooded lower flanks of Moel Hebog and taking in sites of folkloric interest and a lovely valley village, before returning along the banks of a rushing river, via the picturesque Pass of Aberglaslyn.

Spring Snowmelt from the peaks keeps river rapids and waterfalls flowing. The woods are full of bluebells, primroses and aromatic wild garlic.

Summer Look out for birdlife along the riverbanks, including kingfishers and osprey, which breed at Pont Croesor. In the woods, listen for the warbling of chiffchaffs, blackcaps, whitethroats, pied flycatchers and redstarts.

Autumn The woodlands of Coed Aberglaslyn and heather-covered sides of Nant Gwynant put on a dramatic colour show, and the skies throng with migrating birds.

Winter Trees lose their leaves, revealing eye-watering views of Snowdonia's frosted peaks. Spy hardy, winter-defying birds, including robins, bluetits, yellowhammers and reed buntings.

The regular real ales poured at the Prince Llewelyn are Robinson's Cwrw'r Ddraig Aur and Unicorn.

In the footsteps of...
According to legend, in the 13th century, Prince Llywelyn returned from hunting to find his baby's cradle overturned and his dog, Gelert, with a bloody mouth. Believing the hound had savaged the infant he slayed it, only to discover the child unharmed beside a dead wolf. Realising the faithful dog had actually protected his son he was overcome with remorse. The animal was buried in a large grave (which this walk passes), and the prince, it was said, never smiled again.

How to Get There

By Car Park at the National Trust's Nantmor car park, accessed via the A4085 between Beddgelert and Penrhyndeudraeth.

By Public Transport The nearest train stations are at Penrhyndeudraeth (4½ miles/7km) and Porthmadog (5 miles/8km).

OS Map OS Explorer OL17 (Snowdon/ Yr Wyddfa), Landranger 115 (Snowdon & Caernarfon); grid ref (for start): SH 597/462.

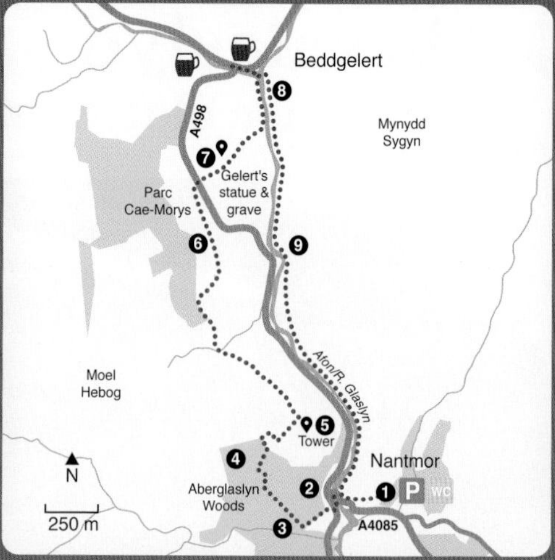

1. From Nantmor car park, go through the gate to the left of the National Trust information board and parking machine. Bear left and climb the steps leading uphill, following an arrow for Aberglaslyn. Trace the rocky and root-runged path through beech and oak woods, until you meet the river, then turn left and go through a metal kissing gate.

2. Walk across the bridge, passing over a set of rapids on Afon Glaslyn, then turn left along the road. There is no footpath here, so be careful, but as soon as you round the corner, cross the road and pick up the path leading away from the road and into woods by the National Trust sign for Coed Aberglaslyn.

3. Follow wooden posts with National Trust waymarkers on them, climbing up to the left, where you will meet a waterfall rampaging down the hill and cascading under a footbridge. Don't cross this bridge; instead walk straight up the steps, through beech and sweet chestnut trees, with the waterfall on your left. Ignore the path leading right to a ruined stone structure and keep following waymarkers up the hill. The path zigs and zags into the woods, which become dominated by tall, straight pines. The route is clearly arrowed, all the way to a ladder stile over a stone wall.

4. Climb over the stile and walk out of the woods onto open ground atop Bryn Du. A spectacular view explodes open in front of you, with Mynydd Sygyn dominating it, towering over the village of Beddgelert way below. Follow the path to a stone turret structure, where the vista can be enjoyed uninterrupted.

5. From this little tower, retrace your steps briefly, then follow arrows pointing down the hill. The undulating path descends and then climbs a stone-clad track. It can be slippery underfoot, but this part of the walk offers great glimpses through the valley and along the river to Beddgelert. Go through a gate and descend through sheep-grazing fields, passing the remains of a ruined stone cottage, now occupied by a tree. Go over a ladder stile and keep to the top-left edge of the next field as you walk down towards the road and railway line. Graig Wen and Yr Aran now dominate the horizon.

6. Go through a metal field gate and continue until you almost reach a wooden field gate. Turn right here, carefully cross the railway line and road, and go through the gate immediately opposite. Follow a double-width track, and when it forks, go left to little wooden gate. On the left is a stone structure, and inside stands Gelert's alert statue. Take the left fork in the path to visit the poor dog's grave, which lies just beyond, below two solemn-looking trees.

7. Continue on, into Beddgelert, joining the path that runs along Afon Glaslyn, walking with the river on your right. Go past the church, through a metal gate and then turn left, passing a craft shop and café and walking up to the pretty stone bridge. The house to the left of the bridge is Tŷ Isaf, a traditional stone cottage and National Trust holiday let. Opposite that is The Tanronnen Inn, another pub with a little garden bar overlooking the river, and great views of the 2,656ft (782m) peak of Moel Hebog. Cross the bridge, walking over the river to The Prince Llewelyn hotel on the far side. The pub signs of both The Tanronnen Inn and The Prince Llewelyn reference the sad story of Gelert.

8. Leaving the pub, cross back over the stone bridge and retrace your footsteps past the craft shop and toilets. Cross the footbridge straight ahead, which spans the dramatic confluence point of the rivers Colwyn and Glaslyn. Turn right and walk with the water rushing along on your right, past the National Trust sign for Aberglaslyn, going through a gate and along a sealed path. Cross the railway line and keep going past a lovely stony beach area by a small set of rapids.

9. The river runs alongside you all the way back, with heather-cloaked hills beyond the water on your right, and the railway line to your left for a while. The path soon turns less pedestrian and much more exciting, with stone slabs, scrambles, and one section where it virtually protrudes out over the river, and steel hand hoops are provided to help walkers remain secure. By a section of wooden walkway, a dark shaft burrows into the bowels of the hill – a reminder of this fascinating area's mining history. When you meet the junction where you turned down to the road at the start of the walk, carry straight on to the car park.

Above: The tragic tale of Gelert is remembered with a statue of the loyal dog.

Below: The rocky riverside trail runs close to the rapids on Afon Glaslyn.

72 Glyderau

The Pen-y-Gwryd Hotel

The Pen-y-Gwryd Hotel
Nant Gwynant
Gwynedd LL55 4NT
01286 870211
www.pyg.co.uk

About this walk
- Mountain peaks and iconic rock features
- Snowdonia National Park
- Challenging sections involving scrambling and route finding
- Lots of ascent

Start/finish PyG Hotel
Distance 7½ miles (12km)
Time to pub At start/end
Walking time 5–6 hours
Terrain Mountain paths, exposed, unmarked and technical in places

The PEN-Y-GWRYD HOTEL (PyG) is steeped in mountaineering history. Built in 1810 as a farmhouse, it became a coaching inn and provided a training base for Edmund Hillary and Tenzing Norgay before their successful first ascent of Mt Everest. Hobnail boots hang from rafters, photos and mountain memorabilia festoon wood-lined walls, while the atmospheric Smoke Room has a reliquary of items from the 1953 Everest expedition. Hillary and Tenzing's signatures adorn the front room ceiling, alongside those of other celebrated climbers. Food and accommodation available.

Visiting the spectacular twin peaks of Glyder Fawr and Glyder Fach atop the Glyderau massif, this is the most technical and challenging walk in this book – as befits a foray finishing at the Pen-y-Gwryd Hotel, home of British mountaineering. Only attempt the full route if you have hill-walking and peak-climbing experience. Wear protective layers, take a map, compass and phone, and don't attempt the adventure in poor weather or low visibility (always check the mountain forecast before setting off). The well-trodden trails to the top of Snowdon (Yr Wyddfa) from Pen-y-Pass are an excellent, easier alternative.

Spring Nature awakes slowly on the chilly and shaded mountain slopes of North Wales, but eventually spring brings hardy arctic-alpine plants including purple saxifrage, moss campion and alpine lady's mantle.

Summer Snowdon lilies flower amid the rocks. Scan blue skies for soaring peregrine falcons and ravens, which nest in the nooks of broken boulders around Snowdonia's summits.

Autumn The Glyderau's grassy lower flanks turn a glorious ginger, and the sun setting over the shoulder of Snowdon bathes the Glyders in a golden hue during ever-earlier evenings.

Winter Ice, snow, wicked winds and freezing temperatures make this a route that shouldn't be attempted in winter unless you're very experienced.

The Pen-y-Gwryd Hotel serves local elixers including Snowdonia Ale (Cwrw Eryri) and Madog's Ale (Cwrw Madog) from Purple Moose Brewery.

Follow in the footsteps of... Noted climbers including George Mallory honed their skills in these mountains. Before the 1953 Everest expedition, Hillary and Norgay trained together here, especially on Tryfan, an extremely technical peak adjacent to Glyder Fach.

How to Get There

By Car There's roadside parking on the A498 opposite the Pen-y-Gwryd Hotel, where this walk starts – a better alternative to the usually full car park at Pen-y-Pass. Shuttle buses operate.

By Public Transport The nearest train station is Betws-y-Coed (9½ miles/15.3km). The Snowdon Sherpa bus service provides an excellent way for walkers and climbers to get around the area (where parking is problematic).

OS Map OS Explorer OL17 (Snowdon & Conwy Valley), Landranger 115 (Snowdon & Caernarfon); grid ref (for start): SH 660/557.

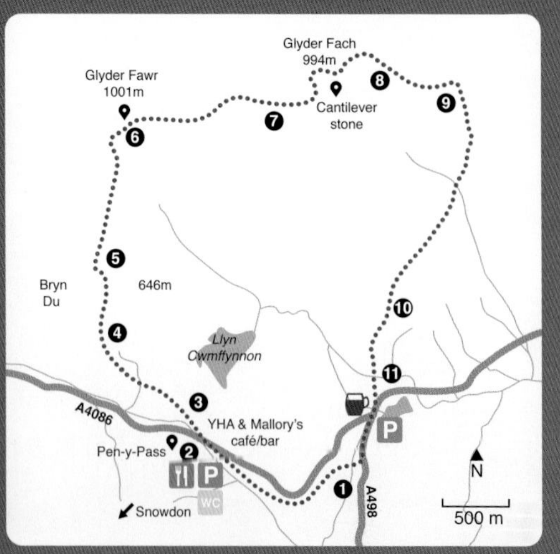

1. From The Pen-y-Gwryd Hotel, cross the A4086 and walk along the grass beside the A498 for 150 yards before going right, across a little footbridge, following a fingerpost pointing along the Llwybr Pen-y-Pass footpath. The well-made track goes up through the Pass of Llanberis, running roughly parallel to the A4086, but out of sight of cars. A path joins from the left, by a fingerpost. Keep climbing, with Afon Trawsnant (a stream) rushing downhill to your left.

2. At the busy Pen-y-Pass car park, turn right and cross the A4086. Contemplate a coffee at Mallory's café/bar in the YHA, a historic building formerly called Gorphwysfa ('resting place'), where a plaque commemorates legendary landlord Owen Rawson Owen, who hosted hillwalkers and climbers here for 60 years. Mallory's is positioned perfectly in a place where a decision must be made: if you're not confident navigating unmarked (and often unclear) paths and crossing open, technical terrain, stick to the well-trammelled trails on Snowdon, south of the A4086, where the Miner's and Pyg tracks both lead to Yr Wyddfa, the summit of Wales' highest mountain. Otherwise, to continue to the Glyderau on the much quieter route shown here, turn right over a ladder stile (or go through the gate) at the far end of the YHA building, following a footpath arrow.

3. Go through a kissing gate and ascend the rugged path. Bear slightly left and go past a prominent, pyramid-shaped rock, where you'll be greeted with views of Llyn Cwmffynnon, a wind-rippled mountain lake, with the steep gun barrel-grey flanks of Glyder Fawr and Glyder Fach on the far side. To your right is the little peak of Moel Berfedd, and over your left shoulder, cloud cover willing, soars the shard of Snowdon/Yr Wyddfa. Continue to the left of the llyn, following a faint, rising path.

4. Head to the left of a rocky outcrop. It's a real scramble in places, but the rough route can commonly be made out from trods (footprints of fellow hill walkers), and when it's wet (often), water trickles down the trail. You'll come to a tongue of scree (loose rock). Ascend this, and when it levels off slightly, look for red paint splats leading through the rock field (unofficial waymarkers daubed on boulders by persons unknown, which upset some climbers, but do prove quite useful ... until they disappear).

5. Join the dots to a near-horizontal slab of rock. Clamber over this, then cross the plateau that follows – carefully dodging deep bogs. Red splats reappear on the far side, leading to a stony path that zig-zags up the steep slope. When you reach a flat, green, boggy plateau, the path becomes clearer for a bit, before the real scrambling begins, up to the summit of Glyder Fawr (3,284ft/1,001m). There's no trig point to indicate the summit, just two particularly prominent, jagged rocks.

Element-sculpted rocks in the Glyderau saddle between Glyder Fawr and Glyder Fach.

6. All around Glyder Fawr, the beautifully bleak highpoint of the Glyderau, shattered rocks form a surreal splintered landscape, all-too-often cloaked in mist and low cloud.

7. Follow a series of stone cairns across the boulder-strewn saddle towards Glyder Fach, passing the Bwlch y Ddwy Glyder and Bwlch Dwglydion track, which leads right, back down to Llyn Cwmffynnon. This section is fiddly, but you basically scramble right, around the spiky crown of Castell y Gwynt, edging along a contour and then climbing. The actual summit of Glyder Fach (3,261ft/994m) is hard to pinpoint and only attainable by clambering and scrambling over lots of rocks, so you might want to skirt around it. If you pass to the left of the peak, look north to see the tops of Tryfan, where Hillary and Norgay sharpened their skills and forged a friendship before heading to the Himalayas in 1953. Don't forget to find the famous Cantilever Stone – a seemingly delicately balanced slab and much-photographed feature of the Glyderau – just beyond Glyder Fach.

8. As you start to descend to the right (south), don't stray left of the big cairn you encounter on the way down – that path leads towards Y Foel Goch. Instead, downclimb across boulders to connect with the Miner's Track.

9. After a steep drop, the route levels off. The track (often faint) bears right before meeting a steeper section, and traverses boggy ground. Pass to the right of a rocky outcrop, then bear slightly left through small gully, by a waterfall.

10. Keep descending along the boggy track, going over a stone wall via a ladder stile. Keep this wall on your right as you progress downwards, ignoring a ladder stile and several gaps.

11. Eventually another wall crosses your path. Climb the ladder stile and cross a footbridge over the river. Continue on to a stile, which takes you out onto the road. Go right and walk to the Pen-y-Gwryd Hotel.

Opposite: A stony path plunges through Stickle Ghyll from The Lakes' Langdale Fells (see page 217).

North West

73 Dunham Massey

Swan with Two Nicks

Swan with Two Nicks
Park Lane, Little Bollington
Cheshire WA14 4TJ
0161 928 2914
www.swanwithtwonicks.co.uk

About this walk

- Country park
- Gorgeous gardens
- Fallow deer
- Bridgewater Canal

Start/finish Dunham Massey car park (National Trust)
Distance 3½ miles (5.5km)
Time to pub 1.5 hours
Walking time 2 hours
Terrain Parkland trails and canal towpaths

The SWAN WITH TWO NICKS is a traditional alehouse between Dunham Massey and the Bridgewater Canal, with a long, somewhat opaque history going back several centuries. The name comes from a 16th-century practice of 'nicking' (marking with a knife) swans' beaks to establish ownership (since the 12th century, the monarch has claimed all unmarked mute swans on open water). The large pub, which has appeared in the Manchester-based TV series *Cold Feet*, has several rooms, with open fires and wooden features, plus a great beer garden. It's dog friendly, and food is served.

After exploring a historic country estate (a deer-populated oasis on Manchester's outskirts) wander over the River Bollin to a historic alehouse with a brilliant beer garden, before returning along the banks of the Bridgewater Canal.

Spring The 'Yellow Meadow' – a carpet of daffodils and Narcissus tête-à-tête – blooms in Dunham Massey garden. Cherry, crab apple and magnolia trees blossom on the main lawn, the woods are awash with bluebells, and tulips line the canal.

Summer Enjoy the profusion of flowers in the gardens, look for woodpeckers in the trees and the iridescent flash of blue kingfishers along the canal.

Autumn Fallow deer stags fight for supremacy during the rut. Japanese maples blush deep red in the garden and falling leaves from the katsura tree emit a sweet, candyfloss-like fragrance.

Winter Wander through Dunham's Winter Garden to see a rotation of ever-changing bulbs, including snowdrops, irises and cyclamen.

The Swan with Two Nicks serves ales from the Dunham Massey Brewing Company, many inspired by local features from the estate and surrounds, including Obelisk, Castle Hill and Bridgewater Blonde.

Follow in the footsteps of ... Dunham Massey's history is entwined with the fortunes of two aristocratic families, the Booths and the Greys. Two Booths spent time in the Tower of London, one for supporting exiled Charles II during the Interregnum, and another for sedition against James II. During the First World War, the house was used as a military hospital and in the 1930s it hosted Haile Selassie – Emperor of Ethiopia and Rastafari messiah – after he was deposed by Mussolini.

How to Get There

By Car There's parking at Dunham Massey (Altrincham WA14 4SJ; National Trust), reached via the A56 and B5160 (M6 exit 19; M56 exit 7).

By Public Transport The nearest train stations are Altrincham (3 miles/5km) and Hale (3 miles/5km). A limited bus service runs from Altrincham Interchange to Warrington, stopping near Dunham Massey.

OS Map OS Explorer 276 (Bolton Central, Wigan & Warrington), Landranger 109 (Manchester, Bolton & Warrington); grid ref (for start): SJ 732/875.

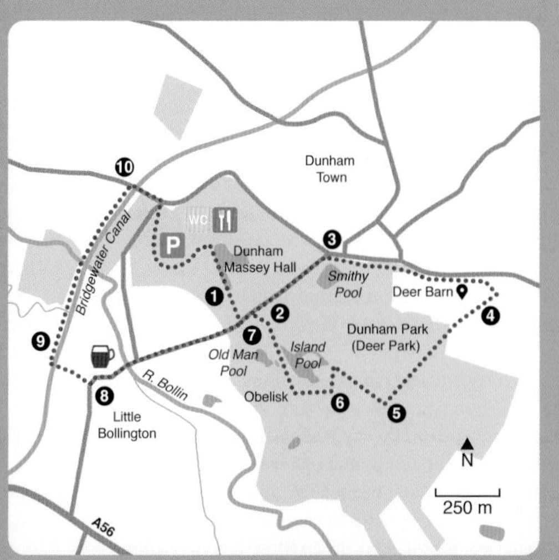

A fallow deer stag grazes in front of Dunham Massey Hall.

1. From the car park, go through the visitor centre, exit from the left and follow signs to the Deer Park. Dunham Massey began life as a medieval park, where deer and wild boar were hunted in the 14th century, and a large population of fallow deer have remained within the walls of the estate since the boundaries were walled in 1748. The deer wander around freely, and you will encounter lots of them (keep all dogs on a short lead). Head up to the lake and turn right to walk with the water and hall on your left. Go through a gate and past a 500-year-old oak tree. Pass the clocktower and stable buildings on your left and continue, bearing left around the end of the moat.

2. Walk past the front of the hall and continue along Smithy Drive, an avenue lined by beech trees. The gardens are off to the left, but elsewhere in the park fallow deer roam freely.

3. Bear right to walk around the edge of Smithy Pool, a lake graced by swans and other waterfowl. Continue going right, along a path lined by large oaks, sycamore, beech and sweet chestnut trees. Some are fenced to protect them from the deer, including a plantation of American basswoods. Go past the Deer Barn, over on your right.

4. At a cross-tracks, turn right along Charcoal Drive. When you draw level with the Deer Barn, as the track bends to the right, a path goes left along an avenue between beech and oak trees. Go about 50 yards past this, then branch left and walk around the edge of the deer sanctuary, marked out with wooden posts and signs. Keep these posts on your left as the path wends through trees, passing the tall, spooky looking Slaughter House on the right.

5. Meet Main Drive and turn right. Walk until you see a series of wooden posts making a right angle on your left.

6. Turn left, stroll along the path and over a wooden bridge and boardwalk. Continue with Island Pool on your right and posts on the left, until you meet a major track (Farm Walk), and then go right, walking with the water on your right.

7. At a junction, with the hall in front of you, go hard left. Walk past the Mill on the right, and when the lane forks, stay left and go over a set of steps beside a gate, exiting the park.

8. Walk along the track between two fields and at the end, by Bollington Mill, where there is a four-way fingerpost, go straight ahead, across a narrow bridge over the river, with a rushing weir to left. The pub is straight ahead.

9. Leave the pub and continue up the road towards Little Bollington. At a footpath fingerpost, turn right and go along a cobbled lane. Go under the bridge (an aqueduct), then turn immediately right, climbing the steps to meet the Bridgewater Canal. Walk with the water on your right, taking in the boats and bucolic view, which seems far distant from the city, even if Manchester is only 12 miles (19km) away.

10. After about two-thirds of a mile (1km), turn left down a path, then right along a pavement beside the road as it goes under another aqueduct and up to the entrance of Dunham Massey. A small metal gate on the left as you enter takes you back into the car park.

Opened in 1761, the Bridgewater Canal was the first navigation in Britain to be built without following an existing waterway.

74 Formby
The Freshfield

The Freshfield
1 Massams Lane, Freshfield
Merseyside L37 7BD
01704 874871
www.greeneking-pubs.co.uk/pubs/merseyside/freshfield

About this walk
- Sandy beaches and dunes
- Woodlands
- Wildlife
- Prehistoric foot prints

Start/finish Victoria Road car park (National Trust)
Distance 5½ miles (9km)
Time to pub 2–2.5 hours
Walking time 3–3.5 hours
Terrain Woodland paths, sand and some road

A multiple CAMRA award-winning inn, THE FRESHFIELD is a large pub with a bright and breezy feel, located a few roads back from the beach. A regular weekend watering hole for walkers exploring the Formby and Ainsdale coast and woodlands, it has a dedicated area for people with dogs to sit inside, and a big beer garden. Besides a comprehensive offering of drinks, it serves good, reasonably priced food from a varied menu offering burgers, brunch and bar snacks, with vegan and vegetarian options.

Explore wonderful woodlands full of scampering red squirrels, before walking through historic asparagus fields and one of Europe's best sand dune habitats to reach the beach, where tides deposit treasure and reveal secrets, including prehistoric footprints frozen in time. Return via a nature reserve and an iconic pub.

Spring Listen for the rasping mating call of the natterjack toad and look for the green flash of male sand lizards amid Ainsdale Sand Dunes National Nature Reserve. Buzzing vernal mining bees, hovering skylarks, green woodpeckers and warblers all add to the spring symphony.

Summer Picnic in the pinewoods and run through epic sand dunes to golden beaches for a dip in the Irish Sea.

Autumn Red squirrels busily bury nuts in secret corners of the Formby woodlands, while deer tiptoe through the trees. Stunning sunsets can be enjoyed from the beach.

Winter Crisp days deliver some of the clearest views out across the Irish Sea, and beachcombing is most fruitful after stormy weather.

A Greene King pub, The Freshfield sells the brewery's standard beers, but also offers an impressive selection of real ales on rotation, with eight pumps in the front bar alone (pictured above). Local tipples such as Big Bog Hinkypunk join options from Yorkshire, Lancashire and further afield. Ale platters are available and there's a large gin menu.

Follow in the footsteps of ... Preserved human footprints from the Mesolithic period can sometimes be seen on the beach, but Formby is now renowned for rich and famous residents, from footballers to actors. Mansion-lined Victoria Road is known as Merseyside's 'Millionaire's Row'.

How to Get There

By Car Park at the Victoria Road car park (National Trust), reached via Victoria Road, 2 miles (3.2km) off the A565 (follow the brown signs); it can be very busy in summer.

By Public Transport Freshfield train station is on this route, and can be used as an alternative starting point.

OS Map OS Explorer 285 (Southport & Chorley), Landranger 108 (Southport & Wigan); grid ref (for start): SD 280/082.

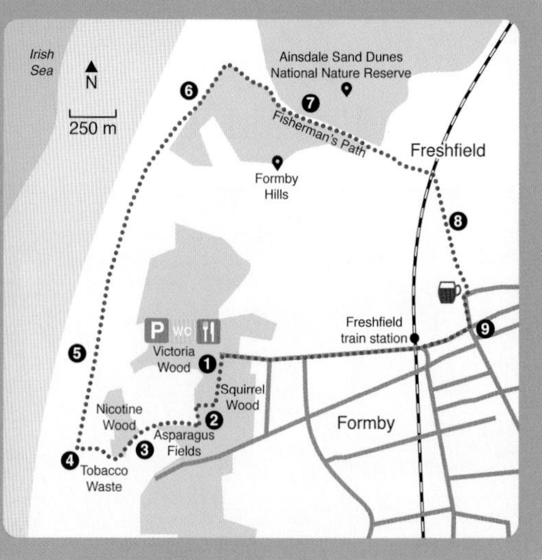

1. From the information board opposite the toilets in the car park, walk into the trees and turn left to go along the top of Squirrel Wood, with pines on your right and beech trees on your left. Ignore the initial turnings left and right and continue straight along a path carpeted in pine needles.

2. When the woods open up at a sandy field, go right, along a matted section of the Asparagus Trail, where the path is fringed by pines. Pass a bench boasting a carving of a donkey and farm worker, and just before meeting the sheep grazing fields, turn left along a sandy single-track path into Horse Jennings Wood, walking with a fence on your right. At the T-junction, turn right and walk along a track towards the sound of the sea, eventually passing between two fenced-off fields – the remains of the Old Asparagus Fields. The tradition of cultivating this labour-intensive crop, which changed the local landscape, is kept alive with asparagus still being grown on the National Trust's Sandfield Farm and Larkhill Farm, nearby.

3. When you meet Nicotine Wood, turn left and walk below the tall, arrow-straight pines. Just before you reach the road, turn right along a wide track. When another track crosses, go straight ahead towards the dunes. The noticeably different vegetation that grows green here in spring and summer is a legacy of the waste tobacco leaf historically dumped from the British Nicotine Company's plant in Bootle.

4. Walk through the gap in the sand dunes to the wide windswept beach. Turn right and continue along the shell-strewn expanse, which sometimes reveals secrets from prehistoric times. Occasionally the tide pulls back the top layer of beach to expose silt beds (about 100–150 yards

from the base of the dunes), which feature footprints left by humans, deer, wolves, aurochs (an ancestor of the modern cow) and other animals, back in the late Mesolithic to Neolithic periods (7500–4500 years ago).

5. Pass the crumbly cliff with signs warning against climbing (the rubble and debris here are the remnants of an old car park, revealed as the dunes roll back at a rate of around 8ft/2.5m a year), and the marker indicating you are passing the bottom of Victoria Road. Out to sea, you might spot a gas rig on the horizon looking like something from War of the Worlds. Keep going, past the indicator for the Gypsy Path that heads into the dunes on your right.

6. When you notice the trees beginning to creep closer to the back of the beach, and the faces of the dunes starting to look slightly steeper, look out for a yellow marker on a post indicating the start of the Fisherman's Path. Follow this and climb up through Ainsdale Sand Dunes National Nature Reserve – home to all sorts of creatures from natterjack toads and sand lizards to tiger beetles and red squirrels – and pick up the path that goes through the pines.

7. Pass the information board about the Sefton Coast dunescape and continue straight, ignoring tracks leading off on the right, and later the left. When you reach the gate at the end of the nature reserve, with a fingerpost pointing towards the train station, go straight, crossing Formby Golf Course. After crossing the railway line, don't go hard right along the path tracing the tracks – instead take the less acute right, to walk with the fence of Freshfield Dune Heath Nature Reserve on your immediate left.

8. Walk through oak woodland, and when a bridleway crosses your path, continue straight. Go past the back of some houses and then emerge into Rimmer's Avenue. Just down the road, on the right, is The Freshfield.

9. After leaving the pub, carefully cross Massams Lane and walk straight along Gore's Lane to the Junction with Victoria Road – also known as Merseyside's 'Millionaire Row'. Turn right here and walk back to the train station or car park.

Opposite: Squirrel Wood, at the outset of this walk, is home to rare red squirrels.

Below: Formby's fantastic foreshore is backed by rolling sand dunes, home to wildlife including sand lizards and great crested newts.

75 Heysham Coast

The Royal

Built in 1502 as a grain store, and transformed into an inn a century later, **THE ROYAL** is regally positioned in the heart of Heysham, a port town on the edge of Morecambe Bay. This storied pub was best known for nettle beer, once brewed in the cottage next door. The recently refurbished interior is now very modern, with trendy touches like demijohn lampshades in open-plan rooms offering restaurant-quality food. There's still a locals' bar where walkers are always welcome, and an extensive beer garden. Accommodation is available.

The Royal
7 Main Street
Heysham, Morecambe
Lancashire LA3 2RN
01524 859298
www.theroyalheysham.co.uk

About this walk

- Coast views
- Historic ruins
- Outdoor art installations

Start/finish Half Moon Bay car park
Distance 1½ miles (2.4km)
Time to pub 45 minutes
Walking time 1–1.5 hours
Terrain Coastal trails, footpaths and pavement

This short adventure across a sandstone headland between Half Moon Bay and Heysham, offers spectacular views over Morecambe Bay to Cumbria. From an evocative modern sculpture, traverse Lancashire's only sea cliffs to an ancient place of pilgrimage with mysterious rock-cut graves, before visiting a 16th-century pub.

Spring Migrant birds including willow warblers start to arrive. The Wildlife Trust has recorded rarer visitors too, like yellow-browed warblers from Siberia.

Summer Listen for whitethroats, warblers, greenfinches, chiffchaffs, meadow pipits and linnets. Flowering yellow-wort and wild orchids attract pollinators including small skipper, common blue and small copper butterflies, plus five- and six-spot burnet moths.

Autumn Watch the sun set over the Irish Sea, setting the Lake District fells ablaze. Various thrush species arrive to overwinter around Heysham Nature Reserve.

Winter Witness storms from the headland, and watch waves race across Morecambe Bay. On calmer days, scan the shoreline for water rails, snipe and woodcock.

The Royal offers six ales from Lancashire brewery Thwaites, with favourites including IPA, Gold, Amber, Mild and Best Bitter.

Follow in the footsteps of ...
St Patrick is Ireland's patron saint, but one story claims he was born in Ravenglass, Cumbria, before being enslaved by pirates. In the 5th century, he's believed to have built a chapel at Heysham, after being shipwrecked off the headland. A small structure still stands, although it dates to several centuries after St Patrick, and was possibly a sheltering place for pilgrims visiting the mysterious stone graves here.

How to Get There

By Car Drive towards Heysham Ferry Port and park in Half Moon Bay car park (LA3 2LA; not National Trust).

By Public Transport Buses serve Heysham from Lancaster and Morecambe. There is a train station at Heysham Port, close to the start of the walk, although services are infrequent and timed around ferries.

OS Map OS Explorer 296 (Lancaster, Morecambe & Fleetwood), Landranger 97 (Kendal & Morecambe); grid ref (for start): SD 409/608.

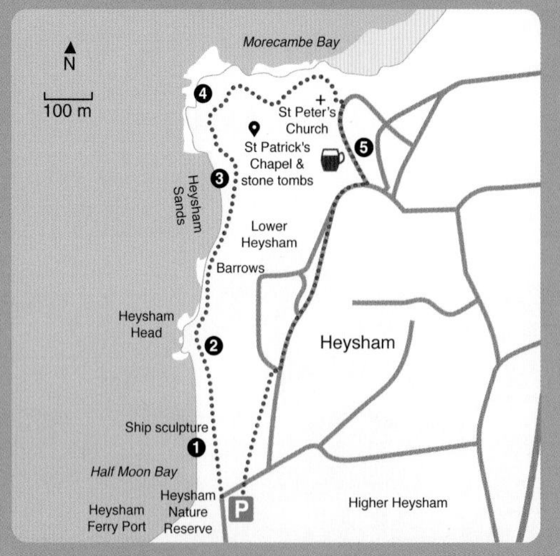

1. From Half Moon Bay car park, carefully cross the road. Heysham Ferry Port is just to your left, with ferries departing to and arriving from the Isle of Man, and Heysham Nature Reserve is nearby. Turn right along the coast path, with a sprawling beach of sand and mudflats stretching away to your left. (Note: Morecambe and Half Moon Bay are notorious for fast-moving tides and shifting sands and can be extremely dangerous – avoid walking out at low tide.) Walk past a large and extraordinary sculpture called *SHIP* (pictured opposite), by artist Anna Gillespie, depicting a boat with a man sat on either end, looking towards opposite horizons, one looking south, the other gazing north. Continue on, past the National Trust sign for the Heysham Coast, walking around Heysham Head. Over the top of the gorse, you can (weather permitting) see Lake District fells forming the line of the horizon.

2. Stroll on, across the grassland of the Barrows, Lancashire's only sea cliffs. Keep to the left when the sandy path braids, to get the best views of the Heysham Sands shoreline right in front of you, and the curvy Cumbrian coast on the opposite side of Morecambe Bay.

3. As you round the headland, the fractured outline of St Patrick's Chapel becomes clear, straight ahead on Chapel Hill. Take the track up to the ruins and explore. If you stand in the right spot and the weather behaves, you can frame the taller peaks of the Lake District through the chapel doorway. Just south of the chapel are eight, body-shaped, open stone graves, carved into the sandstone headland. It's thought these unique rock-cut graves were created around the 11th century and were used for burying very high-status people.

4. Go through the stone entrance of the chapel, follow the path leading left, pass through a gate and walk down to meet a path. This leads to St Peter's Church, which looks modern next to the ancient chapel, but parts of the building are Anglo-Saxon in origin and have been here for 1,000 years. Explore the church (in the south chancel aisle, there's an amazing, intricately carved Viking hogback stone dating to the 10th century) and graveyard. Then take the path around to meet Main Street in Heysham town. Turn right and The Royal is just down the road, on the right.

5. Leave the pub and turn right. As you enter the town triangle, check out the 3-D, mural-style sculpture *Spirit of Heysham* by Michael Edwards, which features on the front wall of Heysham Jubilee Institute on your left. Cross Barrows Lane by the bus stop, turn right and follow the road around as it bends left, walking on pavement. After a few hundred yards, cross the road and cut across the grass towards the port, until you are opposite the car park.

76 Crummock Water

Kirkstile Inn

Kirkstile Inn
Loweswater
Cumbria CA13 0RU
01900 85219
www.kirkstile.com

About this walk

- Lake District National Park
- Waterfalls and fells
- Wainwright views
- Bluebells
- Wild swimming

Start/finish Lanthwaite Wood car park (National Trust)
Distance 11 miles (17.5km)
Time to pub 4.5 hours
Walking time 5 hours
Terrain Lake and fellside trails, lanes, some road

A legendary Lake District pub located between Loweswater and Crummock Water, the **KIRKSTILE INN** dates to the 16th century and welcomes walkers with an open fire, wonderful local food and drink, and spectacular views of surrounding fells, including several Wainwrights. A regular winner of CAMRA's regional pub of the year, the inn has two low-beamed rooms with snugs. The terrace and garden look up at Brackenthwaite Fell, Grasmoor, Mellbreak, Hen Comb, Black Crag, Carling Knott, Darling and Low Fell, among other peaks, and Park Beck flows past the back garden.

Circumnavigate Crummock Water, walking out along the lake's east bank and across the lower flanks of Grasmoor and Whiteless Pike (compared to Switzerland's Wiesshorn by Alfred Wainwright) to Buttermere. Return via tall waterfalls and crags, along the west bank, to a classic pub.

Spring In April–May, the 'secret valley' of Rannerdale Knotts explodes with bluebells. Listen for larks and stonechats.

Summer The Lakes are busy, but these trails are less trampled than many. Cool your heels in Crummock Water or Buttermere.

Autumn Red squirrels scamper around increasingly colourful Lanthwaite Wood. The early setting sun behind Mellbreak casts wonderful shadows across Grasmoor.

Winter Sour Milk Ghyll and Scale Force waterfalls run fast, the trails are quieter, snow dusts the fells and lake views are crystal clear in the crisp, cold air.

The Kirkstile Inn is the tap bar for Cumbrian Legendary Ales (famous for its award-winning Loweswater Gold), which was housed here until recently. Six handpumps dispense different ales from the brewery, with locally inspired names like Esthwaite Bitter, Grasmoor Dark Ale, Buttermere Beauty, Langdale and Life of a Mountain.

Follow in the footsteps of... In 1930, local writer and publican Nicholas Size published a historical novel, *The Secret Valley*, colourfully depicting Rannerdale Knotts as the scene of a bloody battle between local defenders and invading Normans after 1066. In Size's (admittedly unsubstantiated) story, the locals were victorious, and the profusion of bluebells that floods the site every autumn is supposedly enriched by the spilt blood of slain interlopers.

How to Get There

By Car Park at Lanthwaite Wood (CA13 0RT; National Trust) between Loweswater and Brackenthwaite.

By Public Transport The closest train stations are Workington (20 miles/32.2km west) and Penrith (28 miles/45km east). The 77/77A bus travels between Buttermere and Keswick; in summer there's a free shuttle bus from Cockermouth to Buttermere valley.

OS Map OS Explorer OL4 (The English Lakes North-Western Area), Landranger 89 (West Cumbria, Cockermouth & Wast Water); grid ref (for start): NY 150/214.

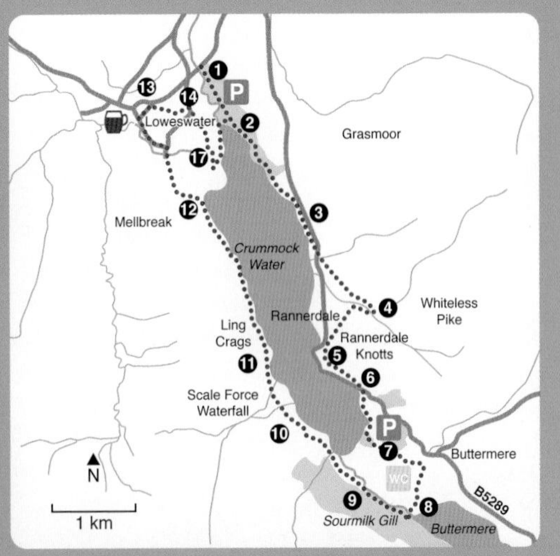

1. From the car park, walk into Lanthwaite Wood, past the National Trust information sign. As the path forks, keep right, with the River Cocker on your right, until you meet Crummock Water at a beach. Go left, up a path to the main track, then turn right.

2. Walk with the lake on your right, enjoying views across the water to Raven and White Crag, and the monstrous dome of Mellbreak. Go right at a fork, passing a boathouse and bench. At the next fork, go left, along a smaller path through High Wood. Cross a stone wall, stream and wooden stile, and continue straight, as the path arcs back towards the water. Go through a gate, emerge from the woods and walk under the arms of several large oaks. Stunning views open up along the lake, and Grasmoor towers to your left. The path skirts the lapping water and crosses a little wooden footbridge. Keep going, past a left turn and through a gate to reach a little beach. After crossing two more wooden footbridges, Rannerdale Knots appears ahead.

3. At a stone wall, go left and ascend to the road. Cross, turn right and walk to a car park. Here, follow a footpath arrow pointing slightly left across the grass and over Cinderdale Beck (a stream).

4. Walk towards the valley between Rannerdale Knotts and Whiteless Pike, which reaches for the clouds on the left. Turn right to cross Squat Beck via a wide wooden footbridge. Ignore the gate on the other side, bear right and follow the stream as it rushes to meet the lake. The path leads through bracken, meets a stone wall and goes through a kissing gate. Keep walking with the wall on your right.

5. Go through a small car park, meet the road and turn left. After about 75 yards, take the footpath leading left, ascending and walking over Low Bank, which offers stunning views across Crummock Water. Ahead, beyond Buttermere, looms Fleetwith Pike.

6. Descend to the road, carefully cross, go through a gate and along a permitted footpath beside the lake. Another gate leads to a lovely path running through Wood House. Cross a bridge, walk around the beach and cross a second bridge over Mill Beck, which flows into the lake.

7. Go through a gate and turn left, following a path running parallel to the river. Pass a campsite and go through the car park to Buttermere. Meet the road by Buttermere Court Hotel and Croft House café, and turn right, going through a gate and along a lane. At a junction, follow the fingerpost pointing to Buttermere and walk along a lane with fields on your right.

8. Go through a gate and walk around the beach at Buttermere's northern end, gazing across the water

The setting sun projects the outline of Mellbreak onto the flanks of Grasmoor, across Crummock Water.

to Fleetwith Pike and Haystacks. Cross the bridge over Buttermere Dubs and continue across a second, smaller bridge. Walk up a flight of stone steps, turn right and go through a gate and over the bridge, crossing the cascade at Sour Milk Ghyll.

9. Walk with the river on your right. Pass Scale Bridge and continue to Crummock Water. Stroll along a rocky path, crossing two bridges. After the track bends left, towards the valley, another path crosses your route. Go right here and walk parallel to the lakeshore.

10. Cross a stream and another bridge. To the left, shyly hidden away, Scale Force (the Lakes' highest waterfall, with a single drop of 170ft/52m) tumbles off the fells.

11. Pass the almost-island at Low Ling Crag and continue along the lakeside to a stone wall by an attractive pebble beach. There is a gate in the wall, but don't go through (except to skim stones from the beach if you wish).

12. Turn left, walk up and over a steep grassy hill, keeping the wall on your right. Descend into a small group of oaks, bear right and walk down towards a cottage. Go through a gate, turn left just before the cottage, go through another gate and walk along a lane. Cross a bridge over Park Beck, and when the lane forks go left. Walk up to the Kirkstile Inn.

13. Exit the pub and walk along the road with the church on your left. At the phone box and Kirkstile Inn sign, you can walk straight down the road to the car park, but for a more scenic route, turn right down the lane, following a footpath fingerpost. Pass a cottage, hop over a stile and, at a fingerpost, turn left and cross a sequence of fields and stiles to meet a lane by Muncaster House.

14. Go right and, after 50 yards, continue straight ahead through a gate following a footpath fingerpost. Carry on through a second gate, walking along a broad track. Go through several more gates, then across a wide bridge over Park Beck.

15. At the lake, turn left and walk along the shore, before crossing a narrow footbridge. Walk through trees and cross another two footbridges, where outflowing lake water rushes over a weir and fish ladder. Enter a clearing with benches and a great view up Crummock Water. Turn left and walk back through Lanthwaite Wood to the car park.

77 Langdale Fells

The Old Dungeon Ghyll Hotel

The Old Dungeon Ghyll
Great Langdale
Cumbria LA22 9JY
015394 37272
www.odg.co.uk

About this walk
- Wainwright peak bagging
- Lake District National Park
- Waterfalls
- Lots of steep ascents

Start/finish Old Dungeon Ghyll car park (National Trust)
Distance 6½ miles (10.5km)
Time to pub 5 hours
Walking time 5 hours
Terrain Fellside paths, peaks, rocky scrambles

Named for a feature on the flanks of Langdon Fell, which towers behind, the National Trust-owned **OLD DUNGEON GHYLL** is forever full of fell walkers and climbers. Outside tables offer ace views and inside the iconic Hiker's Bar, a converted cowshed (shippon), you'll find a fireplace, snugs, wooden beams, benches and tables engraved by generations of penknife-wielding adventurers. Charts of the Wainwrights line walls, alongside pictures of climbers and crags, and equipment like crampons and climbing nuts. The bar sells both maps and hearty food.

Four Wainwrights can be bagged on this fell walk, which is short in distance but epic in elevation. The rugged route clambers above Stickle Tarn to explore Pavey Ark, Harrison Stickle and the Langdale Pikes, before descending via Dungeon Ghyll.

Spring Herdwick sheep, native to The Lakes, lamb in fields below fells. Spot blue tits, wrens, woodpeckers, cuckoos and treecreepers at Sticklebarn's bird-feeding station.

Summer Spy butterflies (green-veined white, orange-tip, painted lady, red admiral) and dragonflies (common darter, common hawker and golden-ringed). Cool your heels in Stickle Tarn before climbing Pavey Ark.

Autumn Waterfalls, including Dungeon Ghyll Force, are in full flow, and the Stickle Ghyll crossing gets exciting. Thousands of thrushes (including redwings and fieldfares) feast on juniper berries.

Winter This walk can be challenging in winter. If you're experienced and equipped, icy fells, frozen waterfalls and white-topped Wainwrights look wonderful. See snow buntings around Pike of Stickle, and whooper swans and pink-footed geese on the tarn.

Nine handpumps line the serving hatch in the Hiker's Bar, dispensing local ales including Hawkshead Brewery's Windermere Pale Ale and Cumbrian Ales' Loweswater Gold.

Follow in the footsteps of ...
In his seven-volume series, *A Pictorial Guide to the Lakeland Fells,* Alfred Wainwright lovingly described 214 Lake District fells (peaks) that would, thereafter, be collectively known by his name. This walk takes in four (Pavey Ark, Harrison Stickle, Pike of Stickle and Loft Crag) and you could easily bag Thunacar Knott and Sergeant Man too.

How to Get There

By Car Approach via the A591, between Kendal and Keswick, turning off at Ambleside and following signs for Langdale. Use the National Trust car park outside The Old Dungeon Ghyll Hotel. If that's full, there's more parking by Sticklebarn (also National Trust).

By Public Transport Stagecoach bus 516 serves Dungeon Ghyll from Kendal, which has a train station.

OS Map OS Explorer OL6 (The Lake District: South-western area), Landranger 90 (Penrith & Keswick); grid ref (for start): NY 286/061.

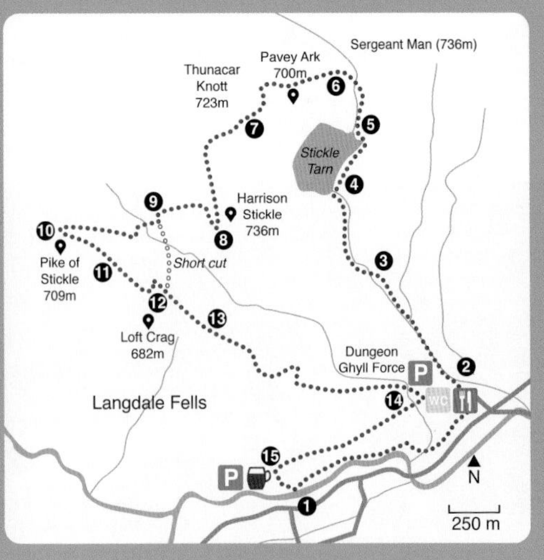

1. Leave the car park via a gate facing away from Langdale Fell and Raven Crag. Turn left and walk across a field, go through a gate and along the path with Mickleden Beck flowing on your right. Pass through another gate, cross a field, hop over a stile and walk around another field. Turn right, cross a bridge and go left, through more gates to reach the National Trust car park by Sticklebarn and the New Dungeon Ghyll Hotel (not to be confused with the Old Dungeon Ghyll Hotel).

2. Walk to the left of the Sticklebarn café (a great place for a coffee and breakfast), go through a gate and along a path, passing the National Trust sign for Stickle Ghyll. Climb a flight of stone steps, passing a waterfall on your right. Cross a wooden bridge and continue, with the cascading water running through Stickle Ghyll on your left.

3. Walk up the footpath towards ever-more impressive falls. Cross a little stone bridge over a stream coming in from the right, and clamber through the rocky architecture of Tarn Crag. Keep climbing and scrambling, crossing to the opposite bank at a waterfall, before continuing to Stickle Tarn.

4. At the water's edge, cross back over the stream and walk around the right bank of the tarn, along a well-formed path with Pavey Ark and Harrison Stickle to your left.

5. Approaching the bottom of Pavey Ark, stay to the right of the stream (Bright Beck). Pass a waterfall and continue to a ford. Cross the stream and take the steep track ascending the fell.

6. Clamber to the small stone cairn marking the sensational 1,127ft (700m) summit of Pavey Ark. Peer through a gap in the rock with views over the tarn, then turn right and follow a sequence of cairns up the steep, rubbly hill. The peaks of Thunacar Knott (2,372ft/723m) and Sergeant Man (2,415ft/736m) are off to your right – two more Wainwrights ripe for bagging, but not part of this walk.

7. Pick your way along the rocky ridge. The way here is indistinct, but occasional cairns indicate a rough route (in poor visibility, be careful not to stray too far left, where there are drop-offs). The path leans left and drops slightly, before becoming more defined, with a series of pebble piles lining the climb to the 2,415ft (736m) peak of Harrison Stickle, the highpoint of this adventure, marked by a couple of stone cairns. If you have any breath remaining, the view from here will steal it.

8. After gazing over Stickle Tarn, turn 180 degrees and look across to Pike of Stickle. Descend towards this distinctive peak, bearing slightly right, following a gully, and going past a stone cairn. At a second cairn, head left and walk directly towards the Pike.

9. In the dip between the peaks, at an obvious junction, go right and head towards the Pike.

Shortcut: to skip the next two peaks, descend directly to the stream (which plummets left over Thorn Crag into Dungeon Ghyll), cross and then trace the path along the lower side of Loft Crag to meet the rest of the route at point 12.

10. There's a short set of steps at the beginning of the ascent but reaching Pike of Stickle's 2,325ft (709m) summit involves a proper scramble – with a wonderful vista as a reward.

11. Descend and bear right, crossing a minor hilltop and clambering up on to 2,237ft (682m) Loft Crag, the fourth and final Wainwright of this fellwalking adventure.

12. Continue right over the top of Loft Crag and descend via a scree-strewn path on the other side, turning right when you get to the bottom.

13. At a large stone cairn, go straight on, descending dramatically through a gully. Walk along a path punctuated by cairns, with a precipitous drop on the right, through Mark Gate. Just before a wall comes in to meet the path on your right, a turning offers you the chance to see Dungeon Ghyll Force waterfall, which is a short diversion from the main path, off to the left.

14. Continue over a river crossing and stile. At the T-junction, turn right and walk with a lovely stone wall on your left and Raven Crag soaring to the right. This stony path is part of the 70-mile (112-km) Cumbria Way that crosses the Lake District National Park between Ulverston and Carlisle.

15. Cross a bridge and go through several gates. Pass a cottage on the left, go through a gate then bear left. Another gate takes you to a path leading to a road. The Old Dungeon Ghyll hotel is on the left.

A pair of Wainwrights, Harrison Stickle and Pavey Ark, reflected in Stickle Tarn.

78 Sizergh Castle
The Strickland Arms

The Strickland Arms
Nannypie Lane
Sizergh, Kendal
Cumbria LA8 8DZ
015395 61010
www.thestricklandarms.com

About this walk
- Wildflowers
- Woodlands
- Deer
- Butterflies

Start/finish Sizergh Castle car park (National Trust)
Distance 4½ miles (7km)
Time to pub 2 hours
Walking time 2.5 hours
Terrain Countryside paths, fields, woodlands

With a flagstone floor, high ceilings, heavy curtains and antique décor, **THE STRICKLAND ARMS** is not your average pub. Well-used to walkers popping in after a wander around the woodlands surrounding Sizergh Castle (above), and owned by the National Trust, the pub specialises in local craft ales and gins, served in a friendly bar area, where an open fire crackles in colder months and candles burn on the tables. There's also a dining area, but food is served throughout. On sunny days you can relax on the front patio or in the orchard garden.

Wander around the wildlife-rich wetlands and woodlands surrounding Sizergh Castle, a 750-year-old manor perched on the edge of the Lake District, before enjoying a local ale in a splendid pub.

Spring Buzzards soar and pheasants fuss around Chapel Wood. Blossom fills the orchards. Look out for roe deer, especially early in the morning, on Sizergh Fell.

Summer Sizergh Fell is resplendent with swathes of purple field scabious and harebells, and a yellow haze of buttercups, bedstraw and cowslips. Bees, green woodpeckers and fritillary butterflies are all active in the woodland glades.

Autumn In Sizergh's woods, oak, hazel, birch, chestnut and ash trees blaze, while in the gardens, Japanese maple ranges from flame yellow to burnt orange. Ripe damsons can be scrumped around Holeslack, and squirrels forage for sweet chestnuts along Ashbank Lane. Look out for roe deer, particularly around Sizergh Fell.

Winter Sizergh is a nationally important breeding site for hawfinches, shy birds best seen between February and April, when they search for hornbeam seeds on bare boughs. Also look out for fieldfares and redwings.

The Strickland Arms sells Swan Blonde from Bowness Bay Brewery and rotates five other local real ales, including Harvest Moon from Ulverston and Union Specific pale from Fell Brewery. There's also a massive gin menu.

Follow in the footsteps of ...
The Strickland family has occupied Sizergh Castle for eight centuries. Catherine Parr, Henry VIII's sixth wife and a relative of the Stricklands, is believed to have lived here after the death of her first husband in 1533.

How to Get There

By Car Use exit 36 from the M6, drive the A590 towards Kendal, take the Barrow-in-Furness turning and follow brown signs for Sizergh.

By public transport Buses from Kendal stop at Brettagh Holt roundabout, a 10-minute walk from Sizergh; take care crossing the busy roads.

OS Map OS Explorer OL7 (The English Lakes – South Eastern area), Landranger 97 (Kendal & Morecambe); grid ref (for start): SD 498/878.

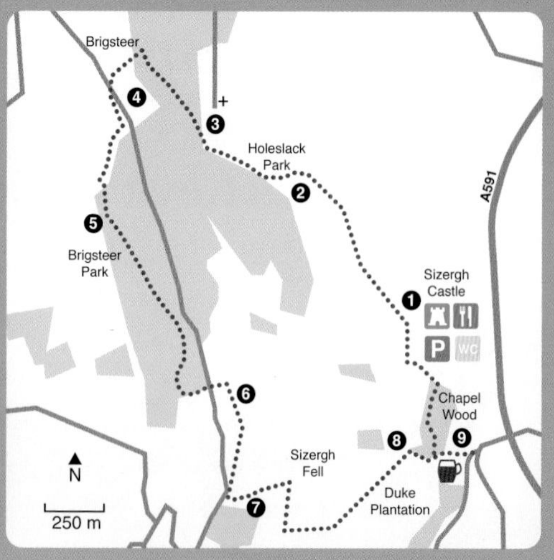

1. From the car park, walk to the left of the visitor centre, by the disabled parking spots. At a three-way fingerpost, head towards Helsington Church and Holeslack, strolling through a gate and along a straight path.

2. Follow blue arrows for Church Fell, through several gates, into mixed woodlands. The path gently ascends through more gates and past farm buildings.

3. Join a lane, cross a cattle grid and, at a fingerpost, bear right to stay on the lane. After 150 yards, veer left, following a fingerpost for Brigsteer Road (a path). Descend across grass, bear left and take a path through trees.

4. At the bottom, by a gate, go left along a narrow stony path by a stone wall, wending downhill to a gate, then descending across a grassy field to a farmhouse and Parkend Lane. Follow purple arrows for Park End Walk and pass through a couple of gates by farm buildings. Cross the road, go through a gate and bear left across the field, following a fingerpost pointing towards Brigsteer. With woods on your left, walk right down to the bottom left corner of the field, to a wide gate. Pass through and go along a broad track into the trees.

5. At a fork, turn left and walk up through leafy Brigsteer Park. Go straight, past a couple of junctions, to a National Trust information sign about the woodlands. Pass a large gate, cross the road, hop over a stone stile and stroll straight ahead, along a gravel lane.

6. After 100 yards, turn right through a wooden gate and walk across a field with a wall on your right. Pass through another gate, go straight, bear right through a gate and follow a path uphill with a wall initially on your left. Keep going straight.

7. Go through a gate, turn left and walk up a track past a lonely sycamore tree. Climb the hill – Sizergh Fell – to the corner of the field and turn right. Go through a gate and veer left, passing through another gate by a wooden post. Keep walking up the hill to another wooden post, bear left, go through a gate and follow a path across the field, through the fenceline and downhill towards Chapel Wood, enjoying a view of the castle over to the left.

8. Go through a gate and follow a footpath snaking downhill, with Chapel Wood on your left. Just before a gate, turn left, cross two little footbridges and go through a kissing gate. At the lane, go straight ahead. Bear right, past some cottages, meet the road, go left and then immediately right through a gate into The Strickland Arms garden.

9. Leaving the pub, return the way you came, but turn right through a gate into Chapel Wood, which is full of forest features for big and little kids. Exit the woods, turn left and walk up to the car park.

79 Cautley Spout & The Calf

The Cross Keys Temperance Inn

Located in a 16th-century former farm building, **THE CROSS KEYS** was a licensed alehouse until 1902, when the landlord drowned helping a drinker who'd fallen in the river. The pub was turned into a temperance inn and left to the National Trust in 1949, on the condition alcohol was never sold. Visitors now enjoy great food, warm hospitality and non-boozy beverages in rooms full of character, artefacts and antique furniture. An open fire warms walkers in winter, while a garden offers intoxicating views of Cautley Spout and Howgill Fells. B&B accommodation available.

The Cross Keys
Cautley, Sedbergh
Cumbria LA10 5NE
015396 20284
www.cautleyspout.co.uk

About this walk

- Epic waterfalls
- Fell and dale views
- Pub with no beer
- Prehistoric site
- Includes a steep climb

Start/finish The Cross Keys
Distance 6½ miles (10.5km)
Time to pub The pub is at the start/finish
Walking time 3 hours
Terrain River and hillside footpaths

Ascend a path beside England's tallest cascade, then hike to the roof of Howgill Fells, on the scenic seam between the Yorkshire Dales and Cumbrian Lake District. Climb The Calf, and return to a pub with no beer (but plenty of cheer).

Spring Streams and waterfalls run fast, wildflowers bloom across The Calf and butterflies flutter by.

Summer Still something of a secret, the Howgill Fells offer crowd-free picnics and perambulations on lazy, hazy, sunny days. Enjoy views to the Lake District from The Calf, before ice cream and cold drinks in the Cross Keys' garden.

Autumn The cascade at Cautley Spout is most dramatic after becks have been fed by autumn rains. Look out for white-breasted dippers bobbing on the rocks of the River Rawthey.

Winter Snow often covers The Calf, Great Dummacks and the wider Howgill Fells, while icicles sprout around Cautley Spout. A roaring fire and warm welcome await in The Cross Keys.

While you can't buy booze at the Cross Keys, the inn does sell a wide range of non-alcoholic beers, alongside top-quality coffee, tea and soft drinks. (B&B guests and diners can BYO wine.)

Follow in the footsteps of ... Alfred Wainwright described 32 ambles in this area in *Walks on the Howgill Fells*. Nearby Sedbergh has become the literary centre of the North, with an August Festival of Books and Drama. The Cross Keys is also a book café.

How to Get There

By Car The Cross Keys has a small car park (customers only) and there's roadside parking. The pub and trailhead are located between Sedbergh and Kirkby Stephen, on the A683.

By Public Transport Buses run between Kendal and Sedbergh, going via Oxenholme train station, (10 miles/16km from Sedbergh), which is on the West Coast Mainline between London and Scotland.

OS Map OS Explorer OL19 (Howgill Fells & Upper Eden Valley), Landranger 98 (Wensleydale & Upper Wharfedale); grid ref (for start): SD 698/969.

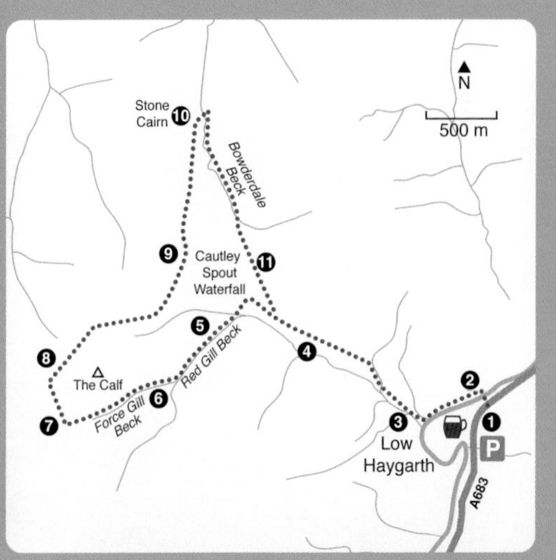

1. The trailhead is about 100 yards up the road from The Cross Keys. Follow the footpath fingerpost pointing towards Cautley Spout and cross the bridge over the River Rawthey.

2. On the other side of the river, at the T-junction with the Pennine Journey (a 247-mile/397-km long-distance walking trail), turn left and follow the path along the Rawthey, heading towards the imposing mounds of Great Dummacks (2,175ft/663m) and Calders (2,211ft/674m), on the horizon directly ahead.

3. When the path forks at a ford, leave the Pennine Journey (which carries straight on towards a footbridge) and follow the better-trodden path as it arcs right, towards the now very visible waterfall. Walk to an information sign about the formation of the falls and the Iron Age settlement that occupied this valley 2,000 years ago. Continue along the path, crossing the stream (Cautley Holme Beck) several times. Scree-scattered Cautley Crags now loom on the left, and the waterfall is often audible from here.

4. The path starts to climb. When it forks, go left and explore the fantastic falls below Cautley Spout, England's tallest cascade, which drops 550ft (200m). Ash and hawthorn trees overhang the pool and gorge below the tumbling water. A sign politely asks people to vary their route up the hill to avoid erosion – try and do this as you ascend to a set of

Enjoy great coffee and homemade cake in the atmospheric lounge of The Cross Keys.

NORTH WEST

The view from the top of Cautley Spout, the highest cascade in the country.

steep steps that zig-zag up the right-hand side of the waterfall. At the top, bear left.

5. As the route levels, a single-track path leads around a contour line, crossing a brook before dropping and then heading along a lovely chattering section of Red Gill Beck, a stream with lots of little falls and pools.

6. Go past a ruined croft building and, after the stream forks, keep walking with the water on your left, along the banks of Force Gill Beck. The path climbs steadily, then leaves the stream and ascends a grassy hill to the right. Emerge at a T-junction with A Dale's Highway (a 90-mile/145-km long-distance footpath) and turn right. Walk uphill, ignoring the smaller path going down to the right, and ascend to the trig point at the top of The Calf (2,217ft/676m), Howgill Fells' highest point. From here, on a good day, you can enjoy views right across Cumbria to the famous fells of The Lakes.

7. Continue walking north along A Dale's Highway. A valley plunges to your left here, between the hilltops of Howell Fells, which Wainwright likened to 'a huddle of squatting elephants'.

8. Keep walking along the ridge. When the path forks by a little tarn, go right and follow the distinct bridleway, as it runs down a long descent into Bowderdale.

9. Keep following the path, descending into the dale for around 1 mile (1.6km), until you spot a big stone cairn way down on the right.

10. Turn right towards this cairn before you meet Ram's Gill, and right again along a grassy path just before actually reaching the cairn. The path runs uphill, parallel to Bowderdale Beck, to Bowderdale Head, with several minor stream crossings along the way. Look out for some stone sheepfolds over on the right.

11. Ignore little paths on the right and go straight ahead into the dale that brought you here. From this spot there's an amazing perspective on Cautley Spout waterfall, with the eponymous crag forming the backdrop behind the cascade. Descend along the path, with the waterfall over to your far right. The route becomes steep, then snakes down to the junction where you began the ascent earlier. From here, retrace your footsteps to The Cross Keys.

80 Scafell
Wasdale Head Inn

Perched betwixt famous fells, including England's tallest peak, the **WASDALE HEAD INN** claims to be the 'birthplace of British climbing' (although it is also where the World's Biggest Liar contest began). That the inn is a legendary hangout for walkers and rock climbers is, however, beyond doubt. Hearty fell fuel and real ale is served, amid an adventure-soaked ambience created by the many images and references to crag-clambering and peak-bagging. A log burner keeps Ritson's Bar cosy. In summer sit out by the beck and order from the bistro. Accommodation available.

Wasdale Head Inn
Wasdale Head
Cumbria CA20 1EX
019467 26229
www.wasdale.com

About this walk
- England's highest peak
- Lake District National Park
- Stunning views
- Steep climb (3,247ft/990m of ascent)
- Rock scrambling

Start/finish Lake Head car park (National Trust)
Distance 9 miles (14.5km)
Time to pub 4 hours
Walking time 5 hours
Terrain High fell footpaths, technical trails

NORTH WEST

Climb to England's rooftop and absorb Lake District views, before traversing the adventurous Corridor Route to Sty Head and wandering back through Wasdale, past Great Gable and Kirk Fell, to a church that commemorates fallen climbers and a fantastic fell-walkers' pub.

Spring Ravens rock hop and skylarks soar. Buzzards, kestrels, even golden eagles can be seen.

Summer Car parks and paths are busy – start early and finish in time for a beer by the beck in the sun. Wastwater shimmers, inviting post-walk paddles.

Autumn Sunlight dances in the dale, and cloud inversions are often seen from Scafell summit. Sunsets and star displays are sensational as evenings draw in.

Winter Waterfalls, including Ritson's Force, gush spectacularly. Trails are quiet, and views are serene and often flecked with snow. Conditions can change quickly – check forecasts carefully and only venture out if you're an experienced winter fell walker with the appropriate gear.

Ritson's Bar offers a large rotating range of Cumbrian-made real ales and ciders, including small-batch bespoke beers like The Wasd'Ale (copper), Ritson's Biggest Lie (blonde) and Great Corby (stout).

Follow in the footsteps of ...
Ritson's Bar is named for former landlord, Will Ritson, a raconteur, wrestler, fellsman, guide and farmer, fondly remembered as the 'World's biggest liar' for the outrageously tall tales with which he regaled ramblers and clamberers. He even started an annual international fib-spinning competition, which continues today, albeit in a different pub (Santon's Bridge's Bridge Inn).

How to Get There

By Car Head to Wasdale, 5 miles (8km) east of the A595, turning at Gosforth. Park at Lake Head car park by the National Trust campsite (CA20 1EX; National Trust).

By Public Transport The nearest train station is Seascale (11 miles/ 17.5km). Seasonal shuttle buses operate in Wasdale in August and September.

OS Map OS Explorer OL6 (The Lake District – South-western area), Landranger 89 (West Cumbria, Cockermouth & Wast Water); grid ref (for start): NY 183/075.

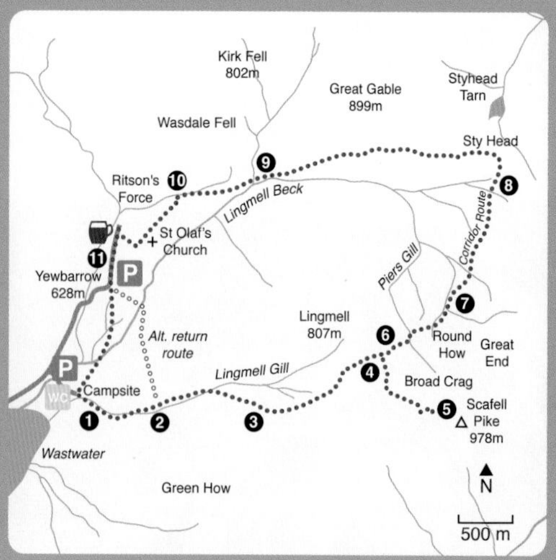

1. Go through the gate at the top of the National Trust car park, by a cattle grid, and take a path running next to Lingmell Gill. You can walk either side, but our route takes you to the right of the rushing water, initially, before crossing a footbridge and continuing up through the valley with wonderful views over Wastwater – England's deepest lake – to the right.

2. A path comes in left, from Wasdale Head. This is the alternative return route if you choose to come back this way instead of taking the Corridor Route, but for now carry on walking uphill, beside the gill. Go through a gate and continue along a stone-clad path, before bearing right, crossing the gill and continuing up a stepped path.

3. When the path forks, stay left and walk up a steep, stone-clad track. The route becomes rougher, but remains distinct, with stone cairns keeping you on the right track as you climb with Pulpit Rock and Pikes Crag above, to the right.

4. As you reach the col in the saddle between Lingmell (left) and Scafell Pike (right), the path bends right and then, where another path leads left, the route to the summit goes straight up, past a large, distinct, dark-coloured boulder. Follow the steep path as it snakes around numerous stone cairns to the 3,209ft/978m peak, where there's a trig point and a stone war memorial summit cairn. In 1918, the peak of Scafell Pike and surrounding land (above the 2,000ft/610m contour line on the Scafell massif) was gifted to the National Trust by Lord Leconfield as a memorial to the men of the Lake District killed in World War I. Standing beside this sombre structure, you can be absolutely sure that you are the highest person on land in England at that moment.

5. Descend via the same route to the T-junction by the boulder where you began the summit approach. Turn right to take the Corridor Route, which has one tricky section requiring a bit of a scramble, but otherwise follows a good path. (Alternatively, if conditions are poor or you'd rather avoid the scramble, go left and descend the same route you just climbed, veering right at the junction at point 2 and following signs to Wasdale Head.)

6. Descend the craggy path, following cairns and crossing Piers Gill, where a waterfall cascades on the left. Ignore a scrappy track going sharp right, up towards the summit, and another that descends left along Piers Gill, and stay right, walking around the bottom of Broad Crag.

7. Disregard a path going right and continue downwards. Cross another stream (Greta Gill) and take care on a craggy section of path with two lovely little waterfalls distracting you to the left as you edge past Round How. Shortly after another gill crossing, you need to scramble up rocks to the right; an arrow etched on the crag points the way,

but it's easy to miss. (If you find yourself clambering around a steep face with a big drop to your left, you've gone wrong – go back.) A short (20-yard), relatively easy scramble up the rocks returns you to a distinct path.

8. The path wends, crosses another gill, and finally meets a T-junction at a large cairn. Turn left and go over a little sign-topped hillock, with Sprinkling Tarn sparkling to your right, and Styhead Tarn straight ahead. Descend and hop over some stone slabs across a bog to Sty Head, where a Keswick Mountain Rescue Team emergency stretcher box huddles by a boulder. Turn left here, walk past a cairn on your right and stroll along an obvious path, descending gradually into the dale with Great Gable and Kirk Fell to your right, and tantalising views of Wasdale Head Inn straight ahead.

9. Go through a gate and meet Lingmell Beck, which runs on your left. Cross a ghyll via a footbridge and walk through a field with a stone wall on your left, past a gate and a National Trust collection box.

10. At Burnthwaite Cottage, go left through a wide gate, walk past the building to meet a lane, turn right and pass a National Trust sign for Burnthwaite Farm. Pass through a kissing gate and turn right at St Olaf's – England's smallest church, where there are graves and memorials to climbers who perished on the crags and during the First World War, including a plaque from the Fell and Rock Climbing Club of the English Lake District that once graced the top of Great Gable. Continue through two more gates to the Wasdale Head Inn.

11. Leave the pub and turn right, walking down the road towards Wastwater. At a bend in the road, go straight ahead, along a signed footpath, through a gate and across a field. Follow an obvious path, crossing a stream, going through a gate and then across two rivers via stepping stones and shallow fords to another gate. At another water crossing, in an area with a pebble beach and a stone cairn, ignore a path coming in from the left and keep going straight ahead, to the National Trust campsite. To reach the car park, follow footpath arrows across the campsite and through a gate leading left at the end, and then go right to loop back in via the gate you took at the very beginning.

Looking down along Piers Gill on the Corridor Route, a more interesting and less trafficked way to descend from Scafell Pike.

81 Windermere

The Tower Bank Arms

Nestled in Near Sawrey, between Esthwaite Water and Windermere, the National Trust-owned **TOWER BANK ARMS** is a charming 17th-century inn. Located next to Beatrix Potter's Hill Top house, the pub appears in *The Tale of Jemima Puddle-duck*. A cosy front bar features slate floors, low oak beams and a blazing fire. The rear room is for dining, while a patio looks across a Lakeland landscape. The pub welcomes walkers – Kendal mint cake sits on the bar and muddy boots and rain-soaked coats don't faze staff. Good food and local ales served. Accommodation available.

The Tower Bank Arms
Near Sawrey
Cumbria LA22 0LF
015394 36334
www.towerbankarms.co.uk

About this walk

- Lake District National Park
- Windermere shore trails
- Wildlife
- Literary interest

Start/finish Ash Landing car park, Windermere west shore (National Trust)
Distance 8 miles (13km)
Time to pub 3 hours
Walking time 4 hours
Terrain Lakeside trails, country footpaths, fields, lanes and some road

Wander the west shore of Windermere, England's largest lake, before heading inland to explore the tarns and trees of Claife Heights. Visit a lovely Lakeland inn beside Beatrix Potter's house and return via Claife Viewing Station.

Spring Bluebells flood Ash Landing Nature Reserve, along with enough daffodils to delight Wordsworth for a lifetime.

Summer Butterflies flutter over the wildflower meadow at Ash Landing, while black darter and downy emerald dragonflies, and common blue damselflies, hover above Moss Eccles Tarn.

Autumn Look for red deer around Bark Barn, and scan conifer trees across Claife Heights for red squirrels. Woodlands around Claife Viewing Station turn yellow and red, while the breeze plays lively tunes on the Aeolian wind harp.

Winter Jemima isn't the only duck in town – tufted ducks live on Windermere all year, while overwintering visitors include goldeneye and pochard. If you're really lucky, you may spot an otter hunting for Arctic char.

The Tower Bank Arms serves Lake District-brewed ales including Hawkshead pale and bitter, Loweswater Gold and Barngates Brewery's Cracker.

Follow in the footsteps of ... Author, conservationist and natural scientist Beatrix Potter bought Hill Top Farm in 1905, with proceeds from *The Tale of Peter Rabbit*. She married William Heelis and moved to nearby Castle Cottage in 1913, but Hill Top remained her writing retreat and muse, with the farmhouse and surrounds – including The Tower Bank Arms – appearing in her enduringly popular stories. When she died in 1943, Potter left Hill Top to the National Trust, and it's been preserved as she kept it.

How to Get There

By Car Take the B5285 from Coniston or come via the ferry from Windermere. Park at Ash Landing car park, Windermere west shore (National Trust).

By Public Transport The nearest train station is Windermere, 3 miles (5km) away via ferry or shuttle bus.

OS Map OS Explorer OL7 (The English Lakes – South Eastern Area), Landranger 97 (Kendal & Morecambe); grid ref (for start): SD 388/954.

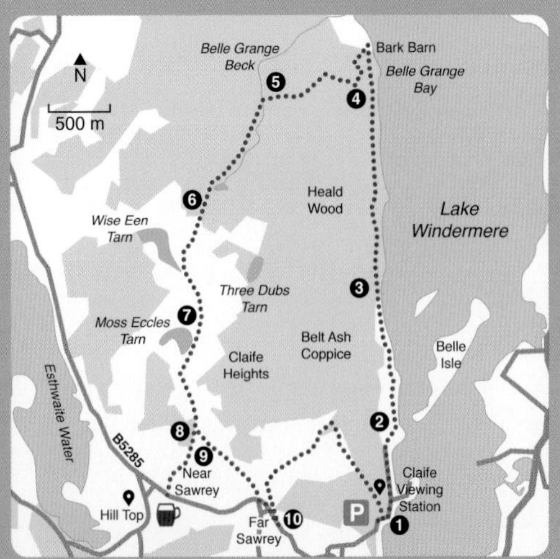

1. From Ash Landing car park, take the path leading away from the water, walking uphill, following a fingerpost pointing to Claife Viewing Station. Go through woods for about 200 yards, then turn left up a set of stone steps. At a junction, you can divert left to immediately check out this extraordinary purpose-built, 200-year-old lookout tower, which originally boasted a drawing room and wine cellar, or you can save it until the end of the walk and turn right along our main route. (It's not often you get the chance to enjoy panoramic views along Windermere through a series of coloured panels, while hearing the breeze blowing across an Aeolian wind harp, so it's worth seeing twice.) Continue, following a fingerpost pointing towards 'Station Cottage Courtyard and Ferry' and descend towards the lake. Walk through the café area, where information boards explain the history of the viewing station and pleasure gardens, and exit through a stone archway. Go past the Windermere ferry jetty – over on your right – and along a sealed lane, walking with Station Scar Wood on the left and the lake on your right.

2. Go over a cattlegrid and past Harrowslack car park, a green area with great lake views. Stroll along a waterside section of gravel footpath, which circles Coatlap Point, then rejoin the lane and continue past National Trust accommodation at Tanner Brow, passing lots of little beaches on your right, all looking out at Belle Isle.

3. Go through a wide gate next to a cattle grid, where National Trust information boards provide a handy snapshot of local flora and fauna. Continue along the lakeshore, past Strawberry Gardens (National Trust accommodation) opposite a wonderful waterfall. Keep going, following fingerposts pointing towards Bark Barn, with beech, sweet chestnut and towering red spruce trees standing sentinel between the track and the lake for a section, before the path descends to skirt the shore, with Windermere lapping to your right.

4. When you reach Bark Barn you'll find more National Trust info boards, and a floating jetty from where boats cross to Brockhole, the Lake District information centre. Turn left here, following a fingerpost pointing towards Hawkshead and climbing up into Fleming Wood, along a rock-plated path that follows Belle Grange Beck. Ignore a turning to the left, which crosses a stream, and continue up. Grange Beck runs along to the right of the track, and then swaps over to the left.

5. Cross a lane and follow a fingerpost pointing left, along a bridleway signed 'Sawrey via Tarns'. Go across another track and keep walking straight along the bridleway. Another track joins from the left, but keep going through the spruce forest of Claife Heights, looking out for red squirrels.

6. Pass through a gate and emerge next to a stone wall, then cross an open expanse of sheep-grazing

Looking north along Windermere, the largest lake in England.

land, going between two tarns – keep your eyes open for dragonflies and damselflies. The bridleway wends left, goes through a wide farm gate and continues along a track.

7. Descend past Moss Eccles Tarn on your right. This was a favourite place for Beatrix Potter and her husband William Heelis – the couple kept a boat here and planted water lilies on this hill lake. Keep going, through farmland and past several tracks and lanes.

8. When the track and bridleway forks, go right, through a wide farm gate and descend past a barn and through another gate into the pretty little village of Near Sawrey, strolling along lanes lined with stone cottages. The Tower Bank Arms is up on your left, beside Hill Top.

9. After leaving the pub, reverse your footsteps back along the same lane. When you pass through the second gate, where the bridleway forked earlier, go sharp right through a gate and along a track. Go through another gate, and walk alongside Wiffin Beck, with the water on your left. Cross a footbridge over the river, join a sealed track coming in from the left, and go through a gate by a cattlegrid. Stroll past a farmhouse and descend into Far Sawrey.

10. Walk along a tarmac lane fringed by stone walls, enjoying great views across rolling green farmland. When you meet the road, turn left and walk past the Cuckoo Brow Inn (a pub and B&B, serving a couple of local ales). Opposite Braithwaite Hall, take the path leading left, following a fingerpost for Belle Grange. Pass the Sawrey Institute and picnic spot and go through a gate. When the path forks, stay right, heeding a bridleway arrow and ascending a track beside a stone wall. Ignore a track leading left and continue straight, following a fingerpost pointing to 'Windermere lakeshore'.

11. After about 500 yards, take the footpath leading right, following a fingerpost pointing towards 'the station and ferry'. Trace this undulating and sometimes technical path through Scar Woods, until it bends, descends and eventually passes through a cleft between large rocks to bring you back out at Claife Viewing Station. Look out once again across Windermere, then descend to the car park, following the fingerpost pointing towards Ash Landing Nature Reserve.

Opposite: Looking back across Milecastle 39 to Crag Lough (see page 253).

North East

82 Longshaw
The Grouse Inn

The Grouse Inn
Longshaw, Sheffield
Yorkshire S11 7TZ
01433 630423
www.thegrouse
inn-froggatt.co.uk

About this walk

- Moorland habitat
- Peak District and valley views
- Red deer
- Climbing crags

Start/finish Haywood car park, Longshaw Estate (National Trust)
Distance 7 miles (11km)
Time to pub 2.5 hours
Walking time 3 hours
Terrain Footpaths, open moorland, cliffs, crags

Close to fantastic footpaths, bridleways and crags, THE GROUSE INN is a post-adventure refuge for Peak District ramblers, scramblers, riders and climbers. Set amid wild open moorland, this family-run pub welcomes walkers warmly, but asks for muddy footwear to be covered (plastic booties provided). The front bar has tables topped by glass-covered bank notes and a fire to keep things cosy. The patio and garden deliver stunning views across the moor, and there's also a vine-entwined conservatory. Famous for its steak pies, food is served all week. Closed 3–6pm weekdays.

This moorland meander traverses the area where Dark Peak meets White Edge. The route tiptoes around the top of iconic inland cliffs, peering over the craggy gritstone escarpment at Froggatt Edge (pictured above) and Curbar Edge to enjoy Derwent Valley views, before strolling back across the plateau along White Edge, which overlooks a wonderfully wild expanse of open moor, to an iconic Peak District pub.

Spring Swallows skim across fields and moorland. As the weather warms, woodland animals including hedgehogs and bats awaken from hibernation.

Summer Longshaw moors blush pink and purple with flowering heather, attracting pollinators and insects, including the iridescent green hairstreak butterfly.

Autumn White Edge and Big Moor are home to red deer, and during the annual September–October rut, the males lock horns, bellow and battle on Big Moor. Meanwhile, rare and vibrant waxcap toadstools pop up across the estate.

Winter Derwent Valley views are crisp and clear, snow often powders the paths, and a roaring fire and warm welcome awaits at The Grouse.

With four handpumps, The Grouse Inn serves Yorkshire's ever-popular tipple Tetley's, plus Marston's Pedigree and Old Empire, and Banks's Amber Ale.

Follow in the footsteps of ...
Longshaw was rescued from the threat of development in 1924 by countryside conservation pioneer and avid walker Ethel Haythornthwaite, who led a public fundraising campaign that allowed the Campaign to Protect Rural England to purchase the 747-acre (302-ha) estate, which was subsequently gifted to the National Trust in 1931.

How to Get There

By Car Head to the National Trust Longshaw Estate car park at Haywood, south-west of Sheffield on the A625 between Nether Padley and Froggatt.

By Public Transport The closest train station is Grindleford, which is a 1½ mile (2.4km) walk from the start of the route, via Tumbling Hill and Hay Wood; Stagecoach bus 65 and First Bus 272/271 also serve the area from Sheffield.

OS Map OS Explorer OL24 (The Peak District – White Peak Area), Landranger 119 (Buxton & Matlock); grid ref (for start): SK 256/777.

1. Exit from the far end of Haywood car park (the opposite end to the way you drove in) and bear left along the footpath. Cross a stream and climb the stone steps to the road. Go through a gate, carefully cross the road, turn right briefly and then pick up the footpath going left through a wooden gate next to a larger white gate. As you pass a large boulder on your right, you will see your first glimpse of the Derwent Valley views that are to come. A path comes in from the left, but keep going straight, through woods full of downy and silver birch trees.

2. Emerge from the trees on the cusp of famous Froggatt Edge, an area of gritstone crags beloved of boulderers and climbers, many of whom you will doubtless see clambering and clinging to the beautiful rockscape, which tumbles down towards the River Derwent on your right. Ignore footpath arrows leading right and continue along the cliff-edge track, which starts to rise.

3. When the path forks, go right and walk along Curbar Edge, another sensational section of gritstone escarpment with spectacular rock formations, over 200 world-class climbing routes, plus unimpeded and stunning views across the Derwent Valley. After ambling along the edge-top trail, go through a gate and follow signs for White Edge, passing through a picnic area to reach Curbar car park, where there is often a van selling coffee and hot drinks.

4. Go right through the car park and out the other side, following a fingerpost pointing towards White Peak, walking with a stone wall on your left. When this wall veers sharp left, carry straight on, tracing the path as it arcs more gently left, passing a stone cairn, crossing a stone bridge and climbing a set of stone steps.

A fingerpost points the way to the pub.

The Grouse Inn is set amongst the picturesque landscape of the Peak District.

5. When you reach the top of the steps, follow a fingerpost pointing left, to White Edge, walking with another wall on your left for a while. When the path forks, go right to take in the trig point overlooking the imaginatively named Big Moor, which rolls expansively away to meet the horizon and is often populated by herds of wild-roaming red deer.

6. After the trig point the path rejoins the main track, which continues through heather and bracken across the open plateau for another mile (1.5km) or so before meeting a stone wall, offering glimpses of The Grouse Inn down to the left as you walk. While White Edge doesn't have the dramatic drop-offs delivered by the crags of Curbar and Froggatt, the vista is wide, wild and thought-provoking, and it differs by the day in mood and colour. Along the way you will encounter a Companion Stone, one of 12 matching rocks placed across the Peak District, envisaged and sculpted by local artists and poets, which bear inscriptions pointing not towards a town or village, but to an intangible future.

7. Go through the gap in the stone wall and turn left, following a fingerpost pointing towards The Grouse Inn. The path descends steeply, beside a stone wall on your left. Towards the bottom, after a particularly rugged section of path, a second fingerpost indicates the way to the pub, pointing straight ahead, through a small patch of woods.

8. Go through a gate, cross a field – which is often boggy – to another gate that brings you out by the road opposite The Grouse Inn.

9. After leaving the pub, go right and hop over a stile by a National Trust sign for Longshaw Estate. Walk across the field, go through two gates, bearing left after the second one, to return to the car park.

83 Hardcastle Crags

The Blue Pig

The Blue Pig
Midgehole Road
Midgehole
Yorkshire HX7 7AL
01422 844052

About this walk

- Woodlands
- River
- Crags
- Birdlife
- Calderdale Way

Start/finish Midgehole car park (National Trust)
Distance 6½ miles (10.5km)
Time to pub 2.5 hours
Walking time 3 hours
Terrain Woodland and riverside footpaths, lanes

Housed in an old dye workers' cottage, THE BLUE PIG is also the Midgehole Working Men's Club. This hideaway in Hebden Woods feels like a fantastic find every time you enter. Run by friendly volunteers, service hours are unusual (phone ahead), but it's typically open early afternoon into the evening on Wednesdays and Friday–Sunday. Visitors are required to become temporary members (£2), but drinks are good value thereafter, with lots of local and regional real ales on tap. There's a garden, an open fire, and the atmosphere is warm and welcoming. Food is served.

Wander through woodlands beside Hebden Water to a series of scenic crags, before clambering out of the south Pennine valley to stroll part of the Calderdale Way into Heptonstall. Drop back into the vale at Midgehole to visit a secret shebeen.

Spring Bluebells flood the valley. Heron hunt around Gibson Mill and dippers bob. Woodpeckers drum, while skylark and song thrush provide vocals. Spot jays, goldcrest, nuthatch, twites, pipits, pied flycatchers and treecreepers.

Summer Look for chiffchaffs, redstarts, willow and wood warblers. Dragonflies hover over ponds, while bees and butterflies buzz around wildflowers beside the Calderdale Way. The Blue Pig beer festival takes place in August.

Autumn Oak and beech burn yellow, gold and red around the crags, while waxcap fungi add green, purple, yellow and scarlet. Spot roe deer at dawn, and pipistrelle bats at dusk.

Winter Bullfinches, blue tits, wagtails, wrens and robins flit between bare trees. Streams and waterfalls are in full spate. In late winter, northern hairy wood ants emerge from hibernation to repair their towering mansions.

The Blue Pig's regular ales are Goose Eye Brewery's Chinook Blonde and Timothy Taylor's Landlord. Guest beers include Hebden Bridge's Nightjar brews.

Follow in the footsteps of ... Hebden Bridge, setting for TV drama *Happy Valley*, was historically a mill town and textile centre. To supplement meagre wages, a group of local weavers began making counterfeit money. The Yorkshire Coiners were betrayed, which led to an execution. The gang's leader, 'King' David Hartley, was hanged in 1770 and is buried in Heptonstall churchyard.

How to Get There

By Car Take the A6033 north from Hebden Bridge, then turn left along Midgehole Road. Park at Midgehole car park (HX7 7AA; National Trust).

By Public Transport Nearby Hebden Bridge (2 miles/3.2km) has a train station.

OS Map OS Explorer OL21 (South Pennines), Landranger 103 (Blackburn & Burnley); grid ref (for start): SD 989/291.

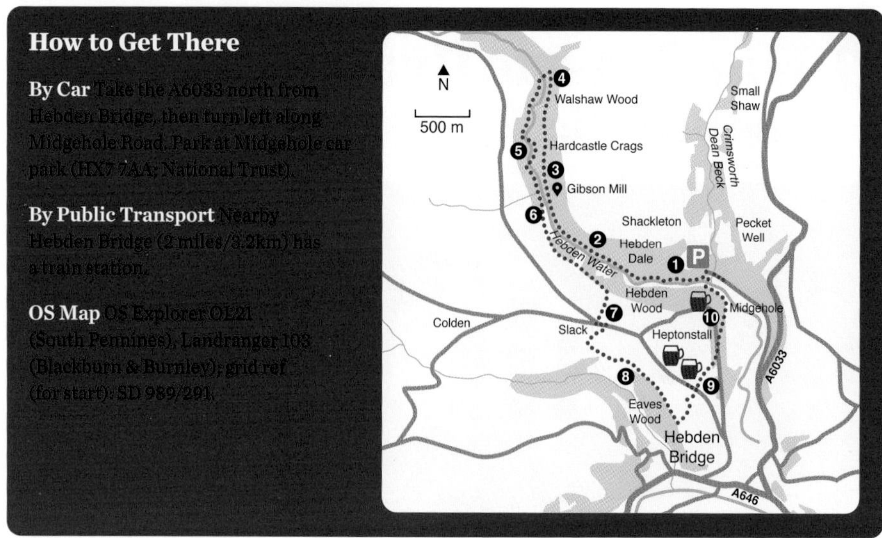

1. From Midgehole car park, follow a fingerpost and red arrows pointing down a track towards the sound of rushing water. At Hebden Water, turn right and walk along a stone-clad, rocky path through beech and oak woods. Ignore steps leading left to the river and keep following red arrows (waymarkers for the Mill Walk). After several stream crossings, the path descends and runs right alongside the river, passing rapids and clambering around rocks leaning over the water, before climbing steps away from the bank.

2. When another path joins from the right, turn left and descend back to the river bank. Emerge into an open area, with stepping stones across the river, but don't cross. Continue along the same bank, crossing several footbridges over streams cascading down Hebden Dale and Foul Hill. Keep the river on your immediate left as the path undulates through the trees to arrive at Gibson Mill, where the Weaving Shed Café offers coffee and cake.

3. From the mill, follow fingerposts pointing towards 'The Crags', ascending the lane to the right of the café and toilets, passing a den-building area. At a picnic area with a wicker horse, turn left up a path with steps, following another fingerpost and yellow arrows. Clamber through the stunning stacks of millstone grit, bearing right when the path forks to reach to the highest point. The descent on the other side is steep and technical, so from the summit, return the way you came to rejoin the main path. Turn left along the broad track, and follow green arrows into Walshaw Wood, keeping left.

4. At a junction, turn left and walk down a tunnel-like track overhung by beech trees, to a footbridge over a steam by a waterfall. Don't cross; instead follow the green arrow left, walking with the water on your right. Cross the main river over a narrow footbridge and go left, following green arrows past a weir house. Keep strolling along the cobbled riverside path with Hebden Water flowing on your left, crossing a couple of footbridges over streams, then walking along a section of boardwalk and up some steps.

5. Cross a bridge going over the river on your left, turn right, and then, after about 100 yards, another footbridge takes you back to the right bank. Walk with the river on your left, as waterfalls gush down the steep hillside on both banks. A footpath comes in from the right, but keep going straight, along a rocky, river-hugging path. Cross several streams, pass a little pool on your right and clamber across a little waterfall that tumbles over the track. Gibson Mill emerges on the opposite bank, but keep going, ignoring the pretty stone bridge. Go past a toilet building and when the track forks, bear right and walk uphill, looking down at a riverside picnic area on your left.

6. At a junction, ignore the path leading downhill on the left, disregard the turning right, up to Clough Hole car park, and go straight ahead, on a hill-hugging track, following footpath arrows. When the path immediately forks, keep walking straight ahead, along a lovely little trail that scampers across the slope. Pass a National Trust sign for Hardcastle Crags, then climb up a series of stone steps. When the path forks, go right, walk along the fence, then hop over a stone stile into a field. A second stile brings you out on to a well-made path. Go right and walk up to the road at Slack.

7. Dogleg across the road and take the path opposite, going past a street sign for 'Slack Top' and following a footpath arrow that looks like it's directing you into someone's house, but actually goes right, over a narrow stone stile and along a little path. When you meet a stone wall, bear left along a path. At a confluence of tracks, take the Calderdale Way.

8. When the lane leans right, keep going straight, until you reach a fingerpost by a hole in the wall on your right. Follow the arm pointing towards Heptonstall, along a rocky path skimming the treetops of Eaves Woods, enjoying great views across Hebden Bridge. Just before a gate, go left towards Heptonstall church. Cross a lane and continue straight, passing to the right of the church, along a cobbled lane. Heptonstall has two good pubs – The White Lion (which offers 170 gins and a wide range of real ales and ciders) and the historic Cross Inn, built in 1617 – both are worth checking out, especially on days The Blue Pig is closed.

9. Walk to the right of The Cross Inn, along Northfield Terrace, passing a footpath turning and then bearing right along a bridleway with Calderdale Way signage. The path widens after meeting a house, and then becomes cobbled and quite steep (and slippery when wet) in sections. Keep going straight, downhill, crossing a couple of paths and a lane.

10. The route bends left as you approach the river and, as it flattens off at Midgehole, passes right by the door of The Blue Pig. After leaving the pub, walk with the river on your right, before crossing the bridge to the car park.

Hebden Water sinuously snakes through a wonderfully wooded valley.

84 Malham Cove, Janet's Foss & Gordale Scar
The Buck Inn

Built in 1874, on the site of an old coaching inn, **THE BUCK INN** straddles the Pennine Way and is in easy walking distance of Malham Cove, Malham Tarn, Janet's Foss and Gordale Scar, so it's only right that it boasts a dedicated Hiker's Bar with low beams, a flagstone floor and a woodburner, where muddy boots and wet dogs are welcome. The stone building also has a lounge with an open fire, outside tables at the front and a beer garden. Food is served (booking advised), and accommodation is available.

The Buck Inn
Cove Road, Malham
Yorkshire BD23 4DA
01729 830317
www.thebuckmalham.co.uk

About this walk
- Limestone crags
- Waterfalls
- Pennine Way
- Dales High Way

Start/finish Malham Watersinks car park (National Trust)
Distance 7½ miles (12km)
Time to pub 1.5 hours
Walking time 3.5 hours
Terrain Footpaths, moorland, crags and lanes

From the edge of a glacial lake, stroll a dramatic section of the Pennine Way to a natural amphitheatre formed by an arc of towering limestone cliffs at Malham Cove. Explore Malham's village inns, before returning along the Dales High Way, via the cascades at Janet's Foss and Gordale Scar.

Spring Ransoms fill the wood at Janet's Foss with the fragrance of wild garlic. Peregrine falcons nest at Malham Cove. Hear sedge warblers sing and curlews call.

Summer Wildflowers – such as sundew, ragged robin, orchids and bugle – abound. Butterflies, including rare northern brown argus, flutter around the cove.

Autumn Janet's Foss and Gordale Scar gush. Great crested grebes, teal and tufted duck visit the tarn, while peregrine falcons hover over the limestone pavement. Pipistrelle bats leave Malham Cove's caves at dusk to go hunting.

Winter Whooper swans and ducks – goldeneye, pochard and wigeon – arrive on the tarn, while redwings and fieldfares joust with thrushes for berries in trees. Look out for short-eared owls, woodcocks and bramblings.

The Buck Inn serves Dark Horse Hetton Pale Ale, alongside guest beers like Settle Brewery's Blonde.

Follow in the footsteps of ... Gordale Scar has inspired artists and writers including J.M.W. Turner and William Wordsworth. Malham Tarn is where Charles Kingsley conceived the idea for his 1863 novel, *The Water-Babies*. According to legend, a fairy queen named Janet (or Jennett) lives in a cave behind Janet's Foss.

How to Get There

By Car Head through Malham, along Cove Road, and turn right to reach Malham Watersinks car park (BD24 9PT; National Trust).

By Public Transport The closest train station is Settle (7 miles/11.3km). Buses run from Skipton.

OS Map OS Explorer OL2 (Yorkshire Dales); Landranger 98 (Wensleydale & Upper Wharfedale); grid ref (for start) SD 894 658.

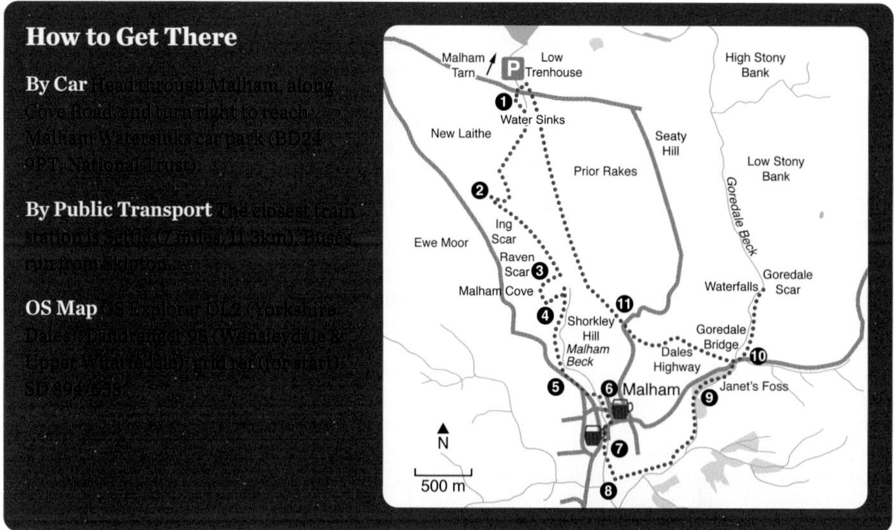

1. From the car park, walk away from Malham Tarn, cross the road and bear right. At a fingerpost, turn left along the Pennine Way, the 268-mile (431-km) long-distance walk between Edale in Derbyshire and Kirk Yetholm in Scotland. You cross Water Sinks here, a limestone plateau where water that becomes the River Aire seeps from the tarn and disappears into underground caves before re-emerging at Aire Head Springs, south of Malham village. Walk across a field, and follow a fingerpost pointing left, towards Malham Cove. At the wall, ignore the stile and turn right. With the wall on your left, walk along a rocky section of path, through a stone chasm, looking out for caves.

2. Follow the Pennine Way as it arcs right below Comb Hill. At a junction, turn sharp left, crossing a stile, walking down into a ravine and passing through crag-fringed Ing Scar and Raven Scar.

3. Follow a long section of level path with a stone wall on your left, passing a National Trust sign for Ewe Moor. Hop over a stile, continue to a fingerpost and go right, staying on the Pennine Way. This brings you out onto a landscape of strange stone slabs a limestone pavement that plunges over an arc of sheer 230ft (70m) high inland cliffs, to form Malham Cove, an extraordinary natural amphitheatre. Follow the Pennine Way as it cuts left, passes through a gate and descends stone steps to the bottom of the cove.

4. Go left along Malham Beck, a waterway lined with lovely ash trees, to explore the undercliff of the great limestone cove, formed 12,000 years ago by glacier meltwater. Cross the head of the beck, loop around and walk back, going over a stile and strolling through a field with the river on your right. Pass through a couple of gates, cross a stone slab bridge and rejoin the Pennine Way. Turn left and walk along a well-formed footpath with the beck babbling on your left. Go through a gate and past a National Trust sign for Malham Estate. Over to your left, stone walls divide green hills into a gorgeous jigsaw.

5. The track rises away from the river, passes through a gate and past a National Trust sign for Malham Fields. Go through another gate and past a second National Trust sign for Malham Estate. When you meet the road, bear left and go straight down the hill for about 200 yards, before following a fingerpost pointing left towards Tarn Road.

6. Cross a beautiful stone bridge over Malham Beck and wend right, around a house. Walk uphill briefly, then turn right along a track, passing the YHA. Turn right on the road, where you will see The Lister Arms, a Grade II-listed, award-winning inn serving Thwaites Brewery ales, which dates to 1723 and makes a good alternative option for a pit stop. Continue across the bridge and over the road to The Buck Inn, which has a dedicated Hiker's Bar and an outdoor shop next door.

7. Leave the pub, turn right and then go left across a stone slab bridge. Turn right and walk along the Pennine Way, with the river on your right. Go through a gate and along a paved path.

8. At a gate and fingerpost, turn left, leaving the Pennine Way and heading towards Janet's Foss and Gordale Scar. Walk along a well-made path, through several kissing gates, tracing the banks of Gordale Beck.

9. Go through another kissing gate and past a National Trust sign for Janet's Foss, walking into woods and continuing along the path until you reach the wonderful waterfall, plunge pool and cave. According to local legend, a fairy queen named Janet (or Jennett) lives in a cave behind Janet's Foss (with foss being a Nordic word for waterfall). The plunge pool here is popular with wild swimmers. Continue through a kissing gate, and when you meet the road, turn right, following a fingerpost for Gordale Scar.

10. At pretty Gordale Bridge, follow a fingerpost for Gordale Scar, going through a gate and walking along the well-made path into the mouth of the amazing canyon. There is a scrambling route up the waterfall, but it's technical and potentially hazardous, so after enjoying the view, retrace your footsteps to Gordale Bridge. Cross and follow a fingerpost pointing to Malham Cove, ambling along the Dales High Way (a 90-mile/145-km walking route from Saltaire in West Yorkshire to Appleby in Cumbria), climbing steadily by a stone wall and going through several kissing gates.

11. When you meet a road, cross and go over a ladder stile. Continue on the Dales High Way for about 200 yards, past Sherriff Hill, before turning right at a fingerpost pointing towards Malham Tarn. Go over a ladder stile by a National Trust sign for Malham Estate and meander across moorland, passing through a little gully. At a fingerpost, follow the arrow for Malham Tarn. Cross a ladder stile, bear left and walk to the car park.

Formed by a waterfall fed by melting glaciers 12,000 years ago, Malham Cove is a dramatic limestone amphitheatre.

85 Upper Wharfedale
The George Inn

The George Inn
Hubberholme, Skipton
Yorkshire BD23 5JE
01756 760223
www.thegeorge-inn.co.uk

About this walk
- Yorkshire Dales National Park
- Wildflowers
- A Pennine Journey
- The Dales Way

Start/finish Buckden village car park
Distance 7½ miles (12km)
Time to pub 2 hours
Walking time 3 hours
Terrain Countryside footpaths, dales, riverside trails, lanes

THE GEORGE INN occupies a cosy 17th-century former farmhouse and vicarage. A community hub steeped in tradition, a candle burns on the bar whenever it's open and, once a year, the Hubberholme Parliament convenes to take bids for a field in an auction lasting as long as the candle stays alight, with proceeds going to the parish poor. Inside you'll find flagstone floors, mullioned windows, bench seats, Toby jugs on low oak beams and a range fire. Outside there's a sunny patio. Food and accommodation available.

From the flanks of Buckden Pike, explore fells, woods and moorland before dropping down to trace the River Wharfe to a delightful Dales' pub.

Spring Yockenthwaite boasts some of Britain's best wildflower meadows, with primroses, bluebells and purple orchids. On Strans Wood's limestone pavement wild thyme and common rock rose bloom. Lapwings, grey wagtails and sand martins swoop by the Wharfe.

Summer Listen for the cry of curlew on the moor, and spy butterflies including common blue, ringlet and meadow brown. Daubenton's bats roost beneath Yockenthwaite Bridge and swoop over the river hunting for insects.

Autumn Rakes and Strans woods turn from green to gold and red. Ducks, goosanders, kingfishers and dippers are active along the Wharfe.

Winter Snowdrops pop up in the woods and blackbirds, blue tits and greater spotted woodpeckers flit between the bare branches. Fieldfares flock and waxwings feast on red hawthorn berries in hedgerows.

The George Inn offers several Yorkshire-made ales including Black Dub (stout) and a bespoke-brewed George Inn session ale from Wensleydale, plus bitters from Black Sheep and Theakston, and rotating beers from Dark Horse.

Follow in the footsteps of ...
Author, playwright and broadcaster J.B. Priestley frequented The George Inn, and his ashes are buried in Hubberholme churchyard. This walk traces a section of 'A Pennine Journey', described in a book of the same name by Alfred Wainwright.

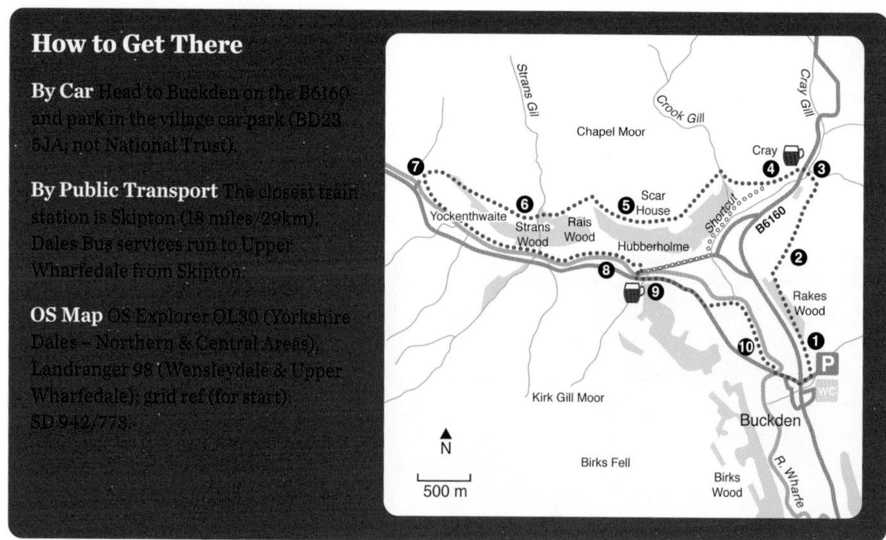

How to Get There

By Car Head to Buckden on the B6160 and park in the village car park (BD23 5JA; not National Trust).

By Public Transport The closest train station is Skipton (18 miles/29km). Dales Bus services run to Upper Wharfedale from Skipton.

OS Map OS Explorer OL30 (Yorkshire Dales – Northern & Central Areas), Landranger 98 (Wensleydale & Upper Wharfedale); grid ref (for start): SD 942/773.

1. Leave the car park through a gate, and walk uphill along Buckden Rake bridleway, following a fingerpost pointing towards Cray High Bridge and Buckden Pike. Pass through a gate and climb steadily up the broad track, through Rakes Wood, with great views left, through gaps in the sycamore, ash and hawthorn trees, down to River Wharfe and along Langstrothdale Chase.

2. Go through a wide field gate and continue along a section of Alfred Wainwright's 'A Pennine Journey', a wandering odyssey undertaken by the trail-blazing author in 1938 and later made into a long-distance walk. The track crosses craggy grazing land and reaches another field gate. There's an option to go right and scale 2,303ft (702m) Buckden Pike here, but our route continues on, across grazing fields with a classic Yorkshire Dales vista straight ahead, formed by a rolling patchwork of green hills stitched together with stone wall seams.

3. Clamber over a stile next to a field gate in a stone wall, then turn left through a gate and descend along a footpath to Cray village. Go through a gate, cross Cray Gill (a stream) and a road, where you'll encounter The White Lion. This pub is well worth checking out. In the main bar, which splits into two areas, (plus a delightful snug), there are stone floors, a beamed ceiling and candles with years' of wax spilling over shelves. Guns and farm-themed pictures hang on the walls, along with an image of a white lion above the fireplace. Four local ales are offered, typically from Dark Horse and Wharfedale breweries, along with food.

4. The path continues, passing right behind the pub. Follow footpath arrows past a farm to a fingerpost. To take a shortcut to The George Inn, go left here and trace the stream down the hill, past waterfalls, to Stubbing Bridge and then go right along the road to Hubberholme (then skip to point 9). Otherwise, continue walking straight on. Pass through several fields and gates, and then walk to the left of a stone wall into a gully. Cross a narrow footbridge over Crook Gill and follow a fingerpost pointing towards Scar House.

5. Walk on a contour line around the middle of Slades Hill, below Chapel Moor, passing through a very narrow gated gap in a stone wall. Be sure to pause and enjoy the sensational views into Langstrothdale on your left. Go through a rock field above Scar House – a Quaker meetinghouse since 1652, when the founder of the movement, George Fox, stayed and converted the farmer. Follow a fingerpost pointing to Yockenthwaite, tracing the path as it arcs left and goes through a gate. Pass through another gate in a moss-covered stone wall and enter the top of Rais Wood, walking along a lovely path through ash and beech trees. Exit the woods and cross a bridge over Strans Gill. Go through a gate and drop to the left.

Some 5,000 miles (8,000km) of ancient dry stone walls criss-cross the Yorkshire Dales.

6. Pass through a succession of walls with gaps and gates and walk past several old stone buildings to your right. In between one of these stone cottages and Little House, as the river comes into clear view down to your left, you meet a fingerpost. Follow this left, descending into the dale and then walking parallel to a fence through woods. When you meet a track, turn left and walk down through farm buildings to the river, where a fingerpost points left towards Hubberholme.

7. Pretty Yockenthwaite Bridge is to your right, but don't cross. Instead, turn left and walk through the lower of two gateways, before following footpath arrows through a couple of small gates to meet the riverside path, which is part of the Dales Way (an 80-mile/129-km route between Ilkley in West Yorkshire and Bowness-on-Windermere in Cumbria). Walk with the river on your right for 1½ miles (2.4km). The water runs with you, while ash, sycamore, beech and hawthorn trees jostle for position on the bank. The path is flat, and the going is easy, as you pass through fields and gates in walls, and cross a little footbridge.

8. As you approach Hubberholme, the path runs between the river and a large, steep bank on the left. Enter the village, pass the church and cross the bridge to The George Inn, famous for its flaming candle, the annual Hubberholme Parliament auction in aid of the parish poor, wonderful Sunday roasts and award-winning pies.

9. When you leave the pub, turn right and walk along the road with the river on your left. After about half a mile (800m), once you've gone past Grange Farm, turn left through a wide gate, following a fingerpost pointing across a field and ambling along the Dales Way towards Buckden Bridge. Go through a little gate and walk with the river on your left and a field fence on the right.

10. Exit fields onto the road via a gate. Turn left, walk over beautiful Buckden Bridge and along the road to the car park, cutting across the village green and passing the village stores on your right.

86 Hudswell Woods

The George & Dragon

The George & Dragon
Hudswell, Richmond
Yorkshire DL11 6BL
01748 518373
www.georgeanddragon
hudswell.co.uk

About this walk

- River access and beaches
- Castle views
- Wildflowers
- Woodland wildlife and birds

Start/finish Round Howe car park
Distance 4 miles (6.5km)
Time to pub 1½ hours
Walking time 2–2½ hours
Terrain Riverside, rural and woodland paths.

The walker-friendly, multi-award-winning GEORGE & DRAGON was Yorkshire's first ever community-owned pub and retains the feel of a true local. There are two main rooms with a bar and an adjoining eating area. In colder months, an open fire keeps drinkers and diners warm. Alongside regional real ales, the pub proudly offers proper pies and Wensleydale cheese-infused menu options, and also sells walking books and other titles by local writers. Food is served every day except Wednesday. The Swale Valley view from the lovely beer garden out the back is beautiful.

Walk through meadows and mixed woodlands beside the River Swale to an 11th-century castle, before looping back across treetops to an award-winning community pub offering local cheeses, pies, real brews and superb views.

Spring Trails are lined with pungent wild garlic, pretty wood anemones and celandines, while bluebells flood Billy Bank Wood. Sand martins search for Swaleside nesting sites, and migratory birds – chiffchaff, blackcap, willow warblers – return from winter sojourns.

Summer Spot the iridescent flash of kingfishers along the river. Red admiral, small tortoiseshell and comma butterflies flutter across meadows, collecting nectar from flowering flora including devil's bit scabious. Late-summer blackberries and sloes attract fruit-loving wildlife.

Autumn Hudswell Woods explode with colour, as beech trees set the river banks ablaze with russet reds, oak trees turn earthy brown, and lime, ash, wych elm and hazel all assume a yellow hue. Fungi are at their beautiful best too.

Winter Spot woodland birds amid bare branches – including treecreepers, nuthatches, woodpeckers and goldcrests – and look for roe deer at dusk.

The George & Dragon serves up to eight regional real ales, with Wensleydale Brewery's Falconer Session Ale a regular, beside beers from Rooster, Small World, Titanic, Rudgate, Brass Castle. Craft ciders also offered.

Follow in the footsteps of ... J.M.W. Turner painted and sketched Richmond Castle from several angles, including across Green Bridge. Watercolourist Walter Stuart Lloyd and landscape painter William Callow also depicted the castle from Hudswell Woods.

How to Get There

By Car Park at Round Howe car park (not National Trust, charges apply for all), off Reeth Road (A6108), a 1½-mile (2.4-km) drive from Richmond.

By Public Transport The nearest train station is Darlington (13 miles/21km), from where buses run to Richmond.

OS Map OS Explorer 304 (Darlington & Richmond); Landranger 92 (Barnard Castle & Richmond); grid ref (for start): NZ 157/009.

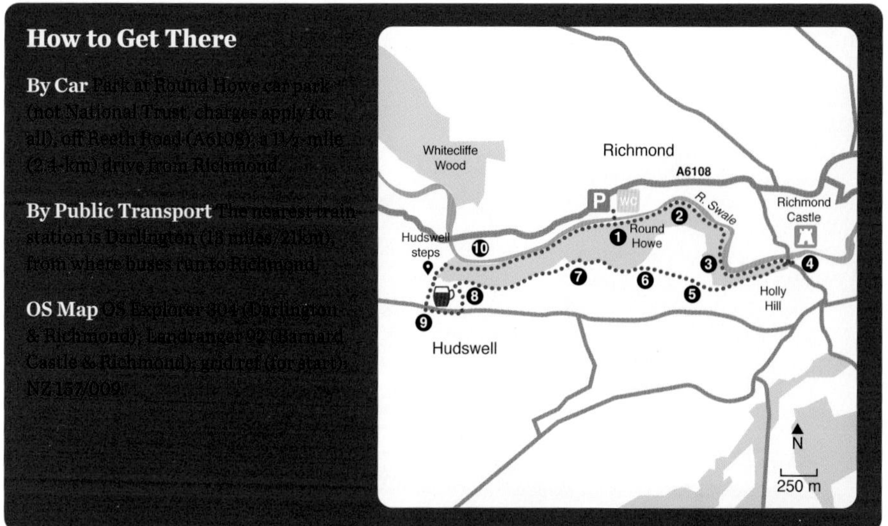

1. From the car park, walk across the bridge over the rushing River Swale. At the National Trust sign, turn left and wander through woods with the river running to your left. Stroll across a broad flood meadow, seasonally full of wildflowers. In summer, there's good access to riverside beaches here, and come autumn the trees put on a kaleidoscopic display of colour. On your right rises Round Howe, a hillock created in the last ice age (Howe comes from *haugr*, meaning 'hill' in old Norse).

2. Walk along the riverside, looking out for birdlife, including flashy kingfishers. Leave the meadow via a metal kissing gate and ramble along the rocky path that hugs the bank, leading into trees. Hudswell Woods includes a rich mix of ancient ash and oak, colourful beech, sycamore, elm, hazel and deciduous yew and holly trees.

3. Turn right up steps and pass the National Trust sign introducing Billy Bank Wood. Cross a bridge and continue, with limestone crags on your right. Walk through the trees to steps leading back down to river bank level, where you'll meet the incoming lower path by a bench.

Alternative route: A lower route can be explored along this stretch by going straight instead of turning right at the steps and hopping across a series of massive stone slabs that run right beside the river. Some of these slabs are broken, however, making it a much more challenging adventure. After rain – when the river runs high and fast – the stones can be slippery, or even submerged.

After the paths (the main and the alternative route) converge, keep walking straight until you meet Bridge Street by the arches of Green Bridge. High on the hill opposite sits Richmond Castle. This imposing fortress was founded in the 1070s by Alan Rufus, a Norman knight who fought at the Battle of Hastings with William the Conqueror, and subsequently helped the king with the horrific 'Harrying of the North', which wiped out around three-quarters of Northern England's population. During the First World War, it housed the Northern Non-Combatant Corps, including a group of conscientious objectors – the Richmond Sixteen – who were court martialled for refusing orders and sentenced to death, until their sentences were commuted to imprisonment.

4. Turn right on the road (Slee Gill). After 20 yards or so, turn right again, following a footpath fingerpost. Walk uphill on the path, into the top section of the woods. The path climbs steadily, then levels off, with beech and holly trees lining the route.

5. Pass through a kissing gate and walk around the edge of a horse-training field. Go over a stile, ignore the stile on the right and continue straight, over another stile. Cross the next field, bear left and follow more footpath arrows across a stile.

Richmond Castle has been a source of artistic inspiration and a place of draconian incarceration.

6. Keep following footpath arrows, bearing right through a field and crossing another four stiles in quick succession. Throughout this part of the walk, you wander through fields, keeping the woodland and river valley on your right and Hudswell Lane on your left. Don't descend into the woods or deviate towards the road.

7. Go through a gate with a small National Trust sign and re-enter the trees. To your right, Hudswell Woods plunge dramatically down the hillside. The path then passes through numerous gates, over many stiles and takes you through a whole series of fields, occasionally entering the top part of the woods and tracing the tree line. Ignore paths leading right and keep to the top of valley.

8. At Scar Close Caravan Site descend a short flight of wooden steps into the woodland and follow the path along the top of the woodland. When you pass the National trust sign for Calfhall Wood, go through the fence and turn left. The path bends right, and then goes left over a streambed, before meeting a T-junction. Turn left and follow the path as it arcs right, goes over a metal stile and passes a playing field to reach the road. Turn right, and The George & Dragon is just past the village hall and cottages on your right.

9. After leaving the pub, turn right and walk past a playground before turning right again, following a footpath fingerpost through a wall. Go through a gate and descend across a farm field to a second gate. This brings you to the top of the infamous Hudswell steps, almost 300 of them. Descend the steps, which are broken up into flights. Just before the end of the last section, turn right, following a fingerpost pointing along a footpath to Round Howe. Cross a little wooden bridge and walk through trees along a footpath that gradually descends to the river.

10. When the path splits, you have the option to walk low, along the riverbank (a lovely stroll in good weather, passing a beach and ascending steps at the end), or stay slightly higher (recommended in wet conditions) and go through woods until the paths reconverge at the top of the aforementioned steps, near a footbridge. Turn left and cross the footbridge over the river, back to the car park.

87 Ravenscar

The Bay Hotel

The Bay Hotel
The Dock
Robin Hood's Bay
Yorkshire YO22 4SJ
01947 880278
www.bayhotel.info

About this walk

- Sea views and beaches
- Marine wildlife
- History
- Wildflowers and fossils

Start/finish Ravenscar Visitor Centre (National Trust)
Distance 7 miles (11.3km)
Time to pub 1.5–2 hours
Walking time 3.5 hours
Terrain Coastal trails, beach, footpaths

Situated at the eastern end of the trail, **THE BAY HOTEL** is popular with Coast-to-Coast walkers and the groundfloor Wainwright Bar has maps showing sections of the route. It has the atmosphere of a sailor's drinking den, with a ship's wheel on the wall, an open fire, stone floor and heavy wooden tables, while the patio looks out over the sea. Upstairs the nautical theme continues, with paintings of sailing scenes, storm lanterns and oars. Beer barrels are built into the bar and there's a tiny snug called the Smoke Room. Home-cooked meals are served from a seafood-heavy menu.

NORTH EAST

Stroll a section of the Cleveland Way, crossing clifftops and ambling through historic alum works, to Boggle Hole beach and The Bay Hotel's Wainwright Bar in Robin Hood's Bay, the official Coast-to-Coast walk trailhead. Return along a stunning shoreline, fossil hunting and seal spotting.

Spring Bluebell Wood lives up to its name. Insects, including the speckled wood butterfly and darting damselfly, are active around water features between the brick and alum works. From April, small birds like dunnocks, yellowhammers, chaffinches and tree sparrows begin nesting in blackthorn bushes.

Summer Grey and common seals can sometimes be spotted between Robin Hood's Bay and Ravenscar. Look for porpoises, dolphins and whales (minke, fin, sei, pilot and humpback).

Autumn Robin Hood's Bay and Boggle Hole are famous fossil-hunting areas; you can also explore rock pools for sea life. The trees in Bluebell Wood transform colour and sloes ripen on blackthorn bushes.

Winter Seals with pups can be viewed on the beach beneath Ravenscar. It's illegal to disturb them. Keep your distance, and ensure dogs are on a lead and under close control.

With four handpumps, the Wainwright Bar sells Wainwright Golden Beer (obviously), two ales from North Yorkshire brewery Theakston (Lightfoot blonde and Best Bitter), and Adnams Ghost Ship is a regular guest.

Follow in the footsteps of ... There's nothing linking Robin Hood to the bay that bears his name, but the 2014 film *Downhill* features four fictional, modern-day merry men tackling the 192-mile (309-km) Coast-to-Coast Walk across Britain from St Bees in Cumbria to Robin Hood's Bay. Shot on the trails, the final scenes are filmed in and around the Bay Hotel.

How to Get There

By Car Ravenscar is signposted from the A171, between Whitby and Scarborough. Free roadside parking is available near the National Trust visitor centre.

By Public Transport The closest train station is Scarborough (11 miles/17.7km), from where East Yorkshire bus 115 travels to Ravenscar.

OS Map OS Explorer OL 27 (North York Moors – Eastern Area); Landranger 94 (Whitby & Esk Dale); grid ref (for start): NZ 980/016.

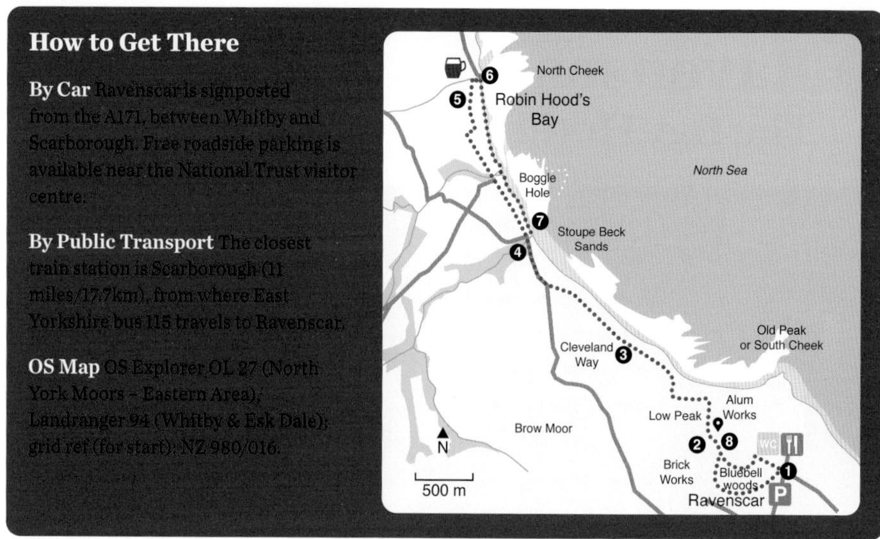

1. As you approach Ravenscar's National Trust visitor centre, turn sharp left, following a fingerpost pointing towards Robin Hood's Bay. Walk down a cobbled track and, at the next fingerpost, continue straight ahead, along the Cleveland Way (a 109-mile/175-km walking route from Helmsley, across the North York Moors National Park to Saltburn-by-the-Sea). When the path forks, go right, following signs for the Alum Works via the Cleveland Way. (The left turn leads to a loop around the old Brick Works and double rail bridge, which will intrigue those with an interest in social history and railways.)

2. Walk with Bluebell Wood on your right until you meet a track. Go left, following Cleveland Way signs. After about 100 yards, turn right at a fingerpost pointing to the Alum Works. Upon reaching the ruins, turn left and walk through the National Trust-maintained site. For over 200 years, from 1650, Ravenscar was a major producer of alum, used as a fixing agent in textile dying and leather tanning. The area has plenty of the fossil-rich shale required to make the agent, but the other crucial ingredient – vast quantities of human urine (which supplies the necessary ammonia) – was shipped in by the barrel-load from London, Hull and Newcastle, and hauled up the cliff on a tramway. After passing a bench with a great view over Robin Hood's Bay, rejoin the Cleveland Way. Descend some steps, cross a section of duckboard, climb more steps, go through a gate and cross a field. Exit via another gate, cross a footbridge and turn right, along the Cleveland Way.

3. Continue over a footbridge and along the cliffs, enjoying wonderful views across the bay to the North Cheek headland. Cross another footbridge and go through a gate by the Ravenscar National Trust sign. The path eventually curls around and goes through a stone wall to meet a tarmac lane. Turn right and walk to Stoupe Bank Farm, where the lane segues into a footpath and bridleway, with paving stone steps on the left for walkers and a muddy track on the right for riders.

4. Drop almost to the beach, cross a footbridge over Stoupe Beck and then bear right along the footpath, following signs for Boggle Hole (boggles are fantastical creatures in northern folklore). Descend the steps to Boggle Hole, where there's access to a wonderful beach. But, for now, cross the footbridge over Mill Beck, pass the YHA and climb the steps following Cleveland Way fingerposts. Walk through a tunnel of blackthorn and pass through a wide gate by the Boggle Hole National Trust sign. Walk with a field on your right, go through a gate and turn right, following Cleveland Way signage along a stone-slab path that rounds the clifftop and rewards with a wonderful view over the vibrant village at Robin Hood's Bay.

5. Descend wooden steps and when the path forks go right, down to the beach. Climb a flight of metal steps, descend the stone steps on the other side and The Bay Hotel is directly in front of you, opposite the National Trust-maintained Old Coastguard Station, coffee shop and visitor centre.

6. Leave the pub and turn left, walking around East Scar and exploring the shoreline and rock pools, if the tide allows. Walk back along the beach to Boggle Hole and High Scar, keeping your eyes peeled for fossils.

7. It is possible to walk further along the beach at low tide, but you can be cut off by the incoming sea, it's dangerous to walk too close to the cliffs, and there is a seal colony at the far end which needs to be given a wide berth (it is illegal to disturb these animals, and dogs must be kept on a lead and under very strict control). This walk turns inland at Stoupe Beck Sands (the last exit from the beach). From here, retrace your steps back to the Alum Works.

8. Just after the Alum Works, when the path forks, go left, leaving the Cleveland Way. Follow this well-defined footpath until you emerge on the golf course. Here the path forks again – go right, and walk up the hill to the right of the castellated edifice of the Raven Hall Hotel and back to the visitor centre.

Opposite: The Bay Hotel's Wainwright Bar, where Coast-to-Coast completers toast their achievement.

Below: Looking across Robin Hood's Bay from the hilltop start at Ravenscar.

88 Roseberry Topping
The King's Head Inn

Positioned directly beneath Roseberry Topping, THE KING'S HEAD INN is integrally paired with the iconic peak. It's also popular with Cleveland Way hikers. This very family-friendly pub was created by joining two 17th-century cottages; accommodation is available in the upstairs rooms, and great food is served in the open-plan, fire-warmed bar (try the chicken parmigiana – the 'Parmo' is a Teesside tradition). There are tables out the front, but peak views are best from the back deck.

The King's Head Inn
The Green
Newton under Roseberry
Yorkshire TS9 6QR
01642 722318
www.kingsheadinn.co.uk

About this walk
- Iconic peak
- Historical interest
- Spectacular views
- Cleveland Way
- Includes a steep climb

Start/finish The King's Head Inn car park
Distance 7 miles (11.5km)
Time to pub 3.5 hours
Walking time 3.5 hours
Terrain Steep trails, countryside and woodland footpaths, sections of road

Climb Roseberry Topping – known as the 'Middlesbrough Matterhorn', because of its distinctive shape. Continue along the Cleveland Way, around Great Ayton Moor, to Captain Cook's Monument, and return to the pub through wonderful woodlands.

Spring In Newton Wood, a tsunami of bluebells surrounds ancient ash and oak trees, while wild garlic lines the trails.

Summer Heather-covered hillsides around Roseberry Topping turn purple. In the woods, listen for laughing green woodpeckers, and the warbling of song thrush and black cap.

Autumn On Roseberry Common and Great Ayton Moor, flocks of fieldfares and redwings feast on blood-red hawthorn berries. Oak and ash trees in Cliff Ridge and Newton Woods change colour, while waxcaps add to the show.

Winter The Topping is often iced like a bun, and with branches bare, small birds including treecreepers, nuthatches and long-tailed tits can be seen in the woodlands. Spy shy roe deer too.

The King's Head Inn serves beers from the local Three Brothers Brewery, including a special Roseberry Pale Ale, developed with input from the landlord. A range of Cleveland Way Gin varietals are available.

Follow in the footsteps of ... Captain James Cook grew up in Great Ayton, beneath Roseberry Topping, and as a boy he would have climbed the peak and dreamed of faraway shores. This walk takes in Captain Cook's Monument on Easby Moor, which celebrates the great explorer's achievements when he sailed off the known map.

How to Get There

By Car Park in the North York Moors National Park Authority car park (fee) on the A173 at Newton under Roseberry or at the pub (let staff know your plans).

By Public Transport Great Ayton train station is on the Middlesbrough–Whitby Esk Valley Line. The Coatham Connect Service 18 bus to Saltburn stops at The King's Head Inn.

OS Map OS Explorer OL26 (North York Moors – Western Area); Landranger 93 (Middlesbrough, Darlington & Hartlepool) and 94 (Whitby & Esk Dale); grid ref (for start): NZ 570/128.

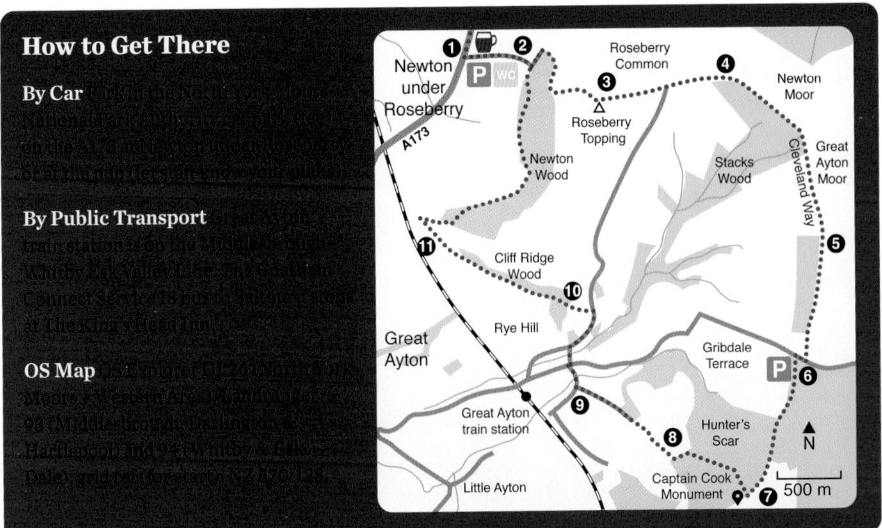

1. Walk up Roseberry Lane, between the car park and the pub, going through a wide gate and along the gravel track.

2. Pass through the gate by a National Trust sign and information board about the peak, and walk into the beech, ash and oak trees of Newton Woods. Go up a small set of steps, then tackle a second steeper flight. At the top, go right and ascend a stone-clad path with little steps, a climb that starts fairly gently but soon gets more challenging. Turn left through a gate and keep going, up more stone steps.

3. From the summit trig point enjoy sensational views all around, but particularly to the south and east, to the obelisk of Captain Cook's Monument and across the North York Moors. Looking at the trig point from your approach route, turn left (east) and walk along the summit ridge, before descending a stone-clad path. When the path forks at the bottom, go right and walk with a stone wall on your right. You're now on the Cleveland Way, a 109-mile (175-km) trail across the North York Moors National Park from Helmsley to Saltburn-by-the-Sea.

4. Walk across Roseberry Common and up a snaking stone-clad path onto Newton Moor, from where there are stunning views back to Roseberry Topping. Go through a gate and, at a fingerpost, continue straight with the stone wall on your right, rather irritatingly obscuring the Roseberry view – although the lovely moorland stretching left compensates for this, especially if roe deer are present.

Try a pint of a unique peak-inspired pale ale brewed for The King's Head Inn by Three Brothers Brewing Co.

NORTH EAST

Looking back at Roseberry Topping from Newton Moor.

5. With Captain Cook's Monument becoming increasingly prominent on the opposite hill, the path descends to meet the road. Carefully cross and turn right then left to walk through the car park, passing an information board, and then going through a gate and past a sign for Gribdale.

6. Follow a Cleveland Way fingerpost pointing to Kildale. Walk up the broad track, crossing Little Ayton Moor, ascending to Easby Moor and passing the crash site where an RAF Lockheed Hudson Bomber collided with the hill in February 1940. Shortly afterwards you reach Captain Cook's Monument, which overlooks Great Ayton, the famous explorer's home from age 8 to 16.

7. From your direction of travel when approaching the monument, turn sharp right and walk towards a scattering of trees, with Roseberry Topping very visible in the distance. Descend along a grassy trail, go through a stone gateway and walk along a single-track path with a stone wall on your left. When the path forks, go left and keep descending into Ayton Banks Wood. Ignore another track going left and keep going down a steep and root-covered path with some steps. Cross a track and go straight on, down another steep drop to a stone wall.

8. Turn left and walk with the wall on your right until you meet a T-junction. Go right on the bridleway, pass through a wide gate and walk along the track, through another gate. The path becomes rugged, then widens into a lane.

9. Ignore a turning left, keep going across a stream and past some houses. Carefully cross Dike Lane (a B-road) and go straight down Aireyholme Lane, briefly descending and crossing a river before steadily climbing.

10. After about 300 yards, look for a stile and footpath on your left. Cross and walk over a field, going through a gate to enter Cliff Ridge Wood, cared for by the National Trust. Walk through the oak, sycamore, holly and beech trees, past a National Trust sign.

11. Shortly after passing a big information board about Cliff Rigg Quarry, turn right through a large wooden kissing gate and walk uphill into Newton Wood. When the path forks, go left. There are myriad ways through these wildlife-rich woods, but if you keep left and walk along the bottom of the trees, there's less climbing. Eventually you'll reach the gate you passed through just before climbing Roseberry Topping. Turn left here, go through another gate and descend along the lane, turning right at the end to go to The King's Head Inn.

89 Hadrian's Wall
The Twice Brewed Inn

A walkers' pub and microbrewery near Hadrian's Wall, **THE TWICE BREWED INN** has a rich history. One story claims ale was double-brewed for Yorkist soldiers here before the Battle of Hexham in 1464, to give it 'fighting strength'. Roman references are ubiquitous, with staff wearing 'For those about to walk, we salute you' T-shirts. There's a drying room and a bike lock-up. The large garden has stilted pods, while inside fires blaze in winter. Accommodation is available, plus guided stargazing experiences. Hearty food is served and walkers can order packed lunches.

The Twice Brewed Inn
Bardon Mill, Hexham
Northumberland
NE47 7AN
01434 344534
www.twicebrewedinn.co.uk

About this walk
- Roman history
- Northumberland National Park
- Dark Sky Park
- Steep climbs

Start/finish The Twice Brewed Inn car park
Distance 7 miles (11.5km)
Time to pub 3.5 hours
Walking time 3–4 hours
Terrain Footpaths, lanes

Hike a spectacular section of Hadrian's Wall, along Whin Sill and part of the Pennine Way, tracing the northern frontier of the Roman Empire past several milecastles and Sycamore Gap to reach Housesteads Fort, then do a loop around Crag Lough to return to a fabulous pub.

Spring Look out for curlews around Crag Lough, kestrels hovering over Hadrian's Wall, and skylarks performing song flights over fields. Wild chive and biting stonecrop start to flower.

Summer Orchids and other wildflowers bloom on the grassland, while under Whin Sill ridge (upon which Hadrian's Wall is built) bog rosemary and asphodel flower. Try to spot the rare large heath butterfly.

Autumn Dunlin arrive from the north. Look out, too, for golden plovers. As evenings arrive ever earlier in this International Dark Sky Park, explore the night sky on astronomer-led star-gazing tours from The Twice Brewed Inn.

Winter Sphagnum moss colours the ridge and Crag Lough is an aquatic hive of avian activity, with whooper swans, goldeneyes, graylag geese, white-fronted geese, lapwings, tufted ducks, teal and widgeons visiting the tarn.

Multiple ales and lagers are brewed on site, with locally pertinent names such as Steel Rigg, and at least five are on handpump at any one time. House-made Sycamore Gap gin is also available.

Follow in the footsteps of ...
Halfway along Hadrian's Wall, Housesteads is Britain's best-preserved Roman fort. Built within 10 years of work beginning on the wall in AD 122, this important fort on the northern edge of the empire garrisoned about 800 soldiers in cramped conditions, up until the Romans abandoned Britain around AD 410.

How to Get There

By Car The Twice Brewed Inn is on the B6318, just off the A69 between Haydon Bridge and Haltwhistle. Use the pub cark park (NE47 7AN; fee payable; not National Trust).

By Public Transport The closest train station is Haltwhistle (5 miles/8km). The AD122 bus service runs daily between April and October, weekends only from November to mid-December, and mid-February to mid-April.

OS Map OS Explorer OL 43 (Hadrian's Wall); Landranger 86 (Haltwhistle & Brampton); grid ref (for start): NY 753/668.

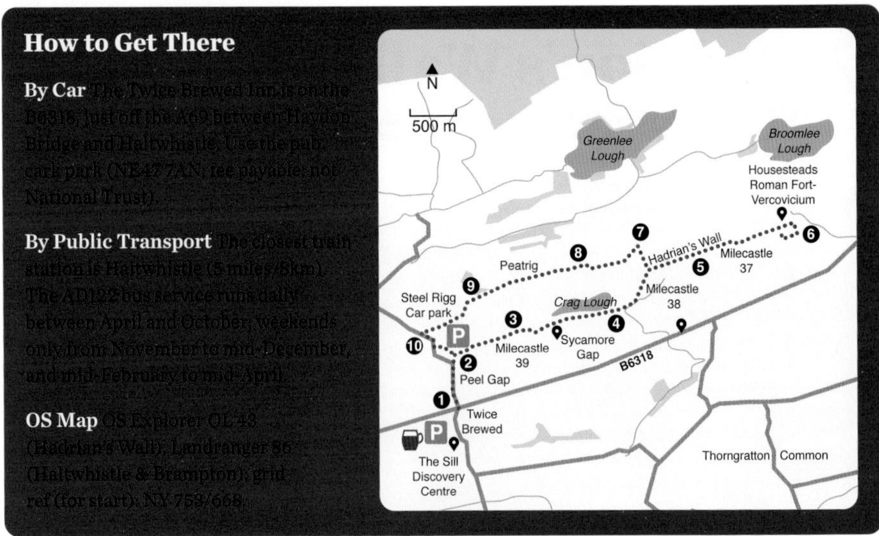

1. With your back to the pub, turn right and go through the car park to the gate and path leading to YHA The Sill. Follow signs to the café, going through a couple of gates, and explore the discovery centre. Afterwards, carefully cross the main road, go through a gate on the opposite side, across a grassy area, through another gate and turn left on the B-road, following a fingerpost pointing towards Hadrian's Wall and Steel Rigg. Walk up the road, passing Springwell Cottage (a National Trust holiday let) on your left. Just past Peel Cottage, at a bend in the road, turn right through a gate. Follow the fingerpost sign for Hadrian's Wall, which points diagonally across a field. (Note: If you want to avoid the steep climbs and descents of the wall path, you can take the footpath fingerpost pointing sharp right, which follows a much flatter, old Roman military road that runs parallel to Hadrian's Wall.)

2. After crossing a wall, the path from Steel Rigg car park comes in from the left. Bear right and join this path, a section of the Pennine Way, descending along the paved stone. When the path starts to climb, look right to see the low-level rectangular remains of Peel Gap Tower. Scramble up the steep, rugged steps to a gate and go through.

3. Cross Peel Crags and keep following the undulating path, with the wall on your immediate left. Descend steeply again to the remains of Milecastle 39 (known as Castle Nick, because it is located by a nick – or gap – in the wall), one of the fortified strongholds built roughly one Roman mile (1,480m) apart along this section of the wall, for defensive purposes and to control the passage of people and goods into and out of the empire. There's still a gap in the wall here, but after exploring the milecastle, ascend the steep rise on the far side, with the wall and views of Crag Lough on your left. March along the wall as the path arcs slightly right and then drops dramatically down into scenic Sycamore Gap, where a solitary, centuries-old sycamore tree stands sentinel by a portal in the wall. This much-photographed tree starred in the 1991 film *Robin Hood: Prince of Thieves* and, as a result, is often referred to as the Robin Hood tree, although it has nothing to do with the original legendary outlaw. Cross through the wall here and climb a section of steep steps on the other side, with the wall on your right. Go through a gate and continue along the ridgeline, walking across Highshield Crags, with a precipitous drop to Crag Lough on your left.

4. Follow the path through woods between the wall and the lough, descending to a gate on your right. Cross a broad farm track, where the old military road comes in from the right, and continue through a gate, following signs for 'Homestead'. Walk uphill on a grassy path, going around Hotbank Farm at Milecastle 38.

5. Keep walking, with the wall on your left. After a descent, the Pennine Way departs north (left), across a ladder stile. Carry on along the wall, going through several gates and following the path as it snakes up a steep bank, climbs a set of steps and continues with Cuddy's Crags on the left. Go past Milecastle 37, pass through another couple of gates and walk with Housesteads Crags dropping vertiginously to your left.

6. After walking along a broad section of wall, go through a gate into Housesteads Roman Fort (Vercovicium). Walk downhill across the grass, between the museum building (on your right) and the extensive remains of the fort. After exploring the site (entry free for National Trust and English Heritage members), start walking back along the wall. You can return to the pub along the wall or take the less undulating military road that runs roughly parallel to it, as mentioned in point 1, but our suggested loop route (described below) traces the north bank of Crag Lough, offering a very different perspective of Hadrian's Wall and Whin Sill.

7. When you reach Hotbank Farm, look for a stone step stile on your right, close to the farm building. Cross, and walk straight ahead, with the farm on your left. Pass through a gate, proceed to a ladder stile by a gate, turn left and hop over a step stile next to a footpath sign. Walk straight across the field, over another stile and through the next field.

8. Turn onto the farm track, following a footpath sign. As you walk, enjoy the stunning view to your left, across the glacial lake to the steep cliffs and crags on the northern side of Whin Sill ridge. When you reach a ladder stile, cross and head over the next field towards an enclosure and barn.

9. Walk with the stone wall on your right, following the path as it becomes a farm track and then reaches a road.

10. Turn left and walk uphill to Steel Rigg car park. From here, descend back down the road to emerge opposite The Sill and The Twice Brewed Inn.

Hadrian's Wall, and the path that runs parallel to it, snake across Sycamore Gap.

90 Dunstanburgh Castle

The Ship Inn

The Ship Inn
Newton Square
Low Newton-by-the-Sea
Northumberland
NE66 3EL
01665 576262
www.shipinnnewton.co.uk

About this walk

- Castle and history
- St Oswald's Way
- Northumberland Coast Path and AONB
- Seals, marine and birdlife

Start/finish Craster Quarry car park
Distance 8 miles (13km)
Time to pub 2 hours
Walking time 3.5 hours
Terrain Coastal paths, dunes and beach

Amid a tiny fishing village, THE SHIP INN is a sanctuary for walkers exploring the Northumberland Coast. Run by a mother-and-daughter team, the pub has an on-site microbrewery, and serves excellent food made with local ingredients, including freshly caught fish and lobsters straight from Newton Bay. The 18th-century National Trust-owned building is cosy, with an open fire, thick stone walls full of stories, and a low-beamed ceiling. Outside tables look across a grassy village square to the North Sea.

From Craster Harbour, amble along a sensational section of the Northumberland Coast Path, past the dramatic ruins of 700-year-old Dunstanburgh Castle, across a beautiful beach and via wildlife-rich Newton Pool, to a picturesque pub.

Spring Wild orchids flower above the beach. Swallows scope out roosts in the castle, while kittiwakes and fulmars flock to Greymare Rock to breed.

Summer Burnet rose and bloody cranesbill bloom in the dunes. Search rock pools for anemones, limpets, crabs and starfish. Spot seals sunbathing around Newton Haven.

Autumn Thousands of birds arrive from the Arctic Circle to overwinter here, including barnacle and pink-footed geese, wigeon, grey plovers and bar-tailed godwits.

Winter Eider ducks (known locally as Cuddy's duck after St Cuthbert) bob around Craster Harbour, with males displaying to females. Linnets and yellowhammers flit across scrub and grassland behind the dunes and castle. Oystercatchers, ringed plovers, redshanks, dunlins and turnstones forage for food along the shore.

Twenty ales are made on rotation by The Ship's micro-brewery, including Sandcastles at Dawn (pale), Red Herring (ruby) and Squid Ink (stout).

Follow in the footsteps of ... This walk traces part of St Oswald's Way, a 97-mile (156-km) route between Holy Island and Hadrian's Wall, joining places of importance to a powerful 7th-century King of Northumbria, credited with bringing Christianity to this corner of the country.

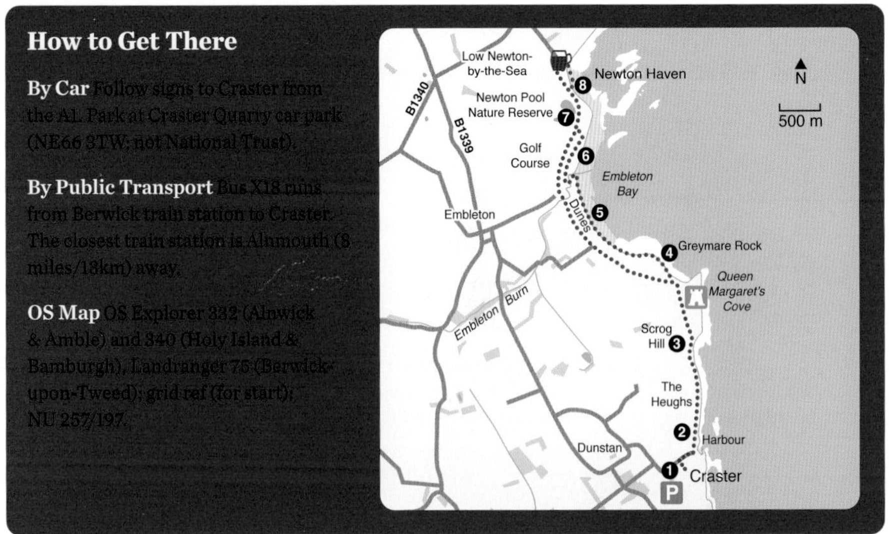

How to Get There

By Car Follow signs to Craster from the A1. Park at Craster Quarry car park (NE66 3TW; not National Trust).

By Public Transport Bus X18 runs from Berwick train station to Craster. The closest train station is Alnmouth (8 miles/13km) away.

OS Map OS Explorer 332 (Alnwick & Amble) and 340 (Holy Island & Bamburgh), Landranger 75 (Berwick-upon-Tweed); grid ref (for start): NU 257/197.

1. From Craster Quarry car park – where interesting information boards explain prehistoric human habitation of Northumbria's coast – turn right and walk downhill, past the village sign towards the pretty little fishing harbour. It's scenic and serene now, but Craster, along with Seahouses, was once the 'kipper capital' of Britain, and in the early 20th century this place would have been buzzing, with boatloads of herring being landed, prepared and smoked. Bear left and walk to a gate with a National Trust sign for Dunstanburgh Castle, and an English Heritage board with entry prices and opening times.

2. Walk across a grassy foreshore, amid clumps of heather that glow yellow in summer and autumn, with the Heughs (derived from a northern English/Scottish word for craggy rises) and Scrog Hill on the left, and white horses cresting the waves of the restless North Sea on your right. The rugged shoreline here is perfect for rock-pooling. Look out for oystercatchers and cormorants, and possibly even the odd seal.

3. Go through a gate and continue straight towards Dunstanburgh Castle, passing slightly to the left of the imposing ruin, hugging the hillside that it's perched upon. This fantastic fortification was built in 1313–22, over the remains of an Iron Age hill fort, by Earl Thomas of Lancaster, who didn't survive to enjoy it. Thomas was engaged in open conflict with his cousin, King Edward II, and was captured after the Battle of Boroughbridge, while attempting to reach the safety of Dunstanburgh. He was executed for treason, and the castle changed hands several times before falling into disrepair after the Wars of the Roses. By 1550 it was already being described as a ruin, but it is still standing, and remains an iconic feature of Northumberland's coast. It's been painted by artists, including J.M.W. Turner, and has inspired poetry and legends including the supernatural story of Sir Guy the Seeker, about a knight who spends his life stuck outside the walls, trying to rescue a noble lady embedded in a crystal tomb beneath the castle. National Trust and English Heritage members can enter the ruins much more easily than poor Guy, and it's well worth exploring.

4. Once you have rounded the fortification, the true strategic magnificence of its hilltop position is revealed. There are steep, exposed slopes to three sides, and to the east a sheer cliff drops down into Queen Margaret's Cove, named after Queen Margaret of Anjou, King Henry VI's wife and the de facto leader of the Lancastrians during the Wars of the Roses, who, according to legend, escaped to France from here, after being lowered down the cliff in a basket. As you walk, look for the distinctive rock formation known as Greymare Rock on your right – a breeding ground for fulmars and kittiwakes. Continue, passing through a gate and walking with a golf course on your left.

Oystercatchers patrol the rocks in front of Dustanburgh Castle.

5. When you reach beautiful Embleton Bay, you can either dawdle through the dunes, or stroll straight over the beach. On warm days it's lovely to shed your shoes and amble across the pale-ale coloured sand, but it is necessary to get back up on the path in order to get over Embleton Burn, which cuts across the bay – unless you're happy to wade through.

6. The path crosses the burn via a bridge, and then rises up over a hill, taking you through a little community of beach huts and chalets. When you get to a junction, go right and walk through a small wooded area with more huts, some of them fairly substantial.

7. Walk past Newton Pool Nature Reserve on your left, where bird hides overlook a lovely lake, offering you the opportunity to spy on geese, swans and various varieties of duck, including pochard, teal and goldeneye. Continue through a gate with a National Trust sign for Embleton Links and walk into the village of Low Newton-by-the-Sea, where there's a little community of whitewashed fishermen's cottages. Carry on to the end of the lane, and then go around the building to the right, where you will be greeted by a gorgeous green village square, presided over by The Ship Inn.

8. After leaving the pub, you can either retrace your footsteps through the cottages, or walk along the beach by Newton Haven, before cutting right along a path by the first wooden hut you see, then turning left to rejoin the main path. Walk back past Newton Pool and reverse your earlier route. If you'd prefer to avoid the dunes, take the path leading slightly more inland as you approach the castle from the bridge over the burn, and walk with the golf course on your left.

91 Lindisfarne
The Ship Inn

The Ship Inn
Marygate, Holy Island
Northumberland TD15 2SJ
01289 389311
www.theshipinn-holy
island.co.uk

About this walk
- Castle and medieval priory
- History
- Seals and birdlife
- St Cuthbert's Way

Start/finish Chare Ends car park
Distance 5½ miles (9km)
Time to pub 2 hours
Walking time 2.5 hours
Terrain Sandy footpaths, dunes, beaches, lanes

For centuries there's been a pub where **THE SHIP INN** stands – at the heart of Holy Island's village, close to the castle, harbour and medieval priory. Until it was re-christened in 1995, The Ship Inn was the Northumberland Arms, but islanders know it as 'the tavern', regardless of what's on the sign. Inside, wood-panelled walls adorned with marine-themed objects give the bar a boat-like ambience. Family run, the pub serves regional ales, food and boasts its own distillery, producing Holy Island Gin. At the back, a wonderful, wind-sheltered garden is popular on sunny afternoons.

NORTH EAST

Circumnavigate Holy Island – exploring shifting dunes, wind-swept beaches, mudflats busy with birds, coves with sunbathing seals, a castle and medieval priory – before grabbing a seat at the atmospheric Ship Inn.

Spring Lindisfarne Castle reopens in March. Skylarks and meadow pipits sing, while fulmars fidget for space on breeding ledges. Sandwich terns arrive with pilgrims at Easter.

Summer Gertrude Jekyll Garden and Castle Crag erupt with wildflowers, orchids bloom in the dunes and grey seals congregate on sand banks. Puffins are sometimes seen passing Castle Point.

Autumn Flocks of birds arrive from the Arctic Circle to feast on mudflat menus at low tide. Ghostly seal song drifts over the Island from Ross Sands.

Winter Wigeon, light-bellied brent and pink-footed geese, grey plover and bar-tailed godwits patrol mudflats. Spot short-eared owls around The Lough, and woodcocks and jacksnipe in dunes. Eider ducks and red-throated divers are active off Castle Point.

The Ship distils Holy Island Gin and stocks regional real ales, including Holy Island Blessed Bitter, Northumbrian Gold and Secret Kingdom from Hadrian Border Brewery.

Follow in the footsteps of ... Lindisfarne, or 'Holy Island', has a long association with Christianity. Irish monk St Aidan founded a monastery here in 635, but the island's best-known hermit, monk and bishop is St Cuthbert, canonised after his perfectly preserved body was exhumed from a grave on Lindisfarne 11 years after his death in 687. This attracted pilgrims and wealth, followed by violent Viking raids from 793, which finally forced the monks to retreat to the mainland.

How to Get There

By Car Note: you can't drive on or off Holy Island at high tide. Check tide times carefully before planning a visit. Park in Chare Ends car park (TD15 2SE, not National Trust), near the village.

By Public Transport Woody's Taxis and Border Buses (477) run seasonal trips to the island from Berwick-upon-Tweed, which has the nearest train station (10 miles/16km).

OS Map OS Explorer 340 (Holy Island & Bamburgh), Landranger 75 (Berwick-upon-Tweed, Holy Island & Wooler); grid ref (for start): NU 126/424

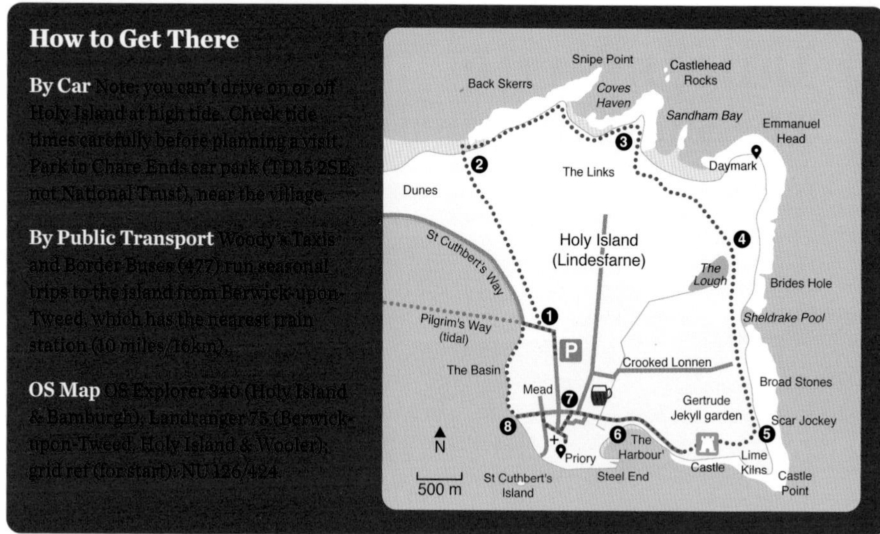

1. Leave the car park via the vehicle entry point, walk north along the roadside grass strip, then bear left towards the causeway. Turn right through a gate in the wall, next to a map and information sign, following a footpath fingerpost.

2. The footpath arcs right, along a wall, but you can continue further, turning along a path between beach and dunes, to enjoy sea views. The maze of sandy hillocks can be befuddling. Hug the coast, stay on the path and be conscious of ground-nesting birds around Snipe Point and Coves Haven.

3. Continue past Castlehead Rocks to Sandham Bay, where seals often lounge at low tide. At Emmanuel Head, a bright white stone pyramid – a 'daymark' – helps ships navigate the tricky channels. From here, bear right and walk slightly inland, on a raised path heading towards the castle.

4. At a bird hide by The Lough, you can spot waterfowl, plus peregrine falcons. Continue, ignoring a path going right, towards the castle, going through several gates, passing Brides Hole, Sheldrake Pool, Broad Stones and Scar Jockey.

5. At Castle Point, spot resident fulmars and look for seals, puffins, eider ducks and red-throated divers. Ringed plovers nest in shingle around the limekilns in spring–summer (heed signs). Explore the castle – a grand Edwardian holiday house built over a defensive Tudor fort – and Gertrude Jekyll Garden, created by the renowned Arts and Crafts garden designer and architect Edwin Lutyens.

6. Walk to the right of the castle, along a tarmac lane into the village, passing the Window on Wild Lindisfarne display and information centre, where Holy Island's extraordinary flora and fauna are detailed. As you enter the village along Marygate, The Ship Inn is on the right.

7. Leaving the pub, continue through the village, passing the National Trust shop and turning left along Crossgate Lane to explore Lindisfarne Priory, a ruined medieval monastery dating to the 7th century and rebuilt by the Normans. Walk along Church Lane, turn right on Lewins Lane, where you'll see Lindisfarne Mead for sale.

8. Take the path leading to the left of the school, turn right along the shore and walk a section of St Cuthbert's Way (a 60-mile/100-km trail from the Scottish Borders, near the saint's birthplace, to Lindisfarne) and St Oswald's Way, which commemorates the 7th-century Northumberland king who gifted Lindisfarne to Irish monks. You may see grey seals in The Basin. At a bench, look left to see the Pilgrim's Way poles, marking a low-tide walking route to the island, then turn right and return to the car park.

Opposite: Looking across Cushendun Bay (see page 268) and the North Channel from the Antrim Coast.

Northern
Ireland

92 Mourne Mountains & Slieve Donard

Harbour House Inn & Macken's Bar

Between the Mourne Mountains and Dundrum Bay, it's hard to know which view to look at from the **HARBOUR HOUSE INN**. This friendly 19th-century pub, located next to the harbour and yacht club at the southern end of Newcastle, opposite the trailhead of the Granite Trail, offers exceptional food, made with local ingredients, and craft Irish beers. The bar has an open fire, there's a choice of dining areas and a sea-facing terrace. Accommodation is available. Opposite, Macken's Bar has traditional music sessions.

Harbour House Inn
4–8 South Promenade
Newcastle, County Down
BT33 0EX; 028 4372 3445
www.harbourhouse newcastle.com

About this walk

- Mourne and Slieve Croob AONB
- Mountain views
- Waterfalls

Start/finish Donard Car Park
Distance 3 miles (5km), Granite Trail loop only; 7½ miles (12km) with Slieve Donard summit
Time to pub 2–4 hours
Walking time 3–5 hours
Terrain Mountain trails

Going from sea to summit and back again, this Mourne Mountains adventure explores the woodlands, waterfalls and moorland beneath Northern Ireland's highest peak, tracing an old quarrying route and pausing for a pint while gazing across Dundrum Bay.

Spring Wheatears arrive from Africa in March and April. Male meadow pipits and skylarks begin their aerial performances and singing sessions, while Irish hares box and emperor moths zoom past, flashing bright red underwings.

Summer Stonechats sing from fenceposts while common heath moths flutter around heather. Bog asphodel bursts into bloom, along with heath spotted orchid and yellow tormentil. Bilberries (or blaeberry as they're locally known) begin to ripen.

Autumn Flowering bell heather and blooming ling transform the sides of the Mourne Mountains into a purple picture. Look for peregrine falcons on the prowl.

Winter Gorse glows gold while ravens croak. If you're very lucky you may spy a snow bunting, or an Irish hare in its winter wardrobe. Be careful if attempting the summit – conditions can be challenging.

The Harbour House Inn and Macken's Bar serve Maggie's Leap IPA from Mourne Mountains-based Whitewater Brewing Company, Chieftain IPA from Cork and Guinness.

Follow in the footsteps of ... The brutal beauty and mystical feel of the Mourne Mountains planted the seed for Narnia in the imagination of *The Lion the Witch and the Wardrobe* author C.S. Lewis, who grew up in Northern Ireland.

How to Get There

By Car Take the A24/A2, head for the centre of Newcastle and park in Donard car park (not National Trust).

By Public Transport Ulsterbus service 520 travels between Belfast and Newcastle.

OSNI Map OSNI Activity Map The Mournes; OS Discoverer Series Sheet 29 The Mournes; grid ref (for start): J373/305.

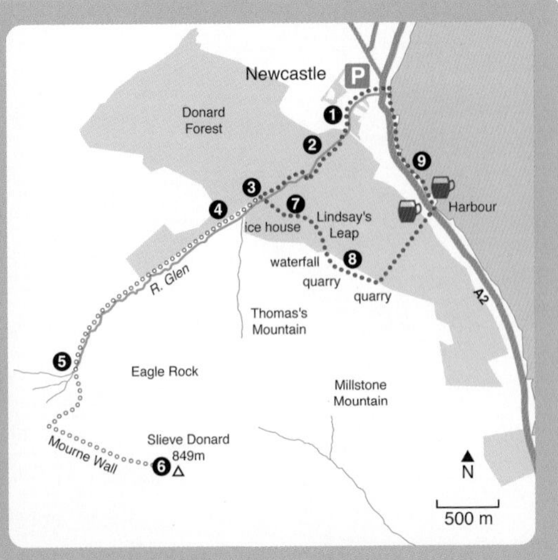

1. From Donard Car Park, walk away from the sea, along a path with sports fields on your right, and pick up the Slieve Donard Trail. You soon meet Glen River, which will be your companion all the way up to the Mourne Wall. Cross Donard's Bridge, turn right and walk uphill with the river on your right. There are several waterfalls to see while wandering the rocky, root-strewn path through Donard Forest, but heed warning signs about unstable banks overhanging the cascades.

2. At Craignagore, cross back over the river via another bridge and continue climbing, with the water now on your left. The path becomes rocky and slippery along this section, especially when wet, and the exact route can be unclear, but hug the river and you can't go wrong.

3. When you meet a track coming in from the right, and a third bridge, it's time to decide whether to head for the summit of Slieve Donard, Northern Ireland's highest peak, a spectacular and rewarding climb if you have sufficient time and energy. It's not a technical mountaintop, and the route is easy to follow, but there's lots of steep ascent, and it's quite exposed. As an out-and-back adventure from this junction, allow at least two hours. If you decide against it, turn left, cross the bridge and skip to point 7.

4. To continue, push on up the path, passing the remains of a 19th-century ice house on the opposite bank, which once served the refrigeration needs of nearby Donard Lodge. Keep climbing the rugged riverside path, with heather and gorse lining the banks. The valley narrows and you pass beneath Eagle Rock on your left. To your right, past another crag, is the second tallest mountain in the Mournes, Slieve Commedagh 2,516ft (767m).

5. As you approach the head of the valley and the source of Glen River, the path crosses the water – now a young stream – and climbs steeply to meet the Mourne Wall. A dry stone wall, built to keep livestock away from streams feeding a reservoir in the Silent Valley, the Mourne Wall (Balla an Mhúrn) stretches for 20 miles (32km) across incredibly steep and exposed terrain, snaking over 15 of the Mourne Mountains' highest peaks, and it took stonemasons 18 years to complete (1904–22). A ladder stile crosses the wall, and you can walk on which ever side you like (depending on where the wind shadow is), but either way, turn left and trace the wall all the way up the mountainside.

6. At the peak, 2,798ft (853m) above sea level, you'll find a trig point standing atop a stone-built summit tower, which offers some shelter when conditions are windy. If luck is with you, views across the Mournes and over deep blue Dundrum Bay are spectacular and can stretch to the Isle of Man and Scotland to the east, deep down into the Republic of Ireland to the south, and across to Donegal in the north-west. There are two stone

The Glen River tumbles over several waterfalls beside the trail, as you ascend towards its source.

cairns on the peak: the Great Cairn near the tower, marking the location of Ireland's highest passage tomb (built over 5,000 years ago), and the Bronze Age Lesser Cairn, overlooking Newcastle. The mountain is named after St Domhanghart (St Donard), a follower of St Patrick who used the summit as a hermitage and oratory, and lived up here until his death in AD 506. The Mourne Wall turns 90 degrees here, and it's possible to follow it south and then turn left along Bloody Bridge River, descending into Bloody Bridge (a beautiful spot with a brutal history, having been the scene of a massacre in the 1641 rebellion, now cared for by the National Trust), but it's impossible to do a loop route this way without walking back along the busy A2 road. Our walk, therefore, returns the way you came, to the junction at the third bridge.

7. Cross the bridge and walk along a forest track, which starts off quite level and then begins to undulate, with some gentle climbing. You're now following a section of the Granite Trail, commemorating the quarrying industry that thrived here in the 19th century. At a viewpoint, above Lindsay's Leap, a circular information stone details the places of interest that can be seen on clear days, including the Isle of Man and Strangford Lough. Divert right here, briefly, up a track and past a quarry to see a sensational waterfall, then return and continue east. Pass through a gate and walk just above the treeline, with sea views left and the slopes of Thomas's and Millstone mountains on your right.

8. After passing another quarry, the path veers left and goes downhill through a wooden gate. Go past an information sign and hut and keep descending. The path steepens and passes another information sign explaining quarrying techniques. Walk down a set of steps, past a quarrying trolley, across a track and down more steps. Cross another track, go through a brick archway and emerge opposite Newcastle lifeboat station and yacht club. Turn left for the Harbour House Inn and Macken's Bar.

9. When you leave the pub, walk into town along the South Promenade, with beaches and Dundrum Bay on your right. Pass the open-air seawater pool, cross over the Glen River bridge and, by the spike sculpture, turn left into Donard Car Park.

93 Minnowburn

The Crown Bar Liquor Saloon

THE CROWN in central Belfast is resplendent with stained glass, ornate tiles, gas lights, brass, decorative woodwork and intimate snugs where you order by buzzing a bell. There's also table seating by the granite-topped bar (backed by beer barrels, mirrors and Irish whiskeys) and in the upstairs restaurant. Opened in 1826, as The Railway Tavern, the pub was transformed into a majestic gin palace in the 1880s. Rocked by blasts during the Troubles, it was acquired by the National Trust and fully restored. Run by Nicholson's, the pub offers food – book ahead to secure a snug.

The Crown Bar
46 Great Victoria Street
Belfast BT2 7BA
028 9024 3187
www.nationaltrust.org.uk/the-crown-bar

About this walk

- Lagan Valley
- Birdlife
- Botanical Gardens

Start Minnowburn car park (National Trust)
Finish The Crown Bar
Distance (one way) 5½ miles (9km)
Time to pub 2–3 hours
Walking time 2–3 hours
Terrain Riverbank footpaths and city streets
Tip Take a bus to the start

Amble along lovely Lagan Valley, through Belfast's Botanical Gardens and Queen's University, into the heart of the modern city, before walking through the decorative doors of The Crown and travelling back in time to a Victorian-era gin palace.

Spring Swifts, swallows and spotted flycatchers arrive. Bluebells flood the valley, while lilac cuckooflower, marsh marigold and common spotted orchids bloom in Lagan Meadows. Spot azure damselflies and speckled wood butterflies.

Summer Kingfishers skim the water and dippers bob on rocks along the Lagan. Skylarks sing and pink ragged-robin and meadowsweet come into flower. Search for signs of otters and, around dusk, look for boisterous badger cubs and hunting owls.

Autumn Red squirrels scamper through beech, oak, sycamore and ash trees in Minnowburn and Belvoir Park Forest, as leaves blaze gold and red. Enchanting (but toxic) fly agaric fungi pop up like fairy houses.

Winter Little grebes linger on the Lagan, while linnets sing and tree sparrows, yellowhammers and reed buntings are easily spotted in leafless trees.

The Crown serves Guinness, Belfast Lager and Belfast Black from Northern Ireland's Whitewater Brewing Co., Nicholson's ales and Chieftain Pale from Cork.

Follow in the footsteps of ...
John Luke Bridge is named after a treasured son of the city. Luke (1906–75) was a multi-award-winning artist who specialised in Regionalism, rendering everyday scenes and local subjects such as Callan Bridge and the locks at Edenderry in his striking, highly coloured style. In Belfast, murals are often political, but several public artworks on the Lagan Towpath depict local wildlife.

How to Get There

By Car Minnowburn car park (National Trust) is just off the A55 ring road from Belfast to Newcastle, in South Belfast.

By Public Transport From central Belfast, buses 6c, 6d, 13 and 513 stop on Milltown Road by the Maxol petrol station, ¾ mile (1.2km) from Minnowburn.

OSNI Map OSNI Discovery 15 Belfast; grid ref (for start): NW 445/242.

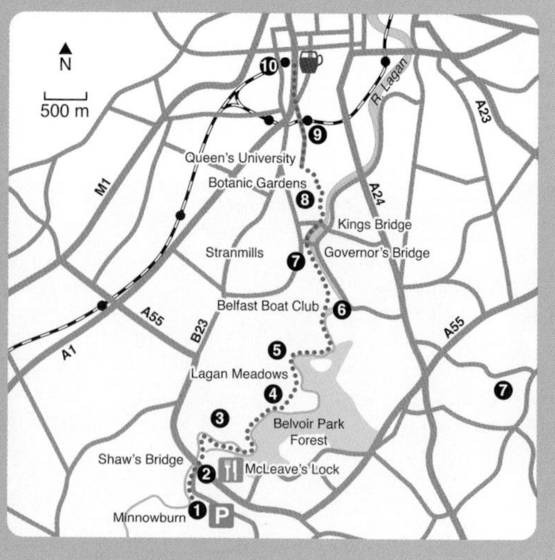

1. From the information sign in the car park at Minnowburn – which explains the history of Lagan Valley Regional Park, Ireland's first such park, founded in 1967 – walk straight down to the river bank and turn right. Stroll along the Lagan, with the river on your left, looking out for kingfishers and herons, and passing beneath branches of oak, beech and sycamore trees that vie for position on the bank.

2. Ascend the ramp on your right and cross old Shaw's Bridge. At the car park, turn acute right and walk beside the river, beneath a larger road bridge, with the water now on your right. Wander through Clement Wilson Park, past rushing rapids (you may see kayakers and canoeists running the white water). The path turns grassy (sometimes muddy) after the kayak pull-out point, but there is a sealed path just over to your left, which runs parallel and is a better option in wet weather.

3. The paths converge at a car park and take you across John Luke Bridge, named after a famous Belfast artist (see Follow in the footsteps of...). Walk along the shared cycling/walking trail through wonderful woodlands, where native species share space with introduced trees such as silver maple. At McLeave's Lock you'll see a beautiful little stone bridge on the right (don't cross), while on your left is The Lock Keeper's Inn – sadly this isn't a pub, but it is a great café serving good coffee and a range of breakfasts and lunch options. You will also find toilets here, and an excellent information centre explaining the history, flora and fauna of the Lagan Valley Regional Park. Continue along the towpath, with the navigation on the right, to a red bridge over the Lagan. Cross this and keep going along the river bank, with the water on your right and beyond that Belvoir Park Forest, where the trees surround a 12th-century Norman motte.

4. Pass a National Cycle Network fingerpost informing you that it's 3½ miles to Belfast, and a bridge leading across the river to Belvoir Park Forest, but keep going along the left bank. You can stay on the river bank and explore the longer way around if you choose, but our walk takes the tarmac towpath that leaves the riverside for a short section here and traces the route of the old navigation, which opened in 1763 and connected Belfast to Lough Neagh. By a tall sign for 'Mickey Taylor's Lock 2', pass a path leading right, across a footbridge into part of Lagan Meadows Park.

5. As you continue, the river comes in to meet the path from the right, and shortly afterwards a fingerpost points left, through a gate, into another section of Lagan Meadows Park. You can explore this urban oasis at your own leisure, but our route continues towards the city. Stroll along a lengthy, lovely, serpentine section of the river, passing another fingerpost pointing left into Lagan Meadows Park.

6. At Molly Ward's Lock, where there is a modern mural-adorned bridge, the path again temporarily leaves the river to go left, around Stranmillis Sluice, Belfast Boat Club and Belfast Rowing Club. Walk along the tarmac path running parallel to Lockview Road, passing Cutter's Wharf, and just beyond Queen's University boathouse, follow the blue sign right to rejoin the river bank pathway.

7. Pass a sign for the Belfast Waterfront Hall and go under Governors Bridge. Walk along Stranmillis Embankment, following a section of pavement between the river and the road, then leave the river and cross to the left side of the road at traffic lights by Kings Bridge.

8. After 50 yards, turn left through a gate along a path crossing the grounds of Queen's University's sports department. Bear left, walking around the circular physical education centre, and then enter Belfast's Botanical Gardens. Take the route that leads right around the gardens, following fingerposts for the Tropical Ravine and Ulster Museum. Pass toilets on the right, then the Tropical Ravine display and, just before the distinctive Palm House, turn right and leave the park, passing McClay Library on your right.

8. Walk along College Park, through Queen's University buildings, cross University Street and continue along Botanic Avenue, a bohemian and culturally rich part of Belfast, bustling with bookshops, bistros and students.

9. At the busy confluence with Donegal Road, dogleg left and then right to walk up Shaftesbury Square and then Great Victoria Street – through a less arty part of the city. At a set of lights, keep going straight, and on the right, opposite the Europa Hotel (once famed as the world's most bombed hotel, having been hit 36 times during the Troubles), on the corner of Amelia Street, is the unmissable Crown Bar.

10. If you parked at Minnowburn and want to walk back, after leaving the pub, you can continue up Great Victoria Street, past the Grand Opera House, and then turn right on Wellington Place and walk via Belfast City Hall and the Waterfront Hall to the Lagan, before bearing right and following the river all the way back. Or you can take a bus or taxi back to the start.

In the verdant Lagan valley, near Minnowburn, Shaw's Bridge crosses the serpentine river that flows into the heart of Belfast.

94 Cushendun

Mary McBride’s

Mary McBride’s
2 Main Street, Cushendun
County Antrim BT44 0PH
028 2176 1511
www.facebook.com/Mcbridescushendun

About this walk

- Castle and history
- Caves and beaches
- Riverside walking
- Wildflowers and butterflies

Start/finish Cushendun National Trust car park
Distance 2½ miles (4km)
Time to pub 1.5 hours
Walking time 1.5 hours
Terrain Beach, riverside footpaths, lanes, some road

MARY MCBRIDE’S is a traditional Irish pub, cared for by the National Trust. A mural in the doorway hall depicts chieftain Somhairle Buide Mac Domhnaill (‘Sorley Boy’ MacDonnell) celebrating victory over his enemy Shane O’Neil, who was slain here in 1567. Historically one of Ireland’s smallest pubs, the cosy original front bar is busy with bohdrans (Irish drums), hurling sticks and tributes to the village Gaelic sports teams. Meals are served upstairs, and there’s seating outside with sensational seaside views. Music sessions take place regularly.

Stroll along a spectacular beach, enjoying views of the Mull of Kintyre in Scotland, to a ruined 14th-century castle with a violent history, before looping past Glenmona House, walking beside the Glendun River, and visiting caves seen in *Game of Thrones*. Finish with a pint of stout in a proper Irish pub.

Spring Wildflowers begin to bloom across The Warren, attracting pollinators including small tortoiseshell butterflies and cinnabar moths. Look out for Irish hares boxing in fields, and listen for cuckoo, chiffchaff, willow warbler and blackcap in the woods behind Glenmona House.

Summer Paddle on Cushendun Beach, scan waves for bottlenose dolphins and look for seals. On The Warren, flowering orchids, yellow rattle and cat’s ear attract six-spot burnet moths and bumblebees.

Autumn Spot red squirrels scurrying for nuts in the woods beside Glenmona House, look for signs of otters along the river and spy foxes and hedgehogs foraging for food.

Winter See dunnock, stonechat, song thrush, and dippers along Glendun River and explore Cushendun’s caves before bagging a seat in Mary McBride’s front bar.

Mary McBride’s sells a large range of Irish whiskeys and excellent Guinness. Other Irish beers include Smithwicks, Hallion Red, Harp and Clonmell lager.

Follow in the footsteps of ...
The Fuldiew Seat at the beginning of this walk commemorates a local tragedy. The tale relates how a young sailor was killed during a voyage in 1803, just before his wedding was due to take place. Days later, his fiancée was found dead, lying atop his grave, having inscribed grief-stricken words into the stone (which can be seen at St Patrick’s Church).

How to Get There

By Car Drive north from Belfast via the stunning coast road from Larne, or take the faster route along the M2/A26/A44 before turning right and following signs for Cushendall and then Cushendun. Use the National Trust car park in Cushendun (BT44 0PH).

By Public Transport Ulsterbus 150 travels between Ballymena and Cushendun.

OSNI Map OSNI Activity Map The Glens of Antrim; grid ref (for start): D 250/327.

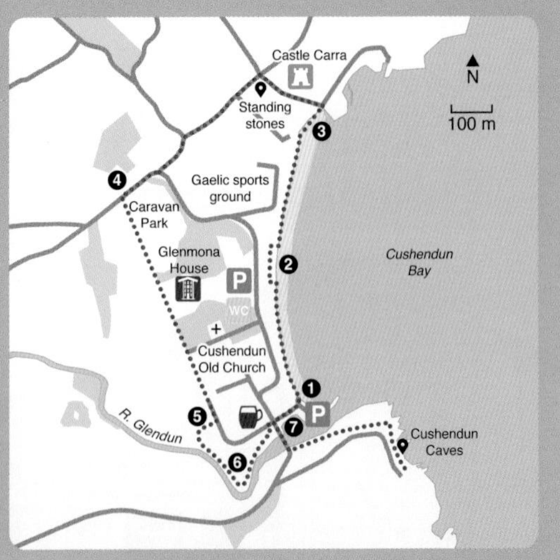

1. From the car park, by the Fuldiew Seat (see opposite), take the path running along the back of the beach, walking through The Warren – a wildflower-rich meadow, part of the Glens Great Grassland Trail.

2. Continue along the top of the beach, passing Robert Emmets GAC Gaelic sports ground on your left. Go over a footbridge across Milltown Burn and pass Seaside Cottages, as the sea laps at an increasingly pebbly beach.

3. When you meet the tarmac road, turn left and walk inland. In the field to the right are the ruins of Castle Carra where Irish chieftain Shane O'Neill was killed by his enemies in 1567. His head was sent to Dublin Castle, and his body was buried at Crosskern Church at Ballyterrim above Cushendun, where a cairn now stands. When you meet Torr Road, turn left and carefully walk along the tarmac. In the field to your immediate left stand a couple of megalithic stones.

4. Continue past the sports ground, go straight across at the junction to briefly walk along Glendun Road. Just past the caravan park, turn left along Church Lane, a lovely track lined with holly, beech and sycamore trees. Walk with grazing fields on your right and, after the caravan park, a long stone wall on your left. Beyond the wall is Glenmona House, a mansion rebuilt after being razed by the Irish Republican Army in 1922. The house was designed by the architect Sir Bertram Clough Williams-Ellis (famous for creating Portmeirion in Wales) for MP Ronald John McNeill, Baron Cushendun, and is now maintained by the National Trust.

5. At a bend, trace the lane left and then immediately turn right, following a footpath arrow along a trail that cuts between fields and then passes behind a row of cottages. Turn right and follow yellow footpath arrows along a path, which bends left and takes you along the Glendun River, initially atop a steep bank with the water on your right.

6. As the river elbows left, the path descends to meet the water and passes two picnic tables. A sign on the grassy corner tells the tale of a terrible battle between Irish and Scottish fairies, which caused the water in the river to run forever brown, stained with the blood of the vanquished Irish fairies (in Gaelic 'dun' or 'donn' means 'brown').

7. At the path's end, go right over Cushendun's iconic five-arch bridge, then turn left and walk down to the beach, with the harbour on your left. At the water's edge, bear right to visit Cushendun's 400-million-year-old caves, now famous for featuring in *Game of Thrones*, but interesting in their own right. After exploring the caverns, walk back across the bridge, and Mary McBride's pub is on your left.

95 White Park Bay & Carrick-a-Rede

Fullerton Arms

Perfectly poised between White Park Bay and Carrick-a-Rede, the **FULLERTON ARMS** offers Irish hospitality, food and drink. Outside, there's a striking Guinness mural, while inside the *Game of Thrones* theme is strong. Ballintoy was used as a filming location for the series, and the pub has a dedicated room with a custom-built throne and one of ten official *Game of Thrones* doors – carved using wood from Northern Ireland's Dark Hedges ('Kingsroad' to fans) blown down by Storm Gertrude in 2016. Accommodation available.

Fullerton Arms
22–24 Main Street
Ballintoy
County Antrim BT54 6LX
028 2076 9613
www.fullerton-arms.com

About this walk

- Causeway Coast
- Historic rope bridge
- Marine and birdlife
- *Game of Thrones* filming locations

Start/finish White Park Bay (National Trust)
Distance 9 miles (14.5km)
Time to pub 3 hours
Walking time 4 hours
Terrain Coastal paths, beach, lanes and some road

Explore a sublime section of the Causeway Coast, strolling across beautiful beaches, bays, headlands and harbours, before reaching a famous rope bridge. Return via a pub where tradition mixes with modern cuisine and popular fantasy fiction.

Spring Cacophonous seabirds including kittiwakes, guillemots, fulmars and razorbills compete for position on the cliff edge. Stonechats, meadow pipits and skylarks sing in the fields, while Irish hares box.

Summer Warblers arrive and wildflowers (meadow cranesbill, kidney vetch, wild thyme, thistles, rock spurrey and sea pinks) bloom, attracting tortoiseshell, red admiral, peacock and common blue butterflies. Bring binoculars to spot Sheep Island's seals. Search waves for fins of porpoises, dolphins and basking sharks.

Autumn Watch cormorants and gannets dive for fish. Look for Irish stoats hunting in hedgerows, roaming red foxes, and circling buzzards.

Winter Oystercatchers strut along the beaches, around eider ducks and ringed plovers. The rocky coast is lashed by wind and battered by big waves.

The Fullerton Arms sells Smithwick's, Guinness, and Chieftain IPA and Rebel Red from Franciscan Well Brewery.

Follow in the footsteps of...
In the 18th century, an illegal 'hedge school' operated at White Park Bay, one of many across Ireland covertly providing primary education to children from 'non-conforming' faiths (Catholic and Presbyterian). Among the graduates from this secret classroom was Robert Stewart, later Lord Castlereagh.

How to Get There

By Car Drive on the Whitepark Road (A2/B15) between Bushmills and Ballycastle. Park at White Park Bay (National Trust).

By public transport Ulsterbus service 172 and Causeway Rambler 402 between Coleraine and Ballycastle stop at White Park Bay and Ballintoy.

OSNI Map OSNI Activity Map Causeway Coast and Rathlin Island; OSNI Discoverer 5 Ballycastle; grid ref (for start): D014/436.

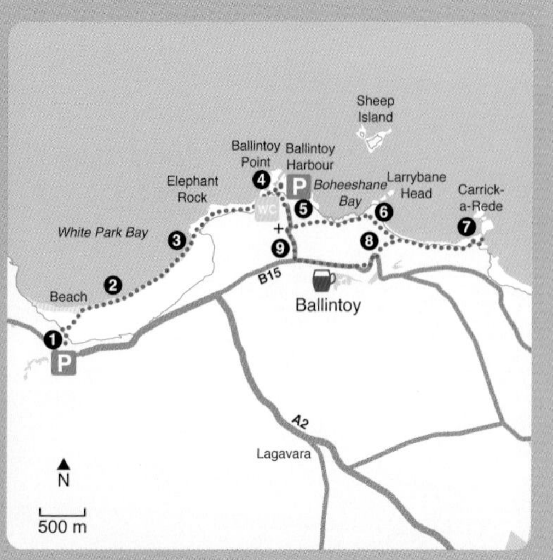

1. From the car park, follow the track down towards White Park Bay beach, which stretches wide left and right, with waves rolling in from the North Atlantic. Go through a gate, pass an information sign and descend the path and steps that zig-zag down to the sand. Pass through a kissing gate and walk to the right of a ruin, where another sign has information on the 'hedge school' that once operated here (see opposite).

2. Stroll through the dunes and turn right along the shore, using a pebble ford to cross the incoming stream and walking along a beautiful blonde expanse of sand towards a tongue of rocks sticking cheekily out into the sea straight head. You're now negotiating a stretch of the Causeway Coast Way (a 30-mile/48-km adventure along the Antrim coast), itself a section of the epic Ulster Way (a 600-mile/960-km circuit of Northern Ireland). While you wander, look for rare meadow cranesbill ('the blue flower of Dunluce'), fossils and White Park's famous beach-dwelling cows.

3. At the end of the beach, go to the right of a large boulder and skirt around the cliff into a rock-strewn cove, with fantastic limestone formations including Elephant Rock on your left. (You may get wet feet here at high tide – it's possible to divert over the headland through fields if that doesn't appeal.) Pass through a gate on the beach, and either walk across the cove, or bear right, clamber over a ladder stile and walk along the sandy path. There are several superb sea-sculpted rocks and arches here, and curious caves disappear darkly into the cliffs.

4. Cross a grassy section and hop over two stiles, both beside distinctive pyramid-shaped rocks. Carry on, looking for seals and seabirds, and enjoying the antics of the rock-climbing sheep (note: dogs are not allowed on this section). Cross another stile and walk around fishermen's cottages into Ballintoy Harbour, passing a couple of large caves. Go through the car park, past toilet facilities and a café. On decent days you can enjoy excellent views of Carrick-a-Rede Island and bridge from the end of the harbour wall here. And, of course, this is a *Game of Thrones* filming location (in the popular show Ballintoy Harbour stars as Lordsport, the main port of Pyke).

5. Following blue Causeway Coast and Ulster Way signs, walk up the road snaking out of Ballintoy. When you reach a church, turn left, heeding more waymarkers, and stroll along the North Antrim Cliff Path, a good track between fields. Shortly, the field on your left is replaced by precipitous cliffs, beyond which lies Sheep Island. Look out for basking sharks, which are big but harmless, unlike the Lig-na-Baste, a terrifying mythical sea serpent said to haunt this coast. As you approach Carrick-a-Rede car park, you will see Larrybane Quarry on your left – this is yet another filming location for scenes in *Game of Thrones*.

The Carrick-a-Rede Bridge has become an icon of Northern Ireland's World Heritage-listed Causeway Coast.

6. At the car park there are more facilities – if you're intending to cross the Carrick-a-Rede Bridge, you can pick up tickets here, but you need to book ahead online, because this is an incredibly popular attraction. National Trust members don't have to pay, but still need to book.

7. It's well worth walking along the cliff-top path to get an eyeful of the island and dramatic bridge, even if you don't want to cross. The famous footbridge was originally a flimsy rope affair, strung up each summer by salmon fishermen, who would edge their way across the terrifying 100ft (30m) drop, holding on to a single rope with one hand, and balancing their gear and catch on their backs with the other. The tradition started in 1755, and the salmon fishery survived for hundreds of years, with as many as 300 fish being netted each day, but the Atlantic salmon population has since been decimated. When you cross the (now much more substantial) modern bridge, you're traversing the mouth of an ancient volcano, which erupted 60 million years ago. Once you've crossed, or simply enjoyed the view, loop around and return along the path to the car park.

8. Walk up the twisting exit lane towards the main coast road (B15). There's a seat near the top so you can stop, catch your breath and enjoy the vista. Just before meeting the road, turn right along a footpath that runs parallel to the tarmac, into Ballintoy. At Knocksoghey Lane bear right and walk into the village, where there are two pubs. The Fullerton Arms, with the huge Guinness mural painted on the wall, offers excellent, modern Irish cuisine, while the more rustic Carrick-a-Rede has a fire-warmed bar and an outside area.

9. Leave the pub and walk out of the village, travelling west along the main street, which has a pavement on the right, following brown signs for Ballintoy Harbour. Turn right along Harbour Road, walk down past the church and then turn left to hike back along the Causeway Coast to the car park. The rock formations and views look totally different when approached from this direction, making the return trek interesting, but if you've walked enough, you can catch a bus from Ballintoy back to White Park Bay.

96 The Giant's Causeway
The Nook

An eccentric little pub, housed in a 19th-century schoolhouse, **THE NOOK** invites visitors to enjoy a pint while contemplating the Causeway Coast and the myths and magic that swirl around it. Near the visitor centre, the stone building features a curved wooden bar and three snug seating areas, warmed by a fire in wilder months and lit by gas-style lamps. The beer garden offers World Heritage views, but if the Northern Irish mists interfere, historic Giant's Causeway photos line the walls. Food is served.

The Nook
48 Causeway Road
Bushmills
County Antrim BT57 8SU
028 2073 2993

About this walk

- Extraordinary rock formations
- Stunning views
- Mythology
- Marine wildlife
- Steep climbs

Start/finish Giant's Causeway car park (National Trust)
Distance 2½ miles (4km)
Time to pub 1–1.5 hours
Walking time Allow 2 hours
Terrain Coastal footpaths

N. IRELAND

Explore a unique coastline, where myths abound, and 40,000 huge polygonal black basalt columns mysteriously march into the waves. Return across colourful cliffs to a cosy pub with views along Antrim's coast, where the Atlantic Ocean meets the Irish Sea.

Spring Sea pinks bloom along basalt rocks. Scan waves for dolphins, porpoises, minke whales and basking sharks. Spy skylarks on cliff-top meadows.

Summer Myriad wildflowers bloom on ledges and in fields, attracting bees and butterflies. Meadow pipits, warblers and stonechats serenade strollers.

Autumn Peregrine falcons and buzzards patrol the sky, while choughs and ravens rock hop.

Winter Trails are quiet and views are clear on calm days. When it's wild, the waves are impressive and curlews, oystercatchers, and eider ducks seek shelter in the bays.

The Nook sells Macardle's Traditional Ale, Guinness and Magners Irish cider on tap, and Whitewater Belfast Ale and Lager by the bottle.

Follow in the footsteps of ...
According to myth, Irish giant Fionn mac Cumhaill (Finn McCool) created the causeway to reach Scotland and battle a rival, Benandonner. Belatedly realising Benandonner was too big, Fionn retreated. The Scottish giant came looking for Fionn and found him snoozing. Fortunately, Fionn's quick-thinking wife, Sadhbh, convinced Benandonner the sleeping figure was her son. Figuring that if his baby was this huge, Fionn himself must be massive, Benandonner scuttled back to Scotland, tearing up the causeway behind him.

How to Get There

By Car The Giant's Causeway is between Coleraine and Ballycastle, near Bushmills village. Take the B147 Causeway road to car park 1 (National Trust). Pre-book parking online.

By Public Transport The closest train stations are Portrush (8 miles/13km) and Coleraine (10 miles/16km). Buses, including Goldline Coach Service 221 and Antrim Coaster Coach Service 252, serve the Causeway Coast from Belfast.

OSNI Map OSNI Activity Map The Causeway Coast and Rathlin Island/ OS Map Sheet 4; grid ref (for start): C944/439.

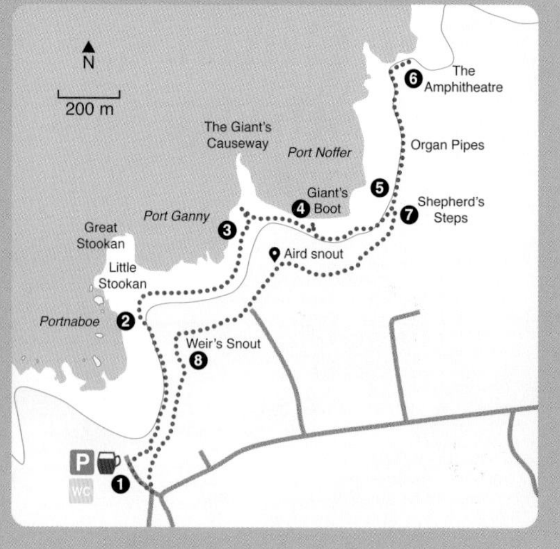

1. From the car park, head towards the visitor centre. You can either go through this innovative building or up the incline and walk right across the glass-panelled roof. From the rear of the centre, follow fingerposts pointing towards the Giant's Causeway, taking the Blue Trail, which leads you on an easy stroll around the top of Portnaboe Bay.

2. The path follows a kerbstone-edged pavement, beside a road used by tourist buses. As you walk, look over your left shoulder, across Portnaboe Bay, and see if you can spot Fionn mac Cumhaill's 'Camel' – the poor, giant-carrying creature was long ago turned to stone and lies frozen in time along the rocky foreshore. Keep going towards the Stookans – a couple of hills on the headland that resemble an old lady with a bent back (said to be the giant's grandmother, whom he turned to stone when she kept nagging him), and follow the footpath as it wends right, around Port Ganny.

3. The famous features of the causeway pop into view here, and at the far end of the bay you can leave the tarmac and explore the beautiful, bizarre basalt rock formations created 50–60 million years ago, by streams of lava hitting the ocean and rapidly cooling. There are three sections – the Little Causeway (an entrée), the Middle Causeway (where the most perfectly shaped hexagonal rocks are found) and the Grand Causeway, with multiple features, including the Wishing Chair (which you can sit in), the Lady's Fan and the Crown.

4. As you walk around to Port Noffer, look for the Giant's Boot on your left – marked on many maps as the Giant's Chair. The Blue Trail stops here, but we carry on, passing the bottom of the Shepherd's Steps and entering a salt marsh environment where coastal wildflowers like sea aster and yellow iris bloom.

5. Pass the Organ Pipes, on your right. These tall, thin columns of basalt rock semi-protrude from the cliff face. From here, the path starts to ascend.

6 A dramatic trail takes you up, through a concrete archway and around to a platform overlooking the Amphitheatre, where the view across the cove to the red-banded cliffs and basalt totem poles beyond is stunning. However, previous rockfalls mean you need to stop here and go back the way you came.

7. Retrace your footsteps to where the path forks and bear left to ascend the Shepherd's Steps (all 162). At the top, bear right, picking up the Red Trail along the windy clifftop, with wildflower-rich meadows to your left and a precipitous drop to your right, down to the Aird headland.

8. Carry on, past the viewpoint at Weir's Snout, back via the visitor centre to take a look in The Nook and enjoy a brew with a view.

Opposite: The River Coe runs through the glen and past the legendary Clachaig Inn (see page 281).

Scotland

97 Rockcliffe & Rough Island

Anchor Hotel

Balanced on the beautiful banks of Urr Water, the family-run ANCHOR HOTEL offers warm Scottish hospitality to hikers, bikers and boaters returning from adventures around the Solway Riviera. The pub has two main areas, with the cosy, fire-warmed, dog-friendly public bar the choice for those fresh from the trails, while the lounge is for dining. The outside area looks across the Urr Estuary to peaks including Screel Hill and Bengairn on the far shore. Good food is offered, and accommodation is available.

Anchor Hotel
Kippford, Dalbeattie
Dumfries and Galloway
DG5 4LN
01556 620205

About this walk
- Solway Riviera views
- Birdlife
- Dark Ages hillfort
- Causeway to an island

Start/finish Rockcliffe public car park
Distance 5 miles (8km)
Time to pub 1.5 hours
Walking time 2.5 hours
Terrain Woodland, coastal and hillside footpaths, lanes, some road

From Rockcliffe, explore a 1,500-year-old fort overlooking spectacular Urr Estuary and Solway Firth, before wandering through wildlife-rich woods to a wonderful waterside inn at Kippford. Walk back on the outgoing tide to visit an island inhabited only by birds.

Spring Listen for the drumming of woodpeckers and spy shelduck, snipe and lapwing along the shore. Spot adders in March and swallows in April.

Summer Yellow rock-roses bloom, attracting rare northern brown argus butterflies. Listen for grasshopper warblers, and the melancholic refrain of willow warblers. Oystercatchers and ringed plovers claim Rough Island for nesting. Scan waves for harbour porpoises.

Autumn Watch wading birds, including dunlin, turnstone, red shank and curlew. Pink-footed geese, whooper swans and various dabbling ducks arrive. Grey seals begin breeding.

Winter Wildfowl, waders and ducks – including wigeon, pintail, scaups, shovelers and teal – fossick for crabs, cockles and worms in the eelgrass around Rough Island. The entire population of the Svalbard barnacle goose overwinters on the estuary's salt marshes.

The Anchor's signature beer is Bitter & Twisted – a golden ale produced by Alva-based Harviestoun Brewery.

Follow in the footsteps of …
The enigmatic Mote of Mark was an important fort in the Celtic kingdom of Rheged, a Brittonic-speaking region in the Solway Firth during the post-Roman era of the 6th century. The lost citadel was destroyed in the 7th century.

How to Get There

By Car

By Public Transport

OS Map

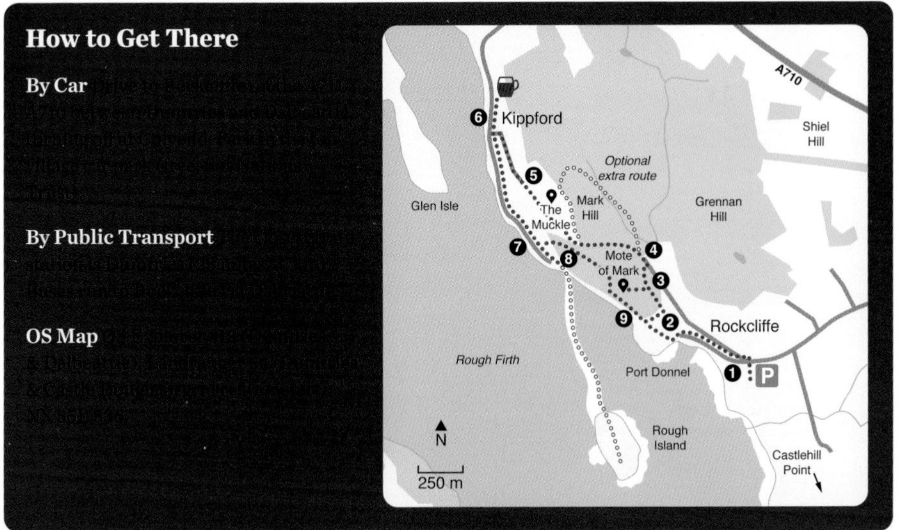

1. From the main car park above Rockcliffe, stroll down the road into the lovely little firth-facing village and enjoy the views out across the Urr Estuary to Rough Island, a tide-protected sanctuary for birds. Just past the information sign and toilets, turn right up the lane to begin the Jubilee Trail that links Rockcliffe and Kippford. Go through a kissing gate, bear left then right through another gate, and pass a large wooden National Trust for Scotland (NTS) sign. As well as tracing a large part of the Jubilee Trail, our walk follows much of the route of the NTS-waymarked Woodpecker Trail through the trees.

2. Follow the path across a grassy area and cross a small footbridge over a rushing stream. Turn immediately right and take the wide track uphill until you reach the NTS information sign for the Mote of Mark. To explore the site of the fort, turn left and walk up to the base of Mote Hill, and left again to ascend the rocky path to the top, where views across Rough Island and Solway Firth to the Lake District in England can be enjoyed on clear days. Return to the base of the hill, go left and continue along the path.

3. Turn right through a wooden gate and walk along a lovely single-track path through a verdant woodland of ivy-covered hawthorn. Go through another gate and pass a wooden sculpture of a woodpecker.

4. At a four-way fingerpost, turn left and walk along a path running parallel to an old moss-cloaked stone wall, following the arm pointing along the Jubilee Path to Kippford (unless you want to do the optional Mark Hill Circular path, also signed, which adds 1¾ miles/2.8km to the overall distance). To your right is mixed woodland of oak, holly, hawthorn and sycamore trees, with bracken, gorse and moss-smothered boulders completing the colour palette. Stroll past several benches, but stay on the main track, ignoring paths leading off to the left. There is an option to divert right and climb up to The Muckle, a 330ft (100m) hillock on the shoulder of Mark Hill, if you're hungry for more views (to do this, look out for a blue arrow on a boulder marking the beginning of the climb).

5. By an NTS sign you emerge onto a tarmac lane. Walk downhill, past several nicely positioned cottages, until you meet Main Street at The Ark café in Kippford. Turn right and walk up the road, with the firth on your left. Continue past the RNLI lifeboat station until you reach the Anchor Hotel, on your right.

6. After leaving the pub, stroll back past the RNLI station and café. Keep going, passing the turn-off that brought you here and walking with the Urr Estuary on your right, fringed by a beach comprised entirely of cockle shells that is well worth pausing to explore.

Rough Island is taken over by ground-nesting oystercatchers and ringed plovers between May and July, when it's off limits to walkers.

7. Continue, past the slipway, a small lookout station and a second slipway. Soon you reach a wooden NTS fingerpost pointing left for the footpath back to Rockcliffe.

Rough Island extension: Before returning to Rockcliffe, however, if the tide is out and you're here outside of the nesting season for oystercatchers and ringed plovers (May–mid-July) don't miss the opportunity to walk out along the causeway to explore Rough Island. A path leads right across the middle of the isle, to reach a stone cairn with great views across the Spring Stones and Solway Firth to the fells of the Lake District, with the Robin Rigg offshore windfarm electricity mills spinning away in the hazy space in between. To your right is Horse Isles and beyond that Hestan Island, home to the intriguingly named Daft Ann's Steps. To your left, on the promontory, is Barcloy Hill and Castlehill Point, where the remains of a prehistoric fort can be explored. Be sure to keep an eye on tide times – the causeway disappears quickly once the tide starts to come in, and you can get trapped.

8. Once back on the mainland, turn up the aforementioned path and follow fingerposts along the footpath to Rockcliffe. Keep to the main trail, ignoring turnings off to the left, and wander through the woods beneath the Mote of Mark.

9. When you meet a T-junction, go left. Pass through a gate by a cattle grid and at the stream turn left, walking up to the footbridge you crossed earlier. Turn right, cross the bridge and reverse your earlier footsteps through two kissing gates and Rockcliffe village to get back to the car park. If you weren't able to get across to Rough Island because of the time of year or tide, or if you simply want to extend your walk, turn right just before you reach the car park to take the signposted 2-mile (3.2-km) return route to Castlehill Point, where similar views to those seen from the island can be enjoyed.

98 Arrochar & Tarbet

The Village Inn

The Village Inn
Loch Long, Shore Road
Arrochar, Argyll and Bute
G83 7AX; 01301 702279
www.classicinns.co.uk/villageinnarrochar

About this walk
- Loch and mountain views
- Viking history
- Wildlife and birdlife
- Heritage Trail and Three Lochs Way

Start/finish Three Villages Hall car park
Distance 5½ miles (9km)
Time to pub 2–2.5 hours
Walking time 2.5–3 hrs
Terrain Lochside trails

SCOTLAND

A wonderful pub on the shores of Loch Long, with views across the water to the Arrochar Alps, THE VILLAGE INN occupies a house built in 1827 as a manse. A favourite hillwalkers' watering hole, there are tables outside, for gazing across the loch when the weather is good. Inside, the cosy bar has a real fire, and a traditional look and feel. Accommodation is available, and good food is served.

From the shore of fjord-like Loch Long, traverse the forested flanks of Cruach Tairbeirt – enjoying views over the Arrochar Alps – to see Ben Lomond's pointy peak from the Loch Lomond-lapped village of Tarbet, before following the Three Lochs Way back to a wonderfully welcoming pub.

Spring Arrochar's lochside is busy with gulls, cormorants and oystercatchers, and blooming spring wildflowers colour the valley trails.

Summer Peregrines are nesting, and ravens circle above the crags. Buzzards soar higher, and you might even spot a golden eagle, or a swooping osprey. Seals swim in Loch Long, with dolphins and whales more occasional visitors. Otters are active along both loch shores.

Autumn Rutting red deer stags bellow on the hills, while smaller roe deer venture lower, to loch level. Around the trails, native red squirrels fight an ongoing turf war with their invasive grey cousins. Elusive pine martens are also present.

Winter The Arrochar Alps and Ben Lomond are snow capped. Eider ducks remain on the lochs, and whitened rock ptarmigan are active in the hills. A fire awaits at The Village Inn.

With five handpumps, The Village Inn serves ales from local breweries including Loch Lomond, Fyne Ales, Fallen and Lerwick. There's an expansive whisky collection – mostly Scottish, but with inclusions from Ireland, Japan and elsewhere.

Follow in the footsteps of ...
In 1263, Vikings under the command of Norwegian King Håkon IV pulled their longboats out of salty Long Loch at Arrochar, dragged them across the isthmus to Tarbet, then sailed south to plunder settlements around Loch Lomond.

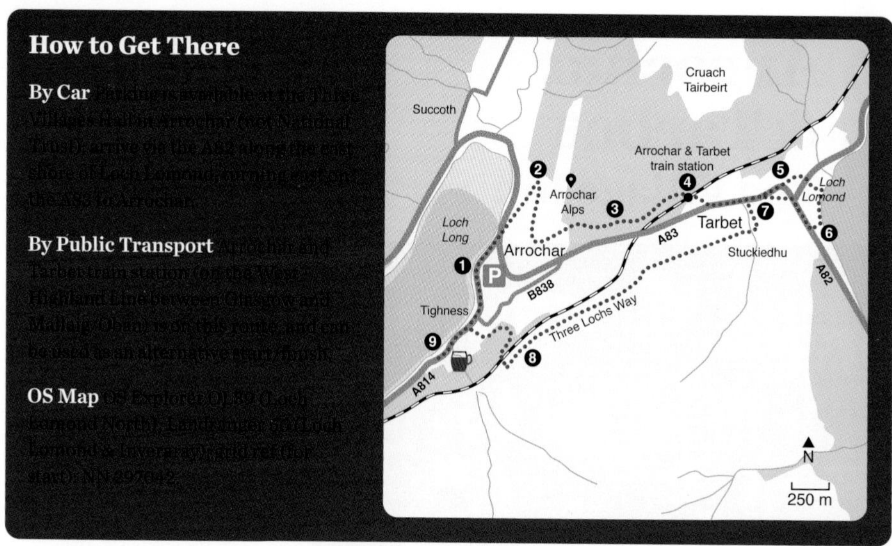

How to Get There

By Car Parking is available at the Three Villages Hall in Arrochar (not National Trust); arrive via the A82 along the east shore of Loch Lomond, turning east on the A83 to Arrochar.

By Public Transport Arrochar and Tarbet train station (on the West Highland Line between Glasgow and Mallaig/Oban) is on this route and can be used as an alternative start/finish.

OS Map OS Explorer OL39 (Loch Lomond North); Landranger 56 (Loch Lomond & Inveraray); grid ref (for start): NN 292042

1. From the Three Villages Hall, walk along the pavement with Loch Long on your left. A main road (A83) joins from the right. Continue to a phone box, then turn right, following a fingerpost with waymakers for the Heritage Trail (a circular walk linking Arrochar and Tarbet) and the Three Lochs Way (a 34-mile/55-km hiking route along the Highland Boundary Fault linking Loch Lomond, Gareloch and Loch Long). Follow the pointer for the 'main trail'.

2. Ascend a pretty, tree-lined path offering fantastic views over Loch Long, following wooden posts topped by yellow rings. Cross straight over a forestry track and continue along the path.

3. The trail rambles around the ankles of Cruach Tairbeirt (which means 'stack of the neck of land', a reference to the isthmus separating the salt water of Loch Long and the fresh water of Loch Lomond). Cross a stream and follow the path around a hairpin bend. Descend, pass beneath the railway track and emerge at Arrochar and Tarbet train station.

4. Turn left and walk down the road. At the main road (A83), turn left, following a fingerpost pointing to Tarbet (a name derived from the Gaelic word for isthmus, *an tairbeart*). Pass a fingerpost pointing right for Glen Douglas – ignore this (for now) and continue straight, towards Tarbet Pier.

5. When the main road bends right, keep going straight ahead, along a path. At the end, carefully cross the road, go through a gap in the wall and along a path to the shore of Loch Lomond. Turn right, walk along the water's edge to the pier. If clouds allow, the spiked 3,195ft (974m) peak of Ben Lomond (looked after by the National Trust for Scotland), looms on the far side of the loch.

6. Loop back around, turning right when you meet the main road (A82). Walk past Tarbet Hotel, then bear left along the A83 until you reach the fingerpost for Glen Douglas you passed earlier.

7. Cross the road, follow this fingerpost through a wide metal gate and walk up the tarmac lane. Go up the hill and then turn right along a gravel path, once again following waymarkers for the Heritage Trail and Three Lochs Way. Go through another wide metal gate and walk along the track.

8. After a mile (1.6km) follow a fingerpost pointing right for Arrochar, passing beneath the railway track and descending across a stream, past houses into the village. Take the path going left of the church, and at the road by the loch, ignore the fingerpost pointing right and instead go left, walking 200 yards to the Village Inn.

9. After leaving the pub, turn right and walk along the loch shore, past the village store and Claymore Hotel, back to Three Villages Hall.

99 Glen Coe & An Torr

Clachaig Inn

Clachaig Inn
Glencoe, Argyll and Bute
PH49 4HX
01855 811252
www.clachaig.com

About this walk

- Mountain and glen views
- History
- Wildlife
- Waterfalls and riverside walking

Start/finish An Torr car park (National Trust for Scotland)
Distance 2 miles (3.2km)
Time to pub 1 hour
Walking time 1.5 hours
Terrain Woodland paths

The CLACHAIG INN is a place of pilgrimage for hillwalkers, rock climbers and mountain bikers. Nestled deep in glorious Glen Coe, it's synonymous with Highland adventures. The Boots Bar, Snug and Bidean Lounge each offer a warm welcome with open fires when the weather's wild, and walls adorned with alpine paraphernalia. Food is served and accommodation is available.

SCOTLAND

This walk is a laid-back browse around An Torr, a hill at the heart of Glen Coe, where the scenery is as beautiful as the history is brutal, and wildlife abounds among woods and waterfalls.

Spring Wildflowers – including bluebells, violets, Scottish primrose, bog asphodel, purple saxifrage, bell heather and yellow 'Scotch' broom – bloom. Ravens, buzzards and even the occasional majestic golden eagle can be seen soaring through the peaks.

Summer Spy shy pine martens in early morning and late evening. Look for dippers on the rocks of the River Coe, golden plover on open moorland and roe deer in the trees.

Autumn Red deer stags (the 'Monarchs of the Glen') roar as the rut gets underway. Rowan berries glow brightly. Red squirrels scamper around An Torr and wild mountain goats forage for food through the glen.

Winter The River Coe's waterfalls are in full spate, snow bunting and ptarmigan patrol the higher hills, while whooper swans fly overhead towards Loch Achtriochtan and red deer seek shelter in the glen.

The Clachaig Inn has multiple handpumps offering Scottish craft ales, lagers, stouts and ciders, plus over 400 malt whiskies and 130 Scottish-distilled gins.

Follow in the footsteps of ... In the freezing pre-dawn of 13 February 1692, a company of government soldiers led by Captain Robert Campbell attacked slumbering members of Glencoe's Clan MacDonald (who'd been feeding them for a fortnight) and mercilessly murdered up to 40 men, women and children. The infamous massacre – commanded and committed in the name of William III who had overthrown the Catholic king James II in 1688 – has never been forgotten.

How to Get There

By Car Park in the National Trust for Scotland's An Torr car park, off the A82 on the way to Glen Coe.

By Public Transport The closest train station is Fort William, from where Shiel Bus N44 travels to Glencoe Junction.

OS Map OS Explorer 384 (Glen Coe & Glen Etive); Landranger 41 (Ben Nevis, Fort William & Glen Coe); grid ref (for start) NN 126/564.

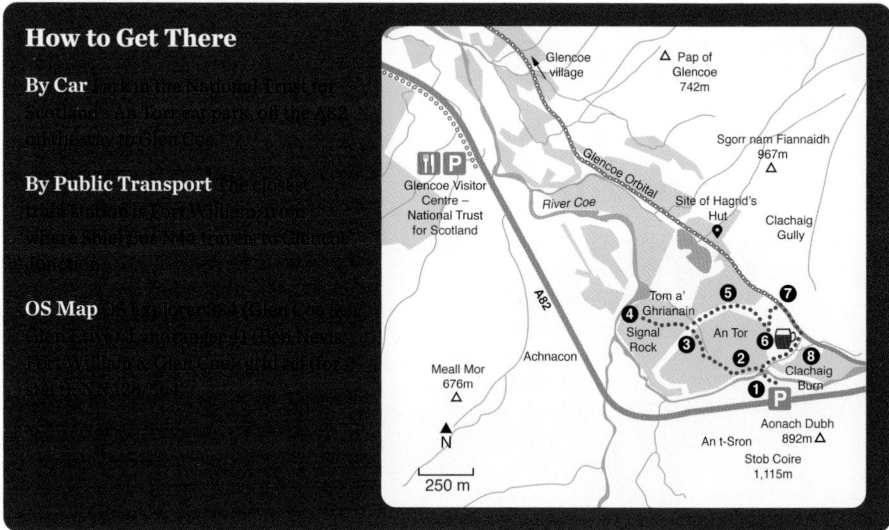

1. From the car park, cross the bridge over the River Coe, where white water rushes across the rocks en route to the sea at Loch Leven, and climb the stone steps opposite. Ignore the yellow arrows pointing along a trail going right and continue straight ahead to a kissing gate. Pass through, and bear left, walking into mixed woodlands.

2. Go along the woodland trail to a colour-coded waymarker where the path forks. Go left here, following blue and black posts towards Tom a' Ghrianain (Hill of the Sun), which is topped by Signal Rock. Stroll through a relatively young plantation of conifers towards a much more ancient section of the woods on your right, where native trees such as Scots pine have stood sentinel for centuries and are now covered with lichen and moss.

3. Keep tracing waymarkers to a second fork in the trail. Here the black posts go right, but our walk bears left, following the blue route through a gate towards Signal Rock. Pass an information sign about the donation of the rock to the National Trust for Scotland and climb the hill towards the rock itself.

4. Circle to the rear of the rock, where steps lead to the top and views can be enjoyed along the glen. It's often claimed that the signal to begin the Glencoe Massacre was given from here although there is no hard evidence that this is true. Over the top of the trees, the mighty Meall Mor rises to the west, while An t-Sron ('the nose') on Stob Coire and the Three Sisters (Aonach Dubh, Beinn Fhada and Gearr Aonach) shape the south side of the glen, and Sgorr na Cìche (the Pap of Glencoe) tickles clouds to the north. After drinking in the view, return the way you came, until you reach the gate.

5. Go through and turn left, following black-topped wooden posts along a path that meanders up and down, wending through the woods around An Torr, occasionally offering up stunning glen views off to the right. At the northernmost extent of the path, you get a good glimpse through trees to a deep tear in the side of Sgorr nam Fiannaidh – this is Clachaig Gully, a famous Scottish gully-climbing route (but one for experienced climbers only). Keep zigging and zagging to reach the apex of An Torr, where more vistas can be enjoyed.

6. Descend from the top of An Torr to a T-junction. Turn left here and follow yellow waymarkers through the woods – looking out for wildlife, including red squirrels – until you reach a tall deer gate and a substantial metal gate, leading out on to the old Glencoe Village road.

7. Harry Potter devotees might want to take a small diversion here, turning left and exploring the lower flanks of Sgorr nam Fiannaidh, where a trail leads right from the road to reach the spot overlooking Torren Lochan, where Hagrid's hut was built for the shooting of the 2004 film *Harry Potter and the Prisoner of Azkaban* – the hut is long gone, but the views remain. Our main route turns right here and follows the road to the sensational sight of the Clachaig Inn, where a warm welcome is extended to all – well, unless your surname happens to be Campbell, in which case it's best to keep that fact quiet (see Follow in the footsteps of...).

8. After leaving the pub, turn right and walk down to a spot where a fingerpost points along an all-ability trail with yellow waymarkers. Follow this right, tracing the alder-lined banks of Clachaig Burn before it tumbles into the River Coe, and looking up at the steep volcanic rock face of Aonach Dubh spiking the sky on your left. Follow the track over a couple of little footbridges, until the river comes to meet you from the left. Cross back over the river via the footbridge to reach the car park.

The Glencoe Orbital

The featured walk is a short stroll around An Torr (Gaelic for 'rocky hill'). A longer walk can be enjoyed from the National Trust for Scotland's excellent Glencoe Visitor Centre, which also incorporates the circuit described here. Waymarked as the Glencoe Orbital, this route explores the woodlands around the visitor centre, before running parallel to the A82 into Glencoe Village, where it turns right, crosses the Bridge of Coe (near a memorial to the Glencoe Massacre) and wanders along a quiet B-road through the glen, beneath the Pap of Glencoe, all the way to An Torr and the Clachaig Inn. At the time of writing, the second part of the orbital, which would ideally cross the River Coe at An Torr car park and lead you back to the visitor centre via a different route, wasn't complete. It's far too dangerous to walk back along the busy A82 (there is no footpath, and it's extremely unadvisable to attempt this), so if you opt to do the longer walk, return the same way you came, after doing the loop of An Torr described here – a total walking distance of 10 miles (16km).

The Clachaig Inn is surrounded by soaring summits, including Aonach Dubh, seen here disappearing into the clouds.

100 Killiecrankie

Moulin Inn

Moulin Inn
11–13 Kirkmichael Road
Moulin, Perth and Kinross
PH16 5EH
01796 472196
www.moulininn.co.uk

About this walk
- Battle site
- Wonderful wildlife
- Optional peak

Start/finish Killiecrankie visitor centre car park (National Trust for Scotland)
Distance 10–11½ miles (16–18.5km)
Time to pub 3 hours
Walking time 5 hours
Terrain River and hillside footpaths, lanes, some road

Dating to 1695, the MOULIN INN is a traditional pub and hotel, which makes its own ales in one of Scotland's first microbreweries, opened in 1995 to celebrate the pub's 300th birthday. A welcoming, atmospheric place, it's frequented by locals and hillhikers, many of them having just climbed nearby Ben Vrakie. The cosy interior features a fire surrounded by antique walking sticks, wooden floors and panelling, and stained-glass images of Highland scenes. Outside tables offer hill views. Good Scottish food is served, and accommodation is available.

Walk with the ghosts of conflicts past, through the Pass of Killiecrankie and Vale of Atholl, along the River Garry and Loch Dunmore to a 300-year-old village inn, returning via the peak of Craigower, enjoying panoramic Perthshire views.

Spring Through the Pass of Killiecrankie and across Craigower, the forest flushes with flowers including wood anemone, primrose, celandine and wood sorrel. Listen for drumming woodpeckers.

Summer Hear pied flycatchers and wood warblers. Spot kingfishers and signs of otters along the river, and elusive pine martens in the woods. Ravens and buzzards circle Craigower, wildflowers attract butterflies and bees, and common lizards sunbathe.

Autumn Trees in the gorge blaze bronze, gold and red. Salmon jump up waterfalls near Soldier's Leap, red squirrels rummage for nuts and fungi pop up in the woods.

Winter Dippers and herons hunt along the River Garry, while woodpeckers and nuthatches raid the feeders at Killiecrankie Visitor Centre

The Moulin Inn sells four signature beers from its microbrewery: Ale of Atholl (ruby), Braveheart (bitter), Moulin Light and the honey-infused rich Old Remedial.

Follow in the footsteps of ...
On 27 July 1689, Killiecrankie saw one of Scotland's bloodiest battles, when Jacobite forces led by John Graham of Claverhouse (Bonnie Dundee) won a famous victory against British soldiers, despite being outnumbered and taking heavy casualties. The Jacobites subsequently chased the retreating redcoats through the Pass of Killiecrankie, among them Donald McBane, whose dramatic escape is remembered at Soldier's Leap.

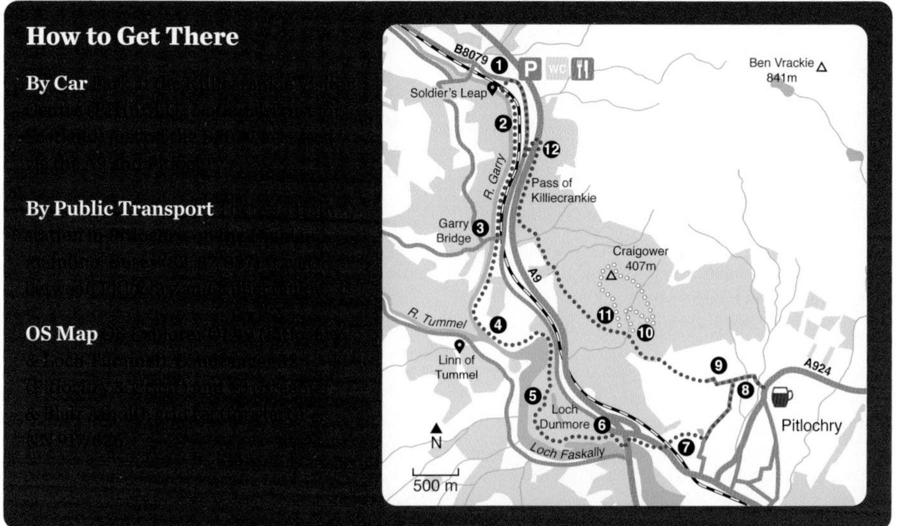

1. From the visitor centre and Jacobite Café, (where there is a wealth of information about the battle, local flora, fauna and geology), follow signs for 'Soldier's Leap and Riverside Walk', passing a National Trust for Scotland (NTS) sign for the Pass of Killiecrankie. Cross Trooper's Den Bridge over a waterfall, from where the first shot of the battle was fired, by a Jacobite sniper, killing a cavalry officer. At a T-junction, turn left and walk past a lookout across the River Garry. Descend steps and follow a path left, signed to Soldier's Leap. Turn right at a second T-junction and visit the spot where redcoat Donald McBane jumped 18ft (5.5m) across the gorge to escape Jacobite pursuers. Retrace your steps, then continue descending, following signs for the Pass of Killiecrankie and Linn of Tummel, and passing the feet of the towering railway viaduct, built in 1863.

2. Stroll a beautiful path through beech woods, with the river rushing across rapids on your right. Pass the NTS charcoal kiln and walk past the Balfour Stone, marking the spot where Brigadier Barthold Balfour is buried. The right bank of the river becomes more dramatic and gorge-like from here, with waterfalls cascading down the rock.

3. Pass a footbridge over the river – walk halfway across to enjoy gorgeous gorge views, but then return (unless you're planning a diversion to the Linn of Tummel) and continue along Bealach Path towards Pitlochry. At a fork, go left, taking the higher route beneath the cacophonous road bridge. The path goes over a little footbridge by a waterfall, then cuts in along a stream and crosses another footbridge. At a fingerpost, turn right and carry on towards Pitlochry, passing a pebble beach. To your left, Craigower raises its head, with Ben Vrackie visible over its right shoulder.

4. A hydroelectric power station appears on the right, as the River Tummel joins the Garry. Just upstream, the Linn of Tummel waterfalls tumble. Continue past Faskally House, following the river right as it widens and segues into Loch Faskally. Walk a section of tarmac road, following wooden posts with green arrows.

5. At a small Scottish Forestry car park, turn right and follow fingerposts pointing towards Pitlochry along Bealach Path (waymarked with green arrows), which enters woods, bears left and skirts past little Loch Dunmore. Climb a section of trail carpeted by pine needles, beneath an umbrella of Douglas fir, following wooden, white-topped posts. When the path forks, go right, heeding green arrows, then bear left at a further fork, following wooden posts towards Loch Faskally. Descend steps and walk along the loch shore. At the next junction, go right, ignoring a sign for Killiecrankie via Faskally woods, and staying beside the loch.

6. Cross a little footbridge and stroll a sealed path, past a lookout point, to the impressive footbridge spanning the loch. Don't cross (except to enjoy the view). Turn left and, at Pitlochry Boating Station, bear right along the tarmac road.

7. Carefully cross the main road and train track at Cuilc Brae, following fingerposts for Craigower. Walk along the lane as it arcs left, around Pitlochry. Ignore a fingerpost pointing left to Craigower, and continue uphill, passing right of the Cuilc (lake). At the end of the lake, go left along the road, ignoring another Craigower sign and following purple, green, orange and blue arrows. Walk past the Red Deer restaurant and golf course to a T-junction.

8. Ignore (for now) the NTS sign for Craigower. Turn right on Craiglunie Road and meander into Moulin, following the road past a standing stone in a field on the left, turning right on Baledmund Road and crossing a brook to reach the Moulin Brewery and Inn.

9. After the pub, walk back to the NTS sign for Craigower. Continue straight, and when the lane forks, go right, passing a tiny car park to reach the golf course, where a fingerpost tries to send you hard right; instead, follow the track up to a wooden gate, where a sign for Craigower and Killiecrankie points left. Take this path through pines, turning left when you meet a track.

10. At a fingerpost, you can either continue straight on to Killiecrankie, or climb Craigower (a 1½-mile/2-km loop, with 500ft/150m of ascent). To climb, turn right along a path snaking up the hill to an NTS sign, then bear right and keep ascending. The path wends left and passes an NTS reptile hibernacula before reaching the summit, where there's an information board and stunning vista to Loch Tummel and Glencoe. Continue over the top and follow signs for a return route on a different path, around the east of the peak, with great views of Ben Vrackie. Turn right when you meet a wide track and walk back to the fingerpost.

11. Carry straight on. Descend until the track forks, then go right, following a blue arrow along the undulating track above the Pass of Killiecrankie, with the river visible down to your left.

13. Turn left at a fingerpost pointing to Killiecrankie, passing beneath the A9, and following a track that zig-zags down to the B8079. Go through a wide gate, carefully cross, turn right and walk along a footpath beside the road to the visitor centre.

The trail along the banks of Loch Faskally in autumn.

Index

All maps by **Barking Dog Art**. All photographs by **Patrick Kinsella**, except for the following: **Shutterstock**: 2–3, 122, 252, 275. **National Trust Images**: 7, 189 (Andrew Butler); 12 (John Millar); 13, 28, 94, 231 (Chris Lacey); 15, 262 (John Miller); 38 (Mel Peters); 46, 167, 261 (Joe Cornish); 51 (Mike Calnan/James Dobson); 63, 73, 76, 146, 205 (James Dobson); 74 (Tony Gill); 85, 143 (Justin Minns); 91, 237 (Paul Harris); 131 (Arnhel de Serra); 145 (Rick Greswell); 156 (Neil Jakeman); 265 (John Hammond); 267 (Paul Moan). **Getty Images**: 27, 51. **Alamy**: 34, 48, 53, 56, 83, 91, 92, 104, 191, 194, 196, 235, 253, 256. **Plough Inn**: 112.

Front cover: Fleece Inn, Bretforton (**National Trust Images/James Dobson**). Back cover, top: The Three Horseshoes, Elsted (**Patrick Kinsella**); middle: Anchor Inn, Seatown (**Alamy**); bottom: The George Inn, Bathampton (**Alamy**).